CFA Institute

CW01677908

ETHICAL AND PROFESSIONAL STANDARDS

CFA® Program Curriculum

2026 • LEVEL I • VOLUME 10

WILEY

ISBN 978-1-961409-92-7

May 2025

Please visit our website at
www.WileyGlobalFinance.com.

WILEY

CONTENTS

How to Use the CFA Program Curriculum

The CFA® Program exams measure your mastery of the core knowledge, skills, and abilities required to succeed as an investment professional. These core competencies are the basis for the Candidate Body of Knowledge (CBOK™). The CBOK consists of four components:

- A broad outline that lists the major CFA Program topic areas (www.cfainstitute.org/programs/cfa/curriculum/cbok/cbok)
- Topic area weights that indicate the relative exam weightings of the top-level topic areas (www.cfainstitute.org/en/programs/cfa/curriculum)
- Learning outcome statements (LOS) that tell you the specific knowledge, skills, and abilities you should gain from each curriculum topic area. You will find these statements at the start of each learning module and lesson. We encourage you to review the information about the LOS on our website (www.cfainstitute.org/programs/cfa/curriculum/study-sessions), including the descriptions of LOS "command words" on the candidate resources page at www.cfainstitute.org/-/media/documents/support/programs/cfa-and-cipm-los-command-words.ashx.
- The CFA Program curriculum that candidates receive access to upon exam registration.

Therefore, the key to your success on the CFA exams is studying and understanding the CBOK. You can learn more about the CBOK on our website: www.cfainstitute.org/programs/cfa/curriculum/cbok.

The curriculum, including the practice questions, is the basis for all exam questions. The curriculum is selected/developed specifically to provide candidates with the knowledge, skills, and abilities reflected in the CBOK.

CFA INSTITUTE LEARNING ECOSYSTEM (LES)

Your exam registration fee includes access to the CFA Institute Learning Ecosystem (LES). This digital learning platform provides access to all the curriculum content and practice questions. The LES is organized as a series of learning modules consisting of short online lessons and associated practice questions. This tool is your source for all study materials, including practice questions and mock exams. The LES is the primary method by which CFA Institute delivers your curriculum experience. Here, you will find additional practice questions to test your knowledge, including some interactive questions.

DESIGNING YOUR PERSONAL STUDY PROGRAM

An orderly, systematic approach to exam preparation is critical. You should dedicate a consistent block of time every week to reading and studying. Review the LOS both before and after you study curriculum content to ensure you can demonstrate the knowledge, skills, and abilities described by the LOS and the assigned learning module. Use the LOS as a self-check to track your progress and highlight areas of weakness for later review.

Successful candidates report an average of more than 300 hours preparing for each exam. Your preparation time will vary based on your prior education and experience, and you will likely spend more time on some topics than on others.

ERRATA

The curriculum development process is rigorous and involves multiple rounds of reviews by content experts. Despite our efforts to produce a curriculum that is free of errors, we must make corrections in some instances. Curriculum errata are periodically updated and posted by exam level and test date on the Curriculum Errata webpage (www.cfainstitute.org/en/programs/submit-errata). If you believe you have found an error in the curriculum, you can submit your concerns through our curriculum errata reporting process found at the bottom of the Curriculum Errata webpage.

OTHER FEEDBACK

Please send any comments or suggestions to info@cfainstitute.org, and we will review your feedback thoughtfully.

Ethical and Professional Standards

LEARNING MODULE

1

Ethics and Trust in the Investment Profession

by Bidhan L. Parmar, PhD, Dorothy C. Kelly, CFA, Colin McLean, MBA, FIA, FSIP, Nitin Mehta, CFA, FSIP, and David B. Stevens, CIMC, CFA.

Bidhan L. Parmar, PhD, is at the University of Virginia (USA). Dorothy C. Kelly, CFA, is at McIntire School of Commerce, University of Virginia (USA). Colin McLean, MBA, FIA, FSIP, is at SVM Asset Management (United Kingdom). Nitin Mehta, CFA, FSIP (United Kingdom). David B. Stevens, CIMC, CFA, is at Wells Fargo Wealth Management (USA).

LEARNING OUTCOMES

Mastery	*The candidate should be able to:*
☐	explain ethics
☐	describe the role of a code of ethics in defining a profession
☐	describe professions and how they establish trust
☐	describe the need for high ethical standards in investment management
☐	explain professionalism in investment management
☐	identify challenges to ethical behavior
☐	compare and contrast ethical standards with legal standards
☐	describe a framework for ethical decision making

INTRODUCTION

1

As a candidate in the CFA Program, you are both expected and required to meet high ethical standards. This reading introduces ideas and concepts that will help you understand the importance of ethical behavior in the investment industry. You will be introduced to various types of ethical issues within the investment profession and learn about the CFA Institute Code of Ethics.

The readings covering ethics and professional standards demonstrate that ethical behavior is central to creating trust. Professional behavior is equally important. Professions help maintain trust in an industry by establishing codes and setting standards that put a framework around ethical behavior and technical competence. Professions also set the wider goal of gaining and maintaining the trust of society as a whole. In this regard, professions have a sense of purpose that society values.

Imagine that you are employed in the research department of a large financial services firm. You and your colleagues spend your days researching, analyzing, and valuing the shares of publicly traded companies and sharing your investment recommendations with clients. You love your work and take great satisfaction in knowing that your recommendations can help the firm's investing clients make informed investment decisions that will help them meet their financial goals and improve their lives.

Several months after starting at the firm, you learn that an analyst at the firm has been terminated for writing and publishing research reports that misrepresented the fundamental risks of some companies to investors. You learn that the analyst wrote the reports with the goal of pleasing the management of the companies that were the subjects of the research reports. He hoped that these companies would hire your firm's investment banking division for its services and he would be rewarded with large bonuses for helping the firm increase its investment banking fees. Some clients bought shares based on the analyst's reports and suffered losses. They posted stories on the internet about their losses and the misleading nature of the reports. When the media investigated and published the story, the firm's reputation for investment research suffered. Investors began to question the firm's motives and the objectivity of its research recommendations. The firm's investment clients started to look elsewhere for investment advice, and company clients begin to transfer their business to firms with untarnished reputations. With business declining, management is forced to trim staff. Along with many other hard-working colleagues, you lose your job—through no fault of your own.

Imagine how you would feel in this situation. Most people would feel upset and resentful that their hard and honest work was derailed by someone else's unethical behavior. Yet, this type of scenario is not uncommon. Around the world, unsuspecting employees at such companies as SAC Capital, Stanford Financial Group, Everbright Securities, Enron, Satyam Computer Services, Arthur Andersen, and other large companies have experienced such career setbacks when someone else's actions destroyed trust in their companies and industries.

Businesses and financial markets thrive on trust—defined as a strong belief in the reliability of a person or institution. In a 2016 study on trust, investors indicated that to earn their trust, the top two attributes of an investment manager should be that it (1) has transparent and open business practices, and (2) has ethical business practices.[1] Although these attributes are valued by customers and clients in any industry, this reading will explore why they are of particular importance to the investment industry.

People may think that ethical behavior is simply about following laws, regulations, and other rules, but throughout our lives and careers we will encounter situations in which there is no definitive rule that specifies how to act, or the rules that exist may be unclear or even in conflict with each other. Responsible people, including investment professionals, must be willing and able to identify potential ethical issues and create solutions to them even in the absence of clearly stated rules.

1 CFA Institute From Trust to Loyalty: A Global Survey of What Investors Want (2013): http://www.cfapubs.org/doi/pdf/10.2469/ccb.v2013.n14.1.(2016): https://www.cfainstitute.org/research/survey-reports/from-trust-to-loyalty

ETHICS 2

☐ explain ethics

Through our individual actions, each of us can affect the lives of others. Our decisions and behavior can harm or benefit a variety of **stakeholders**—individuals or groups of individuals who could be affected either directly or indirectly by a decision and thus have an interest, or stake, in the decision. Examples of stakeholders in decisions made by investment industry professionals include our colleagues, our clients, our employers, the communities in which we live and work, the investment profession, trade associations, regulators, and other financial market participants. In some cases, our actions may benefit all of these stakeholder groups; in other cases, our actions may benefit only some stakeholder groups; and in still other cases, our actions may benefit some stakeholder groups and harm others. For example, recall the research analyst in the introduction who wrote misleading research reports with the aim of increasing the financial benefit to himself and his employer. In the very short term, his conduct seemed to directly benefit some stakeholders (certain clients, himself, and his employer) and to harm other stakeholders (clients who invested based on his reports). Over a longer time period, his conduct resulted in harm to himself and many other stakeholders—his employer, his employer's clients, his colleagues, investors, and through loss of trust when the story was published, the larger financial market.

Ethics encompasses a set of moral principles and rules of conduct that provide guidance for our behavior. The word "ethics" comes from the Greek word "ethos," meaning character, used to describe the guiding beliefs or ideals characterizing a society or societal group. Beliefs are assumptions or thoughts we hold to be true. A principle is defined as a belief or fundamental truth that serves as the foundation for a system of belief or behavior or a chain of reasoning. Our beliefs form our values—those things we deem to have worth or merit.

Moral principles or **ethical principles** are beliefs regarding what is good, acceptable, or obligatory behavior and what is bad, unacceptable, or forbidden behavior. Ethical principles may refer to beliefs regarding behavior that an individual expects of himself or herself, as well as shared beliefs regarding standards of behavior expected or required by a community or societal group.

The study of ethics examines the role of consequences and personal character in defining what is considered good, or ethical, conduct.

Ethical conduct is behavior that follows moral principles and balances self-interest with both the direct and the indirect consequences of the behavior on others. Ethical actions are those actions that are perceived as beneficial and conforming to the ethical expectations of society. An action may be considered beneficial if it improves the outcomes or consequences for stakeholders affected by the action. Telling the truth about the risks or costs associated with a recommended investment, for example, is an ethical action—that is, one that conforms to the ethical expectations of society in general and clients in particular. Telling the truth is also beneficial; telling the truth builds trust with customers and clients and enables them to make more informed decisions, which should lead to better outcomes for them and higher levels of client/customer satisfaction for you and your employer.

Widely acknowledged ethical principles include honesty, transparency, fairness or justice, diligence, and respect for the rights of others. Most societal groups share these fundamental ethical principles and build on them, establishing a shared set of rules regarding how members should behave in certain situations. The principles or rules may take different forms depending on the community establishing them.

Governments and related entities, for example, may establish laws and/or regulations to reflect widely shared beliefs about obligatory and forbidden conduct. Laws and regulations are rules of conduct specified by a governing body, such as a legislature or a regulator, identifying how individuals and entities under its jurisdiction should behave in certain situations. Most countries have laws and regulations governing the investment industry and the conduct of its participants. Differences in laws may reflect differences in beliefs and values.

In some countries, for example, the law requires that an investment adviser act in the best interests of his or her clients. Other countries require that investment professionals recommend investments that are suitable for their clients. These differing requirements can also hold true within one country where some advisers are held to a suitability standard and others to the fiduciary standard of the client's best interests. Investment advisers and portfolio managers who are required by law to act in their clients' best interests must always put their clients' interests ahead of their own or their employers' interests. An investment adviser who is required by law to act in a client's best interest must understand the client's financial objectives and risk tolerance, research and investigate multiple investment opportunities, and recommend the investment or investment portfolio that is *most* suitable for the client in terms of meeting his or her long-term financial objectives. In addition, the investment adviser would be expected to monitor the client's financial situation and investments to ensure that the investments recommended remain the *best* overall option for meeting the client's long-term financial objectives. In countries with only a suitability requirement, it is legal for investment professionals to recommend a suitable investment to a client even if other, similar suitable investments with lower fees are available. These differences in laws reflect differences in beliefs and values.

Specific communities or societal groups in which we live and work sometimes codify their beliefs about obligatory and forbidden conduct in a written set of principles, often called a **code of ethics**. Universities, employers, and professional associations often adopt a code of ethics to communicate the organization's values and overall expectations regarding member behavior. The code of ethics serves as a general guide for how community members should act. Some communities will also expand on their codes of ethics and adopt explicit rules or standards that identify specific behaviors required of community members. These **standards of conduct** serve as benchmarks for the minimally acceptable behavior of community members and can help clarify the code of ethics. Members can choose behaviors that demonstrate even higher standards. By joining the community, members are agreeing to adhere to the community's code of ethics and standards of conduct. To promote their code of ethics and reduce the incidence of violations, communities frequently display their codes in prominent locations and in written materials. In addition, most communities require that members commit to their codes in writing on an annual or more frequent basis.

Violations of a community's established code of ethics and/or standards of conduct can harm the community in a variety of ways. Violations have the potential to damage the community's reputation among external stakeholders and the general public. Violations can also damage the community's reputation internally and lead to reduced trust among community members and can cause the organization to fracture or splinter from within. To protect the reputation of its membership and limit potential harm to innocent members, the community may take corrective actions to investigate possible violations, repair any damages, and attempt to discipline the violator or, in severe cases, revoke the violator's membership in the community.

EXAMPLE 1

Ethics

1. Which of the following statements is *most* accurate? Ethics can be described as:

   A. a commitment to upholding the law.

   B. an individual's personal opinion about right and wrong.

   C. a set of moral principles that provide guidance for our behavior.

Solution:

C is correct. Ethics can be described as a set of moral principles that provide guidance for our behavior; these may be moral principles shared by a community or societal group.

2. Which of the following statements is *most* accurate? Standards of conduct:

   A. are a necessary component of any code of ethics.

   B. serve as a general guide regarding proper conduct by members of a group.

   C. serve as benchmarks for the minimally acceptable behavior required of members of a group.

Solution:

C is correct. Standards of conduct serve as benchmarks for the minimally acceptable behavior required of members of a group. Some organizations will adopt only a code of ethics, which communicates the organization's values and overall expectations regarding member behavior. Others may adopt both a code of ethics and standards of conduct. Standards of conduct identify specific behavior required of community members and serve as benchmarks for the minimally acceptable behavior of community members.

ETHICS AND PROFESSIONALISM 3

- ☐ describe the role of a code of ethics in defining a profession
- ☐ describe professions and how they establish trust
- ☐ describe the need for high ethical standards in investment management
- ☐ explain professionalism in investment management

A **profession** is an occupational community that has specific education, expert knowledge, and a framework of practice and behavior that underpins community trust, respect, and recognition. Most professions emphasize an ethical approach, the importance of good service, and empathy with the client.

Professions have grown in size and number over the last century: the rise of new specialist areas of expertise has created new professions. Driving forces of a new profession include governments and regulators, which encourage the formation of an ethical relationship between professionals and society at large. There is also demand for professions from individuals who see an advantage in working as a professional and from clients who desire to work with professionals.

Professions have not developed in every country. But in most countries, those who work in specialized areas—such as doctors, lawyers, actuaries, accountants, architects, and engineers—are subject to some combination of licensed status and technical standards. These standards distinguish professions from the craft guilds and trade bodies that were established in many countries. In particular, the requirement for members of professions to uphold high ethical standards is one clear difference. Another difference is that trade bodies do not normally have a mission to serve society or to set and enforce professional conduct rules for practitioners.

How Professions Establish Trust

For a profession to be credible, a primary goal is to establish trust among clients and among society in general. In doing so, professions have a number of common characteristics that, when combined, greatly increase confidence and credibility in professionals and their organizations.

Professions normalize practitioner behavior.

Professionalism is underpinned by codes and standards developed by professional bodies. Regulators typically support professional ethics and recognize the framework for ethics that professions can provide. Many regulators around the world have engaged closely with professional bodies to understand their codes and standards, as well as how they are enforced. Codes and standards developed by practitioners can be complementary to regulations, codifying many more individual practices than the high-level principles set by regulation.

Many governments have recognized that a profession can develop a more sophisticated system of standards than a regulator can, via continuous practitioner input and a strong mutual interest within the profession to maintain good standards and adopt best practices. Government support of professions is attributable to the role of professions in helping the public and ensuring expert and principled performance of complex services.

Professions provide a service to society.

There is an obligation for professionals to go beyond codes and standards. Professionals should advocate for higher educational and ethical standards in the industry, individually and through their companies. Professions can widen access to services and support economic activity by encouraging trust in the industries they serve. Professions have realized that earning community trust not only creates professional pride and acceptance but also delivers commercial benefits. A profession that earns trust may ultimately have greater flexibility and independence from government regulators to manage its own affairs, which allows members of the profession to develop service models that are both useful to clients and beneficial to members.

Professions are client focused.

An integral part of a profession's mission is to develop and administer codes, best practice guidelines, and standards that guide an industry. These codes, standards, and guidelines help ensure that all professionals place the integrity of their profession and the interests of clients above their own personal interests. At a minimum, professionals must act in the best interest of the client, exercising a reasonable level of care, skill, and diligence. The obligation to deliver a high standard of care when acting for the benefit of another party is called *fiduciary duty*. Other entities, including employers, regulators, trade associations, and not-for-profit organizations, may also support an industry but are not the same as professional bodies. Unlike professions, these other entities generally do not exist to set and maintain professional standards. Most employers encourage employees to be members of relevant professions, and many give financial support for this membership to ideally improve the quality of client service and reinforce ethical awareness.

Professions have high entry standards.

Membership in a profession is a signal to the market that the professional will deliver high-quality service of a promised standard, going beyond simply academic credentials. Professions develop curricula that equip future professionals with competence, including technical skills, knowledge, and ethics.

Professions possess a body of expert knowledge.

A repository of knowledge, developed by experienced and skilled practitioners, is made available to all members of a profession. This knowledge helps members work effectively and ethically and is based on best practice.

Professions encourage and facilitate continuing education.

Entry into a profession does not, on its own, guarantee that an individual will maintain competency and continue to uphold professional standards. After qualification and throughout the working life of a professional, there will be changes in knowledge and technical skills to perform certain jobs, in technology and standards of ethical behavior, in services that can be offered, and in the legal and business environment in which professional services are delivered. These all require the development of competence and ethical awareness. Most professional bodies make it a condition of membership that a specific amount of new learning is undertaken each year. Typically, such conditions specify a time commitment, which may be separated into different competencies and types of learning activity. This is often referred to as *continuing professional development* and is seen as an important part of maintaining professional standards. The training and education that professionals undertake increase the value of human capital, which can contribute to economic growth and social mobility.

Professions monitor professional conduct.

Members of a profession must be held accountable for their conduct to maintain the integrity and reputation of an industry. Doing so often involves self-regulation by professional bodies through monitoring and imposition of sanctions on members.

Professions are collegial.

Professionals should be respectful to each other, even when they are competing. At the very least, they must respect the rights, dignity, and autonomy of others.

Professions are recognized oversight bodies.

Many professional bodies are not-for-profit organizations with a mission emphasizing excellence, integrity, and public service. Although it is the responsibility of individual professionals to remain competent, an oversight body typically monitors this responsibility. Such bodies provide individuals with ongoing educational resources and access to information about changes in standards and imposes a framework of discipline. Continuing membership indicates sustained competence in (and updating of) practical skills while maintaining ongoing compliance with an ethical code of conduct.

Professions encourage the engagement of members.

Participation by members as volunteers is part of the essence of a profession. Professionals are more likely to refer to, use, and adhere to values that they have helped develop, and they typically have the power as members to revise these values. A good professional will want to mentor and inspire others who recently entered or wish to enter the profession. Professionals should be willing to volunteer to advance the profession and engage with peers to develop expertise and ethics. Professionals should volunteer to help educate new generations in ethical knowledge and ethical decision making and to foster a productive debate about new areas of ethics. Most professionals find that the experience of volunteering within the profession enhances their skills and widens their contacts within the industry. Membership in a professional body allows the necessary engagement with other professionals.

Professions Are Evolving

No profession stands still. Such trends as greater transparency and public accountability force professions to adapt to change. Meanwhile, technology opens up possibilities for new services and different ways of working. In addition, key processes of a profession's responsibilities may need to be reviewed by a government agency or independent public body. In general, professions often engage with non-member individuals. This can help a profession evaluate the viewpoints of the public, clients, or other stakeholders when determining policy and practice and can encourage public trust for a profession's conduct and disciplinary process.

Effective professions continue to develop their role to account for changing best practices. Some medical professional bodies, for instance, have been established for more than 500 years but may now have the same need to adapt as the much younger investment management profession. This means that at any point in time, society may recognize an area of work as a profession even if it has not fully or universally implemented all the expectations. As the requirements for a profession evolve, gaps open up that may take time to remedy. Effective professions also actively learn from other professions, particularly in the area of ethics. New standards of conduct in the accounting profession might be an influence on standards considered in investment management, for example.

Professionalism in Investment Management

> Successful investing professionals are disciplined and consistent and they think a great deal about what they do and how they do it.
>
> —Benjamin Graham, *The Intelligent Investor* (1949)

Investment management is a relatively young profession, which means that public understanding of its practice and codes is still developing. Recognition by regulators and employers also lags established professions. Not everyone engaged in investment management is a professional; some practitioners have not undertaken specific investment training or are not members of a professional body. That creates a challenge for the investment management profession to gain trust, because not all practitioners need to be committed to high ethical standards. However, key elements of the profession have been steadily established over several decades. For example, the publication of Graham and Dodd's *Security Analysis* in 1934 was an important step in establishing a body of knowledge for investment.

The investment management profession meets most, but currently not all, of the expectations of a profession. In most countries, some form of certification or licensing is needed to practice, but there may not be a requirement to join a professional body.

Globally, the trend is to require examined entry to practice investment management and to maintain competence. But few professions have perfect implementation of all the expected attributes. The investment management profession, similar to other professions, is on a journey to improve implementation and keep up with changing demands.

The investment management profession has become increasingly global as capital markets have opened up around the world. Investment management professionals may seek cross-border opportunities or may need to relocate between offices within multinational asset management firms. Regulatory coordination across borders and the emergence of technology are contributing factors to this globalization of investment management. Various investment management professional bodies have developed in individual countries, and several of these bodies have expanded internationally. In addition, several other professional bodies, including those focused on actuarial and accountancy services, have investment management professionals as members.

Trust in Investment Management

The investment management professional today has similarities with professionals in longer-established professions, such as medicine and law. Like doctors and lawyers, investment management professionals are trusted to draw on a body of formal knowledge and apply that knowledge with care and judgement. In comparison to clients, investment professionals are also expected to have superior financial expertise, technical knowledge, and knowledge of the applicable laws and regulations. There is a risk that clients may not be fully aware of the conflicts, risks, and fees involved, so investment management professionals must always handle and fully disclose these issues in a way that serves the best interests of clients. Compliance with codes of ethics and professional standards is essential, and practice must be guided by care, transparency, and integrity.

The investment management profession and investment firms must be interdependent to maintain trust. Employers and regulators have their own standards and practices that may differ from regulations and standards set by professional bodies. The investment management professional bodies typically direct professionals in how to resolve these differences.

In many developed economies, the investment management profession affects many key aspects of the economy, including savings, retirement planning, and the pricing and allocation of capital. In most countries, skilled evaluation of securities leads to more efficient capital allocation and, combined with ethical corporate governance, can assist in attracting investment from international investors. The investment management profession can deliver more value to society when higher levels of trust and better capital allocation reduce transaction costs and help meet client objectives. These reasons explain why practitioners, clients, regulators, and governments have supported the development of an investment management profession.

CFA Institute as an Investment Management Professional Body

CFA Institute is the largest body for investment management professionals.[2] Reflecting the globalization of investment management, CFA Institute moved beyond North America in the 1980s. CFA Institute initiated a number of other changes in line with the growth of investment management. One significant change occurred in 2015, when CFA Institute decided to implement the highest standards of governance in the

2 Eligibility and requirements for becoming a member of CFA Institute vary by jurisdiction. Please consult www.cfainstitute.org for further details.

US not-for-profit sector. The Board of Governors resolved "to implement US Public Company Standards and US not-for-profit leading practices, unless the Board determines that it is not in the best interest of the membership or organization to do so."

The mission of CFA Institute is "to lead the investment profession globally, by promoting the highest standards of ethics, education, and professional excellence for the ultimate benefit of society." The CFA Institute Code of Ethics and Standards of Professional Conduct (Code and Standards) promote the integrity of charterholders and establish a model for ethical behavior. CFA Institute candidates and charterholders must meet the highest standards among those established by CFA Institute, regulators, or the employer. If candidates and charterholders do not meet these standards, there are negative consequences. Where client interests and market interests conflict, the Code and Standards set an investment management professional's duty to market integrity as the overriding obligation. The advocacy efforts of CFA Institute aim to build market integrity by calling for regulations that align the interests of firms and clients.

As a professional body, CFA Institute gathers knowledge from practicing investment professionals, conducts rigorous examinations, and ensures practitioner involvement in developing its codes and values. The CFA Institute Global Body of Investment Knowledge (GBIK) and Candidate Body of Knowledge (CBOK) are updated on an ongoing basis through a process known as *practice analysis*. Through interactions with practicing investment management professionals, practice analysis helps ensure that the body of knowledge for the investment management profession remains current and globally relevant. The CFA Program ensures that candidates have sufficiently mastered the core knowledge, skills, and abilities (competencies) necessary that are generally accepted and applied by investment professionals. CFA Institute also contributes to the dissemination of new research and ideas in finance with the publication of the *Financial Analysts Journal*; CFA Institute Research Foundation books, research briefs, and reviews; and *CFA Institute Magazine*.

CFA Institute encourages charterholders to engage in their professional communities and involves charterholders in its initiatives. CFA Institute local societies keep charterholders connected and engaged in their communities. CFA Institute assists local societies with providing continuing education programs and events that facilitate charterholders engagement. For CFA charterholders, a local CFA society is an important route to maintaining professionalism, particularly for continuing professional development.

CFA charterholders and CFA Program candidates are required to adhere to the Code and Standards and to sign annually a statement attesting to that continued adherence. Charterholders and candidates must maintain and improve their professional competence and strive to maintain and improve the competence of other investment professionals.

EXAMPLE 2

Ethics and Professionalism

1. Which of the following statements is *most* accurate? Investment professionals have a special responsibility to act ethically because:

   A. the industry is heavily regulated.

   B. they are entrusted to protect clients' assets.

   C. the profession requires compliance with its code of ethics.

Solution:

B is correct. Investment professionals have a special responsibility because clients entrust them to protect the clients' assets.

2. Which of the following statements *best* completes the following sentence? Professionals use their specialized knowledge and skills:

   A. in service to others.

   B. to advance their career.

   C. for the exclusive benefit of their employers.

Solution:

A is correct. Professionals use specialized knowledge and skills in service to others. Their career and employer may benefit, but those results are not the primary focus of a professional's use of his or her specialized knowledge and skills.

3. Which of the following statements is *most* accurate? A profession's code of ethics:

   A. includes standards of conduct or specific benchmarks for behavior.

   B. ensures that all members of a profession will act ethically at all times.

   C. publicly communicates the shared principles and expected behaviors of a profession's members.

Solution:

C is correct. A profession's code of ethics publicly communicates the shared principles and expected behaviors of a profession's members. The existence of a code of ethics does not ensure that all members will behave in a manner consistent with the code and act ethically at all times. A profession will often establish a disciplinary process to address alleged violations of the code of ethics. A profession may adopt standards of conduct to enhance and clarify the code of ethics.

CHALLENGES TO ETHICAL CONDUCT 4

☐ identify challenges to ethical behavior

Professionals generally aim to be responsible and to adhere to high moral standards, so what is the benefit of studying ethics? Throughout our careers, we may find ourselves in difficult or at least unfamiliar situations in which an appropriate course of action is not immediately clear and/or there may be more than one seemingly acceptable choice; studying ethics helps us prepare for such situations. This section addresses challenges to engaging in ethical conduct. Failure to acknowledge, understand, or consider these challenges can lead to poor decision making, resulting in unintentional consequences, such as unethical conduct and potential violations of the Code and Standards.

Several challenges can make adherence to ethical conduct difficult. First, people tend to believe that they are ethical people and that their ethical standards are higher than average. Of course, everyone cannot be above average. However, surveys show this belief in above averageness remains.

These survey results illustrate overconfidence, a common behavioral bias that can lead to faulty decision making. Studies have shown that our beliefs and emotions frequently interfere with our cognitive reasoning and result in behavioral bias, a tendency to behave in a way that is not strictly rational. As a result of the overconfidence bias, we are more likely to overestimate the morality of our own behavior, particularly in situations that we have not faced before. The overconfidence bias can result in a failure to consider, explicitly or implicitly, important inputs and variables needed to form the best decision from an ethical perspective. In general, the overconfidence bias leads us to place too much importance on internal traits and intrinsic motivations, such as "I'm honest and would not lie," even though studies have shown that internal traits are generally not the main determinant of whether or not someone will behave ethically in a given situation.

A second challenge is that decision makers often fail to recognize and/or significantly underestimate the effect of situational influences, such as what other people around them are doing. **Situational influences** are external factors, such as environmental or cultural elements, that shape our thinking, decision making, and behavior. Social psychologists have studied how much situational influences affect our behavior and have found that even good people with honorable motives can and often will be influenced to do unethical things when put into difficult situations. Experiments have shown that even people who consider themselves strong, independent, free thinkers will conform to social pressures in many situations. The bystander effect, for example, demonstrates that people are less likely to intervene in an emergency when others are present. Fortunately, experiments have also shown that situational influences can induce people to act more ethically. For example, people tend to behave more ethically when they think someone else is watching or when there is a mirror placed close to them. The important concept to understand is that situational influences have a very powerful and often unrecognized effect on our thinking and behavior. Thus, learning to recognize situational influences is critical to making good decisions.

Common situational influences in the investment industry that can shape thinking and behavior include money and prestige. One experiment found that simply mentioning money can reduce ethical behavior. In the experiment, participants were less likely to cooperate when playing a game if the game was called the Wall Street Game, rather than the Community Game. In the investment industry, large financial rewards—including individual salaries, bonuses, and/or investment gains—can induce honest and well-intentioned individuals to act in ways that others might not consider ethical. Large financial rewards and/or prestige can motivate individuals to act in their own short-term self-interests, ignoring possible short-term risks or consequences to themselves and others as well as long-term risks or consequences for both themselves and others. Another extremely powerful situational influence is loyalty. Loyalty to supervisors or organizations, fellow employees, and other colleagues can tempt individuals to make compromises and take actions that they would reject under different situational influences or judge harshly when taken by others.

Situational influences often blind people to other important considerations. Bonuses, promotions, prestige, and loyalty to employer and colleagues are examples of situational influences that frequently have a disproportionate weight in our decision making. Our brains more easily and quickly identify, recognize, and consider these short-term situational influences than longer-term considerations, such as a commitment to maintaining our integrity and contributing to the integrity of the financial markets. Although absolutely important, these long-term considerations often have less immediate consequences than situational influences, making them less obvious as factors to consider in a decision and, therefore, less likely to influence our overall decision making. Situational influences shift our brain's focus from the long term to the short or immediate term. When our decision making is too narrowly focused on short-term factors and/or self-interest, we tend to ignore and/or minimize the longer-term risks and/or costs and consequences to ourselves and others, and the likelihood of suffering ethical lapses and making poor decisions increases.

Loyalty to employer and/or colleagues is an extremely powerful situational influence. Our colleagues can influence our thinking and behavior in both positive and negative ways. For example, colleagues may have encouraged you to signal your commitment to your career and high ethical standards by enrolling in the CFA Program. If you work for or with people who are not bound by the Code and Standards, they might encourage you to take actions that are consistent with local law, unaware that the recommended conduct falls short of the Code and Standards.

Well-intentioned firms may adopt or develop strong compliance programs to encourage adherence to rules, regulations, and policies. A strong compliance policy is a good start to developing an ethical culture, but a focus on adherence to rules may not be sufficient. A compliance approach may not encourage decision makers to consider the larger picture and can oversimplify decision making. Taken to the extreme, a strong compliance culture can become another situational influence that blinds employees to other important considerations. In a firm focused primarily on compliance, employees may adopt a "check the box" mentality rather than an ethical decision-making approach. Employees may ask the question "What *can* I do?" rather than "What *should* I do?"

EXAMPLE 3

Challenges to Ethical Conduct

1. Which of the following will *most likely* determine whether an individual will behave unethically?

   A. The person's character

   B. The person's internal traits and intrinsic motivation

   C. External factors, such as environmental or cultural elements

Solution:

C is correct. Social psychologists have shown that even good people may behave unethically in difficult situations. Situational influences, which are external factors (e.g., environmental or cultural elements), can shape our thinking, decision making, and behavior and are more likely to lead to unethical behavior than internal traits or character.

2. Which of the following statements is *most* accurate?

   A. Large financial rewards, such as bonuses, are the most powerful situational influences.

   B. When decision making focuses on short-term factors, the likelihood of ethical conduct increases.

   C. Situational influences can motivate individuals to act in their short-term self-interests without recognizing the long-term risks or consequences for themselves and others.

Solution:

C is correct. Situational influences can motivate individuals to act in their short-term self-interests without recognizing the long-term risks or consequences for themselves and others. Large financial rewards are powerful situational influences, but in some situations, other situational influences, such as loyalty to colleagues, may be even more powerful.

5 ETHICAL VS. LEGAL STANDARDS

☐ compare and contrast ethical standards with legal standards

Many times, stakeholders have common ethical expectations. Other times, different stakeholders will have different perceptions and perspectives and use different criteria to decide whether something is beneficial and/or ethical.

Laws and regulations often codify ethical actions that lead to better outcomes for society or specific groups of stakeholders. For example, some laws and regulations require businesses and their representatives to tell the truth. They require specific written disclosures in marketing and other materials. Complying with such rules is considered an ethical action; it creates a more satisfactory outcome that conforms to stakeholders' ethical expectations. As an example, consider disclosure requirements mandated by securities regulators regarding the risks of investing. Complying with such rules creates better outcomes for you, your clients, and your employer. First, compliance with the rule reduces the risk that clients will invest in securities without understanding the risks involved, which, in turn, reduces the risk that clients will file complaints and/or take legal action if their investments decline in value. Complying with the rules also reduces the risk that regulators will initiate an investigation, file charges, or/and discipline or sanction you and/or your employer. Any of these actions could jeopardize the reputation and future prospects of you and your employer. Conduct that reduces these risks (e.g., following disclosure rules) would be considered ethical; it leads to better outcomes for you, your clients, and your employer and conforms to the ethical expectations of various stakeholders.

Although laws frequently codify ethical actions, legal and ethical conduct are not always the same. Think about the diagram in Exhibit 1. Many types of conduct are both legal and ethical, but some conduct may be one and not the other. Some legal behaviors or activities may be considered unethical, and some behaviors or activities considered ethical may be deemed illegal in certain jurisdictions. Acts of civil disobedience, such as peaceful protests, may be in response to laws that individuals consider unethical. The act of civil disobedience may itself be considered ethical, and yet it violates existing local laws.

The investment industry has examples of conduct that may be legal but considered by some to be unethical. Some countries, for example, do not have laws prohibiting trading while in possession of material nonpublic information, but many investment professionals and CFA Institute consider such trading unethical.

Another area in which ethics and laws may conflict is the area of "whistleblowing." Whistleblowing refers to the disclosure by an individual of dishonest, corrupt, or illegal activity by an organization or government. Depending on the circumstances, a whistleblower may violate organizational policies and even local laws with the disclosure; thus, a whistleblower's actions may be deemed illegal and yet considered by some to be ethical.

Exhibit 1: Types of Conduct

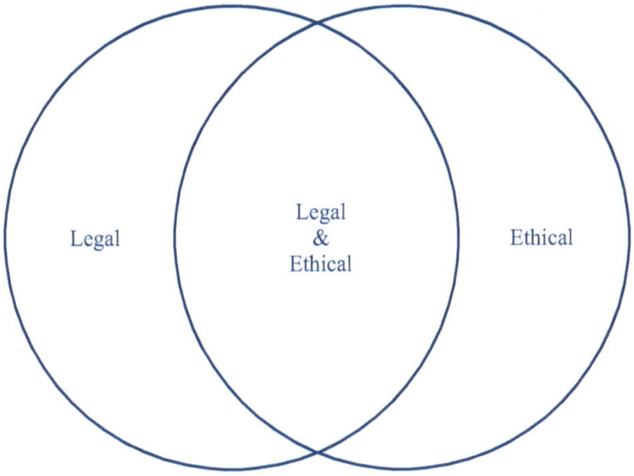

Some people advocate that increased regulation and monitoring of the behavior of participants in the investment industry will increase trust in the financial markets. Although this approach may work in some circumstances, the law is not always the best mechanism to reduce unethical behavior for several reasons. First, laws typically follow market practices; regulators may proactively design laws and regulations to address existing or anticipated practices that may adversely affect the fairness and efficiency of markets or reactively design laws and regulations in response to a crisis or an event that resulted in significant monetary losses and loss of confidence/trust in the financial system. Regulators' responses typically take significant time, during which the problematic practice may continue or even grow. Once enacted, a new law may be vague, conflicting, and/or too narrow in scope. A new law may reduce or even eliminate the existing activity while simultaneously creating an opportunity for a different, but similarly problematic, activity. Additionally, laws vary across countries or jurisdictions, allowing questionable practices to move to places that lack laws relevant to the questionable practice. Laws are also subject to interpretation and compliance by market participants, who may choose to interpret the law in the most advantageous way possible or delay compliance until a later date. For these reasons, laws and regulations are insufficient to ensure the ethical behavior of investment professionals and market participants.

Ethical conduct goes beyond what is legally required and encompasses what different societal groups or communities, including professional associations, consider to be ethically correct behavior. To act ethically, individuals need to be able to think through the facts of the situation and make good choices even in the absence of clear laws or rules. In many cases, there is no simple algorithm or formula that will always lead to an ethical course of action. Ethics requires judgment—the ability to make considered decisions and reach sensible conclusions. Good ethical judgment requires actively considering the interests of stakeholders and trying to benefit multiple stakeholders—clients, family, colleagues, employers, market participants, and so forth—and minimize risks, including reputational risk.

EXAMPLE 4

Ethical vs. Legal Standards

1. Which of the following statements is *most* accurate?

   A. All legal behavior is ethical behavior.

   B. Some ethical behavior may be illegal.

   C. Legal standards represent the highest standard.

Solution:

B is correct. Some ethical behavior may be illegal. Civil disobedience is an example of what may be illegal behavior that some consider to be ethical. Legal and ethical behavior often coincide but not always. Standards of conduct based on ethical principles may represent a higher standard of behavior than the behavior required by law.

2. Which of the following statements is *most* accurate?

   A. Increased regulations are the most useful means to reduce unethical behavior by market participants.

   B. Regulators quickly design and implement laws and regulations to address practices that adversely affect the fairness and efficiency of markets.

   C. New laws designed to reduce or eliminate conduct that adversely affects the markets can create opportunities for different, but similarly problematic, conduct.

Solution:

C is correct. New laws designed to reduce or eliminate conduct that adversely affects the markets can create opportunities for different, but similarly problematic, conduct.

6 ETHICAL DECISION-MAKING FRAMEWORKS

☐ describe a framework for ethical decision making

Laws, regulations, professional standards, and codes of ethics can guide ethical behavior, but individual judgment is a critical ingredient in making principled choices and engaging in appropriate conduct. One strategy to increase trust in the investment industry is to increase the ability and motivation of market participants to act ethically and help them minimize the likelihood of unethical actions. By integrating ethics into the decision-making activities of employees, firms can enhance the ability and the motivation of employees to act ethically, thereby reducing the likelihood of unethical actions. The ability to relate an ethical decision-making framework to a firm's or profession's code of ethics allows investment professionals to bring the principles of the code of ethics to life. An investment professional's natural desire to "do the right thing" can be reinforced by building a culture of integrity and accountability in the workplace. Development, maintenance, and demonstration of a strong culture of integrity within the firm by senior management may be the single most important factor in promoting ethical behavior among the firm's employees.

Adopting a code that clearly lays out the ethical principles that guide the thought processes and conduct the firm expects from its employees is a critical first step. But a code of ethics, although necessary, is insufficient. Simply nurturing an inclination to do right is no match for the multitude of daily decisions that investment professionals make. We need to exercise ethical decision-making skills to develop the muscle memory necessary for fundamentally ethical people to make good decisions despite the reality of conflicts and our natural instinct for self-preservation. Just as coaching and practice transform our natural ability to run across a field into the technique and endurance required to run a race, teaching, reinforcing, and practicing ethical decision-making skills prepare us to confront the hard issues effectively. It is good for business, individuals, firms, the industry, and the markets, as well as society as a whole, to engage in the investment management profession in a highly ethical manner. A strong ethical culture, built on a defined set of principles, that helps honest, ethical people engage in ethical behavior will foster the trust of investors, lead to robust global financial markets, and ultimately benefit society. That is why ethics matter.

The Framework for Ethical Decision-Making

When faced with decisions that can affect multiple stakeholders, investment professionals must have a well-developed set of principles; otherwise, their thought processes can lead to, at best, indecision and, at worst, fraudulent conduct and destruction of the public trust. Establishing an ethical framework to guide your internal thought process regarding how to act is a crucial step to engaging in ethical conduct. Investment professionals are generally comfortable analyzing and making decisions from an economic (profit/loss) perspective. Given the importance of ethical behavior in carrying out professional responsibilities, it is also important to analyze decisions and their potential consequences from an ethical perspective. Using a framework for ethical decision making will help investment professionals to effectively examine their choices in the context of conflicting interests common to their professional obligations (e.g., researching and gathering information, developing investment recommendations, and managing money for others). Such a framework will allow investment professionals to analyze and choose options in a way that allows them to meet high standards of ethical behavior. An ethical decision-making framework provides investment professionals with a tool to help them adhere to a code of ethics. By applying the framework and analyzing the particular circumstances of each available alternative, investment professionals are able to determine the best course of action to fulfill their responsibilities in an ethical manner.

An ethical decision-making framework will help a decision maker see the situation from multiple perspectives and pay attention to aspects of the situation that may be less evident with a short-term, self-focused perspective. The goal of getting a broader picture of a situation is to be able to create a plan of action that is less likely to harm stakeholders and more likely to benefit them. If a decision maker does not know or understand the effects of his or her actions on stakeholders, the likelihood of making a decision and taking action that harms stakeholders is more likely to occur, even if unintentionally. Finally, an ethical decision-making framework helps decision makers explain and justify their actions to a broader audience of stakeholders.

Ethical decision making frameworks are designed to facilitate the decision-making process for all decisions. They help people look at and evaluate a decision from multiple perspectives, enabling them to identify important issues they might not otherwise consider. Using an ethical decision-making framework consistently will help you develop sound judgment and decision-making skills and avoid making decisions that have unanticipated ethical consequences. Ethical decision-making frameworks come in many forms with varying degrees of detail. A general ethical decision-making framework is shown in Exhibit 2.

Exhibit 2: Ethical Decision-Making Framework

- Identify: Relevant facts, stakeholders and duties owed, ethical principles, conflicts of interest
- Consider: Situational influences, additional guidance, alternative actions
- Decide and act
- Reflect: Was the outcome as anticipated? Why or why not?

The ethical decision-making process includes multiple phases, each of which has multiple components. The process is often iterative, and you, the decision maker, may move between phases in an order different from what is presented. For simplicity, we will discuss the phases sequentially. In the initial phase, you will want to identify the important facts that you have available to you, as well as information that you may not have but would like to have to give yourself a more complete understanding of the situation. It is helpful to distinguish between facts and personal opinion, judgements, and biases. You will also want to identify the stakeholders—clients, family, colleagues, your employer, market participants, and so forth—and the duties you have to each of them. You will then want to identify relevant ethical principles and/or legal requirements that might apply to the situation. You should also identify any potential conflicts of interest inherent in the situation or conflicts in the duties you hold to others. For example, your duty to your client may conflict with your duty to your employer.

In the second phase of ethical decision making, you will take time to consider the situational influences as well as personal behavioral biases that could affect your thinking and thus decision making. These situational influences and biases could include a desire to please your boss, to be seen as successful by your peers and family, to gain acceptance, to earn a large bonus, and so on. During this phase, you may seek additional guidance from trusted sources—perhaps a family member, colleague, or mentor who can help you think through the situation and help you identify and evaluate alternative actions. You may turn to your compliance department for assistance or you may even consult outside legal counsel. Seeking additional guidance is a critical step in viewing the situation from different perspectives. You should seek guidance from someone, possibly external to the firm, who is not affected by the same situational influences and behavioral biases as you are and can, therefore, provide a fresh perspective. You should also seek guidance from your firm's policies and procedures and the CFA Institute Code and Standards. A helpful technique might be to imagine how an ethical peer or role model might act in the situation.

The next phase of the framework is to make a decision and act. After you have acted on your decision, you should take the time to reflect on and assess your decision and its outcome. Was the outcome what you anticipated? Why or why not? Had you properly identified all the important facts, stakeholders, duties to stakeholders, conflicts of interest, and relevant ethical principles? Had you considered the situational influences? Did you identify personal behavioral biases that might affect your thinking? Had you sought sufficient guidance? Had you considered and properly evaluated a variety of alternative actions? You may want to reflect on the decision multiple times as the immediate and longer-term consequences of your decision and actions become apparent.

The process is often iterative. After identifying the relevant facts and considering situational influences, you may, for example, decide that you cannot make a decision without more information. You may seek additional guidance on how to obtain the information you need. You may also begin considering alternative actions regarding how to proceed based on expectations of what the additional information will reveal, or you may wait until you have more information, reflect on what you have done and learned so far, and start the process over again. Sometimes cases can be complicated and multiple iterations may reveal that no totally acceptable solution can be created. Applying an ethical decision-making framework can help you evaluate the situation so you can make the best possible decision. The next section shows applications of the framework shown in Exhibit 2.

Applying the Framework

To illustrate how the framework could be applied in your career, consider the scenario in Example 5.

EXAMPLE 5

Applying an Ethical Decision-Making Framework I

1. You have been hired as a junior analyst with a major investment bank. When you join the bank, you receive a copy of the firm's policies as well as training on the policies. Your supervisor is the senior technology analyst for the investment bank. As part of your duties, you gather information, draft documents, conduct analysis, and perform other support functions for the senior analyst.

   Your employer is one of several investment banks working on the initial public offering (IPO) of a well-known technology company. The IPO is expected to generate significant revenues for the investment banks participating in the offering. The IPO has been highly anticipated and is in the news every day.

   You are thrilled when your supervisor asks you to work on several research projects related to analyzing and valuing the upcoming IPO for investors. You eagerly compile information and draft a one-page outline. You stop to consider what other information you could add to improve the report before proceeding. You realize that you have two excellent contacts in the technology industry who could review your work and provide some additional and potentially valuable perspectives. You draft an email to your contacts reading:

   > I am working on an analysis and valuation of Big Tech Company for investors. My employer is one of the banks participating in the IPO, and I want to make sure I have considered everything. I was hoping you could give me feedback on the prospects and risks facing Big Tech. Please treat all the attached material as confidential.

   Before hitting the send button, you stop and think about the ethical decision-making framework you have studied. You decide to apply the framework and jot down some notes as you work through the process: On the first page, you work through the identification phase and make a list of the relevant facts, stakeholders to whom you owe a duty, potential conflicts of interest, and ethical principles. This list is shown is Exhibit 3.

Exhibit 3: Identification Phase

- Relevant facts:
  - *Working on the deal/IPO of the decade*
  - *Employer is one of several investment banks working on IPO*
  - *The IPO is highly anticipated*
  - *A successful IPO could lead to additional investment banking deals and revenues for the firm*
  - *Supervisor is relying on me*
  - *Employer has documented policies and procedures*
  - *Industry is regulated, with many rules and regulations in place*
- Stakeholders and duties owed. I have a duty to the following:
  - *Supervisor*
  - *Employer*
  - *Employer's corporate client, the technology company*
  - *Employer's asset management and other investing clients*
  - *Employer's partners in the IPO*
  - *Investors and market participants interested in the IPO*
  - *All capital market participants*
  - *Profession*
  - *Society as a whole*
- Conflicts or potential conflicts of interest include the following:
  - *Gathering additional research from external sources versus maintaining confidentiality*
  - *Duty to supervisor versus desire to impress*
  - *Duty to corporate client versus duty to other clients of the firm*
  - *The firm's corporate client benefits from a high IPO price whereas the firm's asset management clients would benefit from a low IPO price*
  - *Making the IPO look attractive to the market (sell-side marketing) versus objective analysis of the investment potential of this deal (buy-side analysis)*

- *My bonus, compensation, and career prospects are tied to my supervisor's and the IPO's success; duty to employer, employer's investing clients, profession*

- Ethical principles that are relevant to this situation include the following:
  - *Duty of loyalty to employer*
  - *Client interests come first*
  - *Maintain confidences and confidentiality of information*
  - *Objectivity of analysis*
  - *Fairness to market participants*

On the next page, you write notes relating to the second phase of the framework, considering the various situational factors and the guidance available to you before considering alternative actions. These notes are shown in Exhibit 4.

Exhibit 4: Consideration Phase

- Situational influences:
  - *The firm's written policies*
  - *The bank will earn big fees from the IPO*
  - *I want to impress my boss—and potential future bosses*
  - *My bonus, compensation, and career prospects will be influenced by my contribution to the success of this deal and other deals*
  - *I am one of very few people working on this deal; it is a real honor, and others would be impressed that I am working on this deal*
  - *My employer is filled with successful and wealthy people who are go-getters; I want to be successful and wealthy like them*
- Additional guidance. I could seek guidance from the following:
  - *The firm's code of ethics*
  - *The firm's written policies*
  - *A peer in my firm*
  - *My supervisor, the senior analyst*
  - *The compliance department*
  - *A mentor either at the firm or perhaps from university or industry*
  - *The CFA Institute Code and Standards*

- *Outside legal counsel*

- Alternative actions. I could consider the following:
  - *Asking contacts what they have heard*
  - *Submitting the report as a draft and suggesting that contacts in the industry might be able to provide more perspective*
  - *Sending a survey to various technology industry veterans soliciting their viewpoints on developments*

After completing these steps, you decide to check the firm's policies. Under a section entitled "Research Analyst Role in Securities Offerings," the manual states, "You may not distribute any written (which include email, fax, electronic, and other means) material related to companies and/or their offerings . . . during the course of any offering and the related quiet period."

You read further and note a section entitled "Wall Crossing Policy and Procedures" that states that "employees with confidential information may not communicate the information to anyone who does not have a valid need to know" without first obtaining clearance from the legal and compliance department.

You decide that your contacts do not have a "valid need to know" and that it is unlikely the firm's legal and compliance professionals would approve sharing the information. You then decide to mention your contacts to the senior research analyst. He suggests that they may have some useful perspective and that you might talk to them to hear their perspective and cautions you not to disclose any information about any of the firm's clients, pending deals, or research. You return to your desk, delete the email, and following the senior research analyst's advice, call your contacts on the telephone to discuss the technology sector, its prospects, and its challenges. During the calls, you take care not to reveal any details about Big Tech Company or its offering.

Whatever action you take, you should take time afterward to reflect on the decision and the outcome. Was the outcome as anticipated? Why or why not?

The initial facts presented in the example are based on the real-life experience of a young junior analyst working on a highly anticipated IPO. The junior analyst may or may not have used an ethical decision-making framework to evaluate his situation. Without seeking additional guidance, the junior analyst sent an email similar to the one in the example with an attachment that included confidential, proprietary information, including the senior analyst's analysis and forecasts. Months later, long after the IPO offering, the junior analyst's email was discovered by his employer. When questioned, he admitted that he had received training regarding the firm's policies and that he did not discuss or seek approval from anyone before sending the email. Two days later, the firm terminated the junior analyst's employment and reported to regulatory authorities that he had been terminated for distributing written materials, by email, during a securities offering in violation of firm policies that prohibit the dissemination of any written materials during the course of a securities offering and related periods. The junior analyst's supervisor also lost his job for failing to properly supervise the analyst. Multiple regulators investigated the matter, and the firm was fined millions of dollars for failing to supervise its employees properly. The information regarding the junior analyst's termination was posted and remains available on the regulator's website for all to see. Future employers conducting routine background checks will know that the analyst was terminated for violating firm policies relating to a securities offering.

The example presented is similar to situations faced by many analysts. Using an ethical decision-making framework will help you evaluate situations from multiple perspectives, avoid poor decision making, and avoid the consequences that can result from taking an ill-conceived course of action. Using an ethical decision-making framework is no guarantee of a positive outcome but may help you avoid making unethical decisions.

EXAMPLE 6

Applying an Ethical Decision-Making Framework II

A financial adviser has been saving a portion of his salary to purchase a new vehicle. He is on track to have enough saved within the next three months. His employer has offered a special bonus for this quarter, which will go to the team that attracts the most new investors into the firm's investment funds. In addition to the potential bonus, the firm pays a 5% commission to employees who sell shares in the firm's investment funds. Several of the funds are highly rated, including one designed to provide steady income to investors.

The financial adviser has added only a few new investors to the firm's funds, but his teammates have been very successful in their efforts. The end of the quarter is one week away, and his team is competing closely with another team for the bonus. One of his teammates informs the financial adviser that he really needs the bonus so his elderly mother can receive medical treatment.

Later that day, the financial adviser meets with an elderly client on a limited income who is seeking more income from his investment portfolio. The client is 89 years old and in poor health. According to the client's will, the client's investment portfolio will go to his favorite charity upon his death.

1. Which of the following situational influences is likely to have the *most* effect on the financial adviser's efforts to get new clients to invest in the funds? His relationship with his:

   A. client.

   B. employer.

   C. teammates.

Solution:

C is correct. The financial adviser's relationship with his teammates is likely to have the most effect on the financial adviser's efforts. The teammates share in earning the bonus from the employer. In addition, the team works with each other on a regular basis where there is a likelihood that social influences of working together play a role in decision making and effort.

2. Which of the following statements is *most* accurate? An ethical decision-making framework:

   A. is only beneficial when a firm lacks a code of ethics.

   B. is used to improve compliance with laws and regulations.

C. is a tool for analyzing the potential alternative actions and consequences of a decision.

Solution:

C is correct. An ethical decision-making framework is a tool for analyzing the potential alternative actions and consequences of a decision.

3. Which of the following is *most* accurate? Ethical decision-making frameworks:

   A. raise awareness of different perspectives.

   B. focus attention on short-term consequences.

   C. allocate more weight to those who will directly benefit from the decision.

Solution:

A is correct. Ethical decision-making frameworks raise awareness of different perspectives. The framework should consider short-term consequences, but they are not the focus of the framework. Similarly, the framework may allocate more weight to those who directly benefit from decisions, but this is not the primary goal of an ethical decision-making framework.

4. Which of the following is *most* accurate? Ethical decision-making frameworks:

   A. are not needed if behavior is legal.

   B. identify who gains the most from a decision.

   C. can help reduce unanticipated ethical lapses and unexpected consequences.

Solution:

C is correct. Ethical decision-making frameworks can help avoid unanticipated ethical consequences. As it relates to A, ethics standards are often higher than legal standards so an ethical decision-making framework would be needed. Although B is accurate, identifying who gains most from the decision is a small component of the framework.

5. Using an ethical decision-making framework, which of the following duties would *most likely* take precedence in the scenario described? The financial adviser's duty to his:

   A. client.

   B. employer.

   C. colleagues.

Solution:

A is correct. Using an ethical decision-making framework, the financial adviser's relationship with his client would most likely take precedence in this scenario. The adviser should put his client's interests first. The exception to client interests taking precedence occurs when market integrity effects take precedence.

6. Using an ethical decision-making framework, the financial adviser would *most likely*:

   A. recommend that the elderly client invest at least some of his assets in the highly rated fund.

   B. research other investments that can provide steady income before making a recommendation to his elderly client.

   C. disclose the commission he would earn before recommending that the elderly client invest at least some of his assets in the highly rated fund.

Solution:

B is correct. Using an ethical decision-making framework, the financial adviser would identify the relevant facts, stakeholders, duties owed, and potential conflicts. In this scenario, the financial adviser owes a duty to his client as well as his employer. His client's interests take precedence over all other interests. The bonus and his colleague's desire to help his mother are situational influences. To navigate this situation, the financial adviser should seek additional information; he should research the risk and return parameters and fee structures of other investments that can provide steady income before making a recommendation to his client.

CONCLUSION

7

This reading introduced ideas and concepts that will help you understand the importance of ethical behavior in the investment industry as well as the challenges to adhering to high ethical standards. A code of ethics will communicate an organization's values and the expected behavior of its members as well as provide guidance for decision making. A code of ethics may be further enhanced and clarified by the adoption of standards of conduct. Professions and professional organizations, such as the CFA Institute, can help to establish codes and standards that provide a framework and technical competence for practitioners. An ethical decision-making framework combined with a code of ethics may help investment professionals analyze their decisions in a way that identifies potential conflicts and negative consequences.

Knowing the rules to apply in a particular situation, although important, may not be sufficient to ensure ethical conduct if used alone. Responsible professionals in the investment industry must be able both to recognize areas that are prone to ethical pitfalls and to identify and process those circumstances and influences that can impair judgment and lead to ethical lapses.

SUMMARY

- Ethics refers to the study of making good choices. Ethics encompasses a set of moral principles and rules of conduct that provide guidance for our behavior.
- Situational influences are external factors that may shape our behavior.

- Challenges to ethical behavior include being overconfident in our own morality, underestimating the effect of situational influences, and focusing on the immediate rather than long-term outcomes or consequences of a decision.
- In any given profession, the code of ethics publicly communicates the established principles and expected behavior of its members.
- Members of a profession use specialized knowledge and skills to serve others; they share and agree to adhere to a common code of ethics to serve others and advance the profession.
- A code of ethics helps foster public confidence that members of the profession will use their specialized skills and knowledge to serve their clients and others.
- A profession is an occupational group that has specific education, expert knowledge, and a framework of practice and behavior that underpins community trust, respect, and recognition.
- The requirement to uphold high ethical standards is one clear difference between professions and craft guilds or trade bodies.
- A primary goal of professions is to establish trust among clients and among society in general.
- Common characteristics of professions include normalization of practitioner behavior, service to society, client focus, high entry standards, a body of expert knowledge, encouragement and facilitation of continuing education, monitoring of professional conduct, collegiality, recognized overseeing bodies, and encouragement of member engagement.
- The investment management profession has become increasingly global, driven by the opening of capital markets, coordination of regulation across borders, and the emergence of technology.
- Investment management professionals are trusted to draw on a body of formal knowledge and apply that knowledge with care and judgement. In comparison to clients, investment professionals are also expected to have superior financial expertise, technical knowledge, and knowledge of the applicable laws and regulations.
- As a professional body, CFA Institute gathers knowledge from practicing investment professionals, conducts rigorous examinations, and ensures practitioner involvement in developing its codes and values.
- Investment management professionals are likely to encounter dilemmas, including those with ethical implications. Professionals should consider carefully how to determine the facts of the issue and assess the implications.
- High ethical standards always matter and are of particular importance in the investment management profession, which is based almost entirely on trust. Clients trust investment professionals to use their specialized skills and knowledge to serve clients and protect client assets. All stakeholders gain long-term benefits when investment professionals adhere to high ethical standards.
- Legal standards are often rule based. Ethical conduct goes beyond legal standards, balancing self-interest with the direct and indirect consequences of behavior on others.
- A framework for ethical decision making can help people look at and evaluate a decision from different perspectives, enabling them to identify important issues, make wise decisions, and limit unintended consequences.

PRACTICE PROBLEMS

1. Benchmarks for minimally acceptable behaviors of community members are:

   A. a code of ethics.

   B. laws and regulations.

   C. standards of conduct.

2. Specialized knowledge and skills, a commitment to serve others, and a shared code of ethics *best* characterize a(n):

   A. vocation.

   B. profession.

   C. occupation.

3. When unethical behavior erodes trust in an investment firm, that firm is *more likely* to experience:

   A. lower revenues only.

   B. higher expenses only.

   C. lower revenues and higher expenses.

4. High ethical standards are distinguishing features of which of the following bodies?

   A. Craft guilds

   B. Trade bodies

   C. Professional bodies

5. Fiduciary duty is a standard *most likely* to be upheld by members of a(n):

   A. employer.

   B. profession.

   C. not-for-profit body.

6. Which of the following *best* identifies an internal trait that may lead to poor ethical decision making?

   A. Overconfidence

   B. Loyalty to employer

   C. Promise of money or prestige

7. Situational influences in decision making will *most likely* be minimized if:

   A. strong compliance programs are in place.

   B. longer-term consequences are considered.

C. individuals believe they are truthful and honest.

8. Decision makers who use a compliance approach are *most likely* to:

   A. avoid situational influences.

   B. oversimplify decision making.

   C. consider more factors than when using an ethical decision-making approach.

9. To maintain trust, the investment management profession must be interdependent with:

   A. regulators.

   B. employers.

   C. investment firms.

10. Which is an example of an activity that may be legal but that CFA Institute considers unethical?

    A. Making legally required disclosures in marketing materials

    B. Trading while in possession of material nonpublic information

    C. Disclosure by an employee of his or her own company's dishonest activity

11. An ethical decision-making framework will *most likely*:

    A. include a pre-determined, uniform sequence.

    B. focus exclusively on confirmable facts and relationships.

    C. help avoid a decision that has unanticipated ethical consequences.

12. When an ethical dilemma occurs, an investment professional should *most likely* first raise the issue with a:

    A. mentor outside the firm.

    B. professional body's hotline.

    C. senior individual in the firm.

SOLUTIONS

1. C is correct. Standards of conduct are applied to specific communities or societal groups and identify specific behaviors required of community members. These standards of conduct serve as benchmarks for the minimally acceptable behavior of community members. Codes of ethics serve as a general guide for how community members should act; they communicate the organization's values and overall expectations regarding member behavior, but they do not identify specific behaviors required of community members. Laws and regulations are rules of conduct defined by governments and related entities about obligatory and forbidden conduct broadly applicable for individuals and entities under their jurisdiction.

2. B is correct. A profession has several characteristics that distinguish it from an occupation or vocation, such as specialized knowledge and skills, service to others, and a code of ethics shared by its members. A profession is the ultimate evolution of an occupation, resulting from excellence in practice, a mastery mindest, and expected adherence to a code of ethics and standards of practice.

3. C is correct. Unethical behavior ultimately harms investment firms. Clients are not attracted if they suspect unethical behavior, leading to less business and lower revenues. Investment firms may also experience higher relative costs because regulators are more likely to have cause to initiate costly investigations.

4. C is correct. High ethical standards distinguish professions from the craft guilds or trade bodies. Unlike trade bodies, professional bodies also typically have a mission to serve society and enforce professional conduct rules for practitioners.

5. B is correct. Fiduciary duty is an obligation to deliver a high standard of care when acting for the benefit of another party. Professionals must act in the best interest of the client, exercising a reasonable level of care, skill, and diligence. Other entities—including employers, regulators, trade associations, and not-for-profit bodies—may also support an industry but are not the same as professional bodies. Unlike professions, these other entities generally do not exist to set and maintain professional standards.

6. A is correct. An overconfidence bias can lead individuals to put too much importance on internal traits and intrinsic motivations, such as their own perceptions of personal honesty, that can lead to faulty decision making. Loyalty to an employer and promise of money or prestige are situational influences that can lead to faulty decision making.

7. B is correct. Consciously considering long-term consequences will help offset situational influences. We more easily recognize and consider short-term situational influences than longer-term considerations because longer-term considerations have fewer immediate consequences than situational influences do. When decision making is too narrowly focused on short-term factors, we tend to ignore longer-term risks and consequences, and the likelihood of poor ethical decision making increases. A strong compliance policy is a good first step toward developing an ethical culture; a focus on rules adherence may not be sufficient. Emphasis on compliance may not encourage decision makers to consider the larger picture and can oversimplify decision making. Taken to the extreme, a strong compliance culture can become another situational influence that blinds employees to other important considerations. An overconfidence bias can place too much importance on internal traits and intrinsic motivations, such as "I'm honest and would

not lie," even though studies have shown that internal traits are generally not the main determinant of whether or not someone will behave ethically in a given situation.

8. B is correct. A compliance approach can oversimplify decision making and may not encourage decision makers to consider the larger picture. A strong compliance culture may be a good start in developing an ethical culture but can become another situational influence that may result in employees failing to consider other important factors.

9. C is correct. The investment management profession and investment firms must be interdependent to maintain trust. Employers and regulators have their own standards and practices, which may differ from regulations and standards set by professional bodies.

10. B is correct. The investment industry has examples of conduct that may be legal but that CFA Institute considers unethical. Trading while in possession of material nonpublic information is not prohibited by law worldwide and can, therefore, be legal, but CFA Institute considers such trading unethical.

11. C is correct. Using an ethical decision-making framework consistently will help you develop sound judgment and decision-making skills and avoid making decisions that have unanticipated ethical consequences. The decision-making process is often iterative, and the decision maker may move between phases of the framework. A decision maker should consider more than confirmable facts and relationships; for example, the decision maker should consider situational influences and personal biases.

12. C is correct. When a dilemma occurs, raising an issue internally with a senior employee is often a good starting place and creates an opportunity for an independent internal review. Protecting the client and the firm may take priority over the position of an individual professional raising a concern.

LEARNING MODULE

2

Code of Ethics and Standards of Professional Conduct

LEARNING OUTCOMES	
Mastery	*The candidate should be able to:*
☐	describe the structure of the CFA Institute Professional Conduct Program and the process for the enforcement of the Code and Standards
☐	identify the six components of the Code of Ethics and the seven Standards of Professional Conduct
☐	explain the ethical responsibilities required by the Code and Standards, including the sub-sections of each Standard

PREFACE

1

☐	describe the structure of the CFA Institute Professional Conduct Program and the process for the enforcement of the Code and Standards

The *Standards of Practice Handbook* (*Handbook*) provides guidance to the people who grapple with real ethical dilemmas in the investment profession on a daily basis; the *Handbook* addresses the professional intersection where theory meets practice and where the concept of ethical behavior crosses from the abstract to the concrete. The *Handbook* is intended for a diverse and global audience: CFA Institute members navigating ambiguous ethical situations; supervisors and direct/indirect reports determining the nature of their responsibilities to each other, to existing and potential clients, and to the broader financial markets; and candidates preparing for the Chartered Financial Analyst (CFA) examinations.

Events in global financial markets test the ethical mettle of financial market participants, including CFA Institute members and candidates. The standards taught in the CFA Program and by which CFA Institute members and candidates must abide represent timeless ethical principles and professional conduct for all market conditions.

Through adherence to these standards, which continue to serve as the model for ethical behavior in the investment profession globally, each market participant does his or her part to improve the integrity and efficient operations of the financial markets.

The *Handbook* provides guidance for understanding the interconnectedness of the aspirational and practical principles and provisions of the Code of Ethics and Standards of Professional Conduct (Code and Standards). The Code contains high-level aspirational ethical principles that drive members and candidates to create a positive and reputable investment profession. The Standards contain practical ethical principles of conduct that members and candidates must follow to achieve the broader industry expectations. However, applying the principles individually may not capture the complexity of ethical requirements related to the investment industry. The Code and Standards should be viewed and interpreted as an interwoven tapestry of ethical requirements. Through members' and candidates' adherence to these principles as a whole, the integrity of and trust in the capital markets are improved.

Evolution of the CFA Institute Code of Ethics and Standards of Professional Conduct

The Code and Standards are regularly reviewed and updated so that they remain effective and continue to represent the highest ethical standards in the global investment industry. CFA Institute strongly believes that revisions of the Code and Standards are undertaken not for cosmetic purposes but to add value by addressing legitimate concerns and improving comprehension. In 2023, the CFA Institute Board of Governors approved revisions to the Code and Standards that are fully described later in this learning module.

Changes to the Code and Standards have far-reaching implications for the CFA Institute membership, the CFA Program, and the investment industry as a whole. CFA Institute members and candidates are *required* to adhere to the Code and Standards. In addition, the Code and Standards are often adopted, in whole or in part, by firms and regulatory authorities. Their relevance goes well beyond CFA Institute members and candidates.

Standards of Practice Handbook

The periodic revisions of the *Standards of Practice Handbook* have come in conjunction with updates of the Code and Standards. The *Handbook* is the fundamental element of the ethics education effort of CFA Institute and the primary resource for guidance in interpreting and implementing the Code and Standards. The *Handbook* seeks to educate members and candidates on how to apply the Code and Standards to their professional lives and thereby benefit their clients, employers, and the investing public in general. The *Handbook* explains the purpose of the Code and Standards and how they apply in a variety of situations. The sections discuss and amplify each standard and suggest procedures for compliance.

Examples in the "Application of the Standard" sections are meant to illustrate how the standard applies to hypothetical but factual situations. The names contained in the examples are fictional and are not meant to refer to any actual person or entity. Unless otherwise stated (e.g., one or more people are specifically identified), individuals in each example are subject to the requirements of the Code and Standards. Because factual circumstances vary so widely and often involve gray areas, the explanatory material and examples are not intended to be all inclusive. Many examples set forth in the application sections involve standards that have legal counterparts; ***members***

are strongly urged to discuss with their supervisors and legal and compliance departments the content of the Code and Standards and the members' general obligations under the Code and Standards.

CFA Institute recognizes that the presence of any set of ethical standards may create a false sense of security unless the documents are fully understood, enforced, and made a meaningful part of everyday professional activities. The *Handbook* is intended to provide a useful frame of reference that outlines ethical professional conduct for the organization's members and candidates. The *Handbook* cannot cover every contingency or circumstance, however, and it does not attempt to do so. The development and interpretation of the Code and Standards are evolving processes; the Code and Standards will be subject to continuing refinement.

Summary of the 2023 Revisions to the Code and Standards

In 2023, the CFA Institute Board of Governors revised the Standards of Professional Conduct in three areas, resulting in the inclusion of one new standard and revisions to two existing standards. The following is a summary of the changes:

1. Within Standard I: Professionalism, the Board approved a new standard requiring members to act with and maintain the competence necessary to fulfill their professional responsibilities, thus reinforcing the principle set forth in the Code of Ethics.
2. Within Standard V: Investment Analysis, Recommendations, and Actions, the Board revised Standard V(B) Communication with Clients and Prospective Clients to require disclosures about the nature of the services provided by members and candidates and the costs to the client associated with those services.
3. Within Standard VI: Conflicts of Interest, the Board changed the name of Standard VI(A) to "Standard VI(A) Avoid or Disclose Conflicts" and revised the standard to require members and candidates to either avoid conflicts of interest or disclose those conflicts. Previously, there was no mention of avoiding conflicts of interest in the standard.

New guidance and examples have been added to the *Handbook* to fully explain these new requirements.

New and Revised Standards of Professional Conduct

Competence Standard

I. PROFESSIONALISM

E. Competence

Members and Candidates must:

1. Act with and maintain the competence necessary to fulfill their professional responsibilities.

Given the diverse range of professional services engaged in by members and candidates, the knowledge, skills, and abilities necessary to successfully fulfill their role will vary according to the nature of their professional duties. Over time, a member's role may expand, requiring new or different knowledge, skills, and abilities. Members will develop and refine their skills and abilities throughout their professional careers.

Requiring members and candidates to act with and maintain appropriate levels of competence will help ensure they provide a high standard of professional service for their clients and employers.

Currently, the Code of Ethics requires members and candidates to "act with integrity, competence, and diligence" and to "maintain and improve their professional competence and strive to improve the competence of other investment professionals." This new standard is consistent with and directly supports the requirements of the Code of Ethics. Standard I(E) makes these requirements of the Code of Ethics more explicit and emphasizes the need for members and candidates to continuously maintain or improve the competence required by their professional position.

The skills and abilities necessary for members and candidates to successfully fulfill their role vary according to the nature and complexity of their professional duties. As a result, there will be different criteria for competence for different members. An examination of the facts and circumstances of each member or candidate will dictate their expected conduct under this standard.

Finally, Standard I(E) does not require members and candidates to engage in any specific program of professional development or continuing education. There are a variety of ways members and candidates can demonstrate and maintain competence when engaging in their professional responsibilities.

Disclosure of Nature of Services and Costs to Client

V. INVESTMENT ANALYSIS, RECOMMENDATIONS, AND ACTIONS

B. Communication with Clients and Prospective Clients

Members and Candidates must:

1. Disclose to clients and prospective clients the nature of the services provided, along with information about the costs to the client associated with those services.

A fundamental goal of the Code and Standards is to protect client interests and allow clients to make fully informed decisions about their investments and financial well-being. Providing clients with information about the nature of the services they can expect from investment professionals and the financial impact they can expect from those services is critical to achieving this goal. The disclosures required by this new standard will permit clients to make informed decisions as to whether to engage with the member or candidate and their firm.

Standard V(B) Communication with Clients and Prospective Clients also requires members to disclose the basic format and general principles of the investment processes they use to analyze investments, select securities, and construct portfolios and to promptly disclose any material changes to these processes. The associated financial impact is an important part of the investment process but, until now, was not explicitly addressed as part of this disclosure. The revision to Standard V(B) fills this gap.

Revised Standard Relating to Conflicts

VI. CONFLICTS OF INTEREST

A. Avoid or Disclose Conflicts

Members and Candidates must:

1. Avoid or make full and fair disclosure of all matters that could reasonably be expected to impair their independence and objectivity and interfere with respective duties to their clients, prospective clients, and employer.
2. Ensure that such disclosures are prominent, are delivered in plain language, and communicate the relevant information effectively.

Standard VI(A) has always required members and candidates to disclose conflicts, but previously, the language of the standard made no mention of avoiding conflicts. Nevertheless, the guidance for Standard VI: Conflicts of Interest has long stated that best practice is to avoid conflicts or the appearance of conflicts. Including the option to avoid versus simply disclosing conflicts in the language of the standard emphasizes that members and candidates should avoid conflicts of interest whenever reasonably possible. While avoiding conflicts altogether is preferred, often in the investment industry it may not be reasonable for members and candidates to avoid a conflict or the perception of a conflict. When it is not reasonable for members and candidates to avoid a conflict, Standard VI(A) continues to require clear and complete disclosure of the conflict.

CFA Institute Professional Conduct Program

All CFA Institute members and candidates enrolled in the CFA Program are required to comply with the Code and Standards. The CFA Institute Board of Governors maintains oversight and responsibility for the Professional Conduct Program (PCP), which, in conjunction with the Disciplinary Review Committee (DRC), is responsible for enforcement of the Code and Standards. The DRC is a volunteer committee of CFA charterholders who serve on panels to review conduct and partner with Professional Conduct staff to establish and review professional conduct policies. The CFA Institute Bylaws and Rules of Procedure for Professional Conduct (Rules of Procedure) form the basic structure for enforcing the Code and Standards. The Professional Conduct division is also responsible for enforcing testing policies of other CFA Institute education programs, as well as the professional conduct of Certificate in Investment Performance Measurement (CIPM) certificants.

Professional Conduct inquiries come from a number of sources. First, members and candidates must self-disclose on the annual Professional Conduct Statement all matters that question their professional conduct, such as involvement in civil litigation or a criminal investigation or being the subject of a written complaint. Second, written complaints received by Professional Conduct staff can bring about an investigation. Third, CFA Institute staff may become aware of questionable conduct by a member or candidate through the media, regulatory notices, or another public source. Fourth, candidate conduct is monitored by proctors who complete reports on candidates suspected to have violated testing rules on exam day. Lastly, CFA Institute may also conduct analyses of scores and exam materials after the exam, as well as monitor online and social media to detect disclosure of confidential exam information.

When an inquiry is initiated, the Professional Conduct staff conducts an investigation that may include requesting a written explanation from the member or candidate; interviewing the member or candidate, complaining parties, and third parties; and collecting documents and records relevant to the investigation. Upon reviewing the material obtained during the investigation, the Professional Conduct staff may conclude the inquiry with no disciplinary sanction, issue a cautionary letter, or continue proceedings to discipline the member or candidate. If the Professional Conduct staff believes a violation of the Code and Standards or testing policies has occurred, the member or candidate has the opportunity to reject or accept any charges and the proposed sanctions.

If the member or candidate does not accept the charges and proposed sanction, the matter is referred to a panel composed of DRC members. Panels review materials and presentations from Professional Conduct staff and from the member or candidate. The panel's task is to determine whether a violation of the Code and Standards or testing policies occurred and, if so, what sanction should be imposed.

Sanctions imposed by CFA Institute may have significant consequences; they include public censure, suspension of membership and use of the CFA designation, and revocation of the CFA charter. Candidates enrolled in the CFA Program who have violated the Code and Standards or testing policies may be suspended or prohibited from further participation in the CFA Program.

Adoption of the Code and Standards

The Code and Standards apply to individual members of CFA Institute and candidates in the CFA Program. CFA Institute does encourage firms to adopt the Code and Standards, however, as part of their code of ethics. Those who claim compliance should fully understand the requirements of each of the principles of the Code and Standards.

Once a party—nonmember or firm—ensures its code of ethics meets the principles of the Code and Standards, that party should make the following statement whenever claiming compliance:

> [Insert name of party] claims compliance with the CFA Institute Code of Ethics and Standards of Professional Conduct. This claim has not been verified by CFA Institute.

CFA Institute welcomes public acknowledgement, when appropriate, that firms are complying with the CFA Institute Code of Ethics and Standards of Professional Conduct. For firms that would like to distribute the Code and Standards to clients and potential clients, attractive one-page copies of the Code and Standards, including translations, are available on the CFA Institute website (www.cfainstitute.org).

CFA Institute has also published the Asset Manager Code, which is designed, in part, to help asset managers comply with regulations mandating codes of ethics for investment advisers. Whereas the Code and Standards are aimed at individual investment professionals who are members of CFA Institute or candidates in the CFA Program, the Asset Manager Code applies to firms. The Asset Manager Code provides specific, practical guidelines for asset managers in six areas: loyalty to clients, the investment process, trading, compliance, performance, and disclosure. The Asset Manager Code and the appropriate steps to acknowledge compliance can be found on the CFA Institute website (www.cfainstitute.org).

Acknowledgments

CFA Institute is a not-for-profit organization that is heavily dependent on the expertise and intellectual contributions of member volunteers. Members devote their time because they share a mutual interest in the organization's mission to promote and achieve ethical practice in the investment profession. CFA Institute owes much to the volunteers' abundant generosity and energy in extending ethical integrity.

The CFA Institute Standards of Practice Council (SPC), a group consisting of CFA charterholder volunteers from many different countries, is charged with maintaining and interpreting the Code and Standards and ensuring that they are effective. The SPC draws its membership from a broad spectrum of organizations in the securities field, including brokers, investment advisers, banks, and insurance companies.

The SPC continually evaluates the Code and Standards, as well as the guidance in the *Handbook*, to ensure that they are

- representative of high standards of professional conduct,
- relevant to the changing nature of the investment profession,
- globally applicable,
- sufficiently comprehensive, practical, and specific,
- enforceable, and
- testable for the CFA Program.

Over the years, many volunteer members of the SPC have spent countless hours reviewing and discussing revisions to the Code and Standards and updates to the guidance that make up the *Handbook*. CFA Institute would like to thank all the current and former members of the SPC who generously donated their time and energy to this effort.

ETHICS AND THE INVESTMENT INDUSTRY

2

Society ultimately benefits from efficient markets where capital can freely flow to the most productive or innovative destination. Well-functioning capital markets efficiently match those needing capital with those seeking to invest their assets in revenue-generating ventures. In order for capital markets to be efficient, investors must be able to trust that the markets are fair and transparent and offer them the opportunity to be rewarded for the risk they choose to take. Laws, regulations, and enforcement play a vital role but are insufficient alone to guarantee fair and transparent markets. The markets depend on an ethical foundation to guide participants' judgment and behavior. CFA Institute maintains and promotes the Code of Ethics and Standards of Professional Conduct in order to create a culture of ethics for the ultimate benefit of society.

Why Ethics Matters

Ethics can be defined as a set of moral principles or rules of conduct that provide guidance for our behavior when it affects others. Widely acknowledged fundamental ethical principles include honesty, fairness, diligence, and care and respect for others. Ethical conduct follows those principles and balances self-interest with both the direct and the indirect consequences of that behavior for other people.

Not only does unethical behavior by individuals have serious personal consequences—ranging from job loss and reputational damage to fines and even jail—but unethical conduct from market participants, investment professionals, and those who service investors can damage investor trust and thereby impair the sustainability of the global capital markets as a whole. Unfortunately, there seems to be an unending parade of stories bringing to light accounting frauds and manipulations, Ponzi schemes, insider-trading scandals, and other misdeeds. Not surprisingly, this has led to erosion in public confidence in investment professionals. Empirical evidence from numerous surveys documents the low standing in the eyes of the investing public of banks and financial services firms—the very institutions that are entrusted with the economic well-being and retirement security of society.

Governments and regulators have historically tried to combat misconduct in the industry through regulatory reform, with various levels of success. Global capital markets are highly regulated to protect investors and other market participants. However, compliance with regulation alone is insufficient to fully earn investor trust. Individuals and firms must develop a "culture of integrity" that permeates all levels of operations and promotes the ethical principles of stewardship of investor assets and working in the best interests of clients, above and beyond strict compliance with the law. A strong ethical culture that helps honest, ethical people engage in ethical behavior will foster the trust of investors, lead to robust global capital markets, and ultimately benefit society. That is why ethics matters.

Ethics, Society, and the Capital Markets

CFA Institute includes the concept "for the ultimate benefit of society" as part of its mission. The premise is that we want to live in a socially, politically, and financially stable society that fosters individual well-being and welfare of the public. A key ingredient for this goal is global capital markets that facilitate the efficient allocation of resources so that the available capital finds its way to places where it most benefits that society. These investments are then used to produce goods and services, to fund innovation and jobs, and to promote improvements in standards of living. Indeed, such a function serves the interests of the society. Efficient capital markets, in turn, provide a host of benefits to those providing the investment capital. Investors are provided the opportunity to transfer and transform risk because the capital markets serve as an information exchange, create investment products, provide liquidity, and limit transaction costs.

However, a well-functioning and efficient capital market system is dependent on trust of the participants. If investors believe that capital market participants—investment professionals and firms—cannot be trusted with their financial assets or that the capital markets are unfair such that only insiders can be successful, they will be unlikely to invest or, at the very least, will require a higher risk premium. Decreased investment capital can reduce innovation and job creation and hurt the economy and society as a whole. Reduced trust in capital markets can also result in a less vibrant, if not smaller, investment industry.

Ethics for a global investment industry should be universal and ultimately support trust and integrity above acceptable local or regional customs and culture. Universal ethics for a global industry strongly supports the efficiency, values, and mission of the industry as a whole. Different countries may be at different stages of development in establishing standards of practice, but the end goal must be to achieve rules, regulations, and standards that support and promote fundamental ethical principles on a global basis.

Capital Market Sustainability and the Actions of One

Individuals and firms also have to look at the indirect impacts of their actions on the broader investment community. The increasingly interconnected nature of global finance brings to the fore an added consideration of market sustainability that was, perhaps, less appreciated in years past. In addition to committing to the highest levels of ethical behavior, today's investment professionals and their employers should consider the long-term health of the market as a whole.

Apparently isolated and unrelated decisions, however innocuous when considered on an individual basis, in aggregate can precipitate a market crisis. In an interconnected global economy and marketplace, each participant should strive to be aware of how his or her actions or the products he or she distributes may have an impact on capital market participants in other regions or countries.

Investment professionals should consider how their investment decision-making processes affect the global financial markets in the broader context of how they apply their ethical and professional obligations. Those in positions of authority have a special responsibility to consider the broader context of market sustainability in their development and approval of corporate policies, particularly those involving risk management and product development. In addition, corporate compensation strategies should not encourage otherwise ethically sound individuals to engage in unethical or questionable conduct for financial gain. Ethics, sustainability, and properly functioning capital markets are components of the same concept of protecting the best interests of all. To always place the interests of clients ahead of both investment professionals' own interests and those of their employer remains a key ethos.

The Relationship between Ethics and Regulations

Some equate ethical behavior with legal behavior: If you are following the law, you must be acting appropriately. Ethical principles, like laws and regulations, prescribe appropriate constraints on our natural tendency to pursue self-interest that could harm the interests of others. Laws and regulations often attempt to guide people toward ethical behavior, but they do not cover all unethical behavior. Ethical behavior is often distinguished from legal conduct by describing legal behavior as what is required and ethical behavior as conduct that is morally correct. Ethical principles go beyond that which is legally sufficient and encompass what is the right thing to do.

Given many regulators' lack of sufficient resources to enforce well-conceived rules and regulations, relying on a regulatory framework to lead the charge in establishing ethical behavior has its challenges. Therefore, reliance on compliance with laws and regulation alone is insufficient to ensure ethical behavior of investment professionals or to create a truly ethical culture in the industry.

Inevitably, some individuals will succeed at circumventing the regulatory rules for their personal gain. Only the application of strong ethical principles, at both the individual level and the firm level, will limit abuses. Knowing the rules or regulations to apply in a particular situation, although important, may not be sufficient to ensure ethical conduct. Individuals must be able both to recognize areas that are prone to ethical pitfalls and to identify and process those circumstances and influences that can impair ethical judgment.

Applying an Ethical Framework

Laws, regulations, professional standards, and codes of ethics can guide ethical behavior, but individual judgment is a critical ingredient in making principled choices and engaging in appropriate conduct. When faced with an ethical dilemma, individuals must have a well-developed set of principles; otherwise, their thought processes can lead to, at best, equivocation and indecision and, at worst, fraudulent conduct and destruction of the public trust. Establishing an ethical framework for an internal thought process prior to deciding to act is a crucial step in engaging in ethical conduct.

Most investment professionals are used to making decisions from a business (profit/loss) outlook. But given the importance of ethical behavior in carrying out professional responsibilities, it is critical to also analyze decisions and potential conduct from an ethical perspective. Utilizing a framework for ethical decision making will help investment professionals effectively examine their conduct in the context of conflicting interests common to their professional obligations (e.g., researching and gathering information, developing investment recommendations, and managing money for others). Such a framework will allow investment professionals to analyze their conduct in a way that meets high standards of ethical behavior.

An ethical decision-making framework can come in many forms but should provide investment professionals with a tool for following the principles of the firm's code of ethics. Through analyzing the particular circumstances of each decision, investment professionals are able to determine the best course of action to fulfill their responsibilities in an ethical manner.

Commitment to Ethics by Firms

A firm's code of ethics risks becoming a largely ignored, dusty compilation if it is not truly integrated into the fabric of the business. The ability to relate an ethical decision-making framework to a firm's code of ethics allows investment professionals to bring the aspirations and principles of the code of ethics to life—transforming it from a compliance exercise to something that is at the heart of a firm's culture.

An investment professional's natural desire to "do the right thing" must be reinforced by building a culture of integrity in the workplace. Development, maintenance, and demonstration of a strong culture of integrity within the firm by senior management may be the single most important factor in promoting ethical behavior among the firm's employees. Adopting a code of ethics that clearly lays out the ethical principles that guide the thought processes and conduct the firm expects from its employees is a critical first step. But a code of ethics, while necessary, is insufficient.

Simply nurturing an inclination to do right is no match for the multitude of daily decisions that investment managers make. We need to exercise ethical decision-making skills to develop the muscle memory necessary for fundamentally ethical people to make good decisions despite the reality of conflicts of interest. Just as coaching and practice transform our natural ability to run across a field into the technique and endurance required to run a race, teaching, reinforcing, and practicing ethical decision-making skills prepare us to confront the hard issues effectively. It is good for business, individuals, firms, the industry, and the markets, as well as society as a whole, to engage in the investment management profession in a highly ethical manner.

Ethical Commitment of CFA Institute

An important goal of CFA Institute is to ensure that the organization and its members and candidates develop, promote, and follow the highest ethical standards in the investment industry. The CFA Institute Code of Ethics (Code) and Standards of Professional Conduct (Standards) are the foundation supporting the organization's quest to uphold the industry's highest standards of individual and corporate practice and to help serve the greater good. The Code is a set of principles that define the overarching conduct CFA Institute expects from its members and CFA Program candidates. The Code works in tandem with the Standards, which outline professional conduct that constitutes fair and ethical business practices.

For more than 60 years, CFA Institute members and candidates have been required to abide by the organization's Code and Standards. Periodically, CFA Institute has revised and updated its Code and Standards to ensure that they remain relevant to the changing nature of the investment profession and representative of the highest standard of professional conduct. Within the *Standards of PracticeHandbook*, CFA Institute addresses ethical principles for the profession, including individual professionalism; responsibilities to capital markets, clients, and employers; ethics involved in investment analysis, recommendations, and actions; and possible conflicts of interest. Although the investment world has become a far more complex place since the first publication of the *Standards of Practice Handbook*, distinguishing right from wrong remains the paramount principle of the Code and Standards.

New challenges will continually arise for members and candidates in applying the Code and Standards because many decisions are not unambiguously right or wrong. The dilemma exists because the choice between right and wrong is not always clear. Even well-intentioned investment professionals can find themselves in circumstances that may tempt them to cut corners. Situational influences can overpower the best of intentions.

CFA Institute has made a significant commitment to providing members and candidates with the resources to extend and deepen their understanding of how to appropriately apply the principles of the Code and Standards. The product offerings from CFA Institute offer a wealth of material. Through publications, conferences, webcasts, and podcasts, the ethical challenges of investment professionals are brought to light. Archived issues of these items are available on the CFA Institute website (www.cfainstitute.org).

By reviewing these resources and discussing with their peers, market participants can further enhance their abilities to apply an effective ethical decision-making framework. In time, this should promote the trust of clients, investors, and market participants.

Markets function to an important extent on trust. Investment professionals should remain mindful of the long-term health of financial markets and incorporate this concern for the market's sustainability in their investment decision making. CFA Institute and the Standards of Practice Council hope the *Handbook* will assist and guide investment professionals in meeting the ethical demands of the highly interconnected global capital markets for the ultimate benefit of society.

CFA INSTITUTE CODE OF ETHICS AND STANDARDS OF PROFESSIONAL CONDUCT 3

- [ ] identify the six components of the Code of Ethics and the seven Standards of Professional Conduct
- [ ] explain the ethical responsibilities required by the Code and Standards, including the sub-sections of each Standard

Preamble

The CFA Institute Code of Ethics and Standards of Professional Conduct are fundamental to the values of CFA Institute and essential to achieving its mission to continue to lead the investment profession globally by promoting the highest standards of ethics, education, and professional excellence for the ultimate benefit of society. High ethical standards are critical to maintaining the public's trust in financial markets and in the investment profession. Since their creation in the 1960s, the Code and Standards have promoted the integrity of CFA Institute members and served as a model for measuring the ethics of investment professionals globally, regardless of job function, cultural differences, or local laws and regulations. All CFA Institute members (including holders of the Chartered Financial Analyst [CFA] designation) and CFA candidates have the personal responsibility to embrace and uphold the provisions of the Code and Standards and are encouraged to notify their employer of this responsibility. Violations may result in disciplinary sanctions by CFA Institute. Sanctions can include revocation of membership, revocation of candidacy in the CFA Program, and revocation of the right to use the CFA designation.

The Code of Ethics

Members of CFA Institute (including CFA charterholders) and candidates for the CFA designation ("Members and Candidates") must:

- Act with integrity, competence, diligence, and respect and in an ethical manner with the public, clients, prospective clients, employers, employees, colleagues in the investment profession, and other participants in the global capital markets.
- Place the integrity of the investment profession and the interests of clients above their own personal interests.
- Use reasonable care and exercise independent professional judgment when conducting investment analysis, making investment recommendations, taking investment actions, and engaging in other professional activities.
- Practice and encourage others to practice in a professional and ethical manner that will reflect credit on themselves and the profession.
- Promote the integrity and viability of the global capital markets for the ultimate benefit of society.
- Maintain and improve their professional competence and strive to maintain and improve the competence of other investment professionals.

Standards of Professional Conduct

i. PROFESSIONALISM

A. Knowledge of the Law

Members and Candidates must understand and comply with all applicable laws, rules, and regulations (including the CFA Institute Code of Ethics and Standards of Professional Conduct) of any government, regulatory organization, licensing agency, or professional association governing their professional activities. In the event of conflict, Members and Candidates must comply with the more strict law, rule, or regulation. Members and Candidates must not knowingly participate or assist in and must dissociate from any violation of such laws, rules, or regulations.

B. Independence and Objectivity

Members and Candidates must use reasonable care and judgment to achieve and maintain independence and objectivity in their professional activities. Members and Candidates must not offer, solicit, or accept any gift, benefit, compensation, or consideration that reasonably could be expected to compromise their own or another's independence and objectivity.

C. Misrepresentation

Members and Candidates must not knowingly make any misrepresentations relating to investment analysis, recommendations, actions, or other professional activities.

D. Misconduct

Members and Candidates must not engage in any professional conduct involving dishonesty, fraud, or deceit or commit any act that reflects adversely on their professional reputation, integrity, or competence.

E. Competence

Members and Candidates must act with and maintain the competence necessary to fulfill their professional responsibilities.

ii. INTEGRITY OF CAPITAL MARKETS

A. Material Nonpublic Information

Members and Candidates who possess material nonpublic information that could affect the value of an investment must not act or cause others to act on the information.

B. Market Manipulation

Members and Candidates must not engage in practices that distort prices or artificially inflate trading volume with the intent to mislead market participants.

iii. DUTIES TO CLIENTS

A. Loyalty, Prudence, and Care

Members and Candidates have a duty of loyalty to their clients and must act with reasonable care and exercise prudent judgment. Members and Candidates must act for the benefit of their clients and place their clients' interests before their employer's or their own interests.

B. Fair Dealing

Members and Candidates must deal fairly and objectively with all clients when providing investment analysis, making investment recommendations, taking investment action, or engaging in other professional activities.

C. Suitability

1. When Members and Candidates are in an advisory relationship with a client, they must:

a. Make a reasonable inquiry into a client's or prospective client's investment experience, risk and return objectives, and financial constraints prior to making any investment recommendation or taking investment action and must reassess and update this information regularly.

b. Determine that an investment is suitable to the client's financial situation and consistent with the client's written objectives, mandates, and constraints before making an investment recommendation or taking investment action.

c. Judge the suitability of investments in the context of the client's total portfolio.

2. When Members and Candidates are responsible for managing a portfolio to a specific mandate, strategy, or style, they must make only investment recommendations or take only investment actions that are consistent with the stated objectives and constraints of the portfolio.

D. Performance Presentation

When communicating investment performance information, Members and Candidates must make reasonable efforts to ensure that it is fair, accurate, and complete.

E. Preservation of Confidentiality

Members and Candidates must keep information about current, former, and prospective clients confidential unless:

1. The information concerns illegal activities on the part of the client or prospective client,

2. Disclosure is required by law, or

3. The client or prospective client permits disclosure of the information.

iv. DUTIES TO EMPLOYERS

A. Loyalty

In matters related to their employment, Members and Candidates must act for the benefit of their employer and not deprive their employer of the advantage of their skills and abilities, divulge confidential information, or otherwise cause harm to their employer.

B. Additional Compensation Arrangements

Members and Candidates must not accept gifts, benefits, compensation, or consideration that competes with or might reasonably be expected to create a conflict of interest with their employer's interest unless they obtain written consent from all parties involved.

C. Responsibilities of Supervisors

Members and Candidates must make reasonable efforts to ensure that anyone subject to their supervision or authority complies with applicable laws, rules, regulations, and the Code and Standards.

v. INVESTMENT ANALYSIS, RECOMMENDATIONS, AND ACTIONS

A. Diligence and Reasonable Basis

Members and Candidates must:

1. Exercise diligence, independence, and thoroughness in analyzing investments, making investment recommendations, and taking investment actions.

2. Have a reasonable and adequate basis, supported by appropriate research and investigation, for any investment analysis, recommendation, or action.

B. Communication with Clients and Prospective Clients

Members and Candidates must:

1. Disclose to clients and prospective clients the nature of the services provided, along with information about the costs to the client associated with those services.

2. Disclose to clients and prospective clients the basic format and general principles of the investment processes they use to analyze investments, select securities, and construct portfolios and must promptly disclose any changes that might materially affect those processes.

3. Disclose to clients and prospective clients significant limitations and risks associated with the investment process.

4. Use reasonable judgment in identifying which factors are important to their investment analyses, recommendations, or actions and include those factors in communications with clients and prospective clients.

5. Distinguish between fact and opinion in the presentation of investment analysis and recommendations.

C. Record Retention

Members and Candidates must develop and maintain appropriate records to support their investment analyses, recommendations, actions, and other investment-related communications with clients and prospective clients.

vi. CONFLICTS OF INTEREST

A. Avoid or Disclose Conflicts

Members and Candidates must avoid or make full and fair disclosure of all matters that could reasonably be expected to impair their independence and objectivity and interfere with respective duties to their clients, prospective clients, and employer. Members and Candidates must ensure that such disclosures are prominent, are delivered in plain language, and communicate the relevant information effectively.

B. Priority of Transactions

Investment transactions for clients and employers must have priority over investment transactions in which a Member or Candidate is the beneficial owner.

C. Referral Fees

Members and Candidates must disclose to their employer, clients, and prospective clients, as appropriate, any compensation, consideration, or benefit received from or paid to others for the recommendation of products or services.

vii. RESPONSIBILITIES AS A CFA INSTITUTE MEMBER OR CFA CANDIDATE

A. Conduct as Participants in CFA Institute Programs

Members and Candidates must not engage in any conduct that compromises the reputation or integrity of CFA Institute or the CFA designation or the integrity, validity, or security of CFA Institute programs.

B. Reference to CFA Institute, the CFA Designation, and the CFA Program

When referring to CFA Institute, CFA Institute membership, the CFA designation, or candidacy in the CFA Program, Members and Candidates must not misrepresent or exaggerate the meaning or implications of membership in CFA Institute, holding the CFA designation, or candidacy in the CFA Program.

PRACTICE PROBLEMS

1. Which of the following statements *best* describes an aspect of the Professional Conduct Program process?

   A. Inquiries are not initiated in response to information provided by the media.

   B. Investigations result in Disciplinary Review Committee panels for each case.

   C. Investigations may include requesting a written explanation from the member or candidate.

2. A current Code of Ethics principle reads in full, "Promote the integrity:

   A. and viability of the global capital markets."

   B. of and uphold the rules governing capital markets."

   C. and viability of the global capital markets for the ultimate benefit of society."

3. Which of the following is correct with regard to the Standards of Professional Conduct?

   A. They require supervisors to focus only on the detection and prevention of violations.

   B. They set ethical conduct requirements for members and candidates that have remained unchanged since their creation.

   C. They address the risks and limitations of recommendations being made to clients.

4. Which of the following statements *best* describes an aspect of the Standards of Professional Conduct? Members and candidates are required to:

   A. ensure a portfolio mandate is suitable for all investors.

   B. promptly disclose changes that might materially affect investment processes.

   C. have a reasonable and adequate basis for decisions about client confidentiality.

5. A CFA Institute member or candidate violates Standard II(A) Material Nonpublic Information by:

   A. conducting price distortion practices.

   B. inappropriately causing others to act.

   C. inadequately maintaining investment records.

6. Standard III(C) Suitability requires members and candidates in an advisory relationship with a client to:

   A. place their client's interests before their own interests.

   B. consider investments in the context of the client's total portfolio.

   C. not knowingly make misrepresentations relating to recommendations.

7. Standard III: Duties to Clients states that members and candidates must:
   - **A.** document client financial constraints after an initial investment action.
   - **B.** maintain an equal balance of interests owed to their clients and employers.
   - **C.** deal fairly and objectively with all clients when engaging in professional activities.

8. Standard IV: Duties to Employers states that members and candidates must not:
   - **A.** accept any gifts that might compromise their independence and objectivity.
   - **B.** deprive their employer of their skills and abilities as related to their employment.
   - **C.** accept compensation competing with their employer's interest without the written consent of their employer only.

9. Standard V: Investment Analysis, Recommendations, and Actions states that members and candidates must:
   - **A.** find an investment suitable for their client before making a recommendation.
   - **B.** make reasonable efforts to ensure that performance presentation is fair, accurate, and complete.
   - **C.** distinguish between fact and opinion in the presentation of investment analysis and recommendations.

10. Standard VII: Responsibilities as a CFA Institute Member or CFA Candidate explicitly states a requirement regarding:
    - **A.** loyalty.
    - **B.** responsibility of supervisors.
    - **C.** reference to the CFA Program.

SOLUTIONS

1. C is correct. When an inquiry is initiated, the Professional Conduct staff conducts an investigation that may include requesting a written explanation from the member or candidate.

   A is incorrect because Professional Conduct inquiries can be initiated in response to information provided by the media. CFA Institute staff may become aware of questionable conduct by a member or candidate through the media, regulatory notices, or other public sources.

   B is incorrect because although the Disciplinary Review Committee (DRC) is responsible for enforcement of the Code and Standards in conjunction with the Professional Conduct Program (PCP), only in the event that a member or candidate does not accept the charges and proposed sanction is the matter referred to a panel composed of DRC members.

2. C is correct. One of the principles in the Code of Ethics reflects the role that the capital markets have in society as a whole.

   A is incorrect because it is incomplete, missing the additional language to reflect the role that the capital markets have in society as a whole.

   B is incorrect because the principle as written in the Code of Ethics reflects the role of the capital markets in society as a whole.

3. C is correct. Given the constant development of new and exotic financial instruments and strategies, the standard regarding communicating with clients includes an implicit requirement to disclose to clients the risks and limitations of recommendations being made to clients.

   A is incorrect because the standard for members and candidates with supervision or authority over others within their firms stresses broader compliance expectations beyond the detection and prevention aspects of violations.

   B is incorrect because the standards have evolved over time to remain representative of the highest standards of professional conduct and relevant to the changing nature of the investment profession.

4. B is correct. The Standards of Professional Conduct require members and candidates to promptly disclose any changes that might materially affect investment processes.

   A is incorrect because under Standard III(C) Suitability, when members and candidates are responsible for managing a portfolio according to a specific mandate, they must take only investment actions that are consistent with the stated objectives of the portfolio and not be concerned with whether the mandate is suitable for all investors.

   C is incorrect because under Standard III(E) Preservation of Confidentiality, members and candidates must keep information about current clients confidential unless the information concerns illegal activities on the part of the client, disclosure is required by law, or the client permits disclosure. No decisions on confidentiality are required, with the "reasonable and adequate basis" criterion related to Standard V(A) Diligence and Reasonable Basis.

5. B is correct. Under Standard II(A) Material Nonpublic Information, members who possess material nonpublic information that could affect the value of an investment must not cause others to act on the information.

   A is incorrect because price distortion is mentioned in Standard II(B) Market Manipulation, not Standard II(A) Material Nonpublic Information.

C is incorrect because the maintenance of appropriate records to support investment analyses is noted in Standard V(C) Record Retention, not Standard II(A) Material Nonpublic Information.

6. B is correct. Standard III(C) Suitability states that when members and candidates are in an advisory relationship with a client, they must judge the suitability of investments in the context of the client's total portfolio.

   A is incorrect because this requirement is addressed under Standard III(A) Loyalty, Prudence, and Care, not Standard III(C) Suitability.

   C is incorrect because this requirement is addressed under Standard I(C) Misrepresentation, not Standard III(C) Suitability.

7. C is correct. Under Standard III(B) Fair Dealing, members and candidates must deal fairly and objectively with all clients when providing investment analysis, making investment recommendations, taking investment action, or engaging in other professional activities.

   A is incorrect because under Standard III(C) Suitability, members and candidates in an advisory relationship must make a reasonable inquiry into a client's financial constraints prior to (not after) taking investment action and must reassess and update this regularly.

   B is incorrect because under Standard III(A) Loyalty, Prudence, and Care, members and candidates must act for the benefit of their clients and place their clients' interests before (not maintain an equal balance with) their employer's or their own interests.

8. B is correct. Standard IV(A) Loyalty states that members and candidates cannot deprive their employer of the advantage of their skills and abilities in matters related to their employment.

   A is incorrect because accepting gifts that might compromise a member's or candidate's independence and objectivity is addressed by Standard I: Professionalism, not Standard IV: Duties to Employers.

   C is incorrect because Standard IV(B) Additional Compensation Arrangements permits members and candidates to accept compensation that competes with their employer's interest if they obtain written consent from all parties involved.

9. C is correct. Standard V(B) Communication with Clients and Prospective Clients states that members and candidates must distinguish between fact and opinion in the presentation of investment analysis and recommendations.

   A is incorrect because this standard is discussed in Standard III: Duties to Clients.

   B is incorrect because performance presentation is discussed in Standard III: Duties to Clients.

10. C is correct. Standard VII(B) Reference to CFA Institute, the CFA Designation, and the CFA Program explicitly states the appropriate manner to make reference to CFA Institute, CFA Institute membership, the CFA designation, or candidacy in the CFA Program.

    A is incorrect because Standard VII: Responsibilities as a CFA Institute Member or CFA Candidate does not refer to loyalty. Loyalty is addressed in two other standards, Standard III(A) Loyalty, Prudence, and Care and as part of Standard IV: Duties to Employers.

    B is incorrect because Standard VII does not refer to the responsibility of supervisors. The responsibility of supervisors is addressed in Standard IV(C) Responsibility of Supervisors.

LEARNING MODULE

3

Guidance for Standards I–VII

LEARNING OUTCOMES	
Mastery	***The candidate should be able to:***
☐	demonstrate the application of the Code of Ethics and Standards of Professional Conduct to situations involving issues of professional integrity
☐	recommend practices and procedures designed to prevent violations of the Code of Ethics and Standards of Professional Conduct
☐	identify conduct that conforms to the Code and Standards and conduct that violates the Code and Standards

STANDARD I: PROFESSIONALISM

1

Standard I(A) Knowledge of the Law

Members and Candidates must understand and comply with all applicable laws, rules, and regulations (including the CFA Institute Code of Ethics and Standards of Professional Conduct) of any government, regulatory organization, licensing agency, or professional association governing their professional activities. In the event of conflict, Members and Candidates must comply with the more strict law, rule, or regulation. Members and Candidates must not knowingly participate or assist in and must dissociate from any violation of such laws, rules, or regulations.

Guidance

Highlights:

- *Relationship between the Code and Standards and Applicable Law*
- *Participation in or Association with Violations by Others*
- *Investment Products and Applicable Laws*

Members and candidates must understand the applicable laws and regulations of the countries and jurisdictions where they engage in professional activities. These activities may include, but are not limited to, trading of securities or other financial instruments, providing investment advice, conducting research, or performing other investment services. On the basis of their reasonable and good faith understanding, members and candidates must comply with the laws and regulations that directly govern their professional activities and resulting outcomes and that protect the interests of the clients.

When questions arise, members and candidates should know their firm's policies and procedures for accessing compliance guidance. This standard does not require members and candidates to become experts, however, in compliance. Additionally, members and candidates are not required to have detailed knowledge of or be experts on all the laws that could potentially govern their activities.

During times of changing regulations, members and candidates must remain vigilant in maintaining their knowledge of the requirements for their professional activities. New financial products and processes, along with uncovered ethical missteps, create an environment for recurring and potentially wide-ranging regulatory changes. Members and candidates are also continually provided improved and enhanced methods of communicating with both clients and potential clients, such as mobile applications and web-based social networking platforms. As new local, regional, and global requirements are updated to address these and other changes, members, candidates, and their firms must adjust their procedures and practices to remain in compliance.

Relationship between the Code and Standards and Applicable Law

Some members or candidates may live, work, or provide investment services to clients living in a country that has no law or regulation governing a particular action or that has laws or regulations that differ from the requirements of the Code and Standards. When applicable law and the Code and Standards require different conduct, members and candidates must follow the more strict of the applicable law or the Code and Standards.

"Applicable law" is the law that governs the member's or candidate's conduct. Which law applies will depend on the particular facts and circumstances of each case. The "more strict" law or regulation is the law or regulation that imposes greater restrictions on the action of the member or candidate or calls for the member or candidate to exert a greater degree of action that protects the interests of investors. For example, applicable law or regulation may not require members and candidates to disclose referral fees received from or paid to others for the recommendation of investment products or services. Because the Code and Standards impose this obligation, however, members and candidates must disclose the existence of such fees.

Members and candidates must adhere to the following principles:

- Members and candidates must comply with applicable laws or regulations related to their professional activities.
- Members and candidates must not engage in conduct that constitutes a violation of the Code and Standards, even though it may otherwise be legal.
- In the absence of any applicable law or regulation or when the Code and Standards impose a higher degree of responsibility than applicable laws and regulations, members and candidates must adhere to the Code and Standards. Applications of these principles are outlined in Exhibit 1.

The applicable laws governing the responsibilities of a member or candidate should be viewed as the minimal threshold of acceptable actions. When members and candidates take actions that exceed the minimal requirements, they further support the conduct required of Standard I(A).

CFA Institute members are obligated to abide by the CFA Institute Articles of Incorporation, Bylaws, Code of Ethics, Standards of Professional Conduct, Rules of Procedure, Membership Agreement, and other applicable rules promulgated by CFA Institute, all as amended periodically. CFA candidates who are not members must also abide by these documents (except for the Membership Agreement) as well as rules and regulations related to the administration of the CFA® exam, the Candidate Responsibility Statement, and the Candidate Pledge.

Participation in or Association with Violations by Others

Members and candidates are responsible for violations in which they *knowingly* participate or assist. Although members and candidates are presumed to have knowledge of all applicable laws, rules, and regulations, CFA Institute acknowledges that members may not recognize violations if they are not aware of all the facts giving rise to the violations. Standard I(A) applies when members and candidates know or should know that their conduct may contribute to a violation of applicable laws, rules, or regulations or the Code and Standards.

If a member or candidate has reasonable grounds to believe that imminent or ongoing client or employer activities are illegal or unethical, the member or candidate must dissociate, or separate, from the activity. In extreme cases, dissociation may require a member or candidate to leave his or her employment. Members and candidates may take the following intermediate steps to dissociate from ethical violations of others when direct discussions with the person or persons committing the violation are unsuccessful. The first step should be to attempt to stop the behavior by bringing it to the attention of the employer through a supervisor or the firm's compliance department. If this attempt is unsuccessful, then members and candidates have a responsibility to step away and dissociate from the activity. Dissociation practices will differ on the basis of the member's or candidate's role in the investment industry. It may include removing one's name from written reports or recommendations, asking for a different assignment, or refusing to accept a new client or continue to advise a current client. Inaction combined with continuing association with those involved in illegal or unethical conduct may be construed as participation or assistance in the illegal or unethical conduct.

CFA Institute strongly encourages members and candidates to report potential violations of the Code and Standards committed by fellow members and candidates. Although a failure to report is less likely to be construed as a violation than a failure to dissociate from unethical conduct, the impact of inactivity on the integrity of capital markets can be significant. Although the Code and Standards do not compel members and candidates to report violations to their governmental or regulatory organizations unless such disclosure is mandatory under applicable law (voluntary reporting is often referred to as whistleblowing), such disclosure may be prudent under certain circumstances. Members and candidates should consult their legal and compliance advisers for guidance.

Additionally, CFA Institute encourages members, nonmembers, clients, and the investing public to report violations of the Code and Standards by CFA Institute members or CFA candidates by submitting a complaint in writing to the CFA Institute Professional Conduct Program via e-mail (pcprogram@cfainstitute.org) or the CFA Institute website (www.cfainstitute.org).

Investment Products and Applicable Laws

Members and candidates involved in creating or maintaining investment services or investment products or packages of securities and/or derivatives should be mindful of where these products or packages will be sold as well as their places of origination. The applicable laws and regulations of the countries or regions of origination and expected sale should be understood by those responsible for the supervision of the services or creation and maintenance of the products or packages. Members or candidates should make reasonable efforts to review whether associated firms that are distributing products or services developed by their employing firm also abide by the laws and regulations of the countries and regions of distribution. Members and candidates should undertake the necessary due diligence when transacting cross-border business to understand the multiple applicable laws and regulations in order to protect the reputation of their firm and themselves.

Given the complexity that can arise with business transactions in today's market, there may be some uncertainty surrounding which laws or regulations are considered applicable when activities are being conducted in multiple jurisdictions. Members and candidates should seek the appropriate guidance, potentially including the firm's compliance or legal departments and legal counsel outside the organization, to gain a reasonable understanding of their responsibilities and how to implement them appropriately.

Exhibit 1: Global Application of the Code and Standards

Members and candidates who practice in multiple jurisdictions may be subject to varied securities laws and regulations. If applicable law is stricter than the requirements of the Code and Standards, members and candidates must adhere to applicable law; otherwise, they must adhere to the Code and Standards. The following chart provides illustrations involving a member who may be subject to the securities laws and regulations of three different types of countries:

NS: country with no securities laws or regulations

LS: country with *less* strict securities laws and regulations than the Code and Standards

MS: country with *more* strict securities laws and regulations than the Code and Standards

Applicable Law	Duties	Explanation
Member resides in NS country, does business in LS country; LS law applies.	Member must adhere to the Code and Standards.	Because applicable law is less strict than the Code and Standards, the member must adhere to the Code and Standards.
Member resides in NS country, does business in MS country; MS law applies.	Member must adhere to the law of MS country.	Because applicable law is stricter than the Code and Standards, member must adhere to the more strict applicable law.
Member resides in LS country, does business in NS country; LS law applies.	Member must adhere to the Code and Standards.	Because applicable law is less strict than the Code and Standards, member must adhere to the Code and Standards.
Member resides in LS country, does business in MS country; MS law applies.	Member must adhere to the law of MS country.	Because applicable law is stricter than the Code and Standards, member must adhere to the more strict applicable law.

Applicable Law	Duties	Explanation
Member resides in LS country, does business in NS country; LS law applies, but it states that law of locality where business is conducted governs.	Member must adhere to the Code and Standards.	Because applicable law states that the law of the locality where the business is conducted governs and there is no local law, the member must adhere to the Code and Standards.
Member resides in LS country, does business in MS country; LS law applies, but it states that law of locality where business is conducted governs.	Member must adhere to the law of MS country.	Because applicable law of the locality where the business is conducted governs and local law is stricter than the Code and Standards, member must adhere to the more strict applicable law.
Member resides in MS country, does business in LS country; MS law applies.	Member must adhere to the law of MS country.	Because applicable law is stricter than the Code and Standards, member must adhere to the more strict applicable law.
Member resides in MS country, does business in LS country; MS law applies, but it states that law of locality where business is conducted governs.	Member must adhere to the Code and Standards.	Because applicable law states that the law of the locality where the business is conducted governs and local law is less strict than the Code and Standards, member must adhere to the Code and Standards.
Member resides in MS country, does business in LS country with a client who is a citizen of LS country; MS law applies, but it states that the law of the client's home country governs.	Member must adhere to the Code and Standards.	Because applicable law states that the law of the client's home country governs (which is less strict than the Code and Standards), member must adhere to the Code and Standards.
Member resides in MS country, does business in LS country with a client who is a citizen of MS country; MS law applies, but it states that the law of the client's home country governs.	Member must adhere to the law of MS country.	Because applicable law states that the law of the client's home country governs and the law of the client's home country is stricter than the Code and Standards, the member must adhere to the more strict applicable law.

2 STANDARD I(A): RECOMMENDED PROCEDURES

Members and Candidates

Suggested methods by which members and candidates can acquire and maintain understanding of applicable laws, rules, and regulations include the following:

- *Stay informed*: Members and candidates should establish or encourage their employers to establish a procedure by which employees are regularly informed about changes in applicable laws, rules, regulations, and case law. In many instances, the employer's compliance department or legal counsel can provide such information in the form of memorandums distributed to employees in the organization. Also, participation in an internal or external continuing education program is a practical method of staying current.
- *Review procedures*: Members and candidates should review, or encourage their employers to review, the firm's written compliance procedures on a regular basis to ensure that the procedures reflect current law and provide adequate guidance to employees about what is permissible conduct under the law and/or the Code and Standards. Recommended compliance procedures for specific items of the Code and Standards are discussed in this *Handbook* in the "Guidance" sections associated with each standard.
- *Maintain current files*: Members and candidates should maintain or encourage their employers to maintain readily accessible current reference copies of applicable statutes, rules, regulations, and important cases.

Distribution Area Laws

Members and candidates should make reasonable efforts to understand the applicable laws—both country and regional—for the countries and regions where their investment products are developed and are most likely to be distributed to clients.

Legal Counsel

When in doubt about the appropriate action to undertake, it is recommended that a member or candidate seek the advice of compliance personnel or legal counsel concerning legal requirements. If a potential violation is being committed by a fellow employee, it may also be prudent for the member or candidate to seek the advice of the firm's compliance department or legal counsel.

Dissociation

When dissociating from an activity that violates the Code and Standards, members and candidates should document the violation and urge their firms to attempt to persuade the perpetrator(s) to cease such conduct. To dissociate from the conduct, a member or candidate may have to resign his or her employment.

Firms

The formality and complexity of compliance procedures for firms depend on the nature and size of the organization and the nature of its investment operations. Members and candidates should encourage their firms to consider the following policies and procedures to support the principles of Standard I(A):

- *Develop and/or adopt a code of ethics*: The ethical culture of an organization starts at the top. Members and candidates should encourage their supervisors or managers to adopt a code of ethics. Adhering to a code of ethics facilitates solutions when people face ethical dilemmas and can prevent the need for employees to resort to a "whistleblowing" solution publicly alleging concealed misconduct. CFA Institute has published the *Asset Manager Code of Professional Conduct*, which firms may adopt or use as the basis for their codes (visit www.cfainstitute.org).
- *Provide information on applicable laws*: Pertinent information that highlights applicable laws and regulations might be distributed to employees or made available in a central location. Information sources might include primary information developed by the relevant government, governmental agencies, regulatory organizations, licensing agencies, and professional associations (e.g., from their websites); law firm memorandums or newsletters; and association memorandums or publications (e.g., *CFA Institute Magazine*).
- *Establish procedures for reporting violations*: Firms might provide written protocols for reporting suspected violations of laws, regulations, or company policies.

STANDARD I(A): APPLICATION OF THE STANDARD 3

Example 1 (Notification of Known Violations):

Michael Allen works for a brokerage firm and is responsible for an underwriting of securities. A company official gives Allen information indicating that the financial statements Allen filed with the regulator overstate the issuer's earnings. Allen seeks the advice of the brokerage firm's general counsel, who states that it would be difficult for the regulator to prove that Allen has been involved in any wrongdoing.

> *Comment*: Although it is recommended that members and candidates seek the advice of legal counsel, the reliance on such advice does not absolve a member or candidate from the requirement to comply with the law or regulation. Allen should report this situation to his supervisor, seek an independent legal opinion, and determine whether the regulator should be notified of the error.

Example 2 (Dissociating from a Violation):

Lawrence Brown's employer, an investment banking firm, is the principal underwriter for an issue of convertible debentures by the Courtney Company. Brown discovers that the Courtney Company has concealed severe third-quarter losses in its foreign operations. The preliminary prospectus has already been distributed.

Comment: Knowing that the preliminary prospectus is misleading, Brown should report his findings to the appropriate supervisory persons in his firm. If the matter is not remedied and Brown's employer does not dissociate from the underwriting, Brown should sever all his connections with the underwriting. Brown should also seek legal advice to determine whether additional reporting or other action should be taken.

Example 3 (Dissociating from a Violation):

Kamisha Washington's firm advertises its past performance record by showing the 10-year return of a composite of its client accounts. Washington discovers, however, that the composite omits the performance of accounts that have left the firm during the 10-year period, whereas the description of the composite indicates the inclusion of all firm accounts. This omission has led to an inflated performance figure. Washington is asked to use promotional material that includes the erroneous performance number when soliciting business for the firm.

Comment: Misrepresenting performance is a violation of the Code and Standards. Although she did not calculate the performance herself, Washington would be assisting in violating Standard I(A) if she were to use the inflated performance number when soliciting clients. She must dissociate herself from the activity. If discussing the misleading number with the person responsible is not an option for correcting the problem, she can bring the situation to the attention of her supervisor or the compliance department at her firm. If her firm is unwilling to recalculate performance, she must refrain from using the misleading promotional material and should notify the firm of her reasons. If the firm insists that she use the material, she should consider whether her obligation to dissociate from the activity requires her to seek other employment.

Example 4 (Following the Highest Requirements):

James Collins is an investment analyst for a major Wall Street brokerage firm. He works in a developing country with a rapidly modernizing economy and a growing capital market. Local securities laws are minimal—in form and content—and include no punitive prohibitions against insider trading.

Comment: Collins must abide by the requirements of the Code and Standards, which might be more strict than the rules of the developing country. He should be aware of the risks that a small market and the absence of a fairly regulated flow of information to the market represent to his ability to obtain information and make timely judgments. He should include this factor in formulating his advice to clients. In handling material nonpublic information that accidentally comes into his possession, he must follow Standard II(A) Material Nonpublic Information.

Example 5 (Following the Highest Requirements):

Laura Jameson works for a multinational investment adviser based in the United States. Jameson lives and works as a registered investment adviser in the tiny, but wealthy, island nation of Karramba. Karramba's securities laws state that no investment adviser registered and working in that country can participate in initial public offerings (IPOs) for the adviser's personal account. Jameson, believing that, as a US citizen working for a US-based company, she should comply only with US law, has ignored this Karrambian law. In addition, Jameson believes that as a charterholder, as long as she adheres to the Code and Standards requirement that she disclose her participation in any IPO to her employer and clients when such ownership creates a conflict of interest, she is meeting the highest ethical requirements.

> *Comment*: Jameson is in violation of Standard I(A). As a registered investment adviser in Karramba, Jameson is prevented by Karrambian securities law from participating in IPOs regardless of the law of her home country. In addition, because the law of the country where she is working is stricter than the Code and Standards, she must follow the stricter requirements of the local law rather than the requirements of the Code and Standards.

Example 6 (Laws and Regulations Based on Religious Tenets):

Amanda Janney is employed as a fixed-income portfolio manager for a large international firm. She is on a team within her firm that is responsible for creating and managing a fixed-income hedge fund to be sold throughout the firm's distribution centers to high-net-worth clients. Her firm receives expressions of interest from potential clients from the Middle East who are seeking investments that comply with Islamic law. The marketing and promotional materials for the fixed-income hedge fund do not specify whether or not the fund is a suitable investment for an investor seeking compliance with Islamic law. Because the fund is being distributed globally, Janney is concerned about the reputation of the fund and the firm and believes disclosure of whether or not the fund complies with Islamic law could help minimize potential mistakes with placing this investment.

> *Comment*: As the financial market continues to become globalized, members and candidates will need to be aware of the differences between cultural and religious laws and requirements as well as the different governmental laws and regulations. Janney and the firm could be proactive in their efforts to acknowledge areas where the new fund may not be suitable for clients.

Example 7 (Reporting Potential Unethical Actions):

Krista Blume is a junior portfolio manager for high-net-worth portfolios at a large global investment manager. She observes a number of new portfolios and relationships coming from a country in Europe where the firm did not have previous business and is told that a broker in that country is responsible for this new business. At a meeting on allocation of research resources to third-party research firms, Blume notes that this broker has been added to the list and is allocated payments for research. However, she knows the portfolios do not invest in securities in the broker's country, and she has not seen any research come from this broker. Blume asks her supervisor about the name being on the list and is told that someone in marketing is receiving the research and that the name being on the list is OK. She believes that what may be going on is that the broker is being paid for new business through the inappropriate research payments, and she wishes to dissociate from the misconduct.

> *Comment*: Blume should follow the firm's policies and procedures for reporting potential unethical activity, which may include discussions with her supervisor or someone in a designated compliance department. She should communicate her concerns appropriately while advocating for disclosure between the new broker relationship and the research payments.

Example 8 (Failure to Maintain Knowledge of the Law):

Colleen White is excited to use new technology to communicate with clients and potential clients. She recently began posting investment information, including performance reports and investment opinions and recommendations, to her Facebook page. In addition, she sends out brief announcements, opinions, and thoughts via her X account (for example, "Prospects for future growth of XYZ company look good! #makingmoney4U"). Prior to White's use of these social media platforms, the local regulator had issued new requirements and guidance governing online electronic communication. White's communications appear to conflict with the recent regulatory announcements.

> *Comment*: White is in violation of Standard I(A) because her communications do not comply with the existing guidance and regulation governing use of social media. White must be aware of the evolving legal requirements pertaining to new and dynamic areas of the financial services industry that are applicable to her. She should seek guidance from appropriate, knowledgeable, and reliable sources, such as her firm's compliance department, external service providers, or outside counsel, unless she diligently follows legal and regulatory trends affecting her professional responsibilities.

4 STANDARD I(B) INDEPENDENCE AND OBJECTIVITY

- ☐ demonstrate the application of the Code of Ethics and Standards of Professional Conduct to situations involving issues of professional integrity
- ☐ recommend practices and procedures designed to prevent violations of the Code of Ethics and Standards of Professional Conduct
- ☐ identify conduct that conforms to the Code and Standards and conduct that violates the Code and Standards

> Members and Candidates must use reasonable care and judgment to achieve and maintain independence and objectivity in their professional activities. Members and Candidates must not offer, solicit, or accept any gift, benefit, compensation, or consideration that reasonably could be expected to compromise their own or another's independence and objectivity.

Guidance

Highlights:

- *Buy-Side Clients*
- *Fund Manager and Custodial Relationships*
- *Investment Banking Relationships*
- *Performance Measurement and Attribution*
- *Public Companies*
- *Credit Rating Agency Opinions*

- *Influence during the Manager Selection/Procurement Process*
- *Issuer-Paid Research*
- *Travel Funding*

Standard I(B) states the responsibility of CFA Institute members and candidates in the CFA Program to maintain independence and objectivity so that their clients will have the benefit of their work and opinions unaffected by any potential conflict of interest or other circumstance adversely affecting their judgment. Every member and candidate should endeavor to avoid situations that could cause or be perceived to cause a loss of independence or objectivity in recommending investments or taking investment action.

External sources may try to influence the investment process by offering analysts and portfolio managers a variety of benefits. Corporations may seek expanded research coverage, issuers and underwriters may wish to promote new securities offerings, brokers may want to increase commission business, and independent rating agencies may be influenced by the company requesting the rating. Benefits may include gifts, invitations to lavish functions, tickets, favors, or job referrals. One type of benefit is the allocation of shares in oversubscribed IPOs to investment managers for their personal accounts. This practice affords managers the opportunity to make quick profits that may not be available to their clients. Such a practice is prohibited under Standard I(B). Modest gifts and entertainment are acceptable, but special care must be taken by members and candidates to resist subtle and not-so-subtle pressures to act in conflict with the interests of their clients. Best practice dictates that members and candidates reject any offer of gift or entertainment that could be expected to threaten their independence and objectivity.

Receiving a gift, benefit, or consideration from a *client* can be distinguished from gifts given by entities seeking to influence a member or candidate to the detriment of other clients. In a client relationship, the client has already entered some type of compensation arrangement with the member, candidate, or his or her firm. A gift from a client could be considered supplementary compensation. The potential for obtaining influence to the detriment of other clients, although present, is not as great as in situations where no compensation arrangement exists. When possible, prior to accepting "bonuses" or gifts from clients, members and candidates should disclose to their employers such benefits offered by clients. If notification is not possible prior to acceptance, members and candidates must disclose to their employer benefits previously accepted from clients. Disclosure allows the employer of a member or candidate to make an independent determination about the extent to which the gift may affect the member's or candidate's independence and objectivity.

Members and candidates may also come under pressure from their own firms to, for example, issue favorable research reports or recommendations for certain companies with potential or continuing business relationships with the firm. The situation may be aggravated if an executive of the company sits on the bank or investment firm's board and attempts to interfere in investment decision making. Members and candidates acting in a sales or marketing capacity must be especially mindful of their objectivity in promoting appropriate investments for their clients.

Left unmanaged, pressures that threaten independence place research analysts in a difficult position and may jeopardize their ability to act independently and objectively. One of the ways that research analysts have coped with these pressures in the past is to use subtle and ambiguous language in their recommendations or to temper the tone of their research reports. Such subtleties are lost on some investors, however, who reasonably expect research reports and recommendations to be straightforward and transparent and to communicate clearly an analyst's views based on unbiased analysis and independent judgment.

Members and candidates are personally responsible for maintaining independence and objectivity when preparing research reports, making investment recommendations, and taking investment action on behalf of clients. Recommendations must convey the member's or candidate's true opinions, free of bias from internal or external pressures, and be stated in clear and unambiguous language.

Members and candidates also should be aware that some of their professional or social activities within CFA Institute or its member societies may subtly threaten their independence or objectivity. When seeking corporate financial support for conventions, seminars, or even weekly society luncheons, the members or candidates responsible for the activities should evaluate both the actual effect of such solicitations on their independence and whether their objectivity might be perceived to be compromised in the eyes of their clients.

Buy-Side Clients

One source of pressure on sell-side analysts is buy-side clients. Institutional clients are traditionally the primary users of sell-side research, either directly or with soft dollar brokerage. Portfolio managers may have significant positions in the security of a company under review. A rating downgrade may adversely affect the portfolio's performance, particularly in the short term, because the sensitivity of stock prices to ratings changes has increased in recent years. A downgrade may also affect the manager's compensation, which is usually tied to portfolio performance. Moreover, portfolio performance is subject to media and public scrutiny, which may affect the manager's professional reputation. Consequently, some portfolio managers implicitly or explicitly support sell-side ratings inflation.

Portfolio managers have a responsibility to respect and foster the intellectual honesty of sell-side research. Therefore, it is improper for portfolio managers to threaten or engage in retaliatory practices, such as reporting sell-side analysts to the covered company in order to instigate negative corporate reactions. Although most portfolio managers do not engage in such practices, the perception by the research analyst that a reprisal is possible may cause concern and make it difficult for the analyst to maintain independence and objectivity.

Fund Manager and Custodial Relationships

Research analysts are not the only people who must be concerned with maintaining their independence. Members and candidates who are responsible for hiring and retaining outside managers and third-party custodians should not accepts gifts, entertainment, or travel funding that may be perceived as impairing their decisions. The use of secondary fund managers has evolved into a common practice to manage specific asset allocations. The use of third-party custodians is common practice for independent investment advisory firms and helps them with trading capabilities and reporting requirements. Primary and secondary fund managers, as well as third-party custodians, often arrange educational and marketing events to inform others about their business strategies, investment process, or custodial services. Members and candidates must review the merits of each offer individually in determining whether they may attend yet maintain their independence.

Investment Banking Relationships

Some sell-side firms may exert pressure on their analysts to issue favorable research reports on current or prospective investment banking clients. For many of these firms, income from investment banking has become increasingly important to overall firm profitability because brokerage income has declined as a result of price competition. Consequently, firms offering investment banking services work hard to develop and maintain relationships with investment banking clients and prospects. These companies are often covered by the firm's research analysts because companies often select their investment banks on the basis of the reputation of their research analysts, the quality of their work, and their standing in the industry.

In some countries, research analysts frequently work closely with their investment banking colleagues to help evaluate prospective investment banking clients. In other countries, because of past abuses in managing the obvious conflicts of interest, regulators have established clear rules prohibiting the interaction of these groups. Although collaboration between research analysts and investment banking colleagues may benefit the firm and enhance market efficiency (e.g., by allowing firms to assess risks more accurately and make better pricing assumptions), it requires firms to carefully balance the conflicts of interest inherent in the collaboration. Having analysts work with investment bankers is appropriate only when the conflicts are adequately and effectively managed and disclosed. Firm managers have a responsibility to provide an environment in which analysts are neither coerced nor enticed into issuing research that does not reflect their true opinions. Firms should require public disclosure of actual conflicts of interest to investors.

Members, candidates, and their firms must adopt and follow perceived best practices in maintaining independence and objectivity in the corporate culture and protecting analysts from undue pressure by their investment banking colleagues. The "firewalls" traditionally built between these two functions must be managed to minimize conflicts of interest; indeed, enhanced firewall policies may go as far as prohibiting all communications between these groups. A key element of an enhanced firewall is separate reporting structures for personnel on the research side and personnel on the investment banking side. For example, investment banking personnel should not have any authority to approve, disapprove, or make changes to research reports or recommendations. Another element should be a compensation arrangement that minimizes the pressures on research analysts and rewards objectivity and accuracy. Compensation arrangements should not link analyst remuneration directly to investment banking assignments in which the analyst may participate as a team member. Firms should also regularly review their policies and procedures to determine whether analysts are adequately safeguarded and to improve the transparency of disclosures relating to conflicts of interest. The highest level of transparency is achieved when disclosures are prominent and specific rather than marginalized and generic.

Performance Measurement and Attribution

Members and candidates working within a firm's investment performance measurement department may also be presented with situations that challenge their independence and objectivity. As performance analysts, their analyses may reveal instances where managers may appear to have strayed from their mandate. Additionally, the performance analyst may receive requests to alter the construction of composite indexes owing to negative results for a selected account or fund. The member or candidate must not allow internal or external influences to affect their independence and objectivity as they faithfully complete their performance calculation and analysis-related responsibilities.

Public Companies

Analysts may be pressured to issue favorable reports and recommendations by the companies they follow. Not every stock is a "buy," and not every research report is favorable—for many reasons, including the cyclical nature of many business activities and market fluctuations. For instance, a "good company" does not always translate into a "good stock" rating if the current stock price is fully valued. In making an investment recommendation, the analyst is responsible for anticipating, interpreting, and assessing a company's prospects and stock price performance in a factual manner. Many company managers, however, believe that their company's stock is undervalued, and these managers may find it difficult to accept critical research reports or ratings downgrades. Company managers' compensation may also be dependent on stock performance.

Due diligence in financial research and analysis involves gathering information from a wide variety of sources, including public disclosure documents (such as proxy statements, annual reports, and other regulatory filings) and also company management and investor-relations personnel, suppliers, customers, competitors, and other relevant sources. Research analysts may justifiably fear that companies will limit their ability to conduct thorough research by denying analysts who have "negative" views direct access to company managers and/or barring them from conference calls and other communication venues. Retaliatory practices include companies bringing legal action against analysts personally and/or their firms to seek monetary damages for the economic effects of negative reports and recommendations. Although few companies engage in such behavior, the perception that a reprisal is possible is a reasonable concern for analysts. This concern may make it difficult for them to conduct the comprehensive research needed to make objective recommendations. For further information and guidance, members and candidates should refer to the CFA Institute publication *Best Practice Guidelines Governing Analyst/Corporate Issuer Relations* (www.cfainstitute.org).

Credit Rating Agency Opinions

Credit rating agencies provide a service by grading the fixed-income products offered by companies. Analysts face challenges related to incentives and compensation schemes that may be tied to the final rating and successful placement of the product. Members and candidates employed at rating agencies should ensure that procedures and processes at the agencies prevent undue influences from a sponsoring company during the analysis. Members and candidates should abide by their agencies' and the industry's standards of conduct regarding the analytical process and the distribution of their reports.

The work of credit rating agencies also raises concerns similar to those inherent in investment banking relationships. Analysts may face pressure to issue ratings at a specific level because of other services the agency offers companies—namely, advising on the development of structured products. The rating agencies need to develop the necessary firewalls and protections to allow the independent operations of their different business lines.

When using information provided by credit rating agencies, members and candidates should be mindful of the potential conflicts of interest. And because of the potential conflicts, members and candidates may need to independently validate the rating granted.

Influence during the Manager Selection/Procurement Process

Members and candidates may find themselves on either side of the manager selection process. An individual may be on the hiring side as a representative of a pension organization or an investment committee member of an endowment or a charitable organization. Additionally, other members may be representing their organizations in attempts to earn new investment allocation mandates. The responsibility of members and candidates to maintain their independence and objectivity extends to the hiring or firing of those who provide business services beyond investment management.

When serving in a hiring capacity, members and candidates should not solicit gifts, contributions, or other compensation that may affect their independence and objectivity. Solicitations do not have to benefit members and candidates personally to conflict with Standard I(B). Requesting contributions to a favorite charity or political organization may also be perceived as an attempt to influence the decision-making process. Additionally, members and candidates serving in a hiring capacity should refuse gifts, donations, and other offered compensation that may be perceived to influence their decision-making process.

When working to earn a new investment allocation, members and candidates should not offer gifts, contributions, or other compensation to influence the decision of the hiring representative. The offering of these items with the intent to impair the independence and objectivity of another person would not comply with Standard I(B). Such prohibited actions may include offering donations to a charitable organization or political candidate referred by the hiring representative.

A clear example of improperly influencing hiring representatives was displayed in the "pay-to-play" scandal involving government-sponsored pension funds in the United States. Managers looking to gain lucrative allocations from the large funds made requested donations to the political campaigns of individuals directly responsible for the hiring decisions. This scandal and other similar events have led to new laws requiring additional reporting concerning political contributions and bans on hiring—or hiring delays for—managers that made campaign contributions to representatives associated with the decision-making process.

Issuer-Paid Research

In light of the recent reduction of sell-side research coverage, many companies, seeking to increase visibility both in the financial markets and with potential investors, have hired analysts to produce research reports analyzing their companies. These reports bridge the gap created by the lack of coverage and can be an effective method of communicating with investors.

Issuer-paid research conducted by independent analysts, however, is fraught with potential conflicts. Depending on how the research is written and distributed, investors may be misled into believing that the research is from an independent source when, in reality, it has been paid for by the subject company.

Members and candidates must adhere to strict standards of conduct that govern how the research is to be conducted and what disclosures must be made in the report. Analysts must engage in thorough, independent, and unbiased analysis and must fully disclose potential conflicts of interest, including the nature of their compensation. Otherwise, analysts risk misleading investors.

Investors need clear, credible, and thorough information about companies, and they need research based on independent thought. At a minimum, issuer-paid research should include a thorough analysis of the company's financial statements based on publicly disclosed information, benchmarking within a peer group, and industry analysis. Analysts must exercise diligence, independence, and thoroughness in conducting their research in an objective manner. Analysts must distinguish between fact and opinion in their reports. Conclusions must have a reasonable and adequate basis and must be supported by appropriate research.

Independent analysts must also strictly limit the type of compensation that they accept for conducting issuer-paid research. Otherwise, the content and conclusions of the reports could reasonably be expected to be determined or affected by compensation from the sponsoring companies. Compensation that might influence the research report could be direct, such as payment based on the conclusions of the report, or indirect, such as stock warrants or other equity instruments that could increase in value on the basis of positive coverage in the report. In such instances, the independent analyst has an incentive to avoid including negative information or making negative conclusions. Best practice is for independent analysts, prior to writing their reports, to negotiate only a flat fee for their work that is not linked to their conclusions or recommendations.

Travel Funding

The benefits related to accepting paid travel extend beyond the cost savings to the member or candidate and his firm, such as the chance to talk exclusively with the executives of a company or learning more about the investment options provided by an investment organization. Acceptance also comes with potential concerns; for example, members and candidates may be influenced by these discussions when flying on a corporate or chartered jet or attending sponsored conferences where many expenses, including airfare and lodging, are covered. To avoid the appearance of compromising their independence and objectivity, best practice dictates that members and candidates always use commercial transportation at their expense or at the expense of their firm rather than accept paid travel arrangements from an outside company. Should commercial transportation be unavailable, members and candidates may accept modestly arranged travel to participate in appropriate information-gathering events, such as a property tour.

5 STANDARD I(B): RECOMMENDED PROCEDURES

Members and candidates should adhere to the following practices and should encourage their firms to establish procedures to avoid violations of Standard I(B):

- *Protect the integrity of opinions*: Members, candidates, and their firms should establish policies stating that every research report concerning the securities of a corporate client should reflect the unbiased opinion of the analyst. Firms should also design compensation systems that protect the integrity of the investment decision process by maintaining the independence and objectivity of analysts.
- *Create a restricted list*: If the firm is unwilling to permit dissemination of adverse opinions about a corporate client, members and candidates should encourage the firm to remove the controversial company from the research universe and put it on a restricted list so that the firm disseminates only factual information about the company.
- *Restrict special cost arrangements*: When attending meetings at an issuer's headquarters, members and candidates should pay for commercial transportation and hotel charges. No corporate issuer should reimburse members or candidates for air transportation. Members and candidates should encourage issuers to limit the use of corporate aircraft to situations in which commercial transportation is not available or in which efficient movement could not otherwise be arranged. Members and candidates should take particular care that when frequent meetings are held between an individual issuer and an individual member or candidate, the issuer should not always host the member or candidate.
- *Limit gifts*: Members and candidates must limit the acceptance of gratuities and/or gifts to token items. Standard I(B) does not preclude customary, ordinary business-related entertainment as long as its purpose is not to influence or reward members or candidates. Firms should consider a strict value limit for acceptable gifts that is based on the local or regional customs and should address whether the limit is per gift or an aggregate annual value.
- *Restrict investments*: Members and candidates should encourage their investment firms to develop formal policies related to employee purchases of equity or equity-related IPOs. Firms should require prior approval for

employee participation in IPOs, with prompt disclosure of investment actions taken following the offering. Strict limits should be imposed on investment personnel acquiring securities in private placements.

- *Review procedures*: Members and candidates should encourage their firms to implement effective supervisory and review procedures to ensure that analysts and portfolio managers comply with policies relating to their personal investment activities.
- *Independence policy*: Members, candidates, and their firms should establish a formal written policy on the independence and objectivity of research and implement reporting structures and review procedures to ensure that research analysts do not report to and are not supervised or controlled by any department of the firm that could compromise the independence of the analyst. More detailed recommendations related to a firm's policies regarding research objectivity are set forth in the CFA Institute statement *Research Objectivity Standards* (www.cfainstitute.org).
- *Appointed officer*: Firms should appoint a senior officer with oversight responsibilities for compliance with the firm's code of ethics and all regulations concerning its business. Firms should provide every employee with the procedures and policies for reporting potentially unethical behavior, violations of regulations, or other activities that may harm the firm's reputation.

STANDARD I(B): APPLICATION OF THE STANDARD 6

Example 1 (Travel Expenses):

Steven Taylor, a mining analyst with Bronson Brokers, is invited by Precision Metals to join a group of his peers in a tour of mining facilities in several western US states. The company arranges for chartered group flights from site to site and for accommodations in Spartan Motels, the only chain with accommodations near the mines, for three nights. Taylor allows Precision Metals to pick up his tab, as do the other analysts, with one exception—John Adams, an employee of a large trust company who insists on following his company's policy and paying for his hotel room himself.

> *Comment*: The policy of the company where Adams works complies closely with Standard I(B) by avoiding even the appearance of a conflict of interest, but Taylor and the other analysts were not necessarily violating Standard I(B). In general, when allowing companies to pay for travel and/or accommodations in these circumstances, members and candidates must use their judgment. They must be on guard that such arrangements not impinge on a member's or candidate's independence and objectivity. In this example, the trip was strictly for business and Taylor was not accepting irrelevant or lavish hospitality. The itinerary required chartered flights, for which analysts were not expected to pay. The accommodations were modest. These arrangements are not unusual and did not violate Standard I(B) as long as Taylor's independence and objectivity were not compromised. In the final analysis, members and candidates should consider both whether they can remain objective and whether their integrity might be perceived by their clients to have been compromised.

Example 2 (Research Independence):

Susan Dillon, an analyst in the corporate finance department of an investment services firm, is making a presentation to a potential new business client that includes the promise that her firm will provide full research coverage of the potential client.

> *Comment*: Dillon may agree to provide research coverage, but she must not commit her firm's research department to providing a favorable recommendation. The firm's recommendation (favorable, neutral, or unfavorable) must be based on an independent and objective investigation and analysis of the company and its securities.

Example 3 (Research Independence and Intrafirm Pressure):

Walter Fritz is an equity analyst with Hilton Brokerage who covers the mining industry. He has concluded that the stock of Metals & Mining is overpriced at its current level, but he is concerned that a negative research report will hurt the good relationship between Metals & Mining and the investment banking division of his firm. In fact, a senior manager of Hilton Brokerage has just sent him a copy of a proposal his firm has made to Metals & Mining to underwrite a debt offering. Fritz needs to produce a report right away and is concerned about issuing a less-than-favorable rating.

> *Comment*: Fritz's analysis of Metals & Mining must be objective and based solely on consideration of company fundamentals. Any pressure from other divisions of his firm is inappropriate. This conflict could have been eliminated if, in anticipation of the offering, Hilton Brokerage had placed Metals & Mining on a restricted list for its sales force.

Example 4 (Research Independence and Issuer Relationship Pressure):

As in Example 3, Walter Fritz has concluded that Metals & Mining stock is overvalued at its current level, but he is concerned that a negative research report might jeopardize a close rapport that he has nurtured over the years with Metals & Mining's CEO, chief finance officer, and investment relations officer. Fritz is concerned that a negative report might result also in management retaliation—for instance, cutting him off from participating in conference calls when a quarterly earnings release is made, denying him the ability to ask questions on such calls, and/or denying him access to top management for arranging group meetings between Hilton Brokerage clients and top Metals & Mining managers.

> *Comment*: As in Example 3, Fritz's analysis must be objective and based solely on consideration of company fundamentals. Any pressure from Metals & Mining is inappropriate. Fritz should reinforce the integrity of his conclusions by stressing that his investment recommendation is based on relative valuation, which may include qualitative issues with respect to Metals & Mining's management.

Example 5 (Research Independence and Sales Pressure):

As support for the sales effort of her corporate bond department, Lindsey Warner offers credit guidance to purchasers of fixed-income securities. Her compensation is closely linked to the performance of the corporate bond department. Near the quarter's end, Warner's firm has a large inventory position in the bonds of Milton, Ltd., and has been unable to sell the bonds because of Milton's recent announcement of an operating problem. Salespeople have asked her to contact large clients to push the bonds.

> *Comment*: Unethical sales practices create significant potential violations of the Code and Standards. Warner's opinion of the Milton bonds must not be affected by internal pressure or compensation. In this case, Warner must refuse to push the Milton bonds unless she is able to justify that the market price has already adjusted for the operating problem.

Example 6 (Research Independence and Prior Coverage):

Jill Jorund is a securities analyst following airline stocks and a rising star at her firm. Her boss has been carrying a "buy" recommendation on International Airlines and asks Jorund to take over coverage of that airline. He tells Jorund that under no circumstances should the prevailing buy recommendation be changed.

> *Comment*: Jorund must be independent and objective in her analysis of International Airlines. If she believes that her boss's instructions have compromised her, she has two options: She can tell her boss that she cannot cover the company under these constraints, or she can take over coverage of the company, reach her own independent conclusions, and if they conflict with her boss's opinion, share the conclusions with her boss or other supervisors in the firm so that they can make appropriate recommendations. Jorund must issue only recommendations that reflect her independent and objective opinion.

Example 7 (Gifts and Entertainment from Related Party):

Edward Grant directs a large amount of his commission business to a New York–based brokerage house. In appreciation for all the business, the brokerage house gives Grant two tickets to the World Cup in South Africa, two nights at a nearby resort, several meals, and transportation via limousine to the game. Grant fails to disclose receiving this package to his supervisor.

> *Comment*: Grant has violated Standard I(B) because accepting these substantial gifts may impede his independence and objectivity. Every member and candidate should endeavor to avoid situations that might cause or be perceived to cause a loss of independence or objectivity in recommending investments or taking investment action. By accepting the trip, Grant has opened himself up to the accusation that he may give the broker favored treatment in return.

Example 8 (Gifts and Entertainment from Client):

Theresa Green manages the portfolio of Ian Knowlden, a client of Tisbury Investments. Green achieves an annual return for Knowlden that is consistently better than that of the benchmark she and the client previously agreed to. As a reward, Knowlden offers Green two tickets to Wimbledon and the use of Knowlden's flat in London for a week. Green discloses this gift to her supervisor at Tisbury.

> *Comment*: Green is in compliance with Standard I(B) because she disclosed the gift from one of her clients in accordance with the firm's policies. Members and candidates may accept bonuses or gifts from clients as long

as they disclose them to their employer because gifts in a client relationship are deemed less likely to affect a member's or candidate's objectivity and independence than gifts in other situations. Disclosure is required, however, so that supervisors can monitor such situations to guard against employees favoring a gift-giving client to the detriment of other fee-paying clients (such as by allocating a greater proportion of IPO stock to the gift-giving client's portfolio).

Best practices for monitoring include comparing the transaction costs of the Knowlden account with the costs of other accounts managed by Green and other similar accounts within Tisbury. The supervisor could also compare the performance returns with the returns of other clients with the same mandate. This comparison will assist in determining whether a pattern of favoritism by Green is disadvantaging other Tisbury clients or the possibility that this favoritism could affect her future behavior.

Example 9 (Travel Expenses from External Manager):

Tom Wayne is the investment manager of the Franklin City Employees Pension Plan. He recently completed a successful search for a firm to manage the foreign equity allocation of the plan's diversified portfolio. He followed the plan's standard procedure of seeking presentations from a number of qualified firms and recommended that his board select Penguin Advisors because of its experience, well-defined investment strategy, and performance record. The firm claims compliance with the Global Investment Performance Standards (GIPS®) and has been verified. Following the selection of Penguin, a reporter from the *Franklin City Record* calls to ask if there was any connection between this action and the fact that Penguin was one of the sponsors of an "investment fact-finding trip to Asia" that Wayne made earlier in the year. The trip was one of several conducted by the Pension Investment Academy, which had arranged the itinerary of meetings with economic, government, and corporate officials in major cities in several Asian countries. The Pension Investment Academy obtains support for the cost of these trips from a number of investment managers, including Penguin Advisors; the Academy then pays the travel expenses of the various pension plan managers on the trip and provides all meals and accommodations. The president of Penguin Advisors was also one of the travelers on the trip.

Comment: Although Wayne can probably put to good use the knowledge he gained from the trip in selecting portfolio managers and in other areas of managing the pension plan, his recommendation of Penguin Advisors may be tainted by the possible conflict incurred when he participated in a trip partly paid for by Penguin Advisors and when he was in the daily company of the president of Penguin Advisors. To avoid violating Standard I(B), Wayne's basic expenses for travel and accommodations should have been paid by his employer or the pension plan; contact with the president of Penguin Advisors should have been limited to informational or educational events only; and the trip, the organizer, and the sponsor should have been made a matter of public record. Even if his actions were not in violation of Standard I(B), Wayne should have been sensitive to the public perception of the trip when reported in the newspaper and the extent to which the subjective elements of his decision might have been affected by the familiarity that the daily contact of such a trip would encourage. This advantage would probably not be shared by firms competing with Penguin Advisors.

Example 10 (Research Independence and Compensation Arrangements):

Javier Herrero recently left his job as a research analyst for a large investment adviser. While looking for a new position, he was hired by an investor-relations firm to write a research report on one of its clients, a small educational software company. The investor-relations firm hopes to generate investor interest in the technology company. The firm will pay Herrero a flat fee plus a bonus if any new investors buy stock in the company as a result of Herrero's report.

> *Comment*: If Herrero accepts this payment arrangement, he will be in violation of Standard I(B) because the compensation arrangement can reasonably be expected to compromise his independence and objectivity. Herrero will receive a bonus for attracting investors, which provides an incentive to draft a positive report regardless of the facts and to ignore or play down any negative information about the company. Herrero should accept only a flat fee that is not tied to the conclusions or recommendations of the report. Issuer-paid research that is objective and unbiased can be done under the right circumstances as long as the analyst takes steps to maintain his or her objectivity and includes in the report proper disclosures regarding potential conflicts of interest.

Example 11 (Recommendation Objectivity and Service Fees):

Two years ago, Bob Wade, trust manager for Central Midas Bank, was approached by Western Funds about promoting its family of funds, with special interest in the service-fee class of funds. To entice Central to promote this class, Western Funds offered to pay the bank a service fee of 0.25%. Without disclosing the fee being offered to the bank, Wade asked one of the investment managers to review Western's funds to determine whether they were suitable for clients of Central Midas Bank. The manager completed the normal due diligence review and determined that the new funds were fairly valued in the market with fee structures on a par with competitors. Wade decided to accept Western's offer and instructed the team of portfolio managers to exclusively promote these funds and the service-fee class to clients seeking to invest new funds or transfer from their current investments.

Now, two years later, the funds managed by Western begin to underperform their peers. Wade is counting on the fees to reach his profitability targets and continues to push these funds as acceptable investments for Central's clients.

> *Comment*: Wade is violating Standard I(B) because the fee arrangement has affected the objectivity of his recommendations. Wade is relying on the fee as a component of the department's profitability and is unwilling to offer other products that may affect the fees received.
>
> See also Standard VI(A) Disclosure of Conflicts.

Example 12 (Recommendation Objectivity):

Bob Thompson has been doing research for the portfolio manager of the fixed-income department. His assignment is to do sensitivity analysis on securitized subprime mortgages. He has discussed with the manager possible scenarios to use to calculate expected returns. A key assumption in such calculations is housing price appreciation (HPA) because it drives "prepays" (prepayments of mortgages) and losses. Thompson is concerned with the significant appreciation experienced over the previous five years as a result of the increased availability of funds from subprime mortgages. Thompson insists that the analysis should include a scenario run with –10% for Year 1, –5% for Year 2, and then (to project a worst-case scenario) 0% for Years 3 through 5. The manager replies that these assumptions are too dire because there has never been a time in their available database when HPA was negative.

Thompson conducts his research to better understand the risks inherent in these securities and evaluates these securities in the worst-case scenario, an unlikely but possible environment. Based on the results of the enhanced scenarios, Thompson does not recommend the purchase of the securitization. Against the general market trends, the manager follows Thompson's recommendation and does not invest. The following year, the housing market collapses. In avoiding the subprime investments, the manager's portfolio outperforms its peer group that year.

> *Comment*: Thompson's actions in running the worst-case scenario against the protests of the portfolio manager are in alignment with the principles of Standard I(B). Thompson did not allow his research to be pressured by the general trends of the market or the manager's desire to limit the research to historical norms.
>
> See also Standard V(A) Diligence and Reasonable Basis.

Example 13 (Influencing Manager Selection Decisions):

Adrian Mandel, CFA, is a senior portfolio manager for ZZYY Capital Management who oversees a team of investment professionals who manage labor union pension funds. A few years ago, ZZYY sought to win a competitive asset manager search to manage a significant allocation of the pension fund of the United Doughnut and Pretzel Bakers Union (UDPBU). UDPBU's investment board is chaired by a recognized key decision maker and long-time leader of the union, Ernesto Gomez. To improve ZZYY's chances of winning the competition, Mandel made significant monetary contributions to Gomez's union reelection campaign fund. Even after ZZYY was hired as a primary manager of the pension, Mandel believed that his firm's position was not secure. Mandel continued to contribute to Gomez's reelection campaign chest as well as to entertain lavishly the union leader and his family at top restaurants on a regular basis. All of Mandel's outlays were routinely handled as marketing expenses reimbursed by ZZYY's expense accounts and were disclosed to his senior management as being instrumental in maintaining a strong close relationship with an important client.

> *Comment*: Mandel not only offered but actually gave monetary gifts, benefits, and other considerations that reasonably could be expected to compromise Gomez's objectivity. Therefore, Mandel was in violation of Standard I(B).

Example 14 (Influencing Manager Selection Decisions):

Adrian Mandel, CFA, had heard about the manager search competition for the UDPBU Pension Fund through a broker/dealer contact. The contact told him that a well-known retired professional golfer, Bobby "The Bear" Finlay, who had become a licensed broker/dealer serving as a pension consultant, was orchestrating the UDPBU manager search. Finlay had gained celebrity status with several labor union pension fund boards by entertaining their respective board members and regaling them with colorful stories of fellow pro golfers' antics in clubhouses around the world. Mandel decided to improve ZZYY's chances of being invited to participate in the search competition by befriending Finlay to curry his favor. Knowing Finlay's love of entertainment, Mandel wined and dined Finlay at high-profile bistros where Finlay could glow in the fan recognition lavished on him by all the other patrons. Mandel's endeavors paid off handsomely when Finlay recommended to the UDPBU board that ZZYY be entered as one of three finalist asset management firms in its search.

> *Comment*: Similar to Example 13, Mandel lavished gifts, benefits, and other considerations in the form of expensive entertainment that could reasonably be expected to influence the consultant to recommend the hiring of his firm. Therefore, Mandel was in violation of Standard I(B).

Example 15 (Fund Manager Relationships):

Amie Scott is a performance analyst within her firm with responsibilities for analyzing the performance of external managers. While completing her quarterly analysis, Scott notices a change in one manager's reported composite construction. The change concealed the bad performance of a particularly large account by placing that account into a new residual composite. This change allowed the manager to remain at the top of the list of manager performance. Scott knows her firm has a large allocation to this manager, and the fund's manager is a close personal friend of the CEO. She needs to deliver her final report but is concerned with pointing out the composite change.

> *Comment*: Scott would be in violation of Standard I(B) if she did not disclose the change in her final report. The analysis of managers' performance should not be influenced by personal relationships or the size of the allocation to the outside managers. By not including the change, Scott would not be providing an independent analysis of the performance metrics for her firm.

Example 16 (Intrafirm Pressure):

Jill Stein is head of performance measurement for her firm. During the last quarter, many members of the organization's research department were removed because of the poor quality of their recommendations. The subpar research caused one larger account holder to experience significant underperformance, which resulted in the client withdrawing his money after the end of the quarter. The head of sales requests that Stein remove this account from the firm's performance composite because the performance decline can be attributed to the departed research team and not the client's adviser.

> *Comment*: Pressure from other internal departments can create situations that cause a member or candidate to violate the Code and Standards. Stein must maintain her independence and objectivity and refuse to exclude specific accounts from the firm's performance composites to which they belong. As long as the client invested under a strategy similar to that of the defined composite, it cannot be excluded because of the poor stock selections that led to the underperformance and asset withdrawal.

7 STANDARD I(C) MISREPRESENTATION

- ☐ demonstrate the application of the Code of Ethics and Standards of Professional Conduct to situations involving issues of professional integrity
- ☐ recommend practices and procedures designed to prevent violations of the Code of Ethics and Standards of Professional Conduct
- ☐ identify conduct that conforms to the Code and Standards and conduct that violates the Code and Standards

> Members and Candidates must not knowingly make any misrepresentations relating to investment analysis, recommendations, actions, or other professional activities.

Guidance

Highlights:

- *Impact on Investment Practice*
- *Performance Reporting*
- *Social Media*
- *Omissions*
- *Plagiarism*
- *Work Completed for Employer*

Trust is the foundation of the investment profession. Investors must be able to rely on the statements and information provided to them by those with whom the investors have trusted their financial well-being. Investment professionals who make false or misleading statements not only harm investors but also reduce the level of investor confidence in the investment profession and threaten the integrity of capital markets as a whole.

A misrepresentation is any untrue statement or omission of a fact or any statement that is otherwise false or misleading. A member or candidate must not knowingly omit or misrepresent information or give a false impression of a firm, organization, or security in the member's or candidate's oral representations, advertising (whether in the press or through brochures), electronic communications, or written materials (whether publicly disseminated or not). In this context, "knowingly" means that the member or candidate either knows or should have known that the misrepresentation was being made or that omitted information could alter the investment decision-making process.

Written materials include, but are not limited to, research reports, underwriting documents, company financial reports, market letters, newspaper columns, and books. Electronic communications include, but are not limited to, internet communications, webpages, mobile applications, and e-mails. Members and candidates who use webpages should regularly monitor materials posted on these sites to ensure that they contain current information. Members and candidates should also ensure that all reasonable precautions have been taken to protect the site's integrity and security and that the site does not misrepresent any information and does provide full disclosure.

Standard I(C) prohibits members and candidates from guaranteeing clients any specific return on volatile investments. Most investments contain some element of risk that makes their return inherently unpredictable. For such investments, guaranteeing either a particular rate of return or preservation of investment capital (e.g., "I can guarantee that you will earn 8% on equities this year" or "I can guarantee that you will not lose money on this investment") is misleading to investors. Standard I(C) does not prohibit members and candidates from providing clients with information on investment products that have guarantees built into the structure of the products themselves or for which an institution has agreed to cover any losses.

Impact on Investment Practice

Members and candidates must not misrepresent any aspect of their practice, including (but not limited to) their qualifications or credentials, the qualifications or services provided by their firm, their performance record and the record of their firm, and the characteristics of an investment. Any misrepresentation made by a member or candidate relating to the member's or candidate's professional activities is a breach of this standard.

Members and candidates should exercise care and diligence when incorporating third-party information. Misrepresentations resulting from the use of the credit ratings, research, testimonials, or marketing materials of outside parties become the responsibility of the investment professional when it affects that professional's business practices.

Investing through outside managers continues to expand as an acceptable method of investing in areas outside a firm's core competencies. Members and candidates must disclose their intended use of external managers and must not represent those managers' investment practices as their own. Although the level of involvement of outside managers may change over time, appropriate disclosures by members and candidates are important in avoiding misrepresentations, especially if the primary activity is to invest directly with a single external manager. Standard V(B) Communication with Clients and Prospective Clients discusses in further detail communicating the firm's investment practices.

Performance Reporting

The performance benchmark selection process is another area where misrepresentations may occur. Members and candidates may misrepresent the success of their performance record through presenting benchmarks that are not comparable to their strategies. Further, clients can be misled if the benchmark's results are not reported on a basis comparable to that of the fund's or client's results. Best practice is selecting the most appropriate available benchmark from a universe of available options. The transparent presentation of appropriate performance benchmarks is an important aspect in providing clients with information that is useful in making investment decisions.

However, Standard I(C) does not require that a benchmark always be provided in order to comply. Some investment strategies may not lend themselves to displaying an appropriate benchmark because of the complexity or diversity of the investments included. Furthermore, some investment strategies may use reference indexes that do not reflect the opportunity set of the invested assets—for example, a hedge fund comparing its performance with a "cash plus" basis. When such a benchmark is used, members and candidates should make reasonable efforts to ensure that they disclose the reasons behind the use of this reference index to avoid misrepresentations of their performance. Members and candidates should discuss with clients on a continuous basis the appropriate benchmark to be used for performance evaluations and related fee calculations.

Reporting misrepresentations may also occur when valuations for illiquid or non-traded securities are available from more than one source. When different options are available, members and candidates may be tempted to switch providers to obtain higher security valuations. The process of shopping for values may misrepresent a security's worth, lead to misinformed decisions to sell or hold an investment, and result in overcharging clients advisory fees.

Members and candidates should take reasonable steps to provide accurate and reliable security pricing information to clients on a consistent basis. Changing pricing providers should not be based solely on the justification that the new provider reports a higher current value of a security. Consistency in the reported information will improve the perception of the valuation process for illiquid securities. Clients will likely have additional confidence that they were able to make an informed decision about continuing to hold these securities in their portfolios.

Social Media

The advancement of online discussion forums and communication platforms, commonly referred to as "social media," is placing additional responsibilities on members and candidates. When communicating through social media channels, members and candidates should provide only the same information they are allowed to distribute to clients and potential clients through other, traditional forms of communication. The online or interactive aspects of social media do not remove the need to be open and honest about the information being distributed.

Along with understanding and following existing and newly developing rules and regulations regarding the allowed use of social media, members and candidates should also ensure that all communications in this format adhere to the requirements of the Code and Standards. The perceived anonymity granted through these platforms may entice individuals to misrepresent their qualifications or abilities or those of their employer. Actions undertaken through social media that knowingly misrepresent investment recommendations or professional activities are considered a violation of Standard I(C).

Omissions

The omission of a fact or outcome can be misleading, especially given the growing use of models and technical analysis processes. Many members and candidates rely on such models and processes to scan for new investment opportunities, to develop investment vehicles, and to produce investment recommendations and ratings. When inputs are knowingly omitted, the resulting outcomes may provide misleading information to those who rely on it for making investment decisions. Additionally, the outcomes from models shall not be presented as fact because they represent the expected results based on the inputs and analysis process incorporated.

Omissions in the performance measurement and attribution process can also misrepresent a manager's performance and skill. Members and candidates should encourage their firms to develop strict policies for composite development to prevent cherry picking—situations in which selected accounts are presented as representative of the firm's abilities. The omission of any accounts appropriate for the defined composite may misrepresent to clients the success of the manager's implementation of its strategy.

Plagiarism

Standard I(C) also prohibits plagiarism in the preparation of material for distribution to employers, associates, clients, prospects, or the general public. Plagiarism is defined as copying or using in substantially the same form materials prepared by others without acknowledging the source of the material or identifying the author and publisher of such material. Members and candidates must not copy (or represent as their own) original ideas or material without permission and must acknowledge and identify the source of ideas or material that is not their own.

The investment profession uses a myriad of financial, economic, and statistical data in the investment decision-making process. Through various publications and presentations, the investment professional is constantly exposed to the work of others and to the temptation to use that work without proper acknowledgment.

Misrepresentation through plagiarism in investment management can take various forms. The simplest and most flagrant example is to take a research report or study done by another firm or person, change the names, and release the material as one's own original analysis. This action is a clear violation of Standard I(C). Other practices include (1) using excerpts from articles or reports prepared by others either verbatim or with only slight changes in wording without acknowledgment, (2) citing specific quotations as attributable to "leading analysts" and "investment experts" without naming the specific references, (3) presenting statistical estimates of forecasts prepared by others and identifying the sources but without including the qualifying statements or caveats that may have been used, (4) using charts and graphs without stating their sources, and (5) copying proprietary computerized spreadsheets or algorithms without seeking the cooperation or authorization of their creators.

In the case of distributing third-party, outsourced research, members and candidates may use and distribute such reports as long as they do not represent themselves as the report's authors. Indeed, the member or candidate may add value for the client by sifting through research and repackaging it for clients. In such cases, clients should be fully informed that they are paying for the ability of the member or candidate to find the best research from a wide variety of sources. Members and candidates must not misrepresent their abilities, the extent of their expertise, or the extent of their work in a way that would mislead their clients or prospective clients. Members and candidates should disclose whether the research being presented to clients comes from another source—from either within or outside the member's or candidate's firm. This allows clients to understand who has the expertise behind the report or whether the work is being done by the analyst, other members of the firm, or an outside party.

Standard I(C) also applies to plagiarism in oral communications, such as through group meetings; visits with associates, clients, and customers; use of audio/video media (which is rapidly increasing); and telecommunications, including electronic data transfer and the outright copying of electronic media.

One of the most egregious practices in violation of this standard is the preparation of research reports based on multiple sources of information without acknowledging the sources. Examples of information from such sources include ideas, statistical compilations, and forecasts combined to give the appearance of original work. Although there is no monopoly on ideas, members and candidates must give credit where it is clearly due. Analysts should not use undocumented forecasts, earnings projections, asset values, and so on. Sources must be revealed to bring the responsibility directly back to the author of the report or the firm involved.

Work Completed for Employer

The preceding paragraphs address actions that would constitute a violation of Standard I(C). In some situations, however, members or candidates may use research conducted or models developed by others within the same firm without committing a violation. The most common example relates to the situation in which one (or more) of the original analysts is no longer with the firm. Research and models developed while employed by a firm are the property of the firm. The firm retains the right to continue using the work completed after a member or candidate has left the organization. The firm may issue future reports without providing attribution to the prior analysts. A member or candidate cannot, however, reissue a previously released report solely under his or her name.

8 STANDARD I(C): RECOMMENDED PROCEDURES

Factual Presentations

Members and candidates can prevent unintentional misrepresentations of their qualifications or the services they or their firms provide if each member and candidate understands the limit of the firm's or individual's capabilities and the need to be accurate and complete in presentations. Firms can provide guidance for employees who make written or oral presentations to clients or potential clients by providing a written list of the firm's available services and a description of the firm's qualifications. This list should suggest ways of describing the firm's services, qualifications, and compensation that are both accurate and suitable for client or customer presentations. Firms can also help prevent misrepresentation by specifically designating which employees are authorized to speak on behalf of the firm. Regardless of whether the firm provides guidance, members and candidates should make certain that they understand the services the firm can perform and its qualifications.

Qualification Summary

In addition, to ensure accurate presentations to clients, each member and candidate should prepare a summary of his or her own qualifications and experience and a list of the services the member or candidate is capable of performing. Firms can assist member and candidate compliance by periodically reviewing employee correspondence and documents that contain representations of individual or firm qualifications.

Verify Outside Information

When providing information to clients from a third party, members and candidates share a responsibility for the accuracy of the marketing and distribution materials that pertain to the third party's capabilities, services, and products. Misrepresentation by third parties can damage the member's or candidate's reputation, the reputation of the firm, and the integrity of the capital markets. Members and candidates should encourage their employers to develop procedures for verifying information of third-party firms.

Maintain Webpages

Members and candidates who publish a webpage should regularly monitor materials posted on the site to ensure that the site contains current information. Members and candidates should also ensure that all reasonable precautions have been taken to protect the site's integrity, confidentiality, and security and that the site does not misrepresent any information and provides full disclosure.

Plagiarism Policy

To avoid plagiarism in preparing research reports or conclusions of analysis, members and candidates should take the following steps:

- *Maintain copies*: Keep copies of all research reports, articles containing research ideas, material with new statistical methodologies, and other materials that were relied on in preparing the research report.
- *Attribute quotations*: Attribute to their sources any direct quotations, including projections, tables, statistics, model/product ideas, and new methodologies prepared by persons other than recognized financial and statistical reporting services or similar sources.
- *Attribute summaries*: Attribute to their sources any paraphrases or summaries of material prepared by others. For example, to support his analysis of Brown Company's competitive position, the author of a research report on Brown might summarize another analyst's report on Brown's chief competitor, but the author of the Brown report must acknowledge in his own report the reliance on the other analyst's report.

STANDARD I(C): APPLICATION OF THE STANDARD 9

Example 1 (Disclosure of Issuer-Paid Research):

Anthony McGuire is an issuer-paid analyst hired by publicly traded companies to electronically promote their stocks. McGuire creates a website that promotes his research efforts as a seemingly independent analyst. McGuire posts a profile and a strong buy recommendation for each company on the website indicating that the stock is expected to increase in value. He does not disclose the contractual relationships with the companies he covers on his website, in the research reports he issues, or in the statements he makes about the companies in internet chat rooms.

> *Comment*: McGuire has violated Standard I(C) because the website is misleading to potential investors. Even if the recommendations are valid and supported with thorough research, his omissions regarding the true relationship between himself and the companies he covers constitute a misrepresentation. McGuire has also violated Standard VI(A) Disclosure of Conflicts by not disclosing the existence of an arrangement with the companies through which he receives compensation in exchange for his services.

Example 2 (Correction of Unintentional Errors):

Hijan Yao is responsible for the creation and distribution of the marketing materials for his firm, which claims compliance with the GIPS standards. Yao creates and distributes a presentation of performance by the firm's Asian equity composite that states the composite has ¥350 billion in assets. In fact, the composite has only ¥35 billion in assets, and the higher figure on the presentation is a result of a typographical error. Nevertheless, the erroneous material is distributed to a number of clients before Yao catches the mistake.

Comment: Once the error is discovered, Yao must take steps to cease distribution of the incorrect material and correct the error by informing those who have received the erroneous information. Because Yao did not knowingly make the misrepresentation, however, he did not violate Standard I(C). Because his firm claims compliance with the GIPS standards, it must also comply with the GIPS Guidance Statement on Error Correction in relation to the error.

Example 3 (Noncorrection of Known Errors):

Syed Muhammad is the president of an investment management firm. The promotional material for the firm, created by the firm's marketing department, incorrectly claims that Muhammad has an advanced degree in finance from a prestigious business school in addition to the CFA designation. Although Muhammad attended the school for a short period of time, he did not receive a degree. Over the years, Muhammad and others in the firm have distributed this material to numerous prospective clients and consultants.

Comment: Even though Muhammad may not have been directly responsible for the misrepresentation of his credentials in the firm's promotional material, he used this material numerous times over an extended period and should have known of the misrepresentation. Thus, Muhammad has violated Standard I(C).

Example 4 (Plagiarism):

Cindy Grant, a research analyst for a Canadian brokerage firm, has specialized in the Canadian mining industry for the past 10 years. She recently read an extensive research report on Jefferson Mining, Ltd., by Jeremy Barton, another analyst. Barton provided extensive statistics on the mineral reserves, production capacity, selling rates, and marketing factors affecting Jefferson's operations. He also noted that initial drilling results on a new ore body, which had not been made public, might show the existence of mineral zones that could increase the life of Jefferson's main mines, but Barton cited no specific data as to the initial drilling results. Grant called an officer of Jefferson, who gave her the initial drilling results over the telephone. The data indicated that the expected life of the main mines would be tripled. Grant added these statistics to Barton's report and circulated it within her firm as her own report.

Comment: Grant plagiarized Barton's report by reproducing large parts of it in her own report without acknowledgment.

Example 5 (Misrepresentation of Information):

When Ricki Marks sells mortgage-backed derivatives called "interest-only strips" (IOs) to public pension plan clients, she describes them as "guaranteed by the US government." Purchasers of the IOs are entitled only to the interest stream generated by the mortgages, however, not the notional principal itself. One particular municipality's investment policies and local law require that securities purchased by its public pension plans be guaranteed by the US government. Although the underlying mortgages are guaranteed, neither the investor's investment nor the interest stream on the IOs is guaranteed. When interest rates decline, causing an increase in prepayment of mortgages, interest payments to the IOs' investors decline, and these investors lose a portion of their investment.

Comment: Marks violated Standard I(C) by misrepresenting the terms and character of the investment.

Example 6 (Potential Information Misrepresentation):

Khalouck Abdrabbo manages the investments of several high-net-worth individuals in the United States who are approaching retirement. Abdrabbo advises these individuals that a portion of their investments be moved from equity to bank-sponsored certificates of deposit and money market accounts so that the principal will be "guaranteed" up to a certain amount. The interest is not guaranteed.

Comment: Although there is risk that the institution offering the certificates of deposits and money market accounts could go bankrupt, in the United States, these accounts are insured by the US government through the Federal Deposit Insurance Corporation. Therefore, using the term "guaranteed" in this context is not inappropriate as long as the amount is within the government-insured limit. Abdrabbo should explain these facts to the clients.

Example 7 (Plagiarism):

Steve Swanson is a senior analyst in the investment research department of Ballard and Company. Apex Corporation has asked Ballard to assist in acquiring the majority ownership of stock in the Campbell Company, a financial consulting firm, and to prepare a report recommending that stockholders of Campbell agree to the acquisition. Another investment firm, Davis and Company, had already prepared a report for Apex analyzing both Apex and Campbell and recommending an exchange ratio. Apex has given the Davis report to Ballard officers, who have passed it on to Swanson. Swanson reviews the Davis report and other available material on Apex and Campbell. From his analysis, he concludes that the common stocks of Campbell and Apex represent good value at their current prices; he believes, however, that the Davis report does not consider all the factors a Campbell stockholder would need to know to make a decision. Swanson reports his conclusions to the partner in charge, who tells him to "use the Davis report, change a few words, sign your name, and get it out."

Comment: If Swanson does as requested, he will violate Standard I(C). He could refer to those portions of the Davis report that he agrees with if he identifies Davis as the source; he could then add his own analysis and conclusions to the report before signing and distributing it.

Example 8 (Plagiarism):

Claude Browning, a quantitative analyst for Double Alpha, Inc., returns from a seminar in great excitement. At that seminar, Jack Jorrely, a well-known quantitative analyst at a national brokerage firm, discussed one of his new models in great detail, and Browning is intrigued by the new concepts. He proceeds to test the model, making some minor mechanical changes but retaining the concepts, until he produces some very positive results. Browning quickly announces to his supervisors at Double Alpha that he has discovered a new model and that clients and prospective clients should be informed of this positive finding as ongoing proof of Double Alpha's continuing innovation and ability to add value.

Comment: Although Browning tested Jorrely's model on his own and even slightly modified it, he must still acknowledge the original source of the idea. Browning can certainly take credit for the final, practical results; he can also support his conclusions with his own test. The credit for the innovative thinking, however, must be awarded to Jorrely.

Example 9 (Plagiarism):

Fernando Zubia would like to include in his firm's marketing materials some "plain-language" descriptions of various concepts, such as the price-to-earnings (P/E) multiple and why standard deviation is used as a measure of risk. The descriptions come from other sources, but Zubia wishes to use them without reference to the original authors. Would this use of material be a violation of Standard I(C)?

Comment: Copying verbatim any material without acknowledgement, including plain-language descriptions of the P/E multiple and standard deviation, violates Standard I(C). Even though these concepts are general, best practice would be for Zubia to describe them in his own words or cite the sources from which the descriptions are quoted. Members and candidates would be violating Standard I(C) if they either were responsible for creating marketing materials without attribution or knowingly use plagiarized materials.

Example 10 (Plagiarism):

Through a mainstream media outlet, Erika Schneider learns about a study that she would like to cite in her research. Should she cite both the mainstream intermediary source as well as the author of the study itself when using that information?

Comment: In all instances, a member or candidate must cite the actual source of the information. Best practice for Schneider would be to obtain the information directly from the author and review it before citing it in a report. In that case, Schneider would not need to report how she found out about the information. For example, suppose Schneider read in the *Financial Times* about a study issued by CFA Institute; best practice for Schneider would be to obtain a copy of the study from CFA Institute, review it, and then cite it in her report. If she does not use any interpretation of the report from the *Financial Times* and the newspaper does not add value to the report itself, the newspaper is merely a conduit of the original information and does not need to be cited. If she does not obtain the report and review the information, Schneider runs the risk of relying on second-hand information that may misstate facts. If, for example, the *Financial Times* erroneously reported some information from the original CFA Institute study and Schneider copied that erroneous information without acknowledging CFA Institute, she could be the object of complaints. Best practice would be either to obtain the complete study from its original author and cite only that author or to use the information provided by the intermediary and cite both sources.

Example 11 (Misrepresentation of Information):

Paul Ostrowski runs a two-person investment management firm. Ostrowski's firm subscribes to a service from a large investment research firm that provides research reports that can be repackaged by smaller firms for those firms' clients. Ostrowski's firm distributes these reports to clients as its own work.

> *Comment*: Ostrowski can rely on third-party research that has a reasonable and adequate basis, but he cannot imply that he is the author of such research. If he does, Ostrowski is misrepresenting the extent of his work in a way that misleads the firm's clients or prospective clients.

Example 12 (Misrepresentation of Information):

Tom Stafford is part of a team within Appleton Investment Management responsible for managing a pool of assets for Open Air Bank, which distributes structured securities to offshore clients. He becomes aware that Open Air is promoting the structured securities as a much less risky investment than the investment management policy followed by him and the team to manage the original pool of assets. Also, Open Air has procured an independent rating for the pool that significantly overstates the quality of the investments. Stafford communicates his concerns to his supervisor, who responds that Open Air owns the product and is responsible for all marketing and distribution. Stafford's supervisor goes on to say that the product is outside of the US regulatory regime that Appleton follows and that all risks of the product are disclosed at the bottom of page 184 of the prospectus.

> *Comment*: As a member of the investment team, Stafford is qualified to recognize the degree of accuracy of the materials that characterize the portfolio, and he is correct to be worried about Appleton's responsibility for a misrepresentation of the risks. Thus, he should continue to pursue the issue of Open Air's inaccurate promotion of the portfolio according to the firm's policies and procedures.
>
> The Code and Standards stress protecting the reputation of the firm and the sustainability and integrity of the capital markets. Misrepresenting the quality and risks associated with the investment pool may lead to negative consequences for others well beyond the direct investors.

Example 13 (Avoiding a Misrepresentation):

Trina Smith is a fixed-income portfolio manager at a pension fund. She has observed that the market for highly structured mortgages is the focus of salespeople she meets and that these products represent a significant number of trading opportunities. In discussions about this topic with her team, Smith learns that calculating yields on changing cash flows within the deal structure requires very specialized vendor software. After more research, they find out that each deal is unique and that deals can have more than a dozen layers and changing cash flow priorities. Smith comes to the conclusion that, because of the complexity of these securities, the team cannot effectively distinguish between potentially good and bad investment options. To avoid misrepresenting their understanding, the team decides that the highly structured mortgage segment of the securitized market should not become part of the core of the fund's portfolio; they will allow some of the less complex securities to be part of the core.

Comment: Smith is in compliance with Standard I(C) by not investing in securities that she and her team cannot effectively understand. Because she is not able to describe the risk and return profile of the securities to the pension fund beneficiaries and trustees, she appropriately limits the fund's exposure to this sector.

Example 14 (Misrepresenting Composite Construction):

Robert Palmer is head of performance for a fund manager. When asked to provide performance numbers to fund rating agencies, he avoids mentioning that the fund manager is quite liberal in composite construction. The reason accounts are included/excluded is not fully explained. The performance values reported to the rating agencies for the composites, although accurate for the accounts shown each period, may not present a true representation of the fund manager's ability.

Comment: "Cherry picking" accounts to include in either published reports or information provided to rating agencies conflicts with Standard I(C). Moving accounts into or out of a composite to influence the overall performance results materially misrepresents the reported values over time. Palmer should work with his firm to strengthen its reporting practices concerning composite construction to avoid misrepresenting the firm's track record or the quality of the information being provided.

Example 15 (Presenting Out-of-Date Information):

David Finch is a sales director at a commercial bank, where he directs the bank's client advisers in the sale of third-party mutual funds. Each quarter, he holds a division-wide training session where he provides fact sheets on investment funds the bank is allowed to offer to clients. These fact sheets, which can be redistributed to potential clients, are created by the fund firms and contain information about the funds, including investment strategy and target distribution rates.

Finch knows that some of the fact sheets are out of date; for example, one long-only fund approved the use of significant leverage last quarter as a method to enhance returns. He continues to provide the sheets to the sales team without updates because the bank has no control over the marketing material released by the mutual fund firms.

Comment: Finch is violating Standard I(C) by providing information that misrepresents aspects of the funds. By not providing the sales team and, ultimately, the clients with the updated information, he is misrepresenting the potential risks associated with the funds with outdated fact sheets. Finch can instruct the sales team to clarify the deficiencies in the fact sheets with clients and ensure they have the most recent fund prospectus document before accepting orders for investing in any fund.

Example 16 (Overemphasis of Firm Results):

Bob Anderson is chief compliance officer for Optima Asset Management Company, a firm currently offering eight funds to clients. Seven of the eight had 10-year returns below the median for their respective sectors. Anderson approves a recent advertisement, which includes this statement: "Optima Asset Management is achieving excellent returns for its investors. The Optima Emerging Markets Equity fund, for example, has 10-year returns that exceed the sector median by more than 10%."

Comment: From the information provided it is difficult to determine whether a violation has occurred as long as the sector outperformance is correct. Anderson may be attempting to mislead potential clients by citing the performance of the sole fund that achieved such results. Past performance is often used to demonstrate a firm's skill and abilities in comparison to funds in the same sectors.

However, if all the funds outperformed their respective benchmarks, then Anderson's assertion that the company "is achieving excellent returns" may be factual. Funds may exhibit positive returns for investors, exceed benchmarks, and yet have returns below the median in their sectors.

Members and candidates need to ensure that their marketing efforts do not include statements that misrepresent their skills and abilities to remain compliant with Standard I(C). Unless the returns of a single fund reflect the performance of a firm as a whole, the use of a singular fund for performance comparisons should be avoided.

STANDARD I(D) MISCONDUCT

10

- ☐ demonstrate the application of the Code of Ethics and Standards of Professional Conduct to situations involving issues of professional integrity
- ☐ recommend practices and procedures designed to prevent violations of the Code of Ethics and Standards of Professional Conduct
- ☐ identify conduct that conforms to the Code and Standards and conduct that violates the Code and Standards

Members and Candidates must not engage in any professional conduct involving dishonesty, fraud, or deceit or commit any act that reflects adversely on their professional reputation, integrity, or competence.

Guidance

Whereas Standard I(A) addresses the obligation of members and candidates to comply with applicable law that governs their professional activities, Standard I(D) addresses *all* conduct that reflects poorly on the professional integrity, good reputation, or competence of members and candidates. Any act that involves lying, cheating, stealing, or other dishonest conduct is a violation of this standard if the offense reflects adversely on a member's or candidate's professional activities. Although CFA Institute discourages any sort of unethical behavior by members and candidates, the Code and Standards are primarily aimed at conduct and actions related to a member's or candidate's professional life.

Conduct that damages trustworthiness or competence may include behavior that, although not illegal, nevertheless negatively affects a member's or candidate's ability to perform his or her responsibilities. For example, abusing alcohol during business hours might constitute a violation of this standard because it could have a detrimental effect on the member's or candidate's ability to fulfill his or her professional responsibilities.

Personal bankruptcy may not reflect on the integrity or trustworthiness of the person declaring bankruptcy, but if the circumstances of the bankruptcy involve fraudulent or deceitful business conduct, the bankruptcy may be a violation of this standard.

In some cases, the absence of appropriate conduct or the lack of sufficient effort may be a violation of Standard I(D). The integrity of the investment profession is built on trust. A member or candidate—whether an investment banker, rating or research analyst, or portfolio manager—is expected to conduct the necessary due diligence to properly understand the nature and risks of an investment before making an investment recommendation. By not taking these steps and, instead, relying on someone else in the process to perform them, members or candidates may violate the trust their clients have placed in them. This loss of trust may have a significant impact on the reputation of the member or candidate and the operations of the financial market as a whole.

Individuals may attempt to abuse the CFA Institute Professional Conduct Program by actively seeking CFA Institute enforcement of the Code and Standards, and Standard I(D) in particular, as a method of settling personal, political, or other disputes unrelated to professional ethics. CFA Institute is aware of this issue, and appropriate disciplinary policies, procedures, and enforcement mechanisms are in place to address misuse of the Code and Standards and the Professional Conduct Program in this way.

11 STANDARD I(D): RECOMMENDED PROCEDURES

In addition to ensuring that their own behavior is consistent with Standard I(D), to prevent general misconduct, members and candidates should encourage their firms to adopt the following policies and procedures to support the principles of Standard I(D):

- *Code of ethics*: Develop and/or adopt a code of ethics to which every employee must subscribe, and make clear that any personal behavior that reflects poorly on the individual involved, the institution as a whole, or the investment industry will not be tolerated.
- *List of violations*: Disseminate to all employees a list of potential violations and associated disciplinary sanctions, up to and including dismissal from the firm.
- *Employee references*: Check references of potential employees to ensure that they are of good character and not ineligible to work in the investment industry because of past infractions of the law.

12 STANDARD I(D): APPLICATION OF THE STANDARD

Example 1 (Professionalism and Competence):

Simon Sasserman is a trust investment officer at a bank in a small affluent town. He enjoys lunching every day with friends at the country club, where his clients have observed him having numerous drinks. Back at work after lunch, he clearly is intoxicated while making investment decisions. His colleagues make a point of handling any business with Sasserman in the morning because they distrust his judgment after lunch.

Comment: Sasserman's excessive drinking at lunch and subsequent intoxication at work constitute a violation of Standard I(D) because this conduct has raised questions about his professionalism and competence. His behavior reflects poorly on him, his employer, and the investment industry.

Example 2 (Fraud and Deceit):

Howard Hoffman, a security analyst at ATZ Brothers, Inc., a large brokerage house, submits reimbursement forms over a two-year period to ATZ's self-funded health insurance program for more than two dozen bills, most of which have been altered to increase the amount due. An investigation by the firm's director of employee benefits uncovers the inappropriate conduct. ATZ subsequently terminates Hoffman's employment and notifies CFA Institute.

Comment: Hoffman violated Standard I(D) because he engaged in intentional conduct involving fraud and deceit in the workplace that adversely reflected on his integrity.

Example 3 (Fraud and Deceit):

Jody Brink, an analyst covering the automotive industry, volunteers much of her spare time to local charities. The board of one of the charitable institutions decides to buy five new vans to deliver hot lunches to low-income elderly people. Brink offers to donate her time to handle purchasing agreements. To pay a long-standing debt to a friend who operates an automobile dealership—and to compensate herself for her trouble—she agrees to a price 20% higher than normal and splits the surcharge with her friend. The director of the charity ultimately discovers the scheme and tells Brink that her services, donated or otherwise, are no longer required.

Comment: Brink engaged in conduct involving dishonesty, fraud, and misrepresentation and has violated Standard I(D).

Example 4 (Personal Actions and Integrity):

Carmen Garcia manages a mutual fund dedicated to socially responsible investing. She is also an environmental activist. As the result of her participation in nonviolent protests, Garcia has been arrested on numerous occasions for trespassing on the property of a large petrochemical plant that is accused of damaging the environment.

Comment: Generally, Standard I(D) is not meant to cover legal transgressions resulting from acts of civil disobedience in support of personal beliefs because such conduct does not reflect poorly on the member's or candidate's professional reputation, integrity, or competence.

Example 5 (Professional Misconduct):

Meredith Rasmussen works on a buy-side trading desk of an investment management firm and concentrates on in-house trades for a hedge fund subsidiary managed by a team at the investment management firm. The hedge fund has been very successful and is marketed globally by the firm. From her experience as the trader for much of the activity of the fund, Rasmussen has become quite knowledgeable about the hedge fund's strategy, tactics, and performance. When a distinct break in the market occurs and many of the securities involved in the hedge fund's strategy decline markedly in value, Rasmussen observes that the reported performance of the hedge fund does not reflect this decline. In her experience, the lack of effect is a very unlikely occurrence. She approaches the head of trading about her concern and is told that she should not ask any questions and that the fund is big and successful and is not her concern. She is fairly sure something is not right, so she contacts the compliance officer, who also tells her to stay away from the issue of the hedge fund's reporting.

> *Comment*: Rasmussen has clearly come across an error in policies, procedures, and compliance practices within the firm's operations. According to the firm's procedures for reporting potentially unethical activity, she should pursue the issue by gathering some proof of her reason for doubt. Should all internal communications within the firm not satisfy her concerns, Rasmussen should consider reporting the potential unethical activity to the appropriate regulator.
>
> See also Standard IV(A) for guidance on whistleblowing and Standard IV(C) for the duties of a supervisor.

13 STANDARD I(E) COMPETENCE

- ☐ demonstrate the application of the Code of Ethics and Standards of Professional Conduct to situations involving issues of professional integrity
- ☐ recommend practices and procedures designed to prevent violations of the Code of Ethics and Standards of Professional Conduct
- ☐ identify conduct that conforms to the Code and Standards and conduct that violates the Code and Standards

> Members and Candidates must act with and maintain the competence necessary to fulfill their professional responsibilities.

Guidance

Standard I(E) requires members and candidates to act with and maintain appropriate knowledge, skills, and diligence when they carry out their professional responsibilities so that they provide a high standard of professional service for their clients and employers. The Code of Ethics requires members and candidates to "act with integrity, competence, and diligence" and to "maintain and improve their professional competence and strive to improve the competence of other investment professionals." Standard I(E) directly supports these requirements of the Code of Ethics.

Given the diverse range of professional services members and candidates engage in, the knowledge, skills, and abilities necessary to successfully fulfill their roles will vary according to the nature of their professional duties. Determining what conduct specifically constitutes competence will differ for each role and will depend on the facts and circumstances applicable to each member or candidate.

While the specific conduct that leads to competence may be different for each member or candidate, the underlying principle of competence is straightforward. To be competent in your role and meet your duties under this standard means having sufficient knowledge, skills, and abilities suitable for a professional to work in that specific role with success. These attributes govern the expertise, experience, and accomplishments that professionals need to perform at the highest level.

- Knowledge is the body of information applied directly to the performance of a function and how effectively it is applied.
- Skills are capabilities to perform a role-specific act or function to complete specific tasks and achieve professional goals.
- Abilities are capabilities and attitudes that support behaviors that result in observable outcomes.

While competence allows members and candidates the opportunity to undertake an activity successfully, lack of competence cannot necessarily be determined by an unsuccessful or a negative outcome. Many competent investment professionals have experienced failure or loss in their professional lives. For example, a competent investment manager may not always make profitable investment decisions. A competent securities analyst may not accurately predict the future prospects of an investment, despite diligent and thorough analysis.

Competence is not limited to an examination of the education level of a member or candidate. A highly educated investment consultant may not have the experience to undertake consulting activities in an unfamiliar area of practice. An accounting professional supremely competent in providing financial statement audits may not be competent in assessing compliance with performance presentation standards, such as the GIPS standards. Or an investment consultant hired to conduct a search for an investment manager focused on sustainable investing may not have the skills needed to competently evaluate managers with that focus.

Over time, the professional responsibilities of members and candidates may change or expand, requiring new or different knowledge, skills, and abilities. Members and candidates will develop and refine their skills and abilities as their careers progress. Standard I(E) imposes the duty to not simply achieve but also maintain competence, emphasizing the need for members to continuously maintain or improve the competence required of their professional position. Although Standard I(E) contemplates ongoing professional development to maintain proficiency and competence, this standard does not mandate participation in a particular continuing education program or professional development plan. Members and candidates can attain and maintain the competence needed to fulfill their professional responsibilities in a variety of ways.

STANDARD I(E): RECOMMENDED PROCEDURES

14

To achieve and maintain competence, members and candidates should consider the following activities:

- Regularly engaging in a professional development or continuing education program
- Studying for or earning professional certifications or designations
- Attending conferences, seminars, or webinars
- Regularly participating in training offered by their employer
- Diligently engaging in informal continuing education or self-study, such as through outside reading of subject matter articles, treatises, and publications
- Participating in expert groups or organizations

- Becoming proficient with any new skill or knowledge, as necessary, when their professional responsibilities change

15 STANDARD I(E): APPLICATION OF THE STANDARD

Example 1 (Maintaining Competence):

Michelle Lee runs a geopolitical consulting firm where she analyzes international political, social, and economic issues and developments to produce research reports for her clients, many of which are investment management firms. Lee has been closely monitoring news regarding a new multinational trade deal that has the potential to significantly boost commercial activity among countries in a certain region of the world. As soon as the trade deal was officially ratified and announced, she quickly downloaded a copy of the agreement and read it to understand its terms and impact. She also consulted with experts in the field to obtain their opinions on the impacts of the trade deal and confirm her understanding of its terms and implications.

> *Comment*: Lee satisfied the requirement of Standard I(E). Lee was able to write a knowledgeable and informative research report for her clients by keeping abreast of developments in her field through news reports, consulting with experts, and studying the trade deal itself to ensure that her knowledge was up to date.

Example 2 (Improving Competence):

Chris Choe is the director of research at a large sell-side firm. Several of Choe's clients have asked her to incorporate environmental, social, and governance (ESG) ratings into the research reports the firm produces. Until now, the firm's research reports have been based only on traditional quantitative metrics. Choe hires an experienced ESG analyst for her team, and she requires all research analysts, including herself, to attend ESG-focused seminars and obtain an ESG investment specialist certificate. In due time, Choe and her team begin to incorporate ESG considerations into their research reports.

> *Comment*: Choe extended her competence in her field by educating herself on new considerations relevant to her industry and by hiring someone with ESG expertise to fill a knowledge and skills gap before she and her team incorporated ESG considerations into the firm's research reports. As such, Choe satisfied the requirement of Standard I(E).

Example 3 (Change in Role):

Gerhardt Glusker is a regulatory attorney for a hedge fund who sought to transition to a sales role after impressing senior management with his strong business acumen. There is a licensing requirement involving an examination that an individual must first pass before being qualified to serve in a sales function. Among other things, the examination covers technical rules and regulations designed to ensure fairness when dealing with clients and prospects. Glusker was not familiar with these rules and regulations because he was never asked to provide guidance on them as a regulatory attorney. Glusker did not learn the materials or study for the examination and instead relied on his industry knowledge to receive a passing score.

> *Comment*: Glusker failed to satisfy the requirement of Standard I(E). He did receive a passing score on a licensing examination, but passing the examination, by itself, is not adequate to demonstrate competency. Glusker's failure to learn the applicable rules and regulations relating to fairness when dealing with clients and prospects means that he does not possess the required knowledge to serve in his new role, despite passing the licensing examination.

Example 4 (Supervisory Responsibility):

Linda Evans is one member of a five-person team of analysts at a boutique research firm providing independent research to buy-side firms. Evans primarily covers the energy and transportation sectors. Evans's boss leaves the firm to return to academia. Firm management promotes Evans to director of research and hires two junior analysts to replace her. Evans now has supervisory responsibility for four analysts and is responsible for all research produced by the firm. Prior to her promotion date, Evans spends a great deal of time and effort getting up to speed on the research projects of the firm that she was not involved in. Although she has never directly managed others in the past, Evans does not spend any time becoming familiar with effectively managing employees, leading teams, or compliance requirements relating to subordinates.

> *Comment*: Evans's new position demands competence in other skills, abilities, and knowledge beyond those needed for her previous position. Evans must ensure she extends her competence to cover all responsibilities of her new role. She also must now obtain the skills and knowledge needed for fulfilling her supervisory responsibility of the other analysts. This could include attending conferences or taking professional development courses on management, earning compliance credentials, and internal training on supervisory responsibility.

Example 5 (Choosing Investments):

Kwame Mifune is a financial planner for over 150 retail investors. Based on the investment objectives, financial circumstances, and risk tolerance of 40 of his clients, he suggests they purchase life insurance products from Vouchsafe Insurance Company. Mifune researched Vouchsafe and recommended it because it has a high credit rating, strong financials, and a decade-long history of providing affordable, safe insurance products. Within 18 months, as the result of previously unknown financial impropriety and fraud by the company's chief financial officer, Vouchsafe goes bankrupt and the insurance contracts for thousands of policyholders become worthless. Mifune's clients claim that he was incompetent in recommending the Vouchsafe policies.

> *Comment*: Assuming that Mifune's research of Vouchsafe was thorough and appropriate, his failure to uncover the fraudulent practices of the company he recommended, which had misled the investment industry as whole, does not, by itself, indicate that Mifune is an incompetent financial planner.

Example 6 (Understanding New Investment Products):

Alex Halsey is a portfolio manager for a number of high-net-worth individuals. Several of his clients are impressed by the significant gains in a short time frame that they believe can be achieved by investing in cryptocurrency. They urge Halsey to include cryptocurrency products as part of their portfolios. Although Halsey is generally aware of cryptocurrency and has read several articles about the cryptocurrency investment trend in reputable newspapers, Halsey is unfamiliar with the nature of the asset or the difference between the many cryptocurrency products. Not wanting to seem out of touch with current developments in the market, lose clients, or miss out on a hot market trend by delaying an investment decision until he completes research into the asset, Halsey purchases a cryptocurrency product that has been heavily promoted through social media and online advertising for several of his clients.

> *Comment*: Given his limited knowledge, Halsey is not competent to invest in cryptocurrency for his clients. By hastily investing in cryptocurrency products without understanding the nature of the investment or the suitability of the investment for his clients, Halsey has violated Standard I(E).

16 STANDARD II: INTEGRITY OF CAPITAL MARKETS

- ☐ demonstrate the application of the Code of Ethics and Standards of Professional Conduct to situations involving issues of professional integrity
- ☐ recommend practices and procedures designed to prevent violations of the Code of Ethics and Standards of Professional Conduct
- ☐ identify conduct that conforms to the Code and Standards and conduct that violates the Code and Standards

Standard II(A) Material Nonpublic Information

> Members and Candidates who possess material nonpublic information that could affect the value of an investment must not act or cause others to act on the information.

Guidance

Highlights:

- *What Is "Material" Information?*
- *What Constitutes "Nonpublic" Information?*
- *Mosaic Theory*
- *Social Media*
- *Using Industry Experts*
- *Investment Research Reports*

Trading or inducing others to trade on material nonpublic information erodes confidence in capital markets, institutions, and investment professionals by supporting the idea that those with inside information and special access can take unfair advantage of the general investing public. Although trading on inside information may lead to short-term profits, in the long run, individuals and the profession as a whole suffer from such trading. These actions have caused and will continue to cause investors to avoid capital markets because the markets are perceived to be "rigged" in favor of the knowledgeable insider. When the investing public avoids capital markets, the markets and capital allocation become less efficient and less supportive of strong and vibrant economies. Standard II(A) promotes and maintains a high level of confidence in market integrity, which is one of the foundations of the investment profession.

The prohibition on using this information goes beyond the direct buying and selling of individual securities or bonds. Members and candidates must not use material nonpublic information to influence their investment actions related to derivatives (e.g., swaps or option contracts), mutual funds, or other alternative investments. *Any* trading based on material nonpublic information constitutes a violation of Standard II(A). The expansion of financial products and the increasing interconnectivity of financial markets globally have resulted in new potential opportunities for trading on material nonpublic information.

What Is "Material" Information?

Information is "material" if its disclosure would probably have an impact on the price of a security or if reasonable investors would want to know the information before making an investment decision. In other words, information is material if it would significantly alter the total mix of information currently available about a security in such a way that the price of the security would be affected.

The specificity of the information, the extent of its difference from public information, its nature, and its reliability are key factors in determining whether a particular piece of information fits the definition of material. For example, material information may include, but is not limited to, information on the following:

- earnings;
- mergers, acquisitions, tender offers, or joint ventures;
- changes in assets or asset quality;
- innovative products, processes, or discoveries (e.g., new product trials or research efforts);
- new licenses, patents, registered trademarks, or regulatory approval/rejection of a product;
- developments regarding customers or suppliers (e.g., the acquisition or loss of a contract);
- changes in management;
- change in auditor notification or the fact that the issuer may no longer rely on an auditor's report or qualified opinion;
- events regarding the issuer's securities (e.g., defaults on senior securities, calls of securities for redemption, repurchase plans, stock splits, changes in dividends, changes to the rights of security holders, and public or private sales of additional securities);
- bankruptcies;
- significant legal disputes;
- government reports of economic trends (employment, housing starts, currency information, etc.);
- orders for large trades before they are executed; and

- new or changing equity or debt ratings issued by a third party (e.g., sell-side recommendations and credit ratings).

In addition to the substance and specificity of the information, the source or relative reliability of the information also determines materiality. The less reliable a source, the less likely the information provided would be considered material. For example, factual information from a corporate insider regarding a significant new contract for a company is likely to be material, whereas an assumption based on speculation by a competitor about the same contract is likely to be less reliable and, therefore, not material. Additionally, information about trials of a new drug, product, or service under development from qualified personnel involved in the trials is likely to be material, whereas educated conjecture by subject experts not connected to the trials is unlikely to be material.

Also, the more ambiguous the effect of the information on price, the less material that information is considered. If it is unclear whether and to what extent the information will affect the price of a security, the information may not be considered material. The passage of time may also render information that was once important immaterial.

What Constitutes "Nonpublic" Information?

Information is "nonpublic" until it has been disseminated or is available to the marketplace in general (as opposed to a select group of investors). "Disseminated" can be defined as "made known." For example, a company report of profits that is posted on the internet and distributed widely through a press release or accompanied by a filing has been effectively disseminated to the marketplace. Members and candidates must have a reasonable expectation that people have received the information before it can be considered public. It is not necessary, however, to wait for the slowest method of delivery. Once the information is disseminated to the market, it is public information that is no longer covered by this standard.

Members and candidates must be particularly aware of information that is selectively disclosed by corporations to a small group of investors, analysts, or other market participants. Information that is made available to analysts remains nonpublic until it is made available to investors in general. Corporations that disclose information on a limited basis create the potential for insider-trading violations.

Issues of selective disclosure often arise when a corporate insider provides material information to analysts in a briefing or conference call before that information is released to the public. Analysts must be aware that a disclosure made to a room full of analysts does not necessarily make the disclosed information "public." Analysts should also be alert to the possibility that they are selectively receiving material nonpublic information when a company provides them with guidance or interpretation of such publicly available information as financial statements or regulatory filings.

A member or candidate may use insider information provided legitimately by the source company for the specific purpose of conducting due diligence according to the business agreement between the parties for such activities as mergers, loan underwriting, credit ratings, and offering engagements. In such instances, the investment professional would not be considered in violation of Standard II(A) by using the material information. However, the use of insider information provided by the source company for other purposes, especially to trade or entice others to trade the securities of the firm, conflicts with this standard.

Mosaic Theory

A financial analyst gathers and interprets large quantities of information from many sources. The analyst may use significant conclusions derived from the analysis of public and nonmaterial nonpublic information as the basis for investment recommendations and decisions even if those conclusions would have been material inside information had they been communicated directly to the analyst by a company. Under the "mosaic theory," financial analysts are free to act on this collection, or mosaic, of information without risking violation.

The practice of financial analysis depends on the free flow of information. For the fair and efficient operation of the capital markets, analysts and investors must have the greatest amount of information possible to facilitate making well-informed investment decisions about how and where to invest capital. Accurate, timely, and intelligible communication is essential if analysts and investors are to obtain the data needed to make informed decisions about how and where to invest capital. These disclosures must go beyond the information mandated by the reporting requirements of the securities laws and should include specific business information about items used to guide a company's future growth, such as new products, capital projects, and the competitive environment. Analysts seek and use such information to compare and contrast investment alternatives.

Much of the information used by analysts comes directly from companies. Analysts often receive such information through contacts with corporate insiders, especially investor-relations staff and financial officers. Information may be disseminated in the form of press releases, through oral presentations by company executives in analysts' meetings or conference calls, or during analysts' visits to company premises. In seeking to develop the most accurate and complete picture of a company, analysts should also reach beyond contacts with companies themselves and collect information from other sources, such as customers, contractors, suppliers, and the companies' competitors.

Analysts are in the business of formulating opinions and insights that are not obvious to the general investing public about the attractiveness of particular securities. In the course of their work, analysts actively seek out corporate information not generally known to the market for the express purpose of analyzing that information, forming an opinion on its significance, and informing their clients, who can be expected to trade on the basis of the recommendation. Analysts' initiatives to discover and analyze information and communicate their findings to their clients significantly enhance market efficiency, thus benefiting all investors (see *Dirks v. Securities and Exchange Commission*). Accordingly, violations of Standard II(A) will *not* result when a perceptive analyst reaches a conclusion about a corporate action or event through an analysis of public information and items of nonmaterial nonpublic information.

Investment professionals should note, however, that although analysts are free to use mosaic information in their research reports, they should save and document all their research [see Standard V(C) Record Retention]. Evidence of the analyst's knowledge of public and nonmaterial nonpublic information about a corporation strengthens the assertion that the analyst reached his or her conclusions solely through appropriate methods rather than through the use of material nonpublic information.

Social Media

The continuing advancement in technology allows members, candidates, and the industry at large to exchange information at rates not previously available. It is important for investment professionals to understand the implications of using information from the internet and social media platforms because all such information may not actually be considered public.

Some social media platforms require membership in specific groups in order to access the published content. Members and candidates participating in groups with membership limitations should verify that material information obtained from these sources can also be accessed from a source that would be considered available to the public (e.g., company filings, webpages, and press releases).

Members and candidates may use social media platforms to communicate with clients or investors without conflicting with this standard. As long as the information reaches all clients or is open to the investing public, the use of these platforms would be comparable with other traditional forms of communications, such as e-mails and press releases. Members and candidates, as required by Standard I(A), should also complete all appropriate regulatory filings related to information distributed through social media platforms.

Using Industry Experts

The increased demand for insights for understanding the complexities of some industries has led to an expansion of engagement with outside experts. As the level of engagement increased, new businesses formed to connect analysts and investors with individuals who have specialized knowledge of their industry (e.g., technology or pharmaceuticals). These networks offer investors the opportunity to reach beyond their usual business circles to speak with experts regarding economic conditions, industry trends, and technical issues relating to specific products and services.

Members and candidates may provide compensation to individuals for their insights without violating this standard. However, members and candidates are ultimately responsible for ensuring that they are not requesting or acting on confidential information received from external experts, which is in violation of security regulations and laws or duties to others. As the recent string of insider-trading cases displayed, some experts are willing to provide confidential and protected information for the right incentive.

Firms connecting experts with members or candidates often require both parties to sign agreements concerning the disclosure of material nonpublic information. Even with the protections from such compliance practices, if an expert provides material nonpublic information, members and candidates would be prohibited from taking investment actions on the associated firm until the information became publicly known to the market.

Investment Research Reports

When a particularly well-known or respected analyst issues a report or makes changes to his or her recommendation, that information alone may have an effect on the market and thus may be considered material. Theoretically, under Standard II(A), such a report would have to be made public at the time it was distributed to clients. The analyst is not a company insider, however, and does not have access to inside information. Presumably, the analyst created the report from information available to the public (mosaic theory) and by using his or her expertise to interpret the information. The analyst's hard work, paid for by the client, generated the conclusions.

Simply because the public in general would find the conclusions material does not require that the analyst make his or her work public. Investors who are not clients of the analyst can either do the work themselves or become clients of the analyst to gain access to the analyst's expertise.

17 STANDARD II(A): RECOMMENDED PROCEDURES

Achieve Public Dissemination

If a member or candidate determines that information is material, the member or candidate should make reasonable efforts to achieve public dissemination of the information. These efforts usually entail encouraging the issuing company to make the information public. If public dissemination is not possible, the member or candidate must communicate the information only to the designated supervisory and compliance personnel within the member's or candidate's firm and must not take investment action or alter current investment recommendations on the basis of the information. Moreover, members and candidates must not knowingly engage in any conduct that may induce company insiders to privately disclose material nonpublic information.

Adopt Compliance Procedures

Members and candidates should encourage their firms to adopt compliance procedures to prevent the misuse of material nonpublic information. Particularly important is improving compliance in such areas as the review of employee and proprietary trading, the review of investment recommendations, documentation of firm procedures, and the supervision of interdepartmental communications in multiservice firms. Compliance procedures should suit the particular characteristics of a firm, including its size and the nature of its business.

Members and candidates are encouraged to inform their supervisor and compliance personnel of suspected inappropriate use of material nonpublic information as the basis for security trading activities or recommendations being made within their firm.

Adopt Disclosure Procedures

Members and candidates should encourage their firms to develop and follow disclosure policies designed to ensure that information is disseminated to the marketplace in an equitable manner. For example, analysts from small firms should receive the same information and attention from a company as analysts from large firms receive. Similarly, companies should not provide certain information to buy-side analysts but not to sell-side analysts, or vice versa. Furthermore, a company should not discriminate among analysts in the provision of information or "blackball" particular analysts who have given negative reports on the company in the past.

Within investment and research firms, members and candidates should encourage the development of and compliance with procedures for distributing new and updated investment opinions to clients. Recommendations of this nature may represent material market-moving information that needs to be communicated to all clients fairly.

Issue Press Releases

Companies should consider issuing press releases prior to analyst meetings and conference calls and scripting those meetings and calls to decrease the chance that further information will be disclosed. If material nonpublic information is disclosed for the first time in an analyst meeting or call, the company should promptly issue a press release or otherwise make the information publicly available.

Firewall Elements

An information barrier commonly referred to as a "firewall" is the most widely used approach for preventing the communication of material nonpublic information within firms. It restricts the flow of confidential information to those who need to know the information to perform their jobs effectively. The minimum elements of such a system include, but are not limited to, the following:

- substantial control of relevant interdepartmental communications, preferably through a clearance area within the firm in either the compliance or legal department;
- review of employee trading through the maintenance of "watch," "restricted," and "rumor" lists;

- documentation of the procedures designed to limit the flow of information between departments and of the actions taken to enforce those procedures; and
- heightened review or restriction of proprietary trading while a firm is in possession of material nonpublic information.

Appropriate Interdepartmental Communications

Although documentation requirements must, for practical reasons, take into account the differences between the activities of small firms and those of large, multiservice firms, firms of all sizes and types benefit by improving the documentation of their internal enforcement of firewall procedures. Therefore, even at small firms, procedures concerning interdepartmental communication, the review of trading activity, and the investigation of possible violations should be compiled and formalized.

Physical Separation of Departments

As a practical matter, to the greatest extent possible, firms should consider the physical separation of departments and files to prevent the communication of sensitive information that should not be shared. For example, the investment banking and corporate finance areas of a brokerage firm should be separated from the sales and research departments, and a bank's commercial lending department should be segregated from its trust and research departments.

Prevention of Personnel Overlap

There should be no overlap of personnel between the investment banking and corporate finance areas of a brokerage firm and the sales and research departments or between a bank's commercial lending department and its trust and research departments. For a firewall to be effective in a multiservice firm, an employee should be on only one side of the firewall at any time. Inside knowledge may not be limited to information about a specific offering or the current financial condition of a company. Analysts may be exposed to much information about the company, including new product developments or future budget projections that clearly constitute inside knowledge and thus preclude the analyst from returning to his or her research function. For example, an analyst who follows a particular company may provide limited assistance to the investment bankers under carefully controlled circumstances when the firm's investment banking department is involved in a deal with the company. That analyst must then be treated as though he or she were an investment banker; the analyst must remain on the investment banking side of the wall until any information he or she learns is publicly disclosed. In short, the analyst cannot use any information learned in the course of the project for research purposes and cannot share that information with colleagues in the research department.

A Reporting System

A primary objective of an effective firewall procedure is to establish a reporting system in which authorized people review and approve communications between departments. If an employee behind a firewall believes that he or she needs to share confidential information with someone on the other side of the wall, the employee should consult a designated compliance officer to determine whether sharing the information is necessary and how much information should be shared. If the sharing is necessary, the compliance officer should coordinate the process of "looking over the wall" so that the necessary information will be shared and the integrity of the procedure will be maintained.

A single supervisor or compliance officer should have the specific authority and responsibility of deciding whether information is material and whether it is sufficiently public to be used as the basis for investment decisions. Ideally, the supervisor or compliance officer responsible for communicating information to a firm's research or brokerage area would not be a member of that area.

Personal Trading Limitations

Firms should consider restrictions or prohibitions on personal trading by employees and should carefully monitor both proprietary trading and personal trading by employees. Firms should require employees to make periodic reports (to the extent that such reporting is not already required by securities laws) of their own transactions and transactions made for the benefit of family members. Securities should be placed on a restricted list when a firm has or may have material nonpublic information. The broad distribution of a restricted list often triggers the sort of trading the list was developed to avoid. Therefore, a watch list shown to only the few people responsible for compliance should be used to monitor transactions in specified securities. The use of a watch list in combination with a restricted list is an increasingly common means of ensuring effective control of personal trading.

Record Maintenance

Multiservice firms should maintain written records of the communications between various departments. Firms should place a high priority on training and should consider instituting comprehensive training programs, particularly for employees in sensitive areas.

Proprietary Trading Procedures

Procedures concerning the restriction or review of a firm's proprietary trading while the firm possesses material nonpublic information will necessarily depend on the types of proprietary trading in which the firm may engage. A prohibition on all types of proprietary activity when a firm comes into possession of material nonpublic information is *not* appropriate. For example, when a firm acts as a market maker, a prohibition on proprietary trading may be counterproductive to the goals of maintaining the confidentiality of information and market liquidity. This concern is particularly important in the relationships between small, regional broker/dealers and small issuers. In many situations, a firm will take a small issuer public with the understanding that the firm will continue to be a market maker in the stock. In such instances, a withdrawal by the firm from market-making activities would be a clear tip to outsiders. Firms that continue market-making activity while in the possession of material nonpublic information should, however, instruct their market makers to remain passive with respect to the market—that is, to take only the contra side of unsolicited customer trades.

In risk-arbitrage trading, the case for a trading prohibition is more compelling than it is in the case of market making. The impetus for arbitrage trading is neither passive nor reactive, and the potential for illegal profits is greater than in market making. The most prudent course for firms is to suspend arbitrage activity when a security is placed on the watch list. Those firms that continue arbitrage activity face a high hurdle in proving the adequacy of their internal procedures for preventing trading on material nonpublic information and must demonstrate a stringent review and documentation of firm trades.

Communication to All Employees

Members and candidates should encourage their employers to circulate written compliance policies and guidelines to all employees. Policies and guidelines should be used in conjunction with training programs aimed at enabling employees to recognize material nonpublic information. Such information is not always clearly identifiable.

Employees must be given sufficient training to either make an informed decision or to realize they need to consult a supervisor or compliance officer before engaging in questionable transactions. Appropriate policies reinforce that using material nonpublic information is illegal in many countries. Such trading activities based on material nonpublic information undermine the integrity of the individual, the firm, and the capital markets.

18 STANDARD II(A): APPLICATION OF THE STANDARD

Example 1 (Acting on Nonpublic Information):

Frank Barnes, the president and controlling shareholder of the SmartTown clothing chain, decides to accept a tender offer and sell the family business at a price almost double the market price of its shares. He describes this decision to his sister (SmartTown's treasurer), who conveys it to her daughter (who owns no stock in the family company at present), who tells her husband, Staple. Staple, however, tells his stockbroker, Alex Halsey, who immediately buys SmartTown stock for himself.

> *Comment*: The information regarding the pending sale is both material and nonpublic. Staple has violated Standard II(A) by communicating the inside information to his broker. Halsey also has violated the standard by buying the shares on the basis of material nonpublic information.

Example 2 (Controlling Nonpublic Information):

Samuel Peter, an analyst with Scotland and Pierce Incorporated, is assisting his firm with a secondary offering for Bright Ideas Lamp Company. Peter participates, via telephone conference call, in a meeting with Scotland and Pierce investment banking employees and Bright Ideas' CEO. Peter is advised that the company's earnings projections for the next year have significantly dropped. Throughout the telephone conference call, several Scotland and Pierce salespeople and portfolio managers walk in and out of Peter's office, where the telephone call is taking place. As a result, they are aware of the drop in projected earnings for Bright Ideas. Before the conference call is concluded, the salespeople trade the stock of the company on behalf of the firm's clients and other firm personnel trade the stock in a firm proprietary account and in employees' personal accounts.

> *Comment*: Peter has violated Standard II(A) because he failed to prevent the transfer and misuse of material nonpublic information to others in his firm. Peter's firm should have adopted information barriers to prevent the communication of nonpublic information between departments of the firm. The salespeople and portfolio managers who traded on the information have also violated Standard II(A) by trading on inside information.

Example 3 (Selective Disclosure of Material Information):

Elizabeth Levenson is based in Hanoi and covers the Vietnamese market for her firm, which is based in Singapore. She is invited, together with the other 10 largest shareholders of a manufacturing company, to meet the finance director of that company. During the meeting, the finance director states that the company expects its workforce to strike next Friday, which will cripple productivity and distribution. Can Levenson use this information as a basis to change her rating on the company from "buy" to "sell"?

> *Comment*: Levenson must first determine whether the material information is public. According to Standard II(A), if the company has not made this information public (a small group forum does not qualify as a method of public dissemination), she cannot use the information.

Example 4 (Determining Materiality):

Leah Fechtman is trying to decide whether to hold or sell shares of an oil-and-gas exploration company that she owns in several of the funds she manages. Although the company has underperformed the index for some time already, the trends in the industry sector signal that companies of this type might become takeover targets. While she is considering her decision, her doctor, who casually follows the markets, mentions that she thinks that the company in question will soon be bought out by a large multinational conglomerate and that it would be a good idea to buy the stock right now. After talking to various investment professionals and checking their opinions on the company as well as checking industry trends, Fechtman decides the next day to accumulate more stock in the oil-and-gas exploration company.

> *Comment*: Although information on an expected takeover bid may be of the type that is generally material and nonpublic, in this case, the source of information is unreliable, so the information cannot be considered material. Therefore, Fechtman is not prohibited from trading the stock on the basis of this information.

Example 5 (Applying the Mosaic Theory):

Jagdish Teja is a buy-side analyst covering the furniture industry. Looking for an attractive company to recommend as a buy, he analyzes several furniture makers by studying their financial reports and visiting their operations. He also talks to some designers and retailers to find out which furniture styles are trendy and popular. Although none of the companies that he analyzes are a clear buy, he discovers that one of them, Swan Furniture Company (SFC), may be in financial trouble. SFC's extravagant new designs have been introduced at substantial cost. Even though these designs initially attracted attention, the public is now buying more conservative furniture from other makers. Based on this information and on a profit-and-loss analysis, Teja believes that SFC's next-quarter earnings will drop substantially. He issues a sell recommendation for SFC. Immediately after receiving that recommendation, investment managers start reducing the SFC stock in their portfolios.

> *Comment*: Information on quarterly earnings data is material and nonpublic. Teja arrived at his conclusion about the earnings drop on the basis of public information and pieces of nonmaterial nonpublic information (such as opinions of designers and retailers). Therefore, trading based on Teja's correct conclusion is not prohibited by Standard II(A).

Example 6 (Applying the Mosaic Theory):

Roger Clement is a senior financial analyst who specializes in the European automobile sector at Rivoli Capital. Because he has been repeatedly nominated by many leading industry magazines and newsletters as a "best analyst" for the automobile industry, he is widely regarded as an authority on the sector. After speaking with representatives of Turgot Chariots—a European auto manufacturer with sales primarily in South Korea—and after conducting interviews with salespeople, labor leaders, his firm's South Korean currency analysts, and banking officials, Clement analyzed Turgot Chariots and concluded that (1) its newly introduced model will probably not meet sales expectations, (2) its corporate restructuring strategy may well face serious opposition from unions, (3) the depreciation of the South Korean won should lead to pressure on margins for the industry in general and Turgot's market segment in particular, and (4) banks could take a tougher-than-expected stance in the upcoming round of credit renegotiations with the company. For these reasons, he changes his conclusion about the company from "market outperform" to "market underperform." Clement retains the support material used to reach his conclusion in case questions later arise.

> *Comment*: To reach a conclusion about the value of the company, Clement has pieced together a number of nonmaterial or public bits of information that affect Turgot Chariots. Therefore, under the mosaic theory, Clement has not violated Standard II(A) in drafting the report.

Example 7 (Analyst Recommendations as Material Nonpublic Information):

The next day, Clement is preparing to be interviewed on a global financial news television program where he will discuss his changed recommendation on Turgot Chariots for the first time in public. While preparing for the program, he mentions to the show's producers and Mary Zito, the journalist who will be interviewing him, the information he will be discussing. Just prior to going on the air, Zito sells her holdings in Turgot Chariots. She also phones her father with the information because she knows that he and other family members have investments in Turgot Chariots.

> *Comment*: When Zito receives advance notice of Clement's change of opinion, she knows it will have a material impact on the stock price, even if she is not totally aware of Clement's underlying reasoning. She is not a client of Clement but obtains early access to the material nonpublic information prior to publication. Her trades are thus based on material nonpublic information and violate Standard II(A).
>
> Zito further violates the Standard by relaying the information to her father. It would not matter if he or any other family member traded; the act of providing the information violates Standard II(A). The fact that the information is provided to a family member does not absolve someone of the prohibition of using or communicating material nonpublic information.

Example 8 (Acting on Nonpublic Information):

Ashton Kellogg is a retired investment professional who manages his own portfolio. He owns shares in National Savings, a large local bank. A close friend and golfing buddy, John Mayfield, is a senior executive at National. National has seen its stock price drop considerably, and the news and outlook are not good. In a conversation about the economy and the banking industry on the golf course, Mayfield relays the information that National will surprise the investment community in a few days when it announces excellent earnings for the quarter. Kellogg is pleasantly surprised by this information, and thinking that Mayfield, as a senior executive, knows the law and would not disclose inside information, he doubles his position in the bank. Subsequently, National announces that it had good operating earnings but had to set aside reserves for anticipated significant losses on its loan portfolio. The combined news causes the stock to go down 60%.

> *Comment*: Even though Kellogg believes that Mayfield would not break the law by disclosing inside information and money was lost on the purchase, Kellogg should not have purchased additional shares of National. It is the member's or candidate's responsibility to make sure, before executing investment actions, that comments about earnings are not material nonpublic information. Kellogg has violated Standard II(A).

Example 9 (Mosaic Theory):

John Doll is a research analyst for a hedge fund that also sells its research to a select group of paying-client investment firms. Doll's focus is medical technology companies and products, and he has been in the business long enough and has been successful enough to build up a very credible network of friends and experts in the business. Doll has been working on a major research report recommending Boyce Health, a medical device manufacturer. He recently ran into an old acquaintance at a wedding who is a senior executive at Boyce, and Doll asked about the business. Doll was drawn to a statement that the executive, who has responsibilities in the new products area, made about a product: "I would not get too excited about the medium-term prospects; we have a lot of work to do first." Doll incorporated this and other information about the new Boyce product in his long-term recommendation of Boyce.

> *Comment*: Doll's conversation with the senior executive is part of the mosaic of information used in recommending Boyce. When holding discussions with a firm executive, Doll would need to guard against soliciting or obtaining material nonpublic information. Before issuing the report, the executive's statement about the continuing development of the product would need to be weighed against the other known public facts to determine whether it would be considered material.

Example 10 (Materiality Determination):

Larry Nadler, a trader for a mutual fund, gets a text message from another firm's trader, whom he has known for years. The message indicates a software company is going to report strong earnings when the firm publicly announces in two days. Nadler has a buy order from a portfolio manager within his firm to purchase several hundred thousand shares of the stock. Nadler is aggressive in placing the portfolio manager's order and completes the purchases by the following morning, a day ahead of the firm's planned earnings announcement.

> *Comment*: There are often rumors and whisper numbers before a release of any kind. The text message from the other trader would most likely be considered market noise. Unless Nadler knew that the trader had an ongoing business relationship with the public firm, he had no reason to suspect he was receiving material nonpublic information that would prevent him from completing the trading request of the portfolio manager.

Example 11 (Using an Expert Network):

Mary McCoy is the senior drug analyst at a mutual fund. Her firm hires a service that connects her to experts in the treatment of cancer. Through various phone conversations, McCoy enhances her understanding of the latest therapies for successful treatment. This information is critical to Mary making informed recommendations of the companies producing these drugs.

> *Comment*: McCoy is appropriately using the expert networks to enhance her evaluation process. She has neither asked for nor received information that may be considered material and nonpublic, such as preliminary trial results. McCoy is allowed to seek advice from professionals within the industry that she follows.

Example 12 (Using an Expert Network):

Tom Watson is a research analyst working for a hedge fund. To stay informed, Watson relies on outside experts for information on such industries as technology and pharmaceuticals, where new advancements occur frequently. The meetings with the industry experts often are arranged through networks or placement agents that have specific policies and procedures in place to deter the exchange of material nonpublic information.

Watson arranges a call to discuss future prospects for one of the fund's existing technology company holdings, a company that was testing a new semiconductor product. The scientist leading the tests indicates his disappointment with the performance of the new semiconductor. Following the call, Watson relays the insights he received to others at the fund. The fund sells its current position in the company and buys many put options because the market is anticipating the success of the new semiconductor and the share price reflects the market's optimism.

> *Comment*: Watson has violated Standard II(A) by passing along material nonpublic information concerning the ongoing product tests, which the fund used to trade in the securities and options of the related company. Watson cannot simply rely on the agreements signed by individuals who participate in expert networks that state that he has not received information that would prohibit his trading activity. He must make his own determination whether information he received through these arrangements reaches a materiality threshold that would affect his trading abilities.

19 STANDARD II(B) MARKET MANIPULATION

- ☐ demonstrate the application of the Code of Ethics and Standards of Professional Conduct to situations involving issues of professional integrity
- ☐ recommend practices and procedures designed to prevent violations of the Code of Ethics and Standards of Professional Conduct
- ☐ identify conduct that conforms to the Code and Standards and conduct that violates the Code and Standards

Members and Candidates must not engage in practices that distort prices or artificially inflate trading volume with the intent to mislead market participants.

Guidance

Highlights:

- *Information-Based Manipulation*
- *Transaction-Based Manipulation*

Standard II(B) requires that members and candidates uphold market integrity by prohibiting market manipulation. Market manipulation includes practices that distort security prices or trading volume with the intent to deceive people or entities that rely on information in the market. Market manipulation damages the interests of all investors by disrupting the smooth functioning of financial markets and lowering investor confidence.

Market manipulation may lead to a lack of trust in the fairness of the capital markets, resulting in higher risk premiums and reduced investor participation. A reduction in the efficiency of a local capital market may negatively affect the growth and economic health of the country and may also influence the operations of the globally interconnected capital markets. Although market manipulation may be less likely to occur in mature financial markets than in emerging markets, cross-border investing increasingly exposes all global investors to the potential for such practices.

Market manipulation includes (1) the dissemination of false or misleading information and (2) transactions that deceive or would be likely to mislead market participants by distorting the price-setting mechanism of financial instruments. The development of new products and technologies increases the incentives, means, and opportunities for market manipulation. Additionally, the increasing complexity and sophistication of the technologies used for communicating with market participants have created new avenues for manipulation.

Information-Based Manipulation

Information-based manipulation includes, but is not limited to, spreading false rumors to induce trading by others. For example, members and candidates must refrain from "pumping up" the price of an investment by issuing misleading positive information or overly optimistic projections of a security's worth only to later "dump" the investment (i.e., sell it) once the price, fueled by the misleading information's effect on other market participants, reaches an artificially high level.

Transaction-Based Manipulation

Transaction-based manipulation involves instances where a member or candidate knew or should have known that his or her actions could affect the pricing of a security. This type of manipulation includes, but is not limited to, the following:

- transactions that artificially affect prices or volume to give the impression of activity or price movement in a financial instrument, which represent a diversion from the expectations of a fair and efficient market, and
- securing a controlling, dominant position in a financial instrument to exploit and manipulate the price of a related derivative and/or the underlying asset.

Standard II(B) is not intended to preclude transactions undertaken on legitimate trading strategies based on perceived market inefficiencies. The intent of the action is critical to determining whether it is a violation of this standard.

20 STANDARD II(B): APPLICATION OF THE STANDARD

Example 1 (Independent Analysis and Company Promotion):

The principal owner of Financial Information Services (FIS) entered into an agreement with two microcap companies to promote the companies' stock in exchange for stock and cash compensation. The principal owner caused FIS to disseminate e-mails, design and maintain several websites, and distribute an online investment newsletter—all of which recommended investment in the two companies. The systematic publication of purportedly independent analyses and recommendations containing inaccurate and highly promotional and speculative statements increased public investment in the companies and led to dramatically higher stock prices.

> *Comment*: The principal owner of FIS violated Standard II(B) by using inaccurate reporting and misleading information under the guise of independent analysis to artificially increase the stock price of the companies. Furthermore, the principal owner violated Standard V(A) Diligence and Reasonable Basis by not having a reasonable and adequate basis for recommending the two companies and violated Standard VI(A) Disclosure of Conflicts by not disclosing to investors the compensation agreements (which constituted a conflict of interest).

Example 2 (Personal Trading Practices and Price):

John Gray is a private investor in Belgium who bought a large position several years ago in Fame Pharmaceuticals, a German small-cap security with limited average trading volume. He has now decided to significantly reduce his holdings owing to the poor price performance. Gray is worried that the low trading volume for the stock may cause the price to decline further as he attempts to sell his large position.

Gray devises a plan to divide his holdings into multiple accounts in different brokerage firms and private banks in the names of family members, friends, and even a private religious institution. He then creates a rumor campaign on various blogs and social media outlets promoting the company.

Gray begins to buy and sell the stock using the accounts in hopes of raising the trading volume and the price. He conducts the trades through multiple brokers, selling slightly larger positions than he bought on a tactical schedule, and over time, he is able to reduce his holding as desired without negatively affecting the sale price.

> *Comment*: John violated Standard II(B) by fraudulently creating the appearance that there was a greater investor interest in the stock through the online rumors. Additionally, through his trading strategy, he created the appearance that there was greater liquidity in the stock than actually existed. He was able to manipulate the price through both misinformation and trading practices.

Example 3 (Creating Artificial Price Volatility):

Matthew Murphy is an analyst at Divisadero Securities & Co., which has a significant number of hedge funds among its most important brokerage clients. Some of the hedge funds hold short positions on Wirewolf Semiconductor. Two trading days before the publication of a quarter-end report, Murphy alerts his sales force that he is about to issue a research report on Wirewolf that will include the following opinions:

- quarterly revenues are likely to fall short of management's guidance,
- earnings will be as much as 5 cents per share (or more than 10%) below consensus, and
- Wirewolf's highly respected chief financial officer may be about to join another company.

Knowing that Wirewolf has already entered its declared quarter-end "quiet period" before reporting earnings (and thus would be reluctant to respond to rumors), Murphy times the release of his research report specifically to sensationalize the negative aspects of the message in order to create significant downward pressure on Wirewolf's stock—to the distinct advantage of Divisadero's hedge fund clients. The report's conclusions are based on speculation, not on fact. The next day, the research report is broadcast to all of Divisadero's clients and to the usual newswire services.

Before Wirewolf's investor-relations department can assess the damage on the final trading day of the quarter and refute Murphy's report, its stock opens trading sharply lower, allowing Divisadero's clients to cover their short positions at substantial gains.

> *Comment*: Murphy violated Standard II(B) by aiming to create artificial price volatility designed to have a material impact on the price of an issuer's stock. Moreover, by lacking an adequate basis for the recommendation, Murphy also violated Standard V(A) Diligence and Reasonable Basis.

Example 4 (Personal Trading and Volume):

Rajesh Sekar manages two funds—an equity fund and a balanced fund—whose equity components are supposed to be managed in accordance with the same model. According to that model, the funds' holdings in stock of Digital Design Inc. (DD) are excessive. Reduction of the DD holdings would not be easy, however, because the stock has low liquidity in the stock market. Sekar decides to start trading larger portions of DD stock back and forth between his two funds to slowly increase the price; he believes market participants will see growing volume and increasing price and become interested in the stock. If other investors are willing to buy the DD stock because of such interest, then Sekar will be able to get rid of at least some of his overweight position without inducing price decreases. In this way, the whole transaction will be for the benefit of fund participants, even if additional brokers' commissions are incurred.

> *Comment*: Sekar's plan would be beneficial for his funds' participants but is based on artificial distortion of both trading volume and the price of the DD stock and thus constitutes a violation of Standard II(B).

Example 5 ("Pump-Priming" Strategy):

ACME Futures Exchange is launching a new bond futures contract. To convince investors, traders, arbitrageurs, hedgers, and so on, to use its contract, the exchange attempts to demonstrate that it has the best liquidity. To do so, it enters into agreements with members in which they commit to a substantial minimum trading volume on the new contract over a specific period in exchange for substantial reductions of their regular commissions.

> *Comment*: The formal liquidity of a market is determined by the obligations set on market makers, but the actual liquidity of a market is better estimated by the actual trading volume and bid–ask spreads. Attempts to mislead participants about the actual liquidity of the market constitute a violation of Standard II(B). In this example, investors have been intentionally misled to believe they chose the most liquid instrument for some specific purpose, but they could eventually see the actual liquidity of the contract significantly reduced after the term of the agreement expires. If the ACME Futures Exchange fully discloses its agreement with members to boost transactions over some initial launch period, it will not violate Standard II(B). ACME's intent is not to harm investors but, on the contrary, to give them a better service. For that purpose, it may engage in a liquidity-pumping strategy, but the strategy must be disclosed.

Example 6 (Creating Artificial Price Volatility):

Emily Gordon, an analyst of household products companies, is employed by a research boutique, Picador & Co. Based on information that she has gathered during a trip through Latin America, she believes that Hygene, Inc., a major marketer of personal care products, has generated better-than-expected sales from its new product initiatives in South America. After modestly boosting her projections for revenue and for gross profit margin in her worksheet models for Hygene, Gordon estimates that her earnings projection of US$2.00 per diluted share for the current year may be as much as 5% too low. She contacts the chief financial officer (CFO) of Hygene to try to gain confirmation of her findings from her trip and to get some feedback regarding her revised models. The CFO declines to comment and reiterates management's most recent guidance of US$1.95–US$2.05 for the year.

Gordon decides to try to force a comment from the company by telling Picador & Co. clients who follow a momentum investment style that consensus earnings projections for Hygene are much too low; she explains that she is considering raising her published estimate by an ambitious US$0.15 to US$2.15 per share. She believes that when word of an unrealistically high earnings projection filters back to Hygene's investor-relations department, the company will feel compelled to update its earnings guidance. Meanwhile, Gordon hopes that she is at least correct with respect to the earnings direction and that she will help clients who act on her insights to profit from a quick gain by trading on her advice.

> *Comment*: By exaggerating her earnings projections in order to try to fuel a quick gain in Hygene's stock price, Gordon is in violation of Standard II(B). Furthermore, by virtue of previewing her intentions of revising upward her earnings projections to only a select group of clients, she is in violation of Standard III(B) Fair Dealing. However, it would have been acceptable for Gordon to write a report that

- framed her earnings projection in a range of possible outcomes,
- outlined clearly the assumptions used in her Hygene models that took into consideration the findings from her trip through Latin America, and
- was distributed to all Picador & Co. clients in an equitable manner.

Example 7 (Pump and Dump Strategy):

In an effort to pump up the price of his holdings in Moosehead & Belfast Railroad Company, Steve Weinberg logs on to several investor chat rooms on the internet to start rumors that the company is about to expand its rail network in anticipation of receiving a large contract for shipping lumber.

> *Comment*: Weinberg has violated Standard II(B) by disseminating false information about Moosehead & Belfast with the intent to mislead market participants.

Example 8 (Manipulating Model Inputs):

Bill Mandeville supervises a structured financing team for Superior Investment Bank. His responsibilities include packaging new structured investment products and managing Superior's relationship with relevant rating agencies. To achieve the best rating possible, Mandeville uses mostly positive scenarios as model inputs—scenarios that reflect minimal downside risk in the assets underlying the structured products. The resulting output statistics in the rating request and underwriting prospectus support the idea that the new structured products have minimal potential downside risk. Additionally, Mandeville's compensation from Superior is partially based on both the level of the rating assigned and the successful sale of new structured investment products but does not have a link to the long-term performance of the instruments.

Mandeville is extremely successful and leads Superior as the top originator of structured investment products for the next two years. In the third year, the economy experiences difficulties and the values of the assets underlying structured products significantly decline. The subsequent defaults lead to major turmoil in the capital markets, the demise of Superior Investment Bank, and the loss of Mandeville's employment.

> *Comment*: Mandeville manipulates the inputs of a model to minimize associated risk to achieve higher ratings. His understanding of structured products allows him to skillfully decide which inputs to include in support of the desired rating and price. This information manipulation for short-term gain, which is in violation of Standard II(B), ultimately causes significant damage to many parties and the capital markets as a whole. Mandeville should have realized that promoting a rating and price with inaccurate information could cause not only a loss of price confidence in the particular structured product but also a loss of investor trust in the system. Such loss of confidence affects the ability of the capital markets to operate efficiently.

Example 9 (Information Manipulation):

Allen King is a performance analyst for Torrey Investment Funds. King believes that the portfolio manager for the firm's small- and microcap equity fund dislikes him because the manager never offers him tickets to the local baseball team's games but does offer tickets to other employees. To incite a potential regulatory review of the manager, King creates user profiles on several online forums under the portfolio manager's name and starts rumors about potential mergers for several of the smaller companies in the portfolio. As the prices of these companies' stocks increase, the portfolio manager sells the position, which leads to an investigation by the regulator as King desired.

> *Comment*: King has violated Standard II(B) even though he did not personally profit from the market's reaction to the rumor. In posting the false information, King misleads others into believing the companies were likely

to be acquired. Although his intent was to create trouble for the portfolio manager, his actions clearly manipulated the factual information that was available to the market.

21 STANDARD III: DUTIES TO CLIENTS

- ☐ demonstrate the application of the Code of Ethics and Standards of Professional Conduct to situations involving issues of professional integrity
- ☐ recommend practices and procedures designed to prevent violations of the Code of Ethics and Standards of Professional Conduct
- ☐ identify conduct that conforms to the Code and Standards and conduct that violates the Code and Standards

Standard III(A) Loyalty, Prudence, and Care

Members and Candidates have a duty of loyalty to their clients and must act with reasonable care and exercise prudent judgment. Members and Candidates must act for the benefit of their clients and place their clients' interests before their employer's or their own interests.

Guidance

Highlights:

- *Understanding the Application of Loyalty, Prudence, and Care*
- *Identifying the Actual Investment Client*
- *Developing the Client's Portfolio*
- *Soft Commission Policies*
- *Proxy Voting Policies*

Standard III(A) clarifies that client interests are paramount. A member's or candidate's responsibility to a client includes a duty of loyalty and a duty to exercise reasonable care. Investment actions must be carried out for the sole benefit of the client and in a manner the member or candidate believes, given the known facts and circumstances, to be in the best interest of the client. Members and candidates must exercise the same level of prudence, judgment, and care that they would apply in the management and disposition of their own interests in similar circumstances.

Prudence requires caution and discretion. The exercise of prudence by investment professionals requires that they act with the care, skill, and diligence that a reasonable person acting in a like capacity and familiar with such matters would use. In the context of managing a client's portfolio, prudence requires following the investment parameters set forth by the client and balancing risk and return. Acting with care requires members and candidates to act in a prudent and judicious manner in avoiding harm to clients.

Standard III(A) sets minimum expectations for members and candidates when fulfilling their responsibilities to their clients. Regulatory and legal requirements for such duties can vary across the investment industry depending on a variety of factors, including job function of the investment professional, the existence of an adviser/client relationship, and the nature of the recommendations being offered. From the perspective of the end user of financial services, these different standards can be arcane and confusing, leaving investors unsure of what level of service to expect from investment professionals they employ. The single standard of conduct described in Standard III(A) benefits investors by establishing a benchmark for the duties of loyalty, prudence, and care and clarifies that all CFA Institute members and candidates, regardless of job title, local laws, or cultural differences, are required to comply with these fundamental responsibilities. Investors hiring members or candidates who must adhere to the duty of loyalty, prudence, and care set forth in this standard can be confident that these responsibilities are a requirement regardless of any legally imposed fiduciary duties.

Standard III(A), however, is not a substitute for a member's or candidate's legal or regulatory obligations. As stated in Standard I(A), members and candidates must abide by the most strict requirements imposed on them by regulators or the Code and Standards, including any legally imposed fiduciary duty. Members and candidates must also be aware of whether they have "custody" or effective control of client assets. If so, a heightened level of responsibility arises. Members and candidates are considered to have custody if they have any direct or indirect access to client funds. Members and candidates must manage any pool of assets in their control in accordance with the terms of the governing documents (such as trust documents and investment management agreements), which are the primary determinant of the manager's powers and duties. Whenever their actions are contrary to provisions of those instruments or applicable law, members and candidates are at risk of violating Standard III(A).

Understanding the Application of Loyalty, Prudence, and Care

Standard III(A) establishes a minimum benchmark for the duties of loyalty, prudence, and care that are required of all members and candidates regardless of whether a legal fiduciary duty applies. Although fiduciary duty often encompasses the principles of loyalty, prudence, and care, Standard III(A) does not render all members and candidates fiduciaries. The responsibilities of members and candidates for fulfilling their obligations under this standard depend greatly on the nature of their professional responsibilities and the relationships they have with clients. The conduct of members and candidates may or may not rise to the level of being a fiduciary, depending on the type of client, whether the member or candidate is giving investment advice, and the many facts and circumstances surrounding a particular transaction or client relationship.

Fiduciary duties are often imposed by law or regulation when an individual or institution is charged with the duty of acting for the benefit of another party, such as managing investment assets. The duty required in fiduciary relationships exceeds what is acceptable in many other business relationships because a fiduciary is in an enhanced position of trust. Although members and candidates must comply with any legally imposed fiduciary duty, the Code and Standards neither impose such a legal responsibility nor require all members or candidates to act as fiduciaries. However, Standard III(A) requires members and candidates to work in the client's best interest no matter what the job function.

A member or candidate who does not provide advisory services to a client but who acts only as a trade execution professional must prudently work in the client's interest when completing requested trades. Acting in the client's best interest requires these professionals to use their skills and diligence to execute trades in the most favorable terms that can be achieved. Members and candidates operating in such positions must use care to operate within the parameters set by the client's trading instructions.

Members and candidates may also operate in a blended environment where they execute client trades and offer advice on a limited set of investment options. The extent of the advisory arrangement and limitations should be outlined in the agreement with the client at the outset of the relationship. For instance, members and candidates should inform clients that the advice provided will be limited to the propriety products of the firm and not include other products available on the market. Clients who want access to a wider range of investment products would have the information necessary to decide not to engage with members or candidates working under these restrictions.

Members and candidates operating in this blended context would comply with their obligations by recommending the allowable products that are consistent with the client's objectives and risk tolerance. They would exercise care through diligently aligning the client's needs with the attributes of the products being recommended. Members and candidates should place the client's interests first by disregarding any firm or personal interest in motivating a recommended transaction.

There is a large variety of professional relationships that members and candidates have with their clients. Standard III(A) requires them to fulfill the obligations outlined explicitly or implicitly in the client agreements to the best of their abilities and with loyalty, prudence, and care. Whether a member or candidate is structuring a new securitization transaction, completing a credit rating analysis, or leading a public company, he or she must work with prudence and care in delivering the agreed-on services.

Identifying the Actual Investment Client

The first step for members and candidates in fulfilling their duty of loyalty to clients is to determine the identity of the "client" to whom the duty of loyalty is owed. In the context of an investment manager managing the personal assets of an individual, the client is easily identified. When the manager is responsible for the portfolios of pension plans or trusts, however, the client is not the person or entity who hires the manager but, rather, the beneficiaries of the plan or trust. The duty of loyalty is owed to the ultimate beneficiaries.

In some situations, an actual client or group of beneficiaries may not exist. Members and candidates managing a fund to an index or an expected mandate owe the duty of loyalty, prudence, and care to invest in a manner consistent with the stated mandate. The decisions of a fund's manager, although benefiting all fund investors, do not have to be based on an individual investor's requirements and risk profile. Client loyalty and care for those investing in the fund are the responsibility of members and candidates who have an advisory relationship with those individuals.

Situations involving potential conflicts of interest with respect to responsibilities to clients may be extremely complex because they may involve a number of competing interests. The duty of loyalty, prudence, and care applies to a large number of persons in varying capacities, but the exact duties may differ in many respects in accord with the relationship with each client or each type of account in which the assets are managed. Members and candidates must not only put their obligations to clients first in all dealings but also endeavor to avoid all real or potential conflicts of interest.

Members and candidates with positions whose responsibilities do not include direct investment management also have "clients" that must be considered. Just as there are various types of advisory relationships, members and candidates must look at their roles and responsibilities when making a determination of who their clients are. Sometimes the client is easily identifiable; such is the case in the relationship between a company executive and the firm's public shareholders. At other times, the client may be the investing public as a whole, in which case the goals of independence and objectivity of research surpass the goal of loyalty to a single organization.

Developing the Client's Portfolio

The duty of loyalty, prudence, and care owed to the individual client is especially important because the professional investment manager typically possesses greater knowledge in the investment arena than the client does. This disparity places the individual client in a vulnerable position; the client must trust the manager. The manager in these situations should ensure that the client's objectives and expectations for the performance of the account are realistic and suitable to the client's circumstances and that the risks involved are appropriate. In most circumstances, recommended investment strategies should relate to the long-term objectives and circumstances of the client.

Particular care must be taken to detect whether the goals of the investment manager or the firm in conducting business, selling products, and executing security transactions potentially conflict with the best interests and objectives of the client. When members and candidates cannot avoid potential conflicts between their firm and clients' interests, they must provide clear and factual disclosures of the circumstances to the clients.

Members and candidates must follow any guidelines set by their clients for the management of their assets. Some clients, such as charitable organizations and pension plans, have strict investment policies that limit investment options to certain types or classes of investment or prohibit investment in certain securities. Other organizations have aggressive policies that do not prohibit investments by type but, instead, set criteria on the basis of the portfolio's total risk and return.

Investment decisions must be judged in the context of the total portfolio rather than by individual investment within the portfolio. The member's or candidate's duty is satisfied with respect to a particular investment if the individual has thoroughly considered the investment's place in the overall portfolio, the risk of loss and opportunity for gains, tax implications, and the diversification, liquidity, cash flow, and overall return requirements of the assets or the portion of the assets for which the manager is responsible.

Soft Commission Policies

An investment manager often has discretion over the selection of brokers executing transactions. Conflicts may arise when an investment manager uses client brokerage to purchase research services, a practice commonly called "soft dollars" or "soft commissions." A member or candidate who pays a higher brokerage commission than he or she would normally pay to allow for the purchase of goods or services, without corresponding benefit to the client, violates the duty of loyalty to the client.

From time to time, a client will direct a manager to use the client's brokerage to purchase goods or services for the client, a practice that is commonly called "directed brokerage." Because brokerage commission is an asset of the client and is used to benefit that client, not the manager, such a practice does not violate any duty of loyalty. However, a member or candidate is obligated to seek "best price" and "best execution" and be assured by the client that the goods or services purchased from the brokerage will benefit the account beneficiaries. "Best execution" refers to a trading process that seeks to maximize the value of the client's portfolio within the client's stated investment objectives and constraints. In addition, the member or candidate should disclose to the client that the client may not be getting best execution from the directed brokerage.

Proxy Voting Policies

The duty of loyalty, prudence, and care may apply in a number of situations facing the investment professional besides those related directly to investing assets.

Part of a member's or candidate's duty of loyalty includes voting proxies in an informed and responsible manner. Proxies have economic value to a client, and members and candidates must ensure that they properly safeguard and maximize this value. An investment manager who fails to vote, casts a vote without considering the impact of the question, or votes blindly with management on nonroutine governance issues (e.g., a change in company capitalization) may violate this standard. Voting of proxies is an integral part of the management of investments.

A cost–benefit analysis may show that voting all proxies may not benefit the client, so voting proxies may not be necessary in all instances. Members and candidates should disclose to clients their proxy voting policies.

22 STANDARD III(A): RECOMMENDED PROCEDURES

Regular Account Information

Members and candidates with control of client assets (1) should submit to each client, at least quarterly, an itemized statement showing the funds and securities in the custody or possession of the member or candidate plus all debits, credits, and transactions that occurred during the period, (2) should disclose to the client where the assets are to be maintained, as well as where or when they are moved, and (3) should separate the client's assets from any other party's assets, including the member's or candidate's own assets.

Client Approval

If a member or candidate is uncertain about the appropriate course of action with respect to a client, the member or candidate should consider what he or she would expect or demand if the member or candidate were the client. If in doubt, a member or candidate should disclose the questionable matter in writing to the client and obtain client approval.

Firm Policies

Members and candidates should address and encourage their firms to address the following topics when drafting the statements or manuals containing their policies and procedures regarding responsibilities to clients:

- *Follow all applicable rules and laws*: Members and candidates must follow all legal requirements and applicable provisions of the Code and Standards.
- *Establish the investment objectives of the client*: Make a reasonable inquiry into a client's investment experience, risk and return objectives, and financial constraints prior to making investment recommendations or taking investment actions.
- *Consider all the information when taking actions*: When taking investment actions, members and candidates must consider the appropriateness and suitability of the investment relative to (1) the client's needs and circumstances, (2) the investment's basic characteristics, and (3) the basic characteristics of the total portfolio.

- *Diversify*: Members and candidates should diversify investments to reduce the risk of loss, unless diversification is not consistent with plan guidelines or is contrary to the account objectives.
- *Carry out regular reviews*: Members and candidates should establish regular review schedules to ensure that the investments held in the account adhere to the terms of the governing documents.
- *Deal fairly with all clients with respect to investment actions*: Members and candidates must not favor some clients over others and should establish policies for allocating trades and disseminating investment recommendations.
- *Disclose conflicts of interest*: Members and candidates must disclose all actual and potential conflicts of interest so that clients can evaluate those conflicts.
- *Disclose compensation arrangements*: Members and candidates should make their clients aware of all forms of manager compensation.
- *Vote proxies*: In most cases, members and candidates should determine who is authorized to vote shares and vote proxies in the best interests of the clients and ultimate beneficiaries.
- *Maintain confidentiality*: Members and candidates must preserve the confidentiality of client information.
- *Seek best execution*: Unless directed by the client as ultimate beneficiary, members and candidates must seek best execution for their clients. (Best execution is defined in the preceding text.)
- *Place client interests first*: Members and candidates must serve the best interests of clients.

STANDARD III(A): APPLICATION OF THE STANDARD 23

Example 1 (Identifying the Client—Plan Participants):

First Country Bank serves as trustee for the Miller Company's pension plan. Miller is the target of a hostile takeover attempt by Newton, Inc. In attempting to ward off Newton, Miller's managers persuade Julian Wiley, an investment manager at First Country Bank, to purchase Miller common stock in the open market for the employee pension plan. Miller's officials indicate that such action would be favorably received and would probably result in other accounts being placed with the bank. Although Wiley believes the stock is overvalued and would not ordinarily buy it, he purchases the stock to support Miller's managers, to maintain Miller's good favor toward the bank, and to realize additional new business. The heavy stock purchases cause Miller's market price to rise to such a level that Newton retracts its takeover bid.

> *Comment*: Standard III(A) requires that a member or candidate, in evaluating a takeover bid, act prudently and solely in the interests of plan participants and beneficiaries. To meet this requirement, a member or candidate must carefully evaluate the long-term prospects of the company against the short-term prospects presented by the takeover offer and by the ability to invest elsewhere. In this instance, Wiley, acting on behalf of his employer, which was the trustee for a pension plan, clearly violated Standard III(A). He used the pension plan to perpetuate existing management, perhaps to the detriment of plan participants and the company's shareholders, and

to benefit himself. Wiley's responsibilities to the plan participants and beneficiaries should have taken precedence over any ties of his bank to corporate managers and over his self-interest. Wiley had a duty to examine the takeover offer on its own merits and to make an independent decision. The guiding principle is the appropriateness of the investment decision to the pension plan, not whether the decision benefited Wiley or the company that hired him.

Example 2 (Client Commission Practices):

JNI, a successful investment counseling firm, serves as investment manager for the pension plans of several large regionally based companies. Its trading activities generate a significant amount of commission-related business. JNI uses the brokerage and research services of many firms, but most of its trading activity is handled through a large brokerage company, Thompson, Inc., because the executives of the two firms have a close friendship. Thompson's commission structure is high in comparison with charges for similar brokerage services from other firms. JNI considers Thompson's research services and execution capabilities average. In exchange for JNI directing its brokerage to Thompson, Thompson absorbs a number of JNI overhead expenses, including those for rent.

Comment: JNI executives are breaching their responsibilities by using client brokerage for services that do not benefit JNI clients and by not obtaining best price and best execution for their clients. Because JNI executives are not upholding their duty of loyalty, they are violating Standard III(A).

Example 3 (Brokerage Arrangements):

Charlotte Everett, a struggling independent investment adviser, serves as investment manager for the pension plans of several companies. One of her brokers, Scott Company, is close to consummating management agreements with prospective new clients whereby Everett would manage the new client accounts and trade the accounts exclusively through Scott. One of Everett's existing clients, Crayton Corporation, has directed Everett to place securities transactions for Crayton's account exclusively through Scott. But to induce Scott to exert efforts to send more new accounts to her, Everett also directs transactions to Scott from other clients without their knowledge.

Comment: Everett has an obligation at all times to seek best price and best execution on all trades. Everett may direct new client trades exclusively through Scott Company as long as Everett receives best price and execution on the trades or receives a written statement from new clients that she is *not* to seek best price and execution and that they are aware of the consequence for their accounts. Everett may trade other accounts through Scott as a reward for directing clients to Everett only if the accounts receive best price and execution and the practice is disclosed to the accounts. Because Everett does not disclose the directed trading, Everett has violated Standard III(A).

Example 4 (Brokerage Arrangements):

Emilie Rome is a trust officer for Paget Trust Company. Rome's supervisor is responsible for reviewing Rome's trust account transactions and her monthly reports of personal stock transactions. Rome has been using Nathan Gray, a broker, almost exclusively for trust account brokerage transactions. When Gray makes a market in stocks, he has been giving Rome a lower price for personal purchases and a higher price for sales than he gives to Rome's trust accounts and other investors.

> *Comment*: Rome is violating her duty of loyalty to the bank's trust accounts by using Gray for brokerage transactions simply because Gray trades Rome's personal account on favorable terms. Rome is placing her own interests before those of her clients.

Example 5 (Client Commission Practices):

Lauren Parker, an analyst with Provo Advisors, covers South American equities for her firm. She likes to travel to the markets for which she is responsible and decides to go on a trip to Chile, Argentina, and Brazil. The trip is sponsored by SouthAM, Inc., a research firm with a small broker/dealer affiliate that uses the clearing facilities of a larger New York brokerage house. SouthAM specializes in arranging South American trips for analysts during which they can meet with central bank officials, government ministers, local economists, and senior executives of corporations. SouthAM accepts commission dollars at a ratio of 2 to 1 against the hard-dollar costs of the research fee for the trip. Parker is not sure that SouthAM's execution is competitive, but without informing her supervisor, she directs the trading desk at Provo to start giving commission business to SouthAM so she can take the trip. SouthAM has conveniently timed the briefing trip to coincide with the beginning of Carnival season, so Parker also decides to spend five days of vacation in Rio de Janeiro at the end of the trip. Parker uses commission dollars to pay for the five days of hotel expenses.

> *Comment*: Parker is violating Standard III(A) by not exercising her duty of loyalty to her clients. She should have determined whether the commissions charged by SouthAM are reasonable in relation to the benefit of the research provided by the trip. She also should have determined whether best execution and prices could be received from SouthAM. In addition, the five extra days are not part of the research effort because they do not assist in the investment decision making. Thus, the hotel expenses for the five days should not be paid for with client assets.

Example 6 (Excessive Trading):

Vida Knauss manages the portfolios of a number of high-net-worth individuals. A major part of her investment management fee is based on trading commissions. Knauss engages in extensive trading for each of her clients to ensure that she attains the minimum commission level set by her firm. Although the securities purchased and sold for the clients are appropriate and fall within the acceptable asset classes for the clients, the amount of trading for each account exceeds what is necessary to accomplish the client's investment objectives.

> *Comment*: Knauss has violated Standard III(A) because she is using the assets of her clients to benefit her firm and herself.

Example 7 (Managing Family Accounts):

Adam Dill recently joined New Investments Asset Managers. To assist Dill in building a book of clients, both his father and brother opened new fee-paying accounts. Dill followed all the firm's procedures in noting his relationships with these clients and in developing their investment policy statements.

After several years, the number of Dill's clients has grown, but he still manages the original accounts of his family members. An IPO is coming to market that is a suitable investment for many of his clients, including his brother. Dill does not receive the amount of stock he requested, so to avoid any appearance of a conflict of interest, he does not allocate any shares to his brother's account.

> *Comment*: Dill has violated Standard III(A) because he is not acting for the benefit of his brother's account as well as his other accounts. The brother's account is a regular fee-paying account comparable to the accounts of his other clients. By not allocating the shares proportionately across *all* accounts for which he thought the IPO was suitable, Dill is disadvantaging specific clients.
>
> Dill would have been correct in not allocating shares to his brother's account if that account was being managed outside the normal fee structure of the firm.

Example 8 (Identifying the Client):

Donna Hensley has been hired by a law firm to testify as an expert witness. Although the testimony is intended to represent impartial advice, she is concerned that her work may have negative consequences for the law firm. If the law firm is Hensley's client, how does she ensure that her testimony will not violate the required duty of loyalty, prudence, and care to one's client?

> *Comment*: In this situation, the law firm represents Hensley's employer and the aspect of "who is the client" is not well defined. When acting as an expert witness, Hensley is bound by the standard of independence and objectivity in the same manner as an independent research analyst would be bound. Hensley must not let the law firm influence the testimony she provides in the legal proceedings.

Example 9 (Identifying the Client):

Jon Miller is a mutual fund portfolio manager. The fund is focused on the global financial services sector. Wanda Spears is a private wealth manager in the same city as Miller and is a friend of Miller. At a local CFA Institute society meeting, Spears mentions to Miller that her new client is an investor in Miller's fund. She states that the two of them now share a responsibility to this client.

> *Comment*: Spears' statement is not totally correct. Because she provides the advisory services to her new client, she alone is bound by the duty of loyalty to this client. Miller's responsibility is to manage the fund according to the investment policy statement of the fund. His actions should not be influenced by the needs of any particular fund investor.

Example 10 (Client Loyalty):

After providing client account investment performance to the external-facing departments but prior to it being finalized for release to clients, Teresa Nguyen, an investment performance analyst, notices the reporting system missed a trade. Correcting the omission resulted in a large loss for a client that had previously placed the firm on "watch" for potential termination owing to underperformance in prior periods. Nguyen knows this news is unpleasant but informs the appropriate individuals that the report needs to be updated before releasing it to the client.

Comment: Nguyen's actions align with the requirements of Standard III(A). Even though the correction may lead to the firm's termination by the client, withholding information on errors would not be in the best interest of the client.

Example 11 (Execution-Only Responsibilities):

Baftija Sulejman recently became a candidate in the CFA Program. He is a broker who executes client-directed trades for several high-net-worth individuals. Sulejman does not provide any investment advice and only executes the trading decisions made by clients. He is concerned that the Code and Standards impose a fiduciary duty on him in his dealing with clients and sends an e-mail to the CFA Ethics Helpdesk (ethics@cfainstitute.org) to seek guidance on this issue.

Comment: In this instance, Sulejman serves in an execution-only capacity and his duty of loyalty, prudence, and care is centered on the skill and diligence used when executing trades—namely, by seeking best execution and making trades within the parameters set by the clients (instructions on quantity, price, timing, etc.). Acting in the best interests of the client dictates that trades are executed on the most favorable terms that can be achieved for the client. Given this job function, the requirements of the Code and Standards for loyalty, prudence, and care clearly do not impose a fiduciary duty.

STANDARD III(B) FAIR DEALING

24

- ☐ demonstrate the application of the Code of Ethics and Standards of Professional Conduct to situations involving issues of professional integrity
- ☐ recommend practices and procedures designed to prevent violations of the Code of Ethics and Standards of Professional Conduct
- ☐ identify conduct that conforms to the Code and Standards and conduct that violates the Code and Standards

Members and Candidates must deal fairly and objectively with all clients when providing investment analysis, making investment recommendations, taking investment action, or engaging in other professional activities.

Guidance

Highlights:

- *Investment Recommendations*
- *Investment Action*

Standard III(B) requires members and candidates to treat all clients fairly when disseminating investment recommendations or making material changes to prior investment recommendations or when taking investment action with regard to general purchases, new issues, or secondary offerings. Only through the fair treatment of all parties can the investment management profession maintain the confidence of the investing public.

When an investment adviser has multiple clients, the potential exists for the adviser to favor one client over another. This favoritism may take various forms—from the quality and timing of services provided to the allocation of investment opportunities.

The term "fairly" implies that the member or candidate must take care not to discriminate against any clients when disseminating investment recommendations or taking investment action. Standard III(B) does not state "equally" because members and candidates could not possibly reach all clients at exactly the same time—whether by printed mail, telephone (including text messaging), computer (including internet updates and e-mail distribution), facsimile (fax), or wire. Each client has unique needs, investment criteria, and investment objectives, so not all investment opportunities are suitable for all clients. In addition, members and candidates may provide more personal, specialized, or in-depth service to clients who are willing to pay for premium services through higher management fees or higher levels of brokerage. Members and candidates may differentiate their services to clients, but different levels of service must not disadvantage or negatively affect clients. In addition, the different service levels should be disclosed to clients and prospective clients and should be available to everyone (i.e., different service levels should not be offered selectively).

Standard III(B) covers conduct in two broadly defined categories—investment recommendations and investment action.

Investment Recommendations

The first category of conduct involves members and candidates whose primary function is the preparation of investment recommendations to be disseminated either to the public or within a firm for the use of others in making investment decisions. This group includes members and candidates employed by investment counseling, advisory, or consulting firms as well as banks, brokerage firms, and insurance companies. The criterion is that the member's or candidate's primary responsibility is the preparation of recommendations to be acted on by others, including those in the member's or candidate's organization.

An investment recommendation is any opinion expressed by a member or candidate in regard to purchasing, selling, or holding a given security or other investment. The opinion may be disseminated to customers or clients through an initial detailed research report, through a brief update report, by addition to or deletion from a list of recommended securities, or simply by oral communication. A recommendation that is distributed to anyone outside the organization is considered a communication for general distribution under Standard III(B).

Standard III(B) addresses the manner in which investment recommendations or changes in prior recommendations are disseminated to clients. Each member or candidate is obligated to ensure that information is disseminated in such a manner that all clients have a fair opportunity to act on every recommendation. Communicating with all clients on a uniform basis presents practical problems for members and candidates because of differences in timing and methods of communication with various types of customers and clients. Members and candidates should encourage their firms to design an equitable system to prevent selective or discriminatory disclosure and should inform clients about what kind of communications they will receive.

The duty to clients imposed by Standard III(B) may be more critical when members or candidates change their recommendations than when they make initial recommendations. Material changes in a member's or candidate's prior investment recommendations because of subsequent research should be communicated to all current clients; particular care should be taken that the information reaches those clients who the member or candidate knows have acted on or been affected by the earlier advice. Clients who do not know that the member or candidate has changed a recommendation and who, therefore, place orders contrary to a current recommendation should be advised of the changed recommendation before the order is accepted.

Investment Action

The second category of conduct includes those members and candidates whose primary function is taking investment action (portfolio management) on the basis of recommendations prepared internally or received from external sources. Investment action, like investment recommendations, can affect market value. Consequently, Standard III(B) requires that members or candidates treat all clients fairly in light of their investment objectives and circumstances. For example, when making investments in new offerings or in secondary financings, members and candidates should distribute the issues to all customers for whom the investments are appropriate in a manner consistent with the policies of the firm for allocating blocks of stock. If the issue is oversubscribed, then the issue should be prorated to all subscribers. This action should be taken on a round-lot basis to avoid odd-lot distributions. In addition, if the issue is oversubscribed, members and candidates should forgo any sales to themselves or their immediate families in order to free up additional shares for clients. If the investment professional's family-member accounts are managed similarly to the accounts of other clients of the firm, however, the family-member accounts should not be excluded from buying such shares.

Members and candidates must make every effort to treat all individual and institutional clients in a fair and impartial manner. A member or candidate may have multiple relationships with an institution; for example, the member or candidate may be a corporate trustee, pension fund manager, manager of funds for individuals employed by the customer, loan originator, or creditor. A member or candidate must exercise care to treat all clients fairly.

Members and candidates should disclose to clients and prospective clients the documented allocation procedures they or their firms have in place and how the procedures would affect the client or prospect. The disclosure should be clear and complete so that the client can make an informed investment decision. Even when complete disclosure is made, however, members and candidates must put client interests ahead of their own. A member's or candidate's duty of fairness and loyalty to clients can never be overridden by client consent to patently unfair allocation procedures.

Treating clients fairly also means that members and candidates should not take advantage of their position in the industry to the detriment of clients. For instance, in the context of IPOs, members and candidates must make bona fide public distributions of "hot issue" securities (defined as securities of a public offering that are trading at a premium in the secondary market whenever such trading commences because of the great demand for the securities). Members and candidates are prohibited from withholding such securities for their own benefit and must not use such securities as a reward or incentive to gain benefit.

25 STANDARD III(B): RECOMMENDED PROCEDURES

Develop Firm Policies

Although Standard III(B) refers to a member's or candidate's responsibility to deal fairly and objectively with clients, members and candidates should also encourage their firms to establish compliance procedures requiring all employees who disseminate investment recommendations or take investment actions to treat customers and clients fairly. At the very least, a member or candidate should recommend appropriate procedures to management if none are in place. And the member or candidate should make management aware of possible violations of fair-dealing practices within the firm when they come to the attention of the member or candidate.

The extent of the formality and complexity of such compliance procedures depends on the nature and size of the organization and the type of securities involved. An investment adviser who is a sole proprietor and handles only discretionary accounts might not disseminate recommendations to the public, but that adviser should have formal written procedures to ensure that all clients receive fair investment action.

Good business practice dictates that initial recommendations be made available to all customers who indicate an interest. Although a member or candidate need not communicate a recommendation to all customers, the selection process by which customers receive information should be based on suitability and known interest, not on any preferred or favored status. A common practice to assure fair dealing is to communicate recommendations simultaneously within the firm and to customers.

Members and candidates should consider the following points when establishing fair-dealing compliance procedures:

- *Limit the number of people involved*: Members and candidates should make reasonable efforts to limit the number of people who are privy to the fact that a recommendation is going to be disseminated.
- *Shorten the time frame between decision and dissemination*: Members and candidates should make reasonable efforts to limit the amount of time that elapses between the decision to make an investment recommendation and the time the actual recommendation is disseminated. If a detailed institutional recommendation that might take two or three weeks to publish is in preparation, a short summary report including the conclusion might be published in advance. In an organization where both a research committee and an investment policy committee must approve a recommendation, the meetings should be held on the same day if possible. The process of reviewing reports and printing and mailing them, faxing them, or distributing them by e-mail necessarily involves the passage of time, sometimes long periods of time. In large firms with extensive review processes, the time factor is usually not within the control of the analyst who prepares the report. Thus, many firms and their analysts communicate to customers and firm personnel the new or changed recommendations by an update or "flash" report. The communication technique might be fax, e-mail, wire, or short written report.
- *Publish guidelines for pre-dissemination behavior*: Members and candidates should encourage firms to develop guidelines that prohibit personnel who have prior knowledge of an investment recommendation from discussing or taking any action on the pending recommendation.

- *Simultaneous dissemination*: Members and candidates should establish procedures for the timing of dissemination of investment recommendations so that all clients are treated fairly—that is, are informed at approximately the same time. For example, if a firm is going to announce a new recommendation, supervisory personnel should time the announcement to avoid placing any client or group of clients at an unfair advantage relative to other clients. A communication to all branch offices should be sent at the time of the general announcement. (When appropriate, the firm should accompany the announcement of a new recommendation with a statement that trading restrictions for the firm's employees are now in effect. The trading restrictions should stay in effect until the recommendation is widely distributed to all relevant clients.) Once this distribution has occurred, the member or candidate may follow up separately with individual clients, but members and candidates should not give favored clients advance information when such advance notification may disadvantage other clients.
- *Maintain a list of clients and their holdings*: Members and candidates should maintain a list of all clients and the securities or other investments each client holds in order to facilitate notification of customers or clients of a change in an investment recommendation. If a particular security or other investment is to be sold, such a list can be used to ensure that all holders are treated fairly in the liquidation of that particular investment.
- *Develop and document trade allocation procedures*: When formulating procedures for allocating trades, members and candidates should develop a set of guiding principles that ensure

  - fairness to advisory clients, both in priority of execution of orders and in the allocation of the price obtained in execution of block orders or trades,
  - timeliness and efficiency in the execution of orders, and
  - accuracy of the member's or candidate's records as to trade orders and client account positions.

With these principles in mind, members and candidates should develop or encourage their firm to develop written allocation procedures, with particular attention to procedures for block trades and new issues. Procedures to consider are as follows:

- requiring orders and modifications or cancellations of orders to be documented and time stamped;
- processing and executing orders on a first-in, first-out basis with consideration of bundling orders for efficiency as appropriate for the asset class or the security;
- developing a policy to address such issues as calculating execution prices and "partial fills" when trades are grouped, or in a block, for efficiency;
- giving all client accounts participating in a block trade the same execution price and charging the same commission;
- when the full amount of the block order is not executed, allocating partially executed orders among the participating client accounts pro rata on the basis of order size while not going below an established minimum lot size for some securities (e.g., bonds); and
- when allocating trades for new issues, obtaining advance indications of interest, allocating securities by client (rather than portfolio manager), and providing a method for calculating allocations.

Disclose Trade Allocation Procedures

Members and candidates should disclose to clients and prospective clients how they select accounts to participate in an order and how they determine the amount of securities each account will buy or sell. Trade allocation procedures must be fair and equitable, and disclosure of inequitable allocation methods does not relieve the member or candidate of this obligation.

Establish Systematic Account Review

Member and candidate supervisors should review each account on a regular basis to ensure that no client or customer is being given preferential treatment and that the investment actions taken for each account are suitable for each account's objectives. Because investments should be based on individual needs and circumstances, an investment manager may have good reasons for placing a given security or other investment in one account while selling it from another account and should fully document the reasons behind both sides of the transaction. Members and candidates should encourage firms to establish review procedures, however, to detect whether trading in one account is being used to benefit a favored client.

Disclose Levels of Service

Members and candidates should disclose to all clients whether the organization offers different levels of service to clients for the same fee or different fees. Different levels of service should not be offered to clients selectively.

26 STANDARD III(B): APPLICATION OF THE STANDARD

Example 1 (Selective Disclosure):

Bradley Ames, a well-known and respected analyst, follows the computer industry. In the course of his research, he finds that a small, relatively unknown company whose shares are traded over the counter has just signed significant contracts with some of the companies he follows. After a considerable amount of investigation, Ames decides to write a research report on the small company and recommend purchase of its shares. While the report is being reviewed by the company for factual accuracy, Ames schedules a luncheon with several of his best clients to discuss the company. At the luncheon, he mentions the purchase recommendation scheduled to be sent early the following week to all the firm's clients.

> *Comment*: Ames has violated Standard III(B) by disseminating the purchase recommendation to the clients with whom he has lunch a week before the recommendation is sent to all clients.

Example 2 (Fair Dealing between Funds):

Spencer Rivers, president of XYZ Corporation, moves his company's growth-oriented pension fund to a particular bank primarily because of the excellent investment performance achieved by the bank's commingled fund for the prior five-year period. Later, Rivers compares the results of his pension fund with those of the bank's commingled fund. He is startled to learn that, even though the two accounts have the same investment objectives and similar portfolios, his company's pension fund has significantly underperformed the bank's commingled fund. Questioning this result at his next meeting with the pension fund's manager, Rivers is told that, as a matter of policy, when a new security is placed on the recommended list, Morgan Jackson, the pension fund manager, first purchases the security for the commingled account and then purchases it on a pro rata basis for all other pension fund accounts. Similarly, when a sale is recommended, the security is sold first from the commingled account and then sold on a pro rata basis from all other accounts. Rivers also learns that if the bank cannot get enough shares (especially of hot issues) to be meaningful to all the accounts, its policy is to place the new issues only in the commingled account.

Seeing that Rivers is neither satisfied nor pleased by the explanation, Jackson quickly adds that nondiscretionary pension accounts and personal trust accounts have a lower priority on purchase and sale recommendations than discretionary pension fund accounts. Furthermore, Jackson states, the company's pension fund had the opportunity to invest up to 5% in the commingled fund.

> *Comment*: The bank's policy does not treat all customers fairly, and Jackson has violated her duty to her clients by giving priority to the growth-oriented commingled fund over all other funds and to discretionary accounts over nondiscretionary accounts. Jackson must execute orders on a systematic basis that is fair to all clients. In addition, trade allocation procedures should be disclosed to all clients when they become clients. Of course, in this case, disclosure of the bank's policy would not change the fact that the policy is unfair.

Example 3 (Fair Dealing and IPO Distribution):

Dominic Morris works for a small regional securities firm. His work consists of corporate finance activities and investing for institutional clients. Arena, Ltd., is planning to go public. The partners have secured rights to buy an arena football league franchise and are planning to use the funds from the issue to complete the purchase. Because arena football is the current rage, Morris believes he has a hot issue on his hands. He has quietly negotiated some options for himself for helping convince Arena to do the financing through his securities firm. When he seeks expressions of interest, the institutional buyers oversubscribe the issue. Morris, assuming that the institutions have the financial clout to drive the stock up, then fills all orders (including his own) and decreases the institutional blocks.

> *Comment*: Morris has violated Standard III(B) by not treating all customers fairly. He should not have taken any shares himself and should have prorated the shares offered among all clients. In addition, he should have disclosed to his firm and to his clients that he received options as part of the deal [see Standard VI(A) Disclosure of Conflicts].

Example 4 (Fair Dealing and Transaction Allocation):

Eleanor Preston, the chief investment officer of Porter Williams Investments (PWI), a medium-size money management firm, has been trying to retain a client, Colby Company. Management at Colby, which accounts for almost half of PWI's revenues, recently told Preston that if the performance of its account did not improve, it would find a new money manager. Shortly after this threat, Preston purchases mortgage-backed securities (MBSs) for several accounts, including Colby's. Preston is busy with a number of transactions that day, so she fails to allocate the trades immediately or write up the trade tickets. A few days later, when Preston is allocating trades, she notes that some of the MBSs have significantly increased in price and some have dropped. Preston decides to allocate the profitable trades to Colby and spread the losing trades among several other PWI accounts.

> *Comment*: Preston has violated Standard III(B) by failing to deal fairly with her clients in taking these investment actions. Preston should have allocated the trades prior to executing the orders, or she should have had a systematic approach to allocating the trades, such as pro rata, as soon as practical after they were executed. Among other things, Preston must disclose to the client that the adviser may act as broker for, receive commissions from, and have a potential conflict of interest regarding both parties in agency cross-transactions. After the disclosure, she should obtain from the client consent authorizing such transactions in advance.

Example 5 (Selective Disclosure):

Saunders Industrial Waste Management (SIWM) publicly indicates to analysts that it is comfortable with the somewhat disappointing earnings-per-share projection of US$1.16 for the quarter. Bernard Roberts, an analyst at Coffey Investments, is confident that SIWM management has understated the forecasted earnings so that the real announcement will cause an "upside surprise" and boost the price of SIWM stock. The "whisper number" (rumored) estimate based on extensive research and discussed among knowledgeable analysts is higher than US$1.16. Roberts repeats the US$1.16 figure in his research report to all Coffey clients but informally tells his large clients that he expects the earnings per share to be higher, making SIWM a good buy.

> *Comment*: By not sharing his opinion regarding the potential for a significant upside earnings surprise with all clients, Roberts is not treating all clients fairly and has violated Standard III(B).

Example 6 (Additional Services for Select Clients):

Jenpin Weng uses e-mail to issue a new recommendation to all his clients. He then calls his three largest institutional clients to discuss the recommendation in detail.

> *Comment*: Weng has not violated Standard III(B) because he widely disseminated the recommendation and provided the information to all his clients prior to discussing it with a select few. Weng's largest clients received additional personal service because they presumably pay higher fees or because they have a large amount of assets under Weng's management. If Weng had discussed the report with a select group of clients prior to distributing it to all his clients, he would have violated Standard III(B).

Example 7 (Minimum Lot Allocations):

Lynn Hampton is a well-respected private wealth manager in her community with a diversified client base. She determines that a new 10-year bond being offered by Healthy Pharmaceuticals is appropriate for five of her clients. Three clients request to purchase US$10,000 each, and the other two request US$50,000 each. The minimum lot size is established at US$5,000, and the issue is oversubscribed at the time of placement. Her firm's policy is that odd-lot allocations, especially those below the minimum, should be avoided because they may affect the liquidity of the security at the time of sale.

Hampton is informed she will receive only US$55,000 of the offering for all accounts. Hampton distributes the bond investments as follows: The three accounts that requested US$10,000 are allocated US$5,000 each, and the two accounts that requested US$50,000 are allocated US$20,000 each.

> *Comment*: Hampton has not violated Standard III(B), even though the distribution is not on a completely pro rata basis because of the required minimum lot size. With the total allocation being significantly below the amount requested, Hampton ensured that each client received at least the minimum lot size of the issue. This approach allowed the clients to efficiently sell the bond later if necessary.

Example 8 (Excessive Trading):

Ling Chan manages the accounts for many pension plans, including the plan of his father's employer. Chan developed similar but not identical investment policies for each client, so the investment portfolios are rarely the same. To minimize the cost to his father's pension plan, he intentionally trades more frequently in the accounts of other clients to ensure the required brokerage is incurred to continue receiving free research for use by all the pensions.

> *Comment*: Chan is violating Standard III(B) because his trading actions are disadvantaging his clients to enhance a relationship with a preferred client. All clients are benefiting from the research being provided and should incur their fair portion of the costs. This does not mean that additional trading should occur if a client has not paid an equal portion of the commission; trading should occur only as required by the strategy.

Example 9 (Limited Social Media Disclosures):

Mary Burdette was recently hired by Fundamental Investment Management (FIM) as a junior auto industry analyst. Burdette is expected to expand the social media presence of the firm because she is active with various networks, including Facebook, LinkedIn, and X. Although Burdette's supervisor, Joe Graf, has never used social media, he encourages Burdette to explore opportunities to increase FIM's online presence and ability to share content, communicate, and broadcast information to clients. In response to Graf's encouragement, Burdette is working on a proposal detailing the advantages of getting FIM onto X in addition to launching a company Facebook page.

As part of her auto industry research for FIM, Burdette is completing a report on the financial impact of Sun Drive Auto Ltd.'s new solar technology for compact automobiles. This research report will be her first for FIM, and she believes Sun Drive's technology could revolutionize the auto industry. In her excitement, Burdette sends a quick post to FIM X followers summarizing her "buy" recommendation for Sun Drive Auto stock.

> *Comment*: Burdette has violated Standard III(B) by sending an investment recommendation to a select group of contacts prior to distributing it to all clients. Burdette must make sure she has received the appropriate training about FIM's policies and procedures, including the appropriate business use of personal social media networks, before engaging in such activities.
>
> See Standard IV(C) for guidance related to the duties of the supervisor.

Example 10 (Fair Dealing between Clients):

Paul Rove, performance analyst for Alpha-Beta Investment Management, is describing to the firm's chief investment officer (CIO) two new reports he would like to develop to assist the firm in meeting its obligations to treat clients fairly. Because many of the firm's clients have similar investment objectives and portfolios, Rove suggests a report detailing securities owned across several clients and the percentage of the portfolio the security represents. The second report would compare the monthly performance of portfolios with similar strategies. The outliers within each report would be submitted to the CIO for review.

Comment: As a performance analyst, Rove likely has little direct contact with clients and thus has limited opportunity to treat clients differently. The recommended reports comply with Standard III(B) while helping the firm conduct after-the-fact reviews of how effectively the firm's advisers are dealing with their clients' portfolios. Reports that monitor the fair treatment of clients are an important oversight tool to ensure that clients are treated fairly.

27 STANDARD III(C) SUITABILITY

- ☐ demonstrate the application of the Code of Ethics and Standards of Professional Conduct to situations involving issues of professional integrity
- ☐ recommend practices and procedures designed to prevent violations of the Code of Ethics and Standards of Professional Conduct
- ☐ identify conduct that conforms to the Code and Standards and conduct that violates the Code and Standards

1. When Members and Candidates are in an advisory relationship with a client, they must:
   a. Make a reasonable inquiry into a client's or prospective client's investment experience, risk and return objectives, and financial constraints prior to making any investment recommendation or taking investment action and must reassess and update this information regularly.
   b. Determine that an investment is suitable to the client's financial situation and consistent with the client's written objectives, mandates, and constraints before making an investment recommendation or taking investment action.
   c. Judge the suitability of investments in the context of the client's total portfolio.
2. When Members and Candidates are responsible for managing a portfolio to a specific mandate, strategy, or style, they must make only investment recommendations or take only investment actions that are consistent with the stated objectives and constraints of the portfolio.

Guidance

Highlights:

- *Developing an Investment Policy*
- *Understanding the Client's Risk Profile*
- *Updating an Investment Policy*
- *The Need for Diversification*
- *Addressing Unsolicited Trading Requests*
- *Managing to an Index or Mandate*

Standard III(C) requires that members and candidates who are in an investment advisory relationship with clients consider carefully the needs, circumstances, and objectives of the clients when determining the appropriateness and suitability of a given investment or course of investment action. An appropriate suitability determination will not, however, prevent some investments or investment actions from losing value.

In judging the suitability of a potential investment, the member or candidate should review many aspects of the client's knowledge, experience related to investing, and financial situation. These aspects include, but are not limited to, the risk profile of the investment as compared with the constraints of the client, the impact of the investment on the diversity of the portfolio, and whether the client has the means or net worth to assume the associated risk. The investment professional's determination of suitability should reflect only the investment recommendations or actions that a prudent person would be willing to undertake. Not every investment opportunity will be suitable for every portfolio, regardless of the potential return being offered.

The responsibilities of members and candidates to gather information and make a suitability analysis prior to making a recommendation or taking investment action fall on those members and candidates who provide investment advice in the course of an advisory relationship with a client. Other members and candidates may be simply executing specific instructions for retail clients when buying or selling securities, such as shares in mutual funds. These members and candidates and some others, such as sell-side analysts, may not have the opportunity to judge the suitability of a particular investment for the ultimate client.

Developing an Investment Policy

When an advisory relationship exists, members and candidates must gather client information at the inception of the relationship. Such information includes the client's financial circumstances, personal data (such as age and occupation) that are relevant to investment decisions, attitudes toward risk, and objectives in investing. This information should be incorporated into a written investment policy statement (IPS) that addresses the client's risk tolerance, return requirements, and all investment constraints (including time horizon, liquidity needs, tax concerns, legal and regulatory factors, and unique circumstances). Without identifying such client factors, members and candidates cannot judge whether a particular investment or strategy is suitable for a particular client. The IPS also should identify and describe the roles and responsibilities of the parties to the advisory relationship and investment process, as well as schedules for review and evaluation of the IPS. After formulating long-term capital market expectations, members and candidates can assist in developing an appropriate strategic asset allocation and investment program for the client, whether these are presented in separate documents or incorporated in the IPS or in appendices to the IPS.

Understanding the Client's Risk Profile

One of the most important factors to be considered in matching appropriateness and suitability of an investment with a client's needs and circumstances is measuring that client's tolerance for risk. The investment professional must consider the possibilities of rapidly changing investment environments and their likely impact on a client's holdings, both individual securities and the collective portfolio. The risk of many investment strategies can and should be analyzed and quantified in advance.

The use of synthetic investment vehicles and derivative investment products has introduced particular issues of risk. Members and candidates should pay careful attention to the leverage inherent in many of these vehicles or products when considering them for use in a client's investment program. Such leverage and limited liquidity, depending on the degree to which they are hedged, bear directly on the issue of suitability for the client.

Updating an Investment Policy

Updating the IPS should be repeated at least annually and also prior to material changes to any specific investment recommendations or decisions on behalf of the client. The effort to determine the needs and circumstances of each client is not a one-time occurrence. Investment recommendations or decisions are usually part of an ongoing process that takes into account the diversity and changing nature of portfolio and client characteristics. The passage of time is bound to produce changes that are important with respect to investment objectives.

For an individual client, important changes might include the number of dependents, personal tax status, health, liquidity needs, risk tolerance, amount of wealth beyond that represented in the portfolio, and extent to which compensation and other income provide for current income needs. With respect to an institutional client, such changes might relate to the magnitude of unfunded liabilities in a pension fund, the withdrawal privileges in an employee savings plan, or the distribution requirements of a charitable foundation. Without efforts to update information concerning client factors, one or more factors could change without the investment manager's knowledge.

Suitability review can be done most effectively when the client fully discloses his or her complete financial portfolio, including those portions not managed by the member or candidate. If clients withhold information about their financial portfolios, the suitability analysis conducted by members and candidates cannot be expected to be complete; it must be based on the information provided.

The Need for Diversification

The investment profession has long recognized that combining several different investments is likely to provide a more acceptable level of risk exposure than having all assets in a single investment. The unique characteristics (or risks) of an individual investment may become partially or entirely neutralized when it is combined with other individual investments within a portfolio. Some reasonable amount of diversification is thus the norm for many portfolios, especially those managed by individuals or institutions that have some degree of legal fiduciary responsibility.

An investment with high relative risk on its own may be a suitable investment in the context of the entire portfolio or when the client's stated objectives contemplate speculative or risky investments. The manager may be responsible for only a portion of the client's total portfolio, or the client may not have provided a full financial picture. Members and candidates can be responsible for assessing the suitability of an investment only on the basis of the information and criteria actually provided by the client.

Addressing Unsolicited Trading Requests

Members and candidates may receive requests from a client for trades that do not properly align with the risk and return objectives outlined in the client's investment policy statement. These transaction requests may be based on the client's individual biases or professional experience. Members and candidates will need to make reasonable efforts to balance their clients' trading requests with their responsibilities to follow the agreed-on investment policy statement.

In cases of unsolicited trade requests that a member or candidate knows are unsuitable for a client, the member or candidate should refrain from making the trade until he or she discusses the concerns with the client. The discussions and resulting actions may encompass a variety of scenarios depending on how the requested unsuitable investment relates to the client's full portfolio.

Many times, an unsolicited request may be expected to have only a minimum impact on the entire portfolio because the size of the requested trade is small or the trade would result in a limited change to the portfolio's risk profile. In discussing the trade, the member or candidate should focus on educating the investor on how the request deviates from the current policy statement. Following the discussion, the member or candidate may follow his or her firm's policies regarding the necessary client approval for executing unsuitable trades. At a minimum, the client should acknowledge the discussion and accept the conditions that make the recommendation unsuitable.

Should the unsolicited request be expected to have a material impact on the portfolio, the member or candidate should use this opportunity to update the investment policy statement. Doing so would allow the client to fully understand the potential effect of the requested trade on his or her current goals or risk levels.

Members and candidates may have some clients who decline to modify their policy statements while insisting an unsolicited trade be made. In such instances, members or candidates will need to evaluate the effectiveness of their services to the client. The options available to the members or candidates will depend on the services provided by their employer. Some firms may allow for the trade to be executed in a new unmanaged account. If alternative options are not available, members and candidates ultimately will need to determine whether they should continue the advisory arrangement with the client.

Managing to an Index or Mandate

Some members and candidates do not manage money for individuals but are responsible for managing a fund to an index or an expected mandate. The responsibility of these members and candidates is to invest in a manner consistent with the stated mandate. For example, a member or candidate who serves as the fund manager for a large-cap income fund would not be following the fund mandate by investing heavily in small-cap or start-up companies whose stock is speculative in nature. Members and candidates who manage pooled assets to a specific mandate are not responsible for determining the suitability of the *fund* as an investment for investors who may be purchasing shares in the fund. The responsibility for determining the suitability of an investment for clients can be conferred only on members and candidates who have an advisory relationship with clients.

28 STANDARD III(C): RECOMMENDED PROCEDURES

Investment Policy Statement

To fulfill the basic provisions of Standard III(C), a member or candidate should put the needs and circumstances of each client and the client's investment objectives into a written investment policy statement. In formulating an investment policy for the client, the member or candidate should take the following into consideration:

- client identification—(1) type and nature of client, (2) the existence of separate beneficiaries, and (3) approximate portion of total client assets that the member or candidate is managing;
- investor objectives—(1) return objectives (income, growth in principal, maintenance of purchasing power) and (2) risk tolerance (suitability, stability of values);
- investor constraints—(1) liquidity needs, (2) expected cash flows (patterns of additions and/or withdrawals), (3) investable funds (assets and liabilities or other commitments), (4) time horizon, (5) tax considerations, (6) regulatory and legal circumstances, (7) investor preferences, prohibitions, circumstances, and unique needs, and (8) proxy voting responsibilities and guidance; and
- performance measurement benchmarks.

Regular Updates

The investor's objectives and constraints should be maintained and reviewed periodically to reflect any changes in the client's circumstances. Members and candidates should regularly compare client constraints with capital market expectations to arrive at an appropriate asset allocation. Changes in either factor may result in a fundamental change in asset allocation. Annual review is reasonable unless business or other reasons, such as a major change in market conditions, dictate more frequent review. Members and candidates should document attempts to carry out such a review if circumstances prevent it.

Suitability Test Policies

With the increase in regulatory required suitability tests, members and candidates should encourage their firms to develop related policies and procedures. The procedures will differ according to the size of the firm and the scope of the services offered to its clients.

The test procedures should require the investment professional to look beyond the potential return of the investment and include the following:

- an analysis of the impact on the portfolio's diversification,
- a comparison of the investment risks with the client's assessed risk tolerance, and
- the fit of the investment with the required investment strategy.

STANDARD III(C): APPLICATION OF THE STANDARD

29

Example 1 (Investment Suitability—Risk Profile):

Caleb Smith, an investment adviser, has two clients: Larry Robertson, 60 years old, and Gabriel Lanai, 40 years old. Both clients earn roughly the same salary, but Robertson has a much higher risk tolerance because he has a large asset base. Robertson is willing to invest part of his assets very aggressively; Lanai wants only to achieve a steady rate of return with low volatility to pay for his children's education. Smith recommends investing 20% of both portfolios in zero-yield, small-cap, high-technology equity issues.

> *Comment*: In Robertson's case, the investment may be appropriate because of his financial circumstances and aggressive investment position, but this investment is not suitable for Lanai. Smith is violating Standard III(C) by applying Robertson's investment strategy to Lanai because the two clients' financial circumstances and objectives differ.

Example 2 (Investment Suitability—Entire Portfolio):

Jessica McDowell, an investment adviser, suggests to Brian Crosby, a risk-averse client, that covered call options be used in his equity portfolio. The purpose would be to enhance Crosby's income and partially offset any untimely depreciation in the portfolio's value should the stock market or other circumstances affect his holdings unfavorably. McDowell educates Crosby about all possible outcomes, including the risk of incurring an added tax liability if a stock rises in price and is called away and, conversely, the risk of his holdings losing protection on the downside if prices drop sharply.

> *Comment*: When determining suitability of an investment, the primary focus should be the characteristics of the client's entire portfolio, not the characteristics of single securities on an issue-by-issue basis. The basic characteristics of the entire portfolio will largely determine whether investment recommendations are taking client factors into account. Therefore, the most important aspects of a particular investment are those that will affect the characteristics of the total portfolio. In this case, McDowell properly considers the investment in the context of the entire portfolio and thoroughly explains the investment to the client.

Example 3 (IPS Updating):

In a regular meeting with client Seth Jones, the portfolio managers at Blue Chip Investment Advisors are careful to allow some time to review his current needs and circumstances. In doing so, they learn that some significant changes have recently taken place in his life. A wealthy uncle left Jones an inheritance that increased his net worth fourfold, to US$1 million.

> *Comment*: The inheritance has significantly increased Jones's ability (and possibly his willingness) to assume risk and has diminished the average yield required to meet his current income needs. Jones's financial circumstances have definitely changed, so Blue Chip managers must update Jones's investment policy statement to reflect how his investment objectives have changed. Accordingly, the Blue Chip portfolio managers should consider

a somewhat higher equity ratio for his portfolio than was called for by the previous circumstances, and the managers' specific common stock recommendations might be heavily tilted toward low-yield, growth-oriented issues.

Example 4 (Following an Investment Mandate):

Louis Perkowski manages a high-income mutual fund. He purchases zero-dividend stock in a financial services company because he believes the stock is undervalued and is in a potential growth industry, which makes it an attractive investment.

> *Comment*: A zero-dividend stock does not seem to fit the mandate of the fund that Perkowski is managing. Unless Perkowski's investment fits within the mandate or is within the realm of allowable investments the fund has made clear in its disclosures, Perkowski has violated Standard III(C).

Example 5 (IPS Requirements and Limitations):

Max Gubler, chief investment officer of a property/casualty insurance subsidiary of a large financial conglomerate, wants to improve the diversification of the subsidiary's investment portfolio and increase its returns. The subsidiary's investment policy statement provides for highly liquid investments, such as large-cap equities and government, supranational, and corporate bonds with a minimum credit rating of AA and maturity of no more than five years. In a recent presentation, a venture capital group offered very attractive prospective returns on some of its private equity funds that provide seed capital to ventures. An exit strategy was already contemplated, but investors would have to observe a minimum three-year lockup period and a subsequent laddered exit option for a maximum of one-third of their shares per year. Gubler does not want to miss this opportunity. After extensive analysis, with the intent to optimize the return on the equity assets within the subsidiary's current portfolio, he invests 4% in this seed fund, leaving the portfolio's total equity exposure still well below its upper limit.

> *Comment*: Gubler is violating Standard III(A) Loyalty, Prudence, and Care as well as Standard III(C). His new investment locks up part of the subsidiary's assets for at least three years and up to as many as five years and possibly beyond. The IPS requires investments in highly liquid investments and describes accepted asset classes; private equity investments with a lockup period certainly do not qualify. Even without a lockup period, an asset class with only an occasional, and thus implicitly illiquid, market may not be suitable for the portfolio. Although an IPS typically describes objectives and constraints in great detail, the manager must also make every effort to understand the client's business and circumstances. Doing so should enable the manager to recognize, understand, and discuss with the client other factors that may be or may become material in the investment management process.

Example 6 (Submanager and IPS Reviews):

Paul Ostrowski's investment management business has grown significantly over the past couple of years, and some clients want to diversify internationally. Ostrowski decides to find a submanager to handle the expected international investments. Because this will be his first subadviser, Ostrowski uses the CFA Institute model "request for proposal" to design a questionnaire for his search. By his deadline, he receives seven completed questionnaires from a variety of domestic and international firms trying to gain his business. Ostrowski reviews all the applications in detail and decides to select the firm that charges the lowest fees because doing so will have the least impact on his firm's bottom line.

> *Comment*: When selecting an external manager or subadviser, Ostrowski needs to ensure that the new manager's services are appropriate for his clients. This due diligence includes comparing the risk profile of the clients with the investment strategy of the manager. In basing the decision on the fee structure alone, Ostrowski may be violating Standard III(C).
>
> When clients ask to diversify into international products, it is an appropriate time to review and update the clients' IPSs. Ostrowski's review may determine that the risk of international investments modifies the risk profiles of the clients or does not represent an appropriate investment.
>
> See also Standard V(A) Diligence and Reasonable Basis for further discussion of the review process needed in selecting appropriate submanagers.

Example 7 (Investment Suitability—Risk Profile):

Samantha Snead, a portfolio manager for Thomas Investment Counsel, Inc., specializes in managing public retirement funds and defined benefit pension plan accounts, all of which have long-term investment objectives. A year ago, Snead's employer, in an attempt to motivate and retain key investment professionals, introduced a bonus compensation system that rewards portfolio managers on the basis of quarterly performance relative to their peers and to certain benchmark indexes. In an attempt to improve the short-term performance of her accounts, Snead changes her investment strategy and purchases several high-beta stocks for client portfolios. These purchases are seemingly contrary to the clients' investment policy statements. Following their purchase, an officer of Griffin Corporation, one of Snead's pension fund clients, asks why Griffin Corporation's portfolio seems to be dominated by high-beta stocks of companies that often appear among the most actively traded issues. No change in objective or strategy has been recommended by Snead during the year.

> *Comment*: Snead violated Standard III(C) by investing the clients' assets in high-beta stocks. These high-risk investments are contrary to the long-term risk profile established in the clients' IPSs. Snead has changed the investment strategy of the clients in an attempt to reap short-term rewards offered by her firm's new compensation arrangement, not in response to changes in clients' investment policy statements.
>
> See also Standard VI(A) Disclosure of Conflicts.

Example 8 (Investment Suitability):

Andre Shrub owns and operates Conduit, an investment advisory firm. Prior to opening Conduit, Shrub was an account manager with Elite Investment, a hedge fund managed by his good friend Adam Reed. To attract clients to a new Conduit fund, Shrub offers lower-than-normal management fees. He can do so because the fund consists of two top-performing funds managed by Reed. Given his personal friendship with Reed and the prior performance record of these two funds, Shrub believes this new fund is a winning combination for all parties. Clients quickly invest with Conduit to gain access to the Elite funds. No one is turned away because Conduit is seeking to expand its assets under management.

Comment: Shrub has violated Standard III(C) because the risk profile of the new fund may not be suitable for every client. As an investment adviser, Shrub needs to establish an investment policy statement for each client and recommend only investments that match each client's risk and return profile in the IPS. Shrub is required to act as more than a simple sales agent for Elite.

Although Shrub cannot disobey the direct request of a client to purchase a specific security, he should fully discuss the risks of a planned purchase and provide reasons why it might not be suitable for a client. This requirement may lead members and candidates to decline new customers if those customers' requested investment decisions are significantly out of line with their stated requirements.

See also Standard V(A) Diligence and Reasonable Basis.

30 STANDARD III(D) PERFORMANCE PRESENTATION

- ☐ demonstrate the application of the Code of Ethics and Standards of Professional Conduct to situations involving issues of professional integrity
- ☐ recommend practices and procedures designed to prevent violations of the Code of Ethics and Standards of Professional Conduct
- ☐ identify conduct that conforms to the Code and Standards and conduct that violates the Code and Standards

> When communicating investment performance information, Members and Candidates must make reasonable efforts to ensure that it is fair, accurate, and complete.

Guidance

Standard III(D) requires members and candidates to provide credible performance information to clients and prospective clients and to avoid misstating performance or misleading clients and prospective clients about the investment performance of members or candidates or their firms. This standard encourages full disclosure of investment performance data to clients and prospective clients.

Standard III(D) covers any practice that would lead to misrepresentation of a member's or candidate's performance record, whether the practice involves performance presentation or performance measurement. This standard prohibits misrepresentations of past performance or reasonably expected performance. A member or candidate must give a fair and complete presentation of performance information whenever communicating data with respect to the performance history of individual accounts, composites or groups of accounts, or composites of an analyst's or firm's performance results. Furthermore, members and candidates should not state or imply that clients will obtain or benefit from a rate of return that was generated in the past.

The requirements of this standard are not limited to members and candidates managing separate accounts. Whenever a member or candidate provides performance information for which the manager is claiming responsibility, such as for pooled funds, the history must be accurate. Research analysts promoting the success or accuracy of their recommendations must ensure that their claims are fair, accurate, and complete.

If the presentation is brief, the member or candidate must make available to clients and prospects, on request, the detailed information supporting that communication. Best practice dictates that brief presentations include a reference to the limited nature of the information provided.

STANDARD III(D): RECOMMENDED PROCEDURES 31

Apply the GIPS Standards

For members and candidates who are showing the performance history of the assets they manage, compliance with the GIPS standards is the best method to meet their obligations under Standard III(D). Members and candidates should encourage their firms to comply with the GIPS standards.

Compliance without Applying GIPS Standards

Members and candidates can also meet their obligations under Standard III(D) by

- considering the knowledge and sophistication of the audience to whom a performance presentation is addressed,
- presenting the performance of the weighted composite of similar portfolios rather than using a single representative account,
- including terminated accounts as part of performance history with a clear indication of when the accounts were terminated,
- including disclosures that fully explain the performance results being reported (for example, stating, when appropriate, that results are simulated when model results are used, clearly indicating when the performance record is that of a prior entity, or disclosing whether the performance is gross of fees, net of fees, or after tax), and
- maintaining the data and records used to calculate the performance being presented.

STANDARD III(D): APPLICATION OF THE STANDARD 32

Example 1 (Performance Calculation and Length of Time):

Kyle Taylor of Taylor Trust Company, noting the performance of Taylor's common trust fund for the past two years, states in a brochure sent to his potential clients, "You can expect steady 25% annual compound growth of the value of your investments over the year." Taylor Trust's common trust fund did increase at the rate of 25% per year for the past year, which mirrored the increase of the entire market. The fund has never averaged that growth for more than one year, however, and the average rate of growth of all of its trust accounts for five years is 5% per year.

> *Comment*: Taylor's brochure is in violation of Standard III(D). Taylor should have disclosed that the 25% growth occurred only in one year. Additionally, Taylor did not include client accounts other than those in the firm's common trust fund. A general claim of firm performance should take into account the performance of all categories of accounts. Finally, by stating that clients can expect a steady 25% annual compound growth rate, Taylor is also violating Standard I(C) Misrepresentation, which prohibits assurances or guarantees regarding an investment.

Example 2 (Performance Calculation and Asset Weighting):

Anna Judd, a senior partner of Alexander Capital Management, circulates a performance report for the capital appreciation accounts for the years 1988 through 2004. The firm claims compliance with the GIPS standards. Returns are not calculated in accordance with the requirements of the GIPS standards, however, because the composites are not asset weighted.

> *Comment*: Judd is in violation of Standard III(D). When claiming compliance with the GIPS standards, firms must meet *all* of the requirements, make mandatory disclosures, and meet any other requirements that apply to that firm's specific situation. Judd's violation is not from any misuse of the data but from a false claim of GIPS compliance.

Example 3 (Performance Presentation and Prior Fund/ Employer):

Aaron McCoy is vice president and managing partner of the equity investment group of Mastermind Financial Advisors, a new business. Mastermind recruited McCoy because he had a proven six-year track record with G&P Financial. In developing Mastermind's advertising and marketing campaign, McCoy prepares an advertisement that includes the equity investment performance he achieved at G&P Financial. The advertisement for Mastermind does not identify the equity performance as being earned while at G&P. The advertisement is distributed to existing clients and prospective clients of Mastermind.

> *Comment*: McCoy has violated Standard III(D) by distributing an advertisement that contains material misrepresentations about the historical performance of Mastermind. Standard III(D) requires that members and candidates make every reasonable effort to ensure that performance information is a fair, accurate, and complete representation of an individual's or firm's performance. As a general matter, this standard does not prohibit showing past performance of funds managed at a prior firm as part of a performance track record as long as showing that record is accompanied by appropriate disclosures about where the performance took place and the person's specific role in achieving that performance. If McCoy chooses to use his past performance from G&P in Mastermind's advertising, he should make full disclosure of the source of the historical performance.

Example 4 (Performance Presentation and Simulated Results):

Jed Davis has developed a mutual fund selection product based on historical information from the 1990–95 period. Davis tested his methodology by applying it retroactively to data from the 1996–2003 period, thus producing simulated performance results for those years. In January 2004, Davis's employer decided to offer the product and Davis began promoting it through trade journal advertisements and direct dissemination to clients. The advertisements included the performance results for the 1996–2003 period but did not indicate that the results were simulated.

> *Comment*: Davis violated Standard III(D) by failing to clearly identify simulated performance results. Standard III(D) prohibits members and candidates from making any statements that misrepresent the performance achieved by them or their firms and requires members and candidates to make every reasonable effort to ensure that performance information presented to clients is fair, accurate, and complete. Use of simulated results should be accompanied by full disclosure as to the source of the performance data, including the fact that the results from 1995 through 2003 were the result of applying the model retroactively to that time period.

Example 5 (Performance Calculation and Selected Accounts Only):

In a presentation prepared for prospective clients, William Kilmer shows the rates of return realized over a five-year period by a "composite" of his firm's discretionary accounts that have a "balanced" objective. This composite, however, consisted of only a few of the accounts that met the balanced criterion set by the firm, excluded accounts under a certain asset level without disclosing the fact of their exclusion, and included accounts that did not have the balanced mandate because those accounts would boost the investment results. In addition, to achieve better results, Kilmer manipulated the narrow range of accounts included in the composite by changing the accounts that made up the composite over time.

> *Comment*: Kilmer violated Standard III(D) by misrepresenting the facts in the promotional material sent to prospective clients, distorting his firm's performance record, and failing to include disclosures that would have clarified the presentation.

Example 6 (Performance Attribution Changes):

Art Purell is reviewing the quarterly performance attribution reports for distribution to clients. Purell works for an investment management firm with a bottom-up, fundamentals-driven investment process that seeks to add value through stock selection. The attribution methodology currently compares each stock with its sector. The attribution report indicates that the value added this quarter came from asset allocation and that stock selection contributed negatively to the calculated return.

Through running several different scenarios, Purell discovers that calculating attribution by comparing each stock with its industry and then rolling the effect to the sector level improves the appearance of the manager's stock selection activities. Because the firm defines the attribution terms and the results better reflect the stated strategy, Purell recommends that the client reports should use the revised methodology.

Comment: Modifying the attribution methodology without proper notifications to clients would fail to meet the requirements of Standard III(D). Purrell's recommendation is being done solely for the interest of the firm to improve its perceived ability to meet the stated investment strategy. Such changes are unfair to clients and obscure the facts regarding the firm's abilities.

Had Purell believed the new methodology offered improvements to the original model, then he would have needed to report the results of both calculations to the client. The report should also include the reasons why the new methodology is preferred, which would allow the client to make a meaningful comparison to prior results and provide a basis for comparing future attributions.

Example 7 (Performance Calculation Methodology Disclosure):

While developing a new reporting package for existing clients, Alisha Singh, a performance analyst, discovers that her company's new system automatically calculates both time-weighted and money-weighted returns. She asks the head of client services and retention which value would be preferred given that the firm has various investment strategies that include bonds, equities, securities without leverage, and alternatives. Singh is told not to label the return value so that the firm may show whichever value is greatest for the period.

Comment: Following these instructions would lead to Singh violating Standard III(D). In reporting inconsistent return values, Singh would not be providing complete information to the firm's clients. Full information is provided when clients have sufficient information to judge the performance generated by the firm.

Example 8 (Performance Calculation Methodology Disclosure):

Richmond Equity Investors manages a long–short equity fund in which clients can trade once a week (on Fridays). For transparency reasons, a daily net asset value of the fund is calculated by Richmond. The monthly fact sheets of the fund report month-to-date and year-to-date performance. Richmond publishes the performance based on the higher of the last trading day of the month (typically, not the last business day) or the last business day of the month as determined by Richmond. The fact sheet mentions only that the data are as of the end of the month, without giving the exact date. Maggie Clark, the investment performance analyst in charge of the calculations, is concerned about the frequent changes and asks her supervisor whether they are appropriate.

Comment: Clark's actions in questioning the changing performance metric comply with Standard III(D). She has shown concern that these changes are not presenting an accurate and complete picture of the performance generated.

STANDARD III(E) PRESERVATION OF CONFIDENTIALITY

33

- ☐ demonstrate the application of the Code of Ethics and Standards of Professional Conduct to situations involving issues of professional integrity
- ☐ recommend practices and procedures designed to prevent violations of the Code of Ethics and Standards of Professional Conduct
- ☐ identify conduct that conforms to the Code and Standards and conduct that violates the Code and Standards

Members and Candidates must keep information about current, former, and prospective clients confidential unless:

- The information concerns illegal activities on the part of the client;
- Disclosure is required by law; or
- The client or prospective client permits disclosure of the information.

Guidance

Highlights:

- *Status of Client*
- *Compliance with Laws*
- *Electronic Information and Security*
- *Professional Conduct Investigations by CFA Institute*

Standard III(E) requires that members and candidates preserve the confidentiality of information communicated to them by their clients, prospective clients, and former clients. This standard is applicable when (1) the member or candidate receives information because of his or her special ability to conduct a portion of the client's business or personal affairs and (2) the member or candidate receives information that arises from or is relevant to that portion of the client's business that is the subject of the special or confidential relationship. If disclosure of the information is required by law or the information concerns illegal activities by the client, however, the member or candidate may have an obligation to report the activities to the appropriate authorities.

Status of Client

This standard protects the confidentiality of client information even if the person or entity is no longer a client of the member or candidate. Therefore, members and candidates must continue to maintain the confidentiality of client records even after the client relationship has ended. If a client or former client expressly authorizes the member or candidate to disclose information, however, the member or candidate may follow the terms of the authorization and provide the information.

Compliance with Laws

As a general matter, members and candidates must comply with applicable law. If applicable law requires disclosure of client information in certain circumstances, members and candidates must comply with the law. Similarly, if applicable law requires members and candidates to maintain confidentiality, even if the information concerns illegal activities on the part of the client, members and candidates should not disclose such information. Additionally, applicable laws, such as inter-departmental communication restrictions within financial institutions, can impose limitations on information flow about a client within an entity that may lead to a violation of confidentiality. When in doubt, members and candidates should consult with their employer's compliance personnel or legal counsel before disclosing confidential information about clients.

Electronic Information and Security

Because of the ever-increasing volume of electronically stored information, members and candidates need to be particularly aware of possible accidental disclosures. Many employers have strict policies about how to electronically communicate sensitive client information and store client information on personal laptops, mobile devices, or portable disk/flash drives. In recent years, regulatory authorities have imposed stricter data security laws applying to the use of mobile remote digital communication, including the use of social media, that must be considered. Standard III(E) does not require members or candidates to become experts in information security technology, but they should have a thorough understanding of the policies of their employer. The size and operations of the firm will lead to differing policies for ensuring the security of confidential information maintained within the firm. Members and candidates should encourage their firm to conduct regular periodic training on confidentiality procedures for all firm personnel, including portfolio associates, receptionists, and other non-investment staff who have routine direct contact with clients and their records.

Professional Conduct Investigations by CFA Institute

The requirements of Standard III(E) are not intended to prevent members and candidates from cooperating with an investigation by the CFA Institute Professional Conduct Program (PCP). When permissible under applicable law, members and candidates shall consider the PCP an extension of themselves when requested to provide information about a client in support of a PCP investigation into their own conduct. Members and candidates are encouraged to cooperate with investigations into the conduct of others. Any information turned over to the PCP is kept in the strictest confidence. Members and candidates will not be considered in violation of this standard by forwarding confidential information to the PCP.

34 STANDARD III(E): RECOMMENDED PROCEDURES

The simplest, most conservative, and most effective way to comply with Standard III(E) is to avoid disclosing any information received from a client except to authorized fellow employees who are also working for the client. In some instances, however, a member or candidate may want to disclose information received from clients that is outside the scope of the confidential relationship and does not involve illegal activities. Before making such a disclosure, a member or candidate should ask the following:

- In what context was the information disclosed? If disclosed in a discussion of work being performed for the client, is the information relevant to the work?

- Is the information background material that, if disclosed, will enable the member or candidate to improve service to the client?

Members and candidates need to understand and follow their firm's electronic information communication and storage procedures. If the firm does not have procedures in place, members and candidates should encourage the development of procedures that appropriately reflect the firm's size and business operations.

Communicating with Clients

Technological changes are constantly enhancing the methods that are used to communicate with clients and prospective clients. Members and candidates should make reasonable efforts to ensure that firm-supported communication methods and compliance procedures follow practices designed for preventing accidental distribution of confidential information. Given the rate at which technology changes, a regular review of privacy protection measures is encouraged.

Members and candidates should be diligent in discussing with clients the appropriate methods for providing confidential information. It is important to convey to clients that not all firm-sponsored resources may be appropriate for such communications.

STANDARD III(E): APPLICATION OF THE STANDARD 35

Example 1 (Possessing Confidential Information):

Sarah Connor, a financial analyst employed by Johnson Investment Counselors, Inc., provides investment advice to the trustees of City Medical Center. The trustees have given her a number of internal reports concerning City Medical's needs for physical plant renovation and expansion. They have asked Connor to recommend investments that would generate capital appreciation in endowment funds to meet projected capital expenditures. Connor is approached by a local businessman, Thomas Kasey, who is considering a substantial contribution either to City Medical Center or to another local hospital. Kasey wants to find out the building plans of both institutions before making a decision, but he does not want to speak to the trustees.

> *Comment*: The trustees gave Connor the internal reports so she could advise them on how to manage their endowment funds. Because the information in the reports is clearly both confidential and within the scope of the confidential relationship, Standard III(E) requires that Connor refuse to divulge information to Kasey.

Example 2 (Disclosing Confidential Information):

Lynn Moody is an investment officer at the Lester Trust Company. She has an advisory customer who has talked to her about giving approximately US$50,000 to charity to reduce her income taxes. Moody is also treasurer of the Home for Indigent Widows (HIW), which is planning its annual giving campaign. HIW hopes to expand its list of prospects, particularly those capable of substantial gifts. Moody recommends that HIW's vice president for corporate gifts call on her customer and ask for a donation in the US$50,000 range.

Comment: Even though the attempt to help the Home for Indigent Widows was well intended, Moody violated Standard III(E) by revealing confidential information about her client.

Example 3 (Disclosing Possible Illegal Activity):

Government officials approach Casey Samuel, the portfolio manager for Garcia Company's pension plan, to examine pension fund records. They tell her that Garcia's corporate tax returns are being audited and the pension fund is being reviewed. Two days earlier, Samuel had learned in a regular investment review with Garcia officers that potentially excessive and improper charges were being made to the pension plan by Garcia. Samuel consults her employer's general counsel and is advised that Garcia has probably violated tax and fiduciary regulations and laws.

Comment: Samuel should inform her supervisor of these activities, and her employer should take steps, with Garcia, to remedy the violations. If that approach is not successful, Samuel and her employer should seek advice of legal counsel to determine the appropriate steps to be taken. Samuel may well have a duty to disclose the evidence she has of the continuing legal violations and to resign as asset manager for Garcia.

Example 4 (Disclosing Possible Illegal Activity):

David Bradford manages money for a family-owned real estate development corporation. He also manages the individual portfolios of several of the family members and officers of the corporation, including the chief financial officer (CFO). Based on the financial records of the corporation and some questionable practices of the CFO that Bradford has observed, Bradford believes that the CFO is embezzling money from the corporation and putting it into his personal investment account.

Comment: Bradford should check with his firm's compliance department or appropriate legal counsel to determine whether applicable securities regulations require reporting the CFO's financial records.

Example 5 (Accidental Disclosure of Confidential Information):

Lynn Moody is an investment officer at the Lester Trust Company (LTC). She has stewardship of a significant number of individually managed taxable accounts. In addition to receiving quarterly written reports, about a dozen high-net-worth individuals have indicated to Moody a willingness to receive communications about overall economic and financial market outlooks directly from her by way of a social media platform. Under the direction of her firm's technology and compliance departments, she established a new group page on an existing social media platform specifically for her clients. In the instructions provided to clients, Moody asked them to "join" the group so they may be granted access to the posted content. The instructions also advised clients that all comments posted would be available to the public and thus the platform was not an appropriate method for communicating personal or confidential information.

Six months later, in early January, Moody posted LTC's year-end "Market Outlook." The report outlined a new asset allocation strategy that the firm is adding to its recommendations in the new year. Moody introduced the publication with a note informing her clients that she would be discussing the changes with them individually in their upcoming meetings.

One of Moody's clients responded directly on the group page that his family recently experienced a major change in their financial profile. The client described highly personal and confidential details of the event. Unfortunately, all clients that were part of the group were also able to read the detailed posting until Moody was able to have the comment removed.

> *Comment*: Moody has taken reasonable steps for protecting the confidentiality of client information while using the social media platform. She provided instructions clarifying that all information posted to the site would be publicly viewable to all group members and warned against using this method for communicating confidential information. The accidental disclosure of confidential information by a client is not under Moody's control. Her actions to remove the information promptly once she became aware further align with Standard III(E).
>
> In understanding the potential sensitivity clients express surrounding the confidentiality of personal information, this event highlights a need for further training. Moody might advocate for additional warnings or controls for clients when they consider using social media platforms for two-way communications.

STANDARD IV: DUTIES TO EMPLOYERS

36

- ☐ demonstrate the application of the Code of Ethics and Standards of Professional Conduct to situations involving issues of professional integrity
- ☐ recommend practices and procedures designed to prevent violations of the Code of Ethics and Standards of Professional Conduct
- ☐ identify conduct that conforms to the Code and Standards and conduct that violates the Code and Standards

Standard IV(A) Loyalty

In matters related to their employment, Members and Candidates must act for the benefit of their employer and not deprive their employer of the advantage of their skills and abilities, divulge confidential information, or otherwise cause harm to their employer.

Guidance

Highlights:

- *Employer Responsibilities*
- *Independent Practice*
- *Leaving an Employer*
- *Use of Social Media*

- *Whistleblowing*
- *Nature of Employment*

Standard IV(A) requires members and candidates to protect the interests of their firm by refraining from any conduct that would injure the firm, deprive it of profit, or deprive it of the member's or candidate's skills and ability. Members and candidates must always place the interests of clients above the interests of their employer but should also consider the effects of their conduct on the sustainability and integrity of the employer firm. In matters related to their employment, members and candidates must not engage in conduct that harms the interests of their employer. Implicit in this standard is the obligation of members and candidates to comply with the policies and procedures established by their employers that govern the employer–employee relationship—to the extent that such policies and procedures do not conflict with applicable laws, rules, or regulations or the Code and Standards.

This standard is not meant to be a blanket requirement to place employer interests ahead of personal interests in all matters. The standard does not require members and candidates to subordinate important personal and family obligations to their work. Members and candidates should enter into a dialogue with their employer about balancing personal and employment obligations when personal matters may interfere with their work on a regular or significant basis.

Employer Responsibilities

The employer–employee relationship imposes duties and responsibilities on both parties. Employers must recognize the duties and responsibilities that they owe to their employees if they expect to have content and productive employees.

Members and candidates are encouraged to provide their employer with a copy of the Code and Standards. These materials will inform the employer of the responsibilities of a CFA Institute member or a candidate in the CFA Program. The Code and Standards also serve as a basis for questioning employer policies and practices that conflict with these responsibilities.

Employers are not obligated to adhere to the Code and Standards. In expecting to retain competent employees who are members and candidates, however, they should not develop conflicting policies and procedures. The employer is responsible for a positive working environment, which includes an ethical workplace. Senior management has the additional responsibility to devise compensation structures and incentive arrangements that do not encourage unethical behavior.

Independent Practice

Included in Standard IV(A) is the requirement that members and candidates abstain from independent competitive activity that could conflict with the interests of their employer. Although Standard IV(A) does not preclude members or candidates from entering into an independent business while still employed, members and candidates who plan to engage in independent practice for compensation must notify their employer and describe the types of services they will render to prospective independent clients, the expected duration of the services, and the compensation for the services. Members and candidates should not render services until they receive consent from their employer to all of the terms of the arrangement. "Practice" means any service that the employer currently makes available for remuneration. "Undertaking independent practice" means engaging in competitive business, as opposed to making preparations to begin such practice.

Leaving an Employer

When members and candidates are planning to leave their current employer, they must continue to act in the employer's best interest. They must not engage in any activities that would conflict with this duty until their resignation becomes effective. It is difficult to define specific guidelines for those members and candidates who are planning to compete with their employer as part of a new venture. The circumstances of each situation must be reviewed to distinguish permissible preparations from violations of duty. Activities that might constitute a violation, especially in combination, include the following:

- misappropriation of trade secrets,
- misuse of confidential information,
- solicitation of the employer's clients prior to cessation of employment,
- self-dealing (appropriating for one's own property a business opportunity or information belonging to one's employer), and
- misappropriation of clients or client lists.

A departing employee is generally free to make arrangements or preparations to go into a competitive business before terminating the relationship with his or her employer as long as such preparations do not breach the employee's duty of loyalty. A member or candidate who is contemplating seeking other employment must not contact existing clients or potential clients prior to leaving his or her employer for purposes of soliciting their business for the new employer. Once notice is provided to the employer of the intent to resign, the member or candidate must follow the employer's policies and procedures related to notifying clients of his or her planned departure. In addition, the member or candidate must not take records or files to a new employer without the written permission of the previous employer.

Once an employee has left the firm, the skills and experience that an employee obtained while employed are not "confidential" or "privileged" information. Similarly, simple knowledge of the names and existence of former clients is generally not confidential information unless deemed such by an agreement or by law. Standard IV(A) does not prohibit experience or knowledge gained at one employer from being used at another employer. Firm records or work performed on behalf of the firm that is stored in paper copy or electronically for the member's or candidate's convenience while employed, however, should be erased or returned to the employer unless the firm gives permission to keep those records after employment ends.

The standard does not prohibit former employees from contacting clients of their previous firm as long as the contact information does not come from the records of the former employer or violate an applicable "noncompete agreement." Members and candidates are free to use public information after departing to contact former clients without violating Standard IV(A) as long as there is no specific agreement not to do so.

Employers often require employees to sign noncompete agreements that preclude a departing employee from engaging in certain conduct. Members and candidates should take care to review the terms of any such agreement when leaving their employer to determine what, if any, conduct those agreements may prohibit.

In some markets, there are agreements between employers within an industry that outline information that departing employees are permitted to take upon resignation, such as the "Protocol for Broker Recruiting" in the United States. These agreements ease individuals' transition between firms that have agreed to follow the outlined procedures. Members and candidates who move between firms that sign such agreements may rely on the protections provided as long as they faithfully adhere to all the procedures outlined.

For example, under the agreement between many US brokers, individuals are allowed to take some general client contact information when departing. To be protected, a copy of the information the individual is taking must be provided to the local management team for review. Additionally, the specific client information may only be used by the departing employee and not others employed by the new firm.

Use of Social Media

The growth in various online networking platforms, such as LinkedIn, X, and Facebook (commonly referred to as social media platforms), is providing new opportunities and challenges for businesses. Members and candidates should understand and abide by all applicable firm policies and regulations as to the acceptable use of social media platforms to interact with clients and prospective clients. This is especially important when a member or candidate is planning to leave an employer.

Social media use makes determining how and when departure notification is delivered to clients more complex. Members and candidates may have developed profiles on these platforms that include connections with individuals who are clients of the firm, as well as individuals unrelated to their employer. Communications through social media platforms that potentially reach current clients should adhere to the employer's policies and procedures regarding notification of departing employees.

Social media connections with clients are also raising questions concerning the differences between public information and firm property. Specific accounts and user profiles of members and candidates may be created for solely professional reasons, including firm-approved accounts for client engagements. Such firm-approved business-related accounts would be considered part of the firm's assets, thus requiring members and candidates to transfer or delete the accounts as directed by their firm's policies and procedures. Best practice for members and candidates is to maintain separate accounts for their personal and professional social media activities. Members and candidates should discuss with their employers how profiles should be treated when a single account includes personal connections and also is used to conduct aspects of their professional activities.

Whistleblowing

A member's or candidate's personal interests, as well as the interests of his or her employer, are secondary to protecting the integrity of capital markets and the interests of clients. Therefore, circumstances may arise (e.g., when an employer is engaged in illegal or unethical activity) in which members and candidates must act contrary to their employer's interests in order to comply with their duties to the market and clients. In such instances, activities that would normally violate a member's or candidate's duty to his or her employer (such as contradicting employer instructions, violating certain policies and procedures, or preserving a record by copying employer records) may be justified. Such action would be permitted only if the intent is clearly aimed at protecting clients or the integrity of the market, not for personal gain.

Nature of Employment

A wide variety of business relationships exists within the investment industry. For instance, a member or candidate may be an employee or an independent contractor. Members and candidates must determine whether they are employees or independent contractors in order to determine the applicability of Standard IV(A). This issue will be decided largely by the degree of control exercised by the employing entity over the member or candidate. Factors determining control include whether the member's or candidate's hours, work location, and other parameters of the job are set; whether facilities are provided to the member or candidate; whether the member's or candidate's expenses are reimbursed; whether the member or candidate seeks work from other employers; and the number of clients or employers the member or candidate works for.

A member's or candidate's duties within an independent contractor relationship are governed by the oral or written agreement between the member and the client. Members and candidates should take care to define clearly the scope of their responsibilities and the expectations of each client within the context of each relationship. Once a member or candidate establishes a relationship with a client, the member or candidate has a duty to abide by the terms of the agreement.

STANDARD IV(A): RECOMMENDED PROCEDURES

37

Employers may establish codes of conduct and operating procedures for their employees to follow. Members and candidates should fully understand the policies to ensure that they are not in conflict with the Code and Standards. The following topics identify policies that members and candidates should encourage their firms to adopt if the policies are not currently in place.

Competition Policy

A member or candidate must understand any restrictions placed by the employer on offering similar services outside the firm while employed by the firm. The policy may outline the procedures for requesting approval to undertake the outside service or may be a strict prohibition of such service. If a member's or candidate's employer elects to have its employees sign a noncompete agreement as part of the employment agreement, the member or candidate should ensure that the details are clear and fully explained prior to signing the agreement.

Termination Policy

Members and candidates should clearly understand the termination policies of their employer. Termination policies should establish clear procedures regarding the resignation process, including addressing how the termination will be disclosed to clients and staff and whether updates posted through social media platforms will be allowed. The firm's policy may also outline the procedures for transferring ongoing research and account management responsibilities. Finally, the procedures should address agreements that allow departing employees to remove specific client-related information upon resignation.

Incident-Reporting Procedures

Members and candidates should be aware of their firm's policies related to whistleblowing and encourage their firm to adopt industry best practices in this area. Many firms are required by regulatory mandates to establish confidential and anonymous reporting procedures that allow employees to report potentially unethical and illegal activities in the firm.

Employee Classification

Members and candidates should understand their status within their employer firm. Firms are encouraged to adopt a standardized classification structure (e.g., part time, full time, outside contractor) for their employees and indicate how each of the firm's policies applies to each employee class.

38 STANDARD IV(A): APPLICATION OF THE STANDARD

Example 1 (Soliciting Former Clients):

Samuel Magee manages pension accounts for Trust Assets, Inc., but has become frustrated with the working environment and has been offered a position with Fiduciary Management. Before resigning from Trust Assets, Magee asks four big accounts to leave that firm and open accounts with Fiduciary. Magee also persuades several prospective clients to sign agreements with Fiduciary Management. Magee had previously made presentations to these prospects on behalf of Trust Assets.

> *Comment*: Magee violated the employee–employer principle requiring him to act solely for his employer's benefit. Magee's duty is to Trust Assets as long as he is employed there. The solicitation of Trust Assets' current clients and prospective clients is unethical and violates Standard IV(A).

Example 2 (Former Employer's Documents and Files):

James Hightower has been employed by Jason Investment Management Corporation for 15 years. He began as an analyst but assumed increasing responsibilities and is now a senior portfolio manager and a member of the firm's investment policy committee. Hightower has decided to leave Jason Investment and start his own investment management business. He has been careful not to tell any of Jason's clients that he is leaving; he does not want to be accused of breaching his duty to Jason by soliciting Jason's clients before his departure. Hightower is planning to copy and take with him the following documents and information he developed or worked on while at Jason: (1) the client list, with addresses, telephone numbers, and other pertinent client information; (2) client account statements; (3) sample marketing presentations to prospective clients containing Jason's performance record; (4) Jason's recommended list of securities; (5) computer models to determine asset allocations for accounts with various objectives; (6) computer models for stock selection; and (7) personal computer spreadsheets for Hightower's major corporate recommendations, which he developed when he was an analyst.

> *Comment*: Except with the consent of their employer, departing members and candidates may not take employer property, which includes books, records, reports, and other materials, because taking such materials may interfere with their employer's business opportunities. Taking any employer records, even those the member or candidate prepared, violates Standard IV(A). Employer records include items stored in hard copy or any other medium (e.g., home computers, portable storage devices, cell phones).

Example 3 (Addressing Rumors):

Reuben Winston manages all-equity portfolios at Target Asset Management (TAM), a large, established investment counselor. Ten years previously, Philpott & Company, which manages a family of global bond mutual funds, acquired TAM in a diversification move. After the merger, the combined operations prospered in the fixed-income business but the equity management business at TAM languished. Lately, a few of the equity pension accounts that had been with TAM before the merger have terminated their relationships with TAM. One day, Winston finds on his voice mail the following message from a concerned client: "Hey! I just heard that Philpott is close to announcing the sale of your firm's equity management business to Rugged Life. What is going on?" Not being aware of any such deal, Winston and his associates are stunned. Their internal inquiries are met with denials from Philpott management, but the rumors persist. Feeling left in the dark, Winston contemplates leading an employee buyout of TAM's equity management business.

> *Comment*: An employee-led buyout of TAM's equity asset management business would be consistent with Standard IV(A) because it would rest on the permission of the employer and, ultimately, the clients. In this case, however, in which employees suspect the senior managers or principals are not truthful or forthcoming, Winston should consult legal counsel to determine appropriate action.

Example 4 (Ownership of Completed Prior Work):

Laura Clay, who is unemployed, wants part-time consulting work while seeking a full-time analyst position. During an interview at Bradley Associates, a large institutional asset manager, Clay is told that the firm has no immediate research openings but would be willing to pay her a flat fee to complete a study of the wireless communications industry within a given period of time. Clay would be allowed unlimited access to Bradley's research files and would be welcome to come to the offices and use whatever support facilities are available during normal working hours. Bradley's research director does not seek any exclusivity for Clay's output, and the two agree to the arrangement on a handshake. As Clay nears completion of the study, she is offered an analyst job in the research department of Winston & Company, a brokerage firm, and she is pondering submitting the draft of her wireless study for publication by Winston.

> *Comment*: Although she is under no written contractual obligation to Bradley, Clay has an obligation to let Bradley act on the output of her study before Winston & Company or Clay uses the information to their advantage. That is, unless Bradley gives permission to Clay and waives its rights to her wireless report, Clay would be in violation of Standard IV(A) if she were to immediately recommend to Winston the same transactions recommended in the report to Bradley. Furthermore, Clay must not take from Bradley any research file material or other property that she may have used.

Example 5 (Ownership of Completed Prior Work):

Emma Madeline, a recent college graduate and a candidate in the CFA Program, spends her summer as an unpaid intern at Murdoch and Lowell. The senior managers at Murdoch are attempting to bring the firm into compliance with the GIPS standards, and Madeline is assigned to assist in its efforts. Two months into her internship, Madeline applies for a job at McMillan & Company, which has plans to become GIPS compliant. Madeline accepts the job with McMillan. Before leaving Murdoch, she copies the firm's software that she helped develop because she believes this software will assist her in her new position.

> *Comment*: Even though Madeline does not receive monetary compensation for her services at Murdoch, she has used firm resources in creating the software and is considered an employee because she receives compensation and benefits in the form of work experience and knowledge. By copying the software, Madeline violated Standard IV(A) because she misappropriated Murdoch's property without permission.

Example 6 (Soliciting Former Clients):

Dennis Elliot has hired Sam Chisolm, who previously worked for a competing firm. Chisolm left his former firm after 18 years of employment. When Chisolm begins working for Elliot, he wants to contact his former clients because he knows them well and is certain that many will follow him to his new employer. Is Chisolm in violation of Standard IV(A) if he contacts his former clients?

Comment: Because client records are the property of the firm, contacting former clients for any reason through the use of client lists or other information taken from a former employer without permission would be a violation of Standard IV(A). In addition, the nature and extent of the contact with former clients may be governed by the terms of any noncompete agreement signed by the employee and the former employer that covers contact with former clients after employment.

Simple knowledge of the names and existence of former clients is not confidential information, just as skills or experience that an employee obtains while employed are not "confidential" or "privileged" information. The Code and Standards do not impose a prohibition on the use of experience or knowledge gained at one employer from being used at another employer. The Code and Standards also do not prohibit former employees from contacting clients of their previous firm, in the absence of a noncompete agreement. Members and candidates are free to use public information about their former firm after departing to contact former clients without violating Standard IV(A).

In the absence of a noncompete agreement, as long as Chisolm maintains his duty of loyalty to his employer before joining Elliot's firm, does not take steps to solicit clients until he has left his former firm, and does not use material from his former employer without its permission after he has left, he is not in violation of the Code and Standards.

Example 7 (Starting a New Firm):

Geraldine Allen currently works at a registered investment company as an equity analyst. Without notice to her employer, she registers with government authorities to start an investment company that will compete with her employer, but she does not actively seek clients. Does registration of this competing company with the appropriate regulatory authorities constitute a violation of Standard IV(A)?

Comment: Allen's preparation for the new business by registering with the regulatory authorities does not conflict with the work for her employer if the preparations have been done on Allen's own time outside the office and if Allen will not be soliciting clients for the business or otherwise operating the new company until she has left her current employer.

Example 8 (Competing with Current Employer):

Several employees are planning to depart their current employer within a few weeks and have been careful to not engage in any activities that would conflict with their duty to their current employer. They have just learned that one of their employer's clients has undertaken a request for proposal (RFP) to review and possibly hire a new investment consultant. The RFP has been sent to the employer and all of its competitors. The group believes that the new entity to be formed would be qualified to respond to the RFP and be eligible for the business. The RFP submission period is likely to conclude before the employees' resignations are effective. Is it permissible for the group of departing employees to respond to the RFP for their anticipated new firm?

> *Comment*: A group of employees responding to an RFP that their employer is also responding to would lead to direct competition between the employees and the employer. Such conduct violates Standard IV(A) unless the group of employees receives permission from their employer as well as the entity sending out the RFP.

Example 9 (Externally Compensated Assignments):

Alfonso Mota is a research analyst with Tyson Investments. He works part time as a mayor for his hometown, a position for which he receives compensation. Must Mota seek permission from Tyson to serve as mayor?

> *Comment*: If Mota's mayoral duties are so extensive and time-consuming that they might detract from his ability to fulfill his responsibilities at Tyson, he should discuss his outside activities with his employer and come to a mutual agreement regarding how to manage his personal commitments with his responsibilities to his employer.

Example 10 (Soliciting Former Clients):

After leaving her employer, Shawna McQuillen establishes her own money management business. While with her former employer, she did not sign a noncompete agreement that would have prevented her from soliciting former clients. Upon her departure, she does not take any of her client lists or contact information and she clears her personal computer of any employer records, including client contact information. She obtains the phone numbers of her former clients through public records and contacts them to solicit their business.

> *Comment*: McQuillen is not in violation of Standard IV(A) because she has not used information or records from her former employer and is not prevented by an agreement with her former employer from soliciting her former clients.

Example 11 (Whistleblowing Actions):

Meredith Rasmussen works on a buy-side trading desk and concentrates on in-house trades for a hedge fund subsidiary managed by a team at the investment management firm. The hedge fund has been very successful and is marketed globally by the firm. From her experience as the trader for much of the activity of the fund, Rasmussen has become quite knowledgeable about the hedge fund's strategy, tactics, and performance. When a distinct break in the market occurs, however, and many of the securities involved in the hedge fund's strategy decline markedly in value, Rasmussen observes that the reported performance of the hedge fund does not reflect this decline. In her experience, the lack of any effect is a very unlikely occurrence. She approaches the head of trading about her concern and is told that she should not ask any questions and that the fund is big and successful and is not her concern. She is fairly sure something is not right, so she contacts the compliance officer, who also tells her to stay away from the issue of this hedge fund's reporting.

Comment: Rasmussen has clearly come upon an error in policies, procedures, and compliance practices in the firm's operations. Having been unsuccessful in finding a resolution with her supervisor and the compliance officer, Rasmussen should consult the firm's whistleblowing policy to determine the appropriate next step toward informing management of her concerns. The potentially unethical actions of the investment management division are appropriate grounds for further disclosure, so Rasmussen's whistleblowing would not represent a violation of Standard IV(A).

See also Standard I(D) Misconduct and Standard IV(C) Responsibilities of Supervisors.

Example 12 (Soliciting Former Clients):

Angel Crome has been a private banker for YBSafe Bank for the past eight years. She has been very successful and built a considerable client portfolio during that time but is extremely frustrated by the recent loss of reputation by her current employer and subsequent client insecurity. A locally renowned headhunter contacted Crome a few days ago and offered her an interesting job with a competing private bank. This bank offers a substantial signing bonus for advisers with their own client portfolios. Crome figures that she can solicit at least 70% of her clients to follow her and gladly enters into the new employment contract.

Comment: Crome may contact former clients upon termination of her employment with YBSafe Bank, but she is prohibited from using client records built by and kept with her in her capacity as an employee of YBSafe Bank. Client lists are proprietary information of her former employer and must not be used for her or her new employer's benefit. The use of written, electronic, or any other form of records other than publicly available information to contact her former clients at YBSafe Bank will be a violation of Standard IV(A).

Example 13 (Notification of Code and Standards):

Krista Smith is a relatively new assistant trader for the fixed-income desk of a major investment bank. She is on a team responsible for structuring collateralized debt obligations (CDOs) made up of securities in the inventory of the trading desk. At a meeting of the team, senior executives explain the opportunity to eventually separate the CDO into various risk-rated tranches to be sold to the clients of the firm. After the senior executives leave the meeting, the head trader announces various responsibilities of each member of the team and then says, "This is a good time to unload some of the junk we have been stuck with for a while and disguise it with ratings and a thick, unreadable prospectus, so don't be shy in putting this CDO together. Just kidding." Smith is worried by this remark and asks some of her colleagues what the head trader meant. They all respond that he was just kidding but that there is some truth in the remark because the CDO is seen by management as an opportunity to improve the quality of the securities in the firm's inventory.

Concerned about the ethical environment of the workplace, Smith decides to talk to her supervisor about her concerns and provides the head trader with a copy of the Code and Standards. Smith discusses the principle of placing the client above the interest of the firm and the possibility that the development of the new CDO will not adhere to this responsibility. The head trader assures Smith that the appropriate analysis will be conducted when determining the appropriate securities for collateral. Furthermore, the ratings are assigned by an independent firm and the prospectus will include full and factual disclosures. Smith is reassured by the meeting, but she also reviews the company's procedures and requirements for reporting potential violations of company policy and securities laws.

> *Comment*: Smith's review of the company policies and procedures for reporting violations allows her to be prepared to report through the appropriate whistleblower process if she decides that the CDO development process involves unethical actions by others. Smith's actions comply with the Code and Standards principles of placing the client's interests first and being loyal to her employer. In providing her supervisor with a copy of the Code and Standards, Smith is highlighting the high level of ethical conduct she is required to adhere to in her professional activities.

Example 14 (Leaving an Employer):

Laura Webb just left her position as portfolio analyst at Research Systems, Inc. (RSI). Her employment contract included a non-solicitation agreement that requires her to wait two years before soliciting RSI clients for any investment-related services. Upon leaving, Webb was informed that RSI would contact clients immediately about her departure and introduce her replacement.

While working at RSI, Webb connected with clients, other industry associates, and friends through her LinkedIn network. Her business and personal relationships were intermingled because she considered many of her clients to be personal friends. Realizing that her LinkedIn network would be a valuable resource for new employment opportunities, she updated her profile several days following her departure from RSI. LinkedIn automatically sent a notification to Webb's entire network that her employment status had been changed in her profile.

> *Comment*: Prior to her departure, Webb should have discussed any client information contained in her social media networks. By updating her LinkedIn profile after RSI notified clients and after her employment ended, she has appropriately placed her employer's interests ahead of her own personal interests. In addition, she has not violated the non-solicitation agreement with RSI, unless it prohibited any contact with clients during the two-year period.

Example 15 (Confidential Firm Information):

Sanjay Gupta is a research analyst at Naram Investment Management (NIM). NIM uses a team-based research process to develop recommendations on investment opportunities covered by the team members. Gupta, like others, provides commentary for NIM's clients through the company blog, which is posted weekly on the NIM password-protected website. According to NIM's policy, every contribution to the website must be approved by the company's compliance department before posting. Any opinions expressed on the website are disclosed as representing the perspective of NIM.

Gupta also writes a personal blog to share his experiences with friends and family. As with most blogs, Gupta's personal blog is widely available to interested readers through various internet search engines. Occasionally, when he disagrees with the team-based research opinions of NIM, Gupta uses his personal blog to express his own opinions as a counterpoint to the commentary posted on the NIM website. Gupta believes this provides his readers with a more complete perspective on these investment opportunities.

Comment: Gupta is in violation of Standard IV(A) for disclosing confidential firm information through his personal blog. The recommendations on the firm's blog to clients are not freely available across the internet, but his personal blog post indirectly provides the firm's recommendations.

Additionally, by posting research commentary on his personal blog, Gupta is using firm resources for his personal advantage. To comply with Standard IV(A), members and candidates must receive consent from their employer prior to using company resources.

39 STANDARD IV(B) ADDITIONAL COMPENSATION ARRANGEMENTS

- ☐ demonstrate the application of the Code of Ethics and Standards of Professional Conduct to situations involving issues of professional integrity
- ☐ recommend practices and procedures designed to prevent violations of the Code of Ethics and Standards of Professional Conduct
- ☐ identify conduct that conforms to the Code and Standards and conduct that violates the Code and Standards

Members and Candidates must not accept gifts, benefits, compensation, or consideration that competes with or might reasonably be expected to create a conflict of interest with their employer's interest unless they obtain written consent from all parties involved.

Guidance

Standard IV(B) requires members and candidates to obtain permission from their employer before accepting compensation or other benefits from third parties for the services rendered to the employer or for any services that might create a conflict with their employer's interest. Compensation and benefits include direct compensation by the client and any indirect compensation or other benefits received from third parties. "Written consent" includes any form of communication that can be documented (for example, communication via e-mail that can be retrieved and documented).

Members and candidates must obtain permission for additional compensation/benefits because such arrangements may affect loyalties and objectivity and create potential conflicts of interest. Disclosure allows an employer to consider the outside arrangements when evaluating the actions and motivations of members and candidates. Moreover, the employer is entitled to have full knowledge of all compensation/benefit arrangements so as to be able to assess the true cost of the services members or candidates are providing.

There may be instances in which a member or candidate is hired by an employer on a "part-time" basis. "Part-time" status applies to employees who do not commit the full number of hours required for a normal work week. Members and candidates should discuss possible limitations to their abilities to provide services that may be competitive with their employer during the negotiation and hiring process. The requirements of Standard IV(B) would be applicable to limitations identified at that time.

STANDARD IV(B): RECOMMENDED PROCEDURES

40

Members and candidates should make an immediate written report to their supervisor and compliance officer specifying any compensation they propose to receive for services in addition to the compensation or benefits received from their employer. The details of the report should be confirmed by the party offering the additional compensation, including performance incentives offered by clients. This written report should state the terms of any agreement under which a member or candidate will receive additional compensation; "terms" include the nature of the compensation, the approximate amount of compensation, and the duration of the agreement.

STANDARD IV(B): APPLICATION OF THE STANDARD

41

Example 1 (Notification of Client Bonus Compensation):

Geoff Whitman, a portfolio analyst for Adams Trust Company, manages the account of Carol Cochran, a client. Whitman is paid a salary by his employer, and Cochran pays the trust company a standard fee based on the market value of assets in her portfolio. Cochran proposes to Whitman that "any year that my portfolio achieves at least a 15% return before taxes, you and your wife can fly to Monaco at my expense and use my condominium during the third week of January." Whitman does not inform his employer of the arrangement and vacations in Monaco the following January as Cochran's guest.

> *Comment*: Whitman violated Standard IV(B) by failing to inform his employer in writing of this supplemental, contingent compensation arrangement. The nature of the arrangement could have resulted in partiality to Cochran's account, which could have detracted from Whitman's performance with respect to other accounts he handles for Adams Trust. Whitman must obtain the consent of his employer to accept such a supplemental benefit.

Example 2 (Notification of Outside Compensation):

Terry Jones sits on the board of directors of Exercise Unlimited, Inc. In return for his services on the board, Jones receives unlimited membership privileges for his family at all Exercise Unlimited facilities. Jones purchases Exercise Unlimited stock for the client accounts for which it is appropriate. Jones does not disclose this arrangement to his employer because he does not receive monetary compensation for his services to the board.

> *Comment*: Jones has violated Standard IV(B) by failing to disclose to his employer benefits received in exchange for his services on the board of directors. The nonmonetary compensation may create a conflict of interest in the same manner as being paid to serve as a director.

Example 3 (Prior Approval for Outside Compensation):

Jonathan Hollis is an analyst of oil-and-gas companies for Specialty Investment Management. He is currently recommending the purchase of ABC Oil Company shares and has published a long, well-thought-out research report to substantiate his recommendation. Several weeks after publishing the report, Hollis receives a call from the investor-relations office of ABC Oil saying that Thomas Andrews, CEO of the company, saw the report and really liked the analyst's grasp of the business and his company. The investor-relations officer invites Hollis to visit ABC Oil to discuss the industry further. ABC Oil offers to send a company plane to pick Hollis up and arrange for his accommodations while visiting. Hollis, after gaining the appropriate approvals, accepts the meeting with the CEO but declines the offered travel arrangements.

Several weeks later, Andrews and Hollis meet to discuss the oil business and Hollis's report. Following the meeting, Hollis joins Andrews and the investment relations officer for dinner at an upscale restaurant near ABC Oil's headquarters.

Upon returning to Specialty Investment Management, Hollis provides a full review of the meeting to the director of research, including a disclosure of the dinner attended.

> *Comment*: Hollis's actions did not violate Standard IV(B). Through gaining approval before accepting the meeting and declining the offered travel arrangements, Hollis sought to avoid any potential conflicts of interest between his company and ABC Oil. Because the location of the dinner was not available prior to arrival and Hollis notified his company of the dinner upon his return, accepting the dinner should not impair his objectivity. By disclosing the dinner, Hollis has enabled Specialty Investment Management to assess whether it has any impact on future reports and recommendations by Hollis related to ABC Oil.

42 STANDARD IV(C) RESPONSIBILITIES OF SUPERVISORS

- ☐ demonstrate the application of the Code of Ethics and Standards of Professional Conduct to situations involving issues of professional integrity
- ☐ recommend practices and procedures designed to prevent violations of the Code of Ethics and Standards of Professional Conduct
- ☐ identify conduct that conforms to the Code and Standards and conduct that violates the Code and Standards

> Members and Candidates must make reasonable efforts to ensure that anyone subject to their supervision or authority complies with applicable laws, rules, regulations, and the Code and Standards.

Guidance

Highlights:

- *System for Supervision*
- *Supervision Includes Detection*

Standard IV(C) states that members and candidates must promote actions by all employees under their supervision and authority to comply with applicable laws, rules, regulations, and firm policies and the Code and Standards.

Any investment professional who has employees subject to her or his control or influence—whether or not the employees are CFA Institute members, CFA charterholders, or candidates in the CFA Program—exercises supervisory responsibility. Members and candidates acting as supervisors must also have in-depth knowledge of the Code and Standards so that they can apply this knowledge in discharging their supervisory responsibilities.

The conduct that constitutes reasonable supervision in a particular case depends on the number of employees supervised and the work performed by those employees. Members and candidates with oversight responsibilities for large numbers of employees may not be able to personally evaluate the conduct of these employees on a continuing basis. These members and candidates may delegate supervisory duties to subordinates who directly oversee the other employees. A member's or candidate's responsibilities under Standard IV(C) include instructing those subordinates to whom supervision is delegated about methods to promote compliance, including preventing and detecting violations of laws, rules, regulations, firm policies, and the Code and Standards.

At a minimum, Standard IV(C) requires that members and candidates with supervisory responsibility make reasonable efforts to prevent and detect violations by ensuring the establishment of effective compliance systems. However, an effective compliance system goes beyond enacting a code of ethics, establishing policies and procedures to achieve compliance with the code and applicable law, and reviewing employee actions to determine whether they are following the rules.

To be effective supervisors, members and candidates should implement education and training programs on a recurring or regular basis for employees under their supervision. Such programs will assist the employees with meeting their professional obligations to practice in an ethical manner within the applicable legal system. Further, establishing incentives—monetary or otherwise—for employees not only to meet business goals but also to reward ethical behavior offers supervisors another way to assist employees in complying with their legal and ethical obligations.

Often, especially in large organizations, members and candidates may have supervisory responsibility but not the authority to establish or modify firm-wide compliance policies and procedures or incentive structures. Such limitations should not prevent a member or candidate from working with his or her own superiors and within the firm structure to develop and implement effective compliance tools, including but not limited to

- a code of ethics,
- compliance policies and procedures,
- education and training programs,
- an incentive structure that rewards ethical conduct, and
- adoption of firm-wide best practice standards (e.g., the GIPS standards, the CFA Institute Asset Manager Code of Professional Conduct).

A member or candidate with supervisory responsibility should bring an inadequate compliance system to the attention of the firm's senior managers and recommend corrective action. If the member or candidate clearly cannot discharge supervisory responsibilities because of the absence of a compliance system or because of an inadequate compliance system, the member or candidate should decline in writing to accept supervisory responsibility until the firm adopts reasonable procedures to allow adequate exercise of supervisory responsibility.

System for Supervision

Members and candidates with supervisory responsibility must understand what constitutes an adequate compliance system for their firms and make reasonable efforts to see that appropriate compliance procedures are established, documented, communicated to covered personnel, and followed. "Adequate" procedures are those designed to meet industry standards, regulatory requirements, the requirements of the Code and Standards, and the circumstances of the firm. Once compliance procedures are established, the supervisor must also make reasonable efforts to ensure that the procedures are monitored and enforced.

To be effective, compliance procedures must be in place prior to the occurrence of a violation of the law or the Code and Standards. Although compliance procedures cannot be designed to anticipate every potential violation, they should be designed to anticipate the activities most likely to result in misconduct. Compliance programs must be appropriate for the size and nature of the organization. The member or candidate should review model compliance procedures or other industry programs to ensure that the firm's procedures meet the minimum industry standards.

Once a supervisor learns that an employee has violated or may have violated the law or the Code and Standards, the supervisor must promptly initiate an assessment to determine the extent of the wrongdoing. Relying on an employee's statements about the extent of the violation or assurances that the wrongdoing will not reoccur is not enough. Reporting the misconduct up the chain of command and warning the employee to cease the activity are also not enough. Pending the outcome of the investigation, a supervisor should take steps to ensure that the violation will not be repeated, such as placing limits on the employee's activities or increasing the monitoring of the employee's activities.

Supervision Includes Detection

Members and candidates with supervisory responsibility must also make reasonable efforts to detect violations of laws, rules, regulations, firm policies, and the Code and Standards. The supervisors exercise reasonable supervision by establishing and implementing written compliance procedures and ensuring that those procedures are followed through periodic review. If a member or candidate has adopted reasonable procedures and taken steps to institute an effective compliance program, then the member or candidate may not be in violation of Standard IV(C) if he or she does not detect violations that occur despite these efforts. The fact that violations do occur may indicate, however, that the compliance procedures are inadequate. In addition, in some cases, merely enacting such procedures may not be sufficient to fulfill the duty required by Standard IV(C). A member or candidate may be in violation of Standard IV(C) if he or she knows or should know that the procedures designed to promote compliance, including detecting and preventing violations, are not being followed.

43 STANDARD IV(C): RECOMMENDED PROCEDURES

Codes of Ethics or Compliance Procedures

Members and candidates are encouraged to recommend that their employers adopt a code of ethics. Adoption of a code of ethics is critical to establishing a strong ethical foundation for investment advisory firms and their employees. Codes of ethics formally emphasize and reinforce the client loyalty responsibilities of investment firm personnel, protect investing clients by deterring misconduct, and protect the firm's reputation for integrity.

There is a distinction, however, between codes of ethics and the specific policies and procedures needed to ensure compliance with the codes and with securities laws and regulations. Although both are important, codes of ethics should consist of fundamental, principle-based ethical and fiduciary concepts that are applicable to all of the firm's employees. In this way, firms can best convey to employees and clients the ethical ideals that investment advisers strive to achieve. These concepts need to be implemented, however, by detailed, firm-wide compliance policies and procedures. Compliance procedures assist the firm's personnel in fulfilling the responsibilities enumerated in the code of ethics and make probable that the ideals expressed in the code of ethics will be adhered to in the day-to-day operation of the firm.

Standalone codes of ethics should be written in plain language and should address general fiduciary concepts. They should be unencumbered by numerous detailed procedures. Codes presented in this way are the most effective in stressing to employees that they are in positions of trust and must act with integrity at all times. Mingling compliance procedures in the firm's code of ethics goes against the goal of reinforcing the ethical obligations of employees.

Separating the code of ethics from compliance procedures will also reduce, if not eliminate, the legal terminology and "boilerplate" language that can make the underlying ethical principles incomprehensible to the average person. Above all, to ensure the creation of a culture of ethics and integrity rather than one that merely focuses on following the rules, the principles in the code of ethics must be stated in a way that is accessible and understandable to everyone in the firm.

Members and candidates should encourage their employers to provide their codes of ethics to clients. In this case also, a simple, straightforward code of ethics will be best understood by clients. Unencumbered by the compliance procedures, the code of ethics will be effective in conveying that the firm is committed to conducting business in an ethical manner and in the best interests of the clients.

Adequate Compliance Procedures

A supervisor complies with Standard IV(C) by identifying situations in which legal violations or violations of the Code and Standards are likely to occur and by establishing and enforcing compliance procedures to prevent such violations. Adequate compliance procedures should

- be contained in a clearly written and accessible manual that is tailored to the firm's operations,
- be drafted so that the procedures are easy to understand,
- designate a compliance officer whose authority and responsibility are clearly defined and who has the necessary resources and authority to implement the firm's compliance procedures,
- describe the hierarchy of supervision and assign duties among supervisors,
- implement a system of checks and balances,
- outline the scope of the procedures,
- outline procedures to document the monitoring and testing of compliance procedures,
- outline permissible conduct, and
- delineate procedures for reporting violations and sanctions.

Once a compliance program is in place, a supervisor should

- disseminate the contents of the program to appropriate personnel,
- periodically update procedures to ensure that the measures are adequate under the law,
- continually educate personnel regarding the compliance procedures,
- issue periodic reminders of the procedures to appropriate personnel,
- incorporate a professional conduct evaluation as part of an employee's performance review,
- review the actions of employees to ensure compliance and identify violators, and
- take the necessary steps to enforce the procedures once a violation has occurred.

Once a violation is discovered, a supervisor should

- respond promptly,
- conduct a thorough investigation of the activities to determine the scope of the wrongdoing,
- increase supervision or place appropriate limitations on the wrongdoer pending the outcome of the investigation, and
- review procedures for potential changes necessary to prevent future violations from occurring.

Implementation of Compliance Education and Training

No amount of ethics education and awareness will deter someone determined to commit fraud for personal enrichment. But the vast majority of investment professionals strive to achieve personal success with dedicated service to their clients and employers.

Regular ethics and compliance training, in conjunction with adoption of a code of ethics, is critical to investment firms seeking to establish a strong culture of integrity and to provide an environment in which employees routinely engage in ethical conduct in compliance with the law. Training and education assist individuals in both recognizing areas that are prone to ethical and legal pitfalls and identifying those circumstances and influences that can impair ethical judgment.

By implementing educational programs, supervisors can train their subordinates to put into practice what the firm's code of ethics requires. Education helps employees make the link between legal and ethical conduct and the long-term success of the business; a strong culture of compliance signals to clients and potential clients that the firm has truly embraced ethical conduct as fundamental to the firm's mission to serve its clients.

Establish an Appropriate Incentive Structure

Even if individuals want to make the right choices and follow an ethical course of conduct and are aware of the obstacles that may trip them up, they can still be influenced to act improperly by a corporate culture that embraces a "succeed at all costs" mentality, stresses results regardless of the methods used to achieve those results, and does not reward ethical behavior. Supervisors can reinforce an individual's natural desire to "do the right thing" by building a culture of integrity in the workplace.

Supervisors and firms must look closely at their incentive structure to determine whether the structure encourages profits and returns at the expense of ethically appropriate conduct. Reward structures may turn a blind eye to how desired outcomes are achieved and encourage dysfunctional or counterproductive behavior. Only when compensation and incentives are firmly tied to client interests and *how* outcomes are achieved, rather than *how much* is generated for the firm, will employees work to achieve a culture of integrity.

STANDARD IV(C): APPLICATION OF THE STANDARD

44

Example 1 (Supervising Research Activities):

Jane Mattock, senior vice president and head of the research department of H&V, Inc., a regional brokerage firm, has decided to change her recommendation for Timber Products from buy to sell. In line with H&V's procedures, she orally advises certain other H&V executives of her proposed actions before the report is prepared for publication. As a result of Mattock's conversation with Dieter Frampton, one of the H&V executives accountable to Mattock, Frampton immediately sells Timber's stock from his own account and from certain discretionary client accounts. In addition, other personnel inform certain institutional customers of the changed recommendation before it is printed and disseminated to all H&V customers who have received previous Timber reports.

> *Comment*: Mattock has violated Standard IV(C) by failing to reasonably and adequately supervise the actions of those accountable to her. She did not prevent or establish reasonable procedures designed to prevent dissemination of or trading on the information by those who knew of her changed recommendation. She must ensure that her firm has procedures for reviewing or recording any trading in the stock of a corporation that has been the subject of an unpublished change in recommendation. Adequate procedures would have informed the subordinates of their duties and detected sales by Frampton and selected customers.

Example 2 (Supervising Research Activities):

Deion Miller is the research director for Jamestown Investment Programs. The portfolio managers have become critical of Miller and his staff because the Jamestown portfolios do not include any stock that has been the subject of a merger or tender offer. Georgia Ginn, a member of Miller's staff, tells Miller that she has been studying a local company, Excelsior, Inc., and recommends its purchase. Ginn adds that the company has been widely rumored to be the subject of a merger study by a well-known conglomerate and discussions between them are under way. At Miller's request, Ginn prepares a memo recommending the stock. Miller passes along Ginn's memo to the portfolio managers prior to leaving for vacation, and he notes that he has not reviewed the memo. As a result of the memo, the portfolio managers buy Excelsior stock immediately. The day Miller returns to the office, he learns that Ginn's only sources for the report were her brother, who is an acquisitions analyst with Acme Industries, the "well-known conglomerate," and that the merger discussions were planned but not held.

> *Comment*: Miller violated Standard IV(C) by not exercising reasonable supervision when he disseminated the memo without checking to ensure that Ginn had a reasonable and adequate basis for her recommendations and that Ginn was not relying on material nonpublic information.

Example 3 (Supervising Trading Activities):

David Edwards, a trainee trader at Wheeler & Company, a major national brokerage firm, assists a customer in paying for the securities of Highland, Inc., by using anticipated profits from the immediate sale of the same securities. Despite the fact that Highland is not on Wheeler's recommended list, a large volume of its stock is traded through Wheeler in this manner. Roberta Ann Mason is a Wheeler vice president responsible for supervising compliance with the securities laws in the trading department. Part of her compensation from Wheeler is based on commission revenues from the trading department. Although she notices the increased trading activity, she does nothing to investigate or halt it.

> *Comment*: Mason's failure to adequately review and investigate purchase orders in Highland stock executed by Edwards and her failure to supervise the trainee's activities violate Standard IV(C). Supervisors should be especially sensitive to actual or potential conflicts between their own self-interests and their supervisory responsibilities.

Example 4 (Supervising Trading Activities and Record Keeping):

Samantha Tabbing is senior vice president and portfolio manager for Crozet, Inc., a registered investment advisory and registered broker/dealer firm. She reports to Charles Henry, the president of Crozet. Crozet serves as the investment adviser and principal underwriter for ABC and XYZ public mutual funds. The two funds' prospectuses allow Crozet to trade financial futures for the funds for the limited purpose of hedging against market risks. Henry, extremely impressed by Tabbing's performance in the past two years, directs Tabbing to act as portfolio manager for the funds. For the benefit of its employees, Crozet has also organized the Crozet Employee Profit-Sharing Plan (CEPSP), a defined contribution retirement plan. Henry assigns Tabbing to manage 20% of the assets of CEPSP. Tabbing's investment objective for her portion of CEPSP's assets is aggressive growth. Unbeknownst to Henry, Tabbing frequently places S&P 500 Index purchase and sale orders for the funds and the CEPSP without providing the futures commission merchants (FCMs) who take the orders with any prior or simultaneous designation of the account for which the trade has been placed. Frequently, neither Tabbing nor anyone else at Crozet completes an internal trade ticket to record the time an order was placed or the specific account for which the order was intended. FCMs often designate a specific account only after the trade, when Tabbing provides such designation. Crozet has no written operating procedures or compliance manual concerning its futures trading, and its compliance department does not review such trading. After observing the market's movement, Tabbing assigns to CEPSP the S&P 500 positions with more favorable execution prices and assigns positions with less favorable execution prices to the funds.

> *Comment*: Henry violated Standard IV(C) by failing to adequately supervise Tabbing with respect to her S&P 500 trading. Henry further violated Standard IV(C) by failing to establish record-keeping and reporting procedures to prevent or detect Tabbing's violations. Henry must make a reasonable effort to determine that adequate compliance procedures covering all employee trading activity are established, documented, communicated, and followed.

Example 5 (Accepting Responsibility):

Meredith Rasmussen works on a buy-side trading desk and concentrates on in-house trades for a hedge fund subsidiary managed by a team at the investment management firm. The hedge fund has been very successful and is marketed globally by the firm. From her experience as the trader for much of the activity of the fund, Rasmussen has become quite knowledgeable about the hedge fund's strategy, tactics, and performance. When a distinct break in the market occurs and many of the securities involved in the hedge fund's strategy decline markedly in value, however, Rasmussen observes that the reported performance of the hedge fund does not at all reflect this decline. From her experience, this lack of an effect is a very unlikely occurrence. She approaches the head of trading about her concern and is told that she should not ask any questions and that the fund is too big and successful and is not her concern. She is fairly sure something is not right, so she contacts the compliance officer and is again told to stay away from the hedge fund reporting issue.

Comment: Rasmussen has clearly come upon an error in policies, procedures, and compliance practices within the firm's operations. According to Standard IV(C), the supervisor and the compliance officer have the responsibility to review the concerns brought forth by Rasmussen. Supervisors have the responsibility of establishing and encouraging an ethical culture in the firm. The dismissal of Rasmussen's question violates Standard IV(C) and undermines the firm's ethical operations.

See also Standard I(D) Misconduct and, for guidance on whistleblowing, Standard IV(A) Loyalty.

Example 6 (Inadequate Procedures):

Brendan Witt, a former junior sell-side technology analyst, decided to return to school to earn an MBA. To keep his research skills and industry knowledge sharp, Witt accepted a position with On-line and Informed, an independent internet-based research company. The position requires the publication of a recommendation and report on a different company every month. Initially, Witt is a regular contributor of new research and a participant in the associated discussion boards that generally have positive comments on the technology sector. Over time, his ability to manage his educational requirements and his work requirements begin to conflict with one another. Knowing a recommendation is due the next day for On-line, Witt creates a report based on a few news articles and what the conventional wisdom of the markets has deemed the "hot" security of the day.

Comment: Allowing the report submitted by Witt to be posted highlights a lack of compliance procedures by the research firm. Witt's supervisor needs to work with the management of On-line to develop an appropriate review process to ensure that all contracted analysts comply with the requirements.

See also Standard V(A) Diligence and Reasonable Basis because it relates to Witt's responsibility for substantiating a recommendation.

Example 7 (Inadequate Supervision):

Michael Papis is the chief investment officer of his state's retirement fund. The fund has always used outside advisers for the real estate allocation, and this information is clearly presented in all fund communications. Thomas Nagle, a recognized sell-side research analyst and Papis's business school classmate, recently left the investment bank he worked for to start his own asset management firm, Accessible Real Estate.

Nagle is trying to build his assets under management and contacts Papis about gaining some of the retirement fund's allocation. In the previous few years, the performance of the retirement fund's real estate investments was in line with the fund's benchmark but was not extraordinary. Papis decides to help out his old friend and also to seek better returns by moving the real estate allocation to Accessible. The only notice of the change in adviser appears in the next annual report in the listing of associated advisers.

> *Comment*: Papis's actions highlight the need for supervision and review at all levels in an organization. His responsibilities may include the selection of external advisers, but the decision to change advisers appears arbitrary. Members and candidates should ensure that their firm has appropriate policies and procedures in place to detect inappropriate actions, such as the action taken by Papis.
>
> See also Standard V(A) Diligence and Reasonable Basis, Standard V(B) Communication with Clients and Prospective Clients, and Standard VI(A) Disclosure of Conflicts.

Example 8 (Supervising Research Activities):

Mary Burdette was recently hired by Fundamental Investment Management (FIM) as a junior auto industry analyst. Burdette is expected to expand the social media presence of the firm because she is active with various networks, including Facebook, LinkedIn, and X. Although Burdette's supervisor, Joe Graf, has never used social media, he encourages Burdette to explore opportunities to increase FIM's online presence and ability to share content, communicate, and broadcast information to clients. In response to Graf's encouragement, Burdette is working on a proposal detailing the advantages of getting FIM onto X in addition to launching a company Facebook page.

As part of her auto industry research for FIM, Burdette is completing a report on the financial impact of Sun Drive Auto Ltd.'s new solar technology for compact automobiles. This research report will be her first for FIM, and she believes Sun Drive's technology could revolutionize the auto industry. In her excitement, Burdette sends a quick post to FIM X followers summarizing her "buy" recommendation for Sun Drive Auto stock.

> *Comment*: Graf has violated Standard IV(C) by failing to reasonably supervise Burdette with respect to the contents of her post. He did not establish reasonable procedures to prevent the unauthorized dissemination of company research through social media networks. Graf must make sure all employees receive regular training about FIM's policies and procedures, including the appropriate business use of personal social media networks.
>
> See Standard III(B) for additional guidance.

Example 9 (Supervising Research Activities):

Chen Wang leads the research department at YYRA Retirement Planning Specialists. Chen supervises a team of 10 analysts in a fast-paced and understaffed organization. He is responsible for coordinating the firm's approved process to review all reports before they are provided to the portfolio management team for use in rebalancing client portfolios.

One of Chen's direct reports, Huang Mei, covers the banking industry. Chen must submit the latest updates to the portfolio management team tomorrow morning. Huang has yet to submit her research report on ZYX Bank because she is uncomfortable providing a "buy" or "sell" opinion of ZYX on the basis of the completed analysis. Pressed for time and concerned that Chen will reject a "hold" recommendation, she researches various websites and blogs on the banking sector for whatever she can find on ZYX. One independent blogger provides a new interpretation of the recently reported data Huang has analyzed and concludes with a strong "sell" recommendation for ZYX. She is impressed by the originality and resourcefulness of this blogger's report.

Very late in the evening, Huang submits her report and "sell" recommendation to Chen without any reference to the independent blogger's report. Given the late time of the submission and the competence of Huang's prior work, Chen compiles this report with the recommendations from each of the other analysts and meets with the portfolio managers to discuss implementation.

> *Comment*: Chen has violated Standard IV(C) by neglecting to reasonably and adequately follow the firm's approved review process for Huang's research report. The delayed submission and the quality of prior work do not remove Chen's requirement to uphold the designated review process. A member or candidate with supervisory responsibility must make reasonable efforts to see that appropriate procedures are established, documented, communicated to covered personnel, and followed.

STANDARD V: INVESTMENT ANALYSIS, RECOMMENDATIONS, AND ACTIONS

45

- ☐ demonstrate the application of the Code of Ethics and Standards of Professional Conduct to situations involving issues of professional integrity
- ☐ recommend practices and procedures designed to prevent violations of the Code of Ethics and Standards of Professional Conduct
- ☐ identify conduct that conforms to the Code and Standards and conduct that violates the Code and Standards

Standard V(A) Diligence and Reasonable Basis

Members and Candidates must:

1. Exercise diligence, independence, and thoroughness in analyzing investments, making investment recommendations, and taking investment actions.
2. Have a reasonable and adequate basis, supported by appropriate research and investigation, for any investment analysis, recommendation, or action.

Guidance

Highlights:

- *Defining Diligence and Reasonable Basis*
- *Using Secondary or Third-Party Research*

- *Using Quantitatively Oriented Research*
- *Developing Quantitatively Oriented Techniques*
- *Selecting External Advisers and Subadvisers*
- *Group Research and Decision Making*

The application of Standard V(A) depends on the investment philosophy the member, candidate, or firm is following, the role of the member or candidate in the investment decision-making process, and the support and resources provided by the member's or candidate's employer. These factors will dictate the nature of the diligence and thoroughness of the research and the level of investigation required by Standard V(A).

The requirements for issuing conclusions based on research will vary in relation to the member's or candidate's role in the investment decision-making process, but the member or candidate must make reasonable efforts to cover all pertinent issues when arriving at a recommendation. Members and candidates enhance transparency by providing or offering to provide supporting information to clients when recommending a purchase or sale or when changing a recommendation.

Defining Diligence and Reasonable Basis

Every investment decision is based on a set of facts known and understood at the time. Clients turn to members and candidates for advice and expect these advisers to have more information and knowledge than they do. This information and knowledge is the basis from which members and candidates apply their professional judgment in taking investment actions and making recommendations.

At a basic level, clients want assurance that members and candidates are putting forth the necessary effort to support the recommendations they are making. Communicating the level and thoroughness of the information reviewed before the member or candidate makes a judgment allows clients to understand the reasonableness of the recommended investment actions.

As with determining the suitability of an investment for the client, the necessary level of research and analysis will differ with the product, security, or service being offered. In providing an investment service, members and candidates typically use a variety of resources, including company reports, third-party research, and results from quantitative models. A reasonable basis is formed through a balance of these resources appropriate for the security or decision being analyzed.

The following list provides some, but definitely not all, examples of attributes to consider while forming the basis for a recommendation:

- global, regional, and country macroeconomic conditions,
- a company's operating and financial history,
- the industry's and sector's current conditions and the stage of the business cycle,
- a mutual fund's fee structure and management history,
- the output and potential limitations of quantitative models,
- the quality of the assets included in a securitization, and
- the appropriateness of selected peer-group comparisons.

Even though an investment recommendation may be well informed, downside risk remains for any investment. Members and candidates can base their decisions only on the information available at the time decisions are made. The steps taken in developing a diligent and reasonable recommendation should minimize unexpected downside events.

Using Secondary or Third-Party Research

If members and candidates rely on secondary or third-party research, they must make reasonable and diligent efforts to determine whether such research is sound. Secondary research is defined as research conducted by someone else in the member's or candidate's firm. Third-party research is research conducted by entities outside the member's or candidate's firm, such as a brokerage firm, bank, or research firm. If a member or candidate has reason to suspect that either secondary or third-party research or information comes from a source that lacks a sound basis, the member or candidate must not rely on that information.

Members and candidates should make reasonable enquiries into the source and accuracy of all data used in completing their investment analysis and recommendations. The sources of the information and data will influence the level of the review a member or candidate must undertake. Information and data taken from internet sources, such as personal blogs, independent research aggregation websites, or social media websites, likely require a greater level of review than information from more established research organizations.

Criteria that a member or candidate can use in forming an opinion on whether research is sound include the following:

- assumptions used,
- rigor of the analysis performed,
- date/timeliness of the research, and
- evaluation of the objectivity and independence of the recommendations.

A member or candidate may rely on others in his or her firm to determine whether secondary or third-party research is sound and use the information in good faith unless the member or candidate has reason to question its validity or the processes and procedures used by those responsible for the research. For example, a portfolio manager may not have a choice of a data source because the firm's senior managers conducted due diligence to determine which vendor would provide services; the member or candidate can use the information in good faith assuming the due diligence process was deemed adequate.

A member or candidate should verify that the firm has a policy about the timely and consistent review of approved research providers to ensure that the quality of the research continues to meet the necessary standards. If such a policy is not in place at the firm, the member or candidate should encourage the development and adoption of a formal review practice.

Using Quantitatively Oriented Research

Standard V(A) applies to the rapidly expanding use of quantitatively oriented research models and processes, such as computer-generated modeling, screening, and ranking of investment securities; the creation or valuation of derivative instruments; and quantitative portfolio construction techniques. These models and processes are being used for much more than the backtesting of investment strategies, especially with continually advancing technology and techniques. The continued broad development of quantitative methods and models is an important part of capital market developments.

Members and candidates need to have an understanding of the parameters used in models and quantitative research that are incorporated into their investment recommendations. Although they are not required to become experts in every technical aspect of the models, they must understand the assumptions and limitations inherent in any model and how the results were used in the decision-making process.

The reliance on and potential limitations of financial models became clear through the investment crisis that unfolded in 2007 and 2008. In some cases, the financial models used to value specific securities and related derivative products did not adequately demonstrate the level of associated risks. Members and candidates should make reasonable efforts to test the output of investment models and other pre-programmed analytical tools they use. Such validation should occur before incorporating the process into their methods, models, or analyses.

Although not every model can test for every factor or outcome, members and candidates should ensure that their analyses incorporate a broad range of assumptions sufficient to capture the underlying characteristics of investments. The omission from the analysis of potentially negative outcomes or of levels of risk outside the norm may misrepresent the true economic value of an investment. The possible scenarios for analysis should include factors that are likely to have a substantial influence on the investment value and may include extremely positive and negative scenarios.

Developing Quantitatively Oriented Techniques

Individuals who create new quantitative models and services must exhibit a higher level of diligence in reviewing new products than the individuals who ultimately use the analytical output. Members and candidates involved in the development and oversight of quantitatively oriented models, methods, and algorithms must understand the technical aspects of the products they provide to clients. A thorough testing of the model and resulting analysis should be completed prior to product distribution.

Members and candidates need to consider the source and time horizon of the data used as inputs in financial models. The information from many commercially available databases may not effectively incorporate both positive and negative market cycles. In the development of a recommendation, the member or candidate may need to test the models by using volatility and performance expectations that represent scenarios outside the observable databases. In reviewing the computer models or the resulting output, members and candidates need to pay particular attention to the assumptions used in the analysis and the rigor of the analysis to ensure that the model incorporates a wide range of possible input expectations, including negative market events.

Selecting External Advisers and Subadvisers

Financial instruments and asset allocation techniques continue to develop and evolve. This progression has led to the use of specialized managers to invest in specific asset classes or diversification strategies that complement a firm's in-house expertise. Standard V(A) applies to the level of review necessary in selecting an external adviser or subadviser to manage a specifically mandated allocation. Members and candidates must review managers as diligently as they review individual funds and securities.

Members and candidates who are directly involved with the use of external advisers need to ensure that their firms have standardized criteria for reviewing these selected external advisers and managers. Such criteria would include, but would not be limited to, the following:

- reviewing the adviser's established code of ethics,
- understanding the adviser's compliance and internal control procedures,
- assessing the quality of the published return information, and
- reviewing the adviser's investment process and adherence to its stated strategy.

Codes, standards, and guides to best practice published by CFA Institute provide members and candidates with examples of acceptable practices for external advisers and advice in selecting a new adviser. The following guides are available at the CFA Institute website (www.cfainstitute.org): Asset Manager Code of Professional Conduct, Global Investment Performance Standards, and Model Request for Proposal (for equity, credit, or real estate managers).

Group Research and Decision Making

Commonly, members and candidates are part of a group or team that is collectively responsible for producing investment analysis or research. The conclusions or recommendations of the group report represent the consensus of the group and are not necessarily the views of the member or candidate, even though the name of the member or candidate is included on the report. In some instances, a member or candidate will not agree with the view of the group. If, however, the member or candidate believes that the consensus opinion has a reasonable and adequate basis and is independent and objective, the member or candidate need not decline to be identified with the report. If the member or candidate is confident in the process, the member or candidate does not need to dissociate from the report even if it does not reflect his or her opinion.

STANDARD V(A): RECOMMENDED PROCEDURES

46

Members and candidates should encourage their firms to consider the following policies and procedures to support the principles of Standard V(A):

- Establish a policy requiring that research reports, credit ratings, and investment recommendations have a basis that can be substantiated as reasonable and adequate. An individual employee (a supervisory analyst) or a group of employees (a review committee) should be appointed to review and approve such items prior to external circulation to determine whether the criteria established in the policy have been met.
- Develop detailed, written guidance for analysts (research, investment, or credit), supervisory analysts, and review committees that establishes the due diligence procedures for judging whether a particular recommendation has a reasonable and adequate basis.
- Develop measurable criteria for assessing the quality of research, the reasonableness and adequacy of the basis for any recommendation or rating, and the accuracy of recommendations over time. In some cases, firms may consider implementing compensation arrangements that depend on these measurable criteria and that are applied consistently to all related analysts.
- Develop detailed, written guidance that establishes minimum levels of scenario testing of all computer-based models used in developing, rating, and evaluating financial instruments. The policy should contain criteria related to the breadth of the scenarios tested, the accuracy of the output over time, and the analysis of cash flow sensitivity to inputs.
- Develop measurable criteria for assessing outside providers, including the quality of information being provided, the reasonableness and adequacy of the provider's collection practices, and the accuracy of the information over time. The established policy should outline how often the provider's products are reviewed.
- Adopt a standardized set of criteria for evaluating the adequacy of external advisers. The policy should include how often and on what basis the allocation of funds to the adviser will be reviewed.

47 STANDARD V(A): APPLICATION OF THE STANDARD

Example 1 (Sufficient Due Diligence):

Helen Hawke manages the corporate finance department of Sarkozi Securities, Ltd. The firm is anticipating that the government will soon close a tax loophole that currently allows oil-and-gas exploration companies to pass on drilling expenses to holders of a certain class of shares. Because market demand for this tax-advantaged class of stock is currently high, Sarkozi convinces several companies to undertake new equity financings at once, before the loophole closes. Time is of the essence, but Sarkozi lacks sufficient resources to conduct adequate research on all the prospective issuing companies. Hawke decides to estimate the IPO prices on the basis of the relative size of each company and to justify the pricing later when her staff has time.

> *Comment*: Sarkozi should have taken on only the work that it could adequately handle. By categorizing the issuers by general size, Hawke has bypassed researching all the other relevant aspects that should be considered when pricing new issues and thus has not performed sufficient due diligence. Such an omission can result in investors purchasing shares at prices that have no actual basis. Hawke has violated Standard V(A).

Example 2 (Sufficient Scenario Testing):

Babu Dhaliwal works for Heinrich Brokerage in the corporate finance group. He has just persuaded Feggans Resources, Ltd., to allow his firm to do a secondary equity financing at Feggans Resources' current stock price. Because the stock has been trading at higher multiples than similar companies with equivalent production, Dhaliwal presses the Feggans Resources managers to project what would be the maximum production they could achieve in an optimal scenario. Based on these numbers, he is able to justify the price his firm will be asking for the secondary issue. During a sales pitch to the brokers, Dhaliwal then uses these numbers as the base-case production levels that Feggans Resources will achieve.

> *Comment*: When presenting information to the brokers, Dhaliwal should have given a range of production scenarios and the probability of Feggans Resources achieving each level. By giving the maximum production level as the likely level of production, he has misrepresented the chances of achieving that production level and seriously misled the brokers. Dhaliwal has violated Standard V(A).

Example 3 (Developing a Reasonable Basis):

Brendan Witt, a former junior sell-side technology analyst, decided to return to school to earn an MBA. To keep his research skills and industry knowledge sharp, Witt accepted a position with On-line and Informed, an independent internet-based research company. The position requires the publication of a recommendation and report on a different company every month. Initially, Witt is a regular contributor of new research and a participant in the associated discussion boards that generally have positive comments on the technology sector. Over time, his ability to manage his educational requirements and his work requirements begin to conflict with one another. Knowing a recommendation is due the next day for On-line, Witt creates a report based on a few news articles and what the conventional wisdom of the markets has deemed the "hot" security of the day.

> *Comment*: Witt's knowledge of and exuberance for technology stocks, a few news articles, and the conventional wisdom of the markets do not constitute, without more information, a reasonable and adequate basis for a stock recommendation that is supported by appropriate research and investigation. Therefore, Witt has violated Standard V(A).
>
> See also Standard IV(C) Responsibilities of Supervisors because it relates to the firm's inadequate procedures.

Example 4 (Timely Client Updates):

Kristen Chandler is an investment consultant in the London office of Dalton Securities, a major global investment consultant firm. One of her UK pension funds has decided to appoint a specialist US equity manager. Dalton's global manager of research relies on local consultants to cover managers within their regions and, after conducting thorough due diligence, puts their views and ratings in Dalton's manager database. Chandler accesses Dalton's global manager research database and conducts a screen of all US equity managers on the basis of a match with the client's desired philosophy/style, performance, and tracking-error targets. She selects the five managers that meet these criteria and puts them in a briefing report that is delivered to the client 10 days later. Between the time of Chandler's database search and the delivery of the report to the client, Chandler is told that Dalton has updated the database with the information that one of the firms that Chandler has recommended for consideration lost its chief investment officer, the head of its US equity research, and the majority of its portfolio managers on the US equity product—all of whom have left to establish their own firm. Chandler does not revise her report with this updated information.

> *Comment*: Chandler has failed to satisfy the requirement of Standard V(A). Although Dalton updated the manager ratings to reflect the personnel turnover at one of the firms, Chandler did not update her report to reflect the new information.

Example 5 (Group Research Opinions):

Evelyn Mastakis is a junior analyst who has been asked by her firm to write a research report predicting the expected interest rate for residential mortgages over the next six months. Mastakis submits her report to the fixed-income investment committee of her firm for review, as required by firm procedures. Although some committee members support Mastakis's conclusion, the majority of the committee disagrees with her conclusion, and the report is significantly changed to indicate that interest rates are likely to increase more than originally predicted by Mastakis. Should Mastakis ask that her name be taken off the report when it is disseminated?

> *Comment*: The results of research are not always clear, and different people may have different opinions based on the same factual evidence. In this case, the committee may have valid reasons for issuing a report that differs from the analyst's original research. The firm can issue a report that is different from the original report of an analyst as long as there is a reasonable and adequate basis for its conclusions.

Generally, analysts must write research reports that reflect their own opinion and can ask the firm not to put their name on reports that ultimately differ from that opinion. When the work is a group effort, however, not all members of the team may agree with all aspects of the report. Ultimately, members and candidates can ask to have their names removed from the report, but if they are satisfied that the process has produced results or conclusions that have a reasonable and adequate basis, members and candidates do not have to dissociate from the report even when they do not agree with its contents. If Mastakis is confident in the process, she does not need to dissociate from the report even if it does not reflect her opinion.

Example 6 (Reliance on Third-Party Research):

Gary McDermott runs a two-person investment management firm. McDermott's firm subscribes to a service from a large investment research firm that provides research reports. McDermott's firm makes investment recommendations on the basis of these reports.

Comment: Members and candidates can rely on third-party research but must make reasonable and diligent efforts to determine that such research is sound. If McDermott undertakes due diligence efforts on a regular basis to ensure that the research produced by the large firm is objective and reasonably based, McDermott can rely on that research when making investment recommendations to clients.

Example 7 (Due Diligence in Submanager Selection):

Paul Ostrowski's business has grown significantly over the past couple of years, and some clients want to diversify internationally. Ostrowski decides to find a submanager to handle the expected international investments. Because this will be his first subadviser, Ostrowski uses the CFA Institute model "request for proposal" to design a questionnaire for his search. By his deadline, he receives seven completed questionnaires from a variety of domestic and international firms trying to gain his business. Ostrowski reviews all the applications in detail and decides to select the firm that charges the lowest fees because doing so will have the least impact on his firm's bottom line.

Comment: The selection of an external adviser or subadviser should be based on a full and complete review of the adviser's services, performance history, and cost structure. In basing the decision on the fee structure alone, Ostrowski may be violating Standard V(A).

See also Standard III(C) Suitability because it relates to the ability of the selected adviser to meet the needs of the clients.

Example 8 (Sufficient Due Diligence):

Michael Papis is the chief investment officer of his state's retirement fund. The fund has always used outside advisers for the real estate allocation, and this information is clearly presented in all fund communications. Thomas Nagle, a recognized sell-side research analyst and Papis's business school classmate, recently left the investment bank he worked for to start his own asset management firm, Accessible Real Estate. Nagle is trying to build his assets under management and contacts Papis about gaining some of the retirement fund's allocation. In the previous few years, the performance of the retirement fund's real estate investments was in line with the fund's benchmark but was not extraordinary. Papis decides to help out his old friend and also to seek better returns by moving the real estate allocation to Accessible. The only notice of the change in adviser appears in the next annual report in the listing of associated advisers.

> *Comment*: Papis violated Standard V(A). His responsibilities may include the selection of the external advisers, but the decision to change advisers appears to have been arbitrary. If Papis was dissatisfied with the current real estate adviser, he should have conducted a proper solicitation to select the most appropriate adviser.
>
> See also Standard IV(C) Responsibilities of Supervisors, Standard V(B) Communication with Clients and Prospective Clients, and Standard VI(A) Disclosure of Conflicts.

Example 9 (Sufficient Due Diligence):

Andre Shrub owns and operates Conduit, an investment advisory firm. Prior to opening Conduit, Shrub was an account manager with Elite Investment, a hedge fund managed by his good friend Adam Reed. To attract clients to a new Conduit fund, Shrub offers lower-than-normal management fees. He can do so because the fund consists of two top-performing funds managed by Reed. Given his personal friendship with Reed and the prior performance record of these two funds, Shrub believes this new fund is a winning combination for all parties. Clients quickly invest with Conduit to gain access to the Elite funds. No one is turned away because Conduit is seeking to expand its assets under management.

> *Comment*: Shrub violated Standard V(A) by not conducting a thorough analysis of the funds managed by Reed before developing the new Conduit fund. Shrub's reliance on his personal relationship with Reed and his prior knowledge of Elite are insufficient justification for the investments. The funds may be appropriately considered, but a full review of their operating procedures, reporting practices, and transparency are some elements of the necessary due diligence.
>
> See also Standard III(C) Suitability.

Example 10 (Sufficient Due Diligence):

Bob Thompson has been doing research for the portfolio manager of the fixed-income department. His assignment is to do sensitivity analysis on securitized subprime mortgages. He has discussed with the manager possible scenarios to use to calculate expected returns. A key assumption in such calculations is housing price appreciation (HPA) because it drives "prepays" (prepayments of mortgages) and losses. Thompson is concerned with the significant appreciation experienced over the previous five years as a result of the increased availability of funds from subprime mortgages. Thompson insists that the analysis should include a scenario run with –10% for Year 1, –5% for Year 2, and then (to project a worst-case scenario) 0% for Years 3 through 5. The manager replies that these assumptions are too dire because there has never been a time in their available database when HPA was negative.

Thompson conducts his research to better understand the risks inherent in these securities and evaluates these securities in the worst-case scenario, a less likely but possible environment. Based on the results of the enhanced scenarios, Thompson does not recommend the purchase of the securitization. Against the general market trends, the manager follows Thompson's recommendation and does not invest. The following year, the housing market collapses. In avoiding the subprime investments, the manager's portfolio outperforms its peer group that year.

> *Comment*: Thompson's actions in running the scenario test with inputs beyond the historical trends available in the firm's databases adhere to the principles of Standard V(A). His concerns over recent trends provide a sound basis for further analysis. Thompson understands the limitations of his model, when combined with the limited available historical information, to accurately predict the performance of the funds if market conditions change negatively.
>
> See also Standard I(B) Independence and Objectivity.

Example 11 (Use of Quantitatively Oriented Models):

Espacia Liakos works in sales for Hellenica Securities, a firm specializing in developing intricate derivative strategies to profit from particular views on market expectations. One of her clients is Eugenie Carapalis, who has become convinced that commodity prices will become more volatile over the coming months. Carapalis asks Liakos to quickly engineer a strategy that will benefit from this expectation. Liakos turns to Hellenica's modeling group to fulfill this request. Because of the tight deadline, the modeling group outsources parts of the work to several trusted third parties. Liakos implements the disparate components of the strategy as the firms complete them.

Within a month, Carapalis is proven correct: Volatility across a range of commodities increases sharply. But her derivatives position with Hellenica returns huge losses, and the losses increase daily. Liakos investigates and realizes that although each of the various components of the strategy had been validated, they had never been evaluated as an integrated whole. In extreme conditions, portions of the model worked at cross-purposes with other portions, causing the overall strategy to fail dramatically.

> *Comment*: Liakos violated Standard V(A). Members and candidates must understand the statistical significance of the results of the models they recommend and must be able to explain them to clients. Liakos did not take adequate care to ensure a thorough review of the whole model; its components were evaluated only individually. Because Carapalis clearly intended to implement the strategy as a whole rather than as separate parts, Liakos should have tested how the components of the strategy interacted as well as how they performed individually.

Example 12 (Successful Due Diligence/Failed Investment):

Alton Newbury is an investment adviser to high-net-worth clients. A client with an aggressive risk profile in his investment policy statement asks about investing in the Top Shelf hedge fund. This fund, based in Calgary, Alberta, Canada, has reported 20% returns for the first three years. The fund prospectus states that its strategy involves long and short positions in the energy sector and extensive leverage. Based on his analysis of the fund's track record, the principals involved in managing the fund, the fees charged, and the fund's risk profile, Newbury recommends the fund to the client and secures a position in it. The next week, the fund announces that it has suffered a loss of 60% of its value and is suspending operations and redemptions until after a regulatory review. Newbury's client calls him in a panic and asks for an explanation.

Comment: Newbury's actions were consistent with Standard V(A). Analysis of an investment that results in a reasonable basis for recommendation does not guarantee that the investment has no downside risk. Newbury should discuss the analysis process with the client while reminding him or her that past performance does not lead to guaranteed future gains and that losses in an aggressive investment portfolio should be expected.

Example 13 (Quantitative Model Diligence):

Barry Cannon is the lead quantitative analyst at CityCenter Hedge Fund. He is responsible for the development, maintenance, and enhancement of the proprietary models the fund uses to manage its investors' assets. Cannon reads several high-level mathematical publications and blogs to stay informed of current developments. One blog, run by "Expert CFA," presents some intriguing research that may benefit one of CityCenter's current models. Cannon is under pressure from firm executives to improve the model's predictive abilities, and he incorporates the factors discussed in the online research. The updated output recommends several new investments to the fund's portfolio managers.

Comment: Cannon has violated Standard V(A) by failing to have a reasonable basis for the new recommendations made to the portfolio managers. He needed to diligently research the effect of incorporating the new factors before offering the output recommendations. Cannon may use the blog for ideas, but it is his responsibility to determine the effect on the firm's proprietary models.

See Standard VII(B) regarding the violation by "Expert CFA" in the use of the CFA designation.

Example 14 (Selecting a Service Provider):

Ellen Smith is a performance analyst at Artic Global Advisors, a firm that manages global equity mandates for institutional clients. She was asked by her supervisor to review five new performance attribution systems and recommend one that would more appropriately explain the firm's investment strategy to clients. On the list was a system she recalled learning about when visiting an exhibitor booth at a recent conference. The system is highly quantitative and something of a "black box" in how it calculates the attribution values. Smith recommended this option without researching the others because the sheer complexity of the process was sure to impress the clients.

Comment: Smith's actions do not demonstrate a sufficient level of diligence in reviewing this product to make a recommendation for selecting the service. Besides not reviewing or considering the other four potential systems, she did not determine whether the "black box" attribution process aligns with the investment practices of the firm, including its investments in different countries and currencies. Smith must review and understand the process of any software or system before recommending its use as the firm's attribution system.

Example 15 (Subadviser Selection):

Craig Jackson is working for Adams Partners, Inc., and has been assigned to select a hedge fund subadviser to improve the diversification of the firm's large fund-of-funds product. The allocation must be in place before the start of the next quarter. Jackson uses a consultant database to find a list of suitable firms that claim compliance with the GIPS standards. He calls more than 20 firms on the list to confirm their potential interest and to determine their most recent quarterly and annual total return values. Because of the short turnaround, Jackson recommends the firm with the greatest total return values for selection.

> *Comment*: By considering only performance and GIPS compliance, Jackson has not conducted sufficient review of potential firms to satisfy the requirements of Standard V(A). A thorough investigation of the firms and their operations should be conducted to ensure that their addition would increase the diversity of clients' portfolios and that they are suitable for the fund-of-funds product.

Example 16 (Manager Selection):

Timothy Green works for Peach Asset Management, where he creates proprietary models that analyze data from the firm request for proposal questionnaires to identify managers for possible inclusion in the firm's fund-of-funds investment platform. Various criteria must be met to be accepted to the platform. Because of the number of respondents to the questionnaires, Green uses only the data submitted to make a recommendation for adding a new manager.

> *Comment*: By failing to conduct any additional outside review of the information to verify what was submitted through the request for proposal, Green has likely not satisfied the requirements of Standard V(A). The amount of information requested from outside managers varies among firms. Although the requested information may be comprehensive, Green should ensure sufficient effort is undertaken to verify the submitted information before recommending a firm for inclusion. This requires that he goes beyond the information provided by the manager on the request for proposal questionnaire and may include interviews with interested managers, reviews of regulatory filings, and discussions with the managers' custodian or auditor.

Example 17 (Technical Model Requirements):

Jérôme Dupont works for the credit research group of XYZ Asset Management, where he is in charge of developing and updating credit risk models. In order to perform accurately, his models need to be regularly updated with the latest market data.

Dupont does not interact with or manage money for any of the firm's clients. He is in contact with the firm's US corporate bond fund manager, John Smith, who has only very superficial knowledge of the model and who from time to time asks very basic questions regarding the output recommendations. Smith does not consult Dupont with respect to finalizing his clients' investment strategies.

Dupont's recently assigned objective is to develop a new emerging market corporate credit risk model. The firm is planning to expand into emerging credit, and the development of such a model is a critical step in this process. Because Smith seems to follow the model's recommendations without much concern for its quality as he develops his clients' investment strategies, Dupont decides to focus his time on the development of the new emerging market model and neglects to update the US model.

After several months without regular updates, Dupont's diagnostic statistics start to show alarming signs with respect to the quality of the US credit model. Instead of conducting the long and complicated data update, Dupont introduces new codes into his model with some limited new data as a quick "fix." He thinks this change will address the issue without needing to complete the full data update, so he continues working on the new emerging market model.

Several months following the quick "fix," another set of diagnostic statistics reveals nonsensical results and Dupont realizes that his earlier change contained an error. He quickly corrects the error and alerts Smith. Smith realizes that some of the prior trades he performed were due to erroneous model results. Smith rebalances the portfolio to remove the securities purchased on the basis of the questionable results without reporting the issue to anyone else.

Comment: Smith violated Standard V(A) because exercising "diligence, independence, and thoroughness in analyzing investments, making investment recommendations, and taking investment actions" means that members and candidates must understand the technical aspects of the products they provide to clients. Smith does not understand the model he is relying on to manage money. Members and candidates should also make reasonable enquiries into the source and accuracy of all data used in completing their investment analysis and recommendations.

Dupont violated Standard V(A) even if he does not trade securities or make investment decisions. Dupont's models give investment recommendations, and Dupont is accountable for the quality of those recommendations. Members and candidates should make reasonable efforts to test the output of pre-programmed analytical tools they use. Such validation should occur before incorporating the tools into their decision-making process.

See also Standard V(B) Communication with Clients and Prospective Clients.

STANDARD V(B) COMMUNICATION WITH CLIENTS AND PROSPECTIVE CLIENTS

48

- ☐ demonstrate the application of the Code of Ethics and Standards of Professional Conduct to situations involving issues of professional integrity
- ☐ recommend practices and procedures designed to prevent violations of the Code of Ethics and Standards of Professional Conduct
- ☐ identify conduct that conforms to the Code and Standards and conduct that violates the Code and Standards

Members and Candidates must:

1. Disclose to clients and prospective clients the nature of the services provided, along with information about the cost to the client associated with those services.
2. Disclose to clients and prospective clients the basic format and general principles of the investment processes they use to analyze investments, select securities, and construct portfolios and must promptly disclose any changes that might materially affect those processes.
3. Disclose to clients and prospective clients significant limitations and risks associated with the investment process.

4. Use reasonable judgment in identifying which factors are important to their investment analyses, recommendations, or actions and include those factors in communications with clients and prospective clients.
5. Distinguish between fact and opinion in the presentation of investment analyses and recommendations.

Guidance

Highlights:

- *Nature of Services and Information on Cost*
- *Informing Clients of the Investment Process*
- *Different Forms of Communication*
- *Identifying Risk and Limitations*
- *Report Presentation*
- *Distinction between Facts and Opinions in Reports*

Standard V(B) addresses member and candidate conduct with respect to communicating with clients. Developing and maintaining clear, frequent, and thorough communication practices is critical to providing high-quality financial services to clients. When clients understand the information communicated to them, they also can understand exactly how members and candidates are acting on their behalf, which gives clients the opportunity to make well-informed decisions about their investments. Such understanding can be accomplished only through clear communication.

Disclosing Nature of Services and Information about Costs to Clients and Prospective Clients

A fundamental goal of the Code and Standards is to protect client interests and allow clients to make fully informed decisions about their investments and financial well-being. Providing clients with a description of the nature of the services they can expect from investment professionals and information about the costs to the client for those services is critical to achieving this goal. The disclosures required by Standard V(B) will permit clients to make informed decisions as to whether to engage in professional services with members or candidates or their firms.

Full and fair disclosure builds trust with clients, and the disclosure of information about costs benefits clients and protects their interests. Standard V(B) makes clear that required disclosures cover all professional services provided by members and candidates. A clear understanding of the services that members and candidates provide is a foundational element of the client relationship. Clients must understand what services the member or candidate will provide and, critically, what services will not be provided so that members and candidates can set appropriate expectations. It is best practice for members and candidates with client-facing responsibilities to clearly set out in written form at the outset of the engagement a description of the nature and parameters of the professional services as part of the engagement agreement, contract, or other documents memorializing the terms of the client relationship.

In addition to understanding the nature of the services, clients must understand the cost they will be expected to pay for those services so they can make informed decisions about the professional services being provided. This standard requires members and candidates to inform their clients and prospective clients about the services they will receive and the associated costs. Disclosures regarding the cost of the services to clients mandated by Standard V(B) are those expected to be charged to and paid for by the client. Members and candidates should provide a reasonable amount of detail regarding the costs incurred by clients. The standard, however, does not require members and candidates to provide specific dollar amounts. For example, a firm that charges clients a quarterly fee based on the market value of assets under management will be unable to specify a dollar amount in advance. Members and candidates are also not required to disclose a description of the costs to the firm of providing those services. Again, best practice is for members and candidates with client-facing responsibilities to disclose information about the nature of the services and the related costs at the outset of the relationship as part of the client agreement.

The disclosure responsibilities of members and candidates under this standard are ongoing. Initial disclosures at the outset of the relationship alone may not meet the requirements of the standard. If the services or costs change, members and candidates must update the disclosures and provide the updated information to all impacted clients and prospective clients on a timely basis.

In addition, the scope of the disclosures is not limited to only those costs charged by the entity with which the client is in a direct relationship. Members and candidates with client-facing responsibilities must provide disclosures about all of the costs that are associated with the investment services and products that are provided to the client. This includes information on costs arising out of services provided by affiliates, related entities, or third parties for products and services utilized by members, candidates, or their firms in providing their services to clients. Members and candidates may not rely on the sophistication of clients and their supposed understanding of the nature and details of the investment process as a reason for not providing the information required by this standard. However, the information may be tailored to the knowledge and sophistication of each individual client.

The manner in which members and candidates provide the disclosures required by Standard V(B) is at their individual discretion so long as the disclosures are appropriate, accurate, timely, and complete. Best practice dictates that such disclosures be made in written form. Often, in large firms, disclosures about charges to and payments expected by clients are dictated by firm policy and practice. However, this does not relieve members or candidates of their responsibility to provide this information when that is part of their professional responsibilities. While members and candidates rely on and can be directed to use firm-generated disclosures, members and candidates should ensure that these disclosures meet the requirements of the Code and Standards. They have the responsibility to call to their firm's attention when the communication is lacking, flawed, or insufficient to meet the members' and candidates' responsibilities under the Code and Standards. In such a case, members and candidates should, when possible, supplement disclosures from the firm that they consider insufficient to meet the requirements of this standard. Ultimately, if members or candidates cannot rectify or supplement inadequate disclosures mandated by the firm, they should document their objections and take steps to dissociate from the activity.

Generally, this standard affects only client-facing members. While CFA Institute encourages all investment professionals to help ensure that clients receive sufficient disclosures, the standard does not impose a duty on members and candidates who do not interact with clients to ensure that others, not subject to the Code and Standards, comply with Standard V(B). As with other standards that may not be applicable to the professional responsibilities of all members and candidates (e.g., investment performance, suitability), those members and candidates who are part of a team of investment professionals providing services to clients but who do not have client-facing responsibilities need not expand their realm of responsibility to ensure appropriate disclosures to clients are made regarding the nature of services and the associated costs.

Informing Clients of the Investment Process

Members and candidates must adequately describe to clients and prospective clients the manner in which they conduct the investment decision-making process. Such disclosure should address factors that have positive and negative influences on the recommendations, including significant risks and limitations of the investment process used. The member or candidate must keep clients and other interested parties informed on an ongoing basis about changes to the investment process, especially newly identified significant risks and limitations. Only by thoroughly understanding the nature of the investment product or service can a client determine whether changes to that product or service could materially affect his or her investment objectives.

Understanding the basic characteristics of an investment is of great importance in judging the suitability of that investment on a standalone basis, but it is especially important in determining the impact each investment will have on the characteristics of a portfolio. Although the risk and return characteristics of a common stock might seem to be essentially the same for any investor when the stock is viewed in isolation, the effects of those characteristics greatly depend on the other investments held. For instance, if the particular stock will represent 90% of an individual's investments, the stock's importance in the portfolio is vastly different from what it would be to an investor with a highly diversified portfolio for whom the stock will represent only 2% of the holdings.

A firm's investment policy may include the use of outside advisers to manage various portions of clients' assets under management. Members and candidates should inform the clients about the specialization or diversification expertise provided by the external adviser(s). This information allows clients to understand the full mix of products and strategies being applied that may affect their investment objectives.

Different Forms of Communication

For purposes of Standard V(B), communication is not confined to a written report of the type traditionally generated by an analyst researching a security, company, or industry. A presentation of information can be made via any means of communication, including in-person recommendation or description, telephone conversation, media broadcast, or transmission by computer (e.g., on the internet).

Computer and mobile device communications have rapidly evolved over the past few years. Members and candidates using any social media service to communicate business information must be diligent in their efforts to avoid unintended problems because these services may not be available to all clients. When providing information to clients through new technologies, members and candidates should take reasonable steps to ensure that such delivery would treat all clients fairly and, if necessary, be considered publicly disseminated.

The nature of client communications is highly diverse—from one word ("buy" or "sell") to in-depth reports of more than 100 pages. A communication may contain a general recommendation about the market, asset allocations, or classes of investments (e.g., stocks, bonds, real estate) or may relate to a specific security. If recommendations are contained in capsule form (such as a recommended stock list), members and candidates should notify clients that additional information and analyses are available from the producer of the report.

Identifying Risks and Limitations

Members and candidates must outline to clients and prospective clients significant risks and limitations of the analysis contained in their investment products or recommendations. The type and nature of significant risks will depend on the investment process that members and candidates are following and on the personal circumstances of the client. In general, the use of leverage constitutes a significant risk and should be disclosed.

Members and candidates must adequately disclose the general market-related risks and the risks associated with the use of complex financial instruments that are deemed significant. Other types of risks that members and candidates may consider disclosing include, but are not limited to, counterparty risk, country risk, sector or industry risk, security-specific risk, and credit risk.

Investment securities and vehicles may have limiting factors that influence a client's or potential client's investment decision. Members and candidates must report to clients and prospective clients the existence of limitations significant to the decision-making process. Examples of such factors and attributes include, but are not limited to, investment liquidity and capacity. Liquidity is the ability to liquidate an investment on a timely basis at a reasonable cost. Capacity is the investment amount beyond which returns will be negatively affected by new investments.

The appropriateness of risk disclosure should be assessed on the basis of what was known at the time the investment action was taken (often called an *ex ante* basis). Members and candidates must disclose significant risks known to them at the time of the disclosure. Members and candidates cannot be expected to disclose risks they are unaware of at the time recommendations or investment actions are made. In assessing compliance with Standard V(B), it is important to establish knowledge of a purported significant risk or limitation. A one-time investment loss that occurs after the disclosure does not constitute a pertinent factor in assessing whether significant risks and limitations were properly disclosed. Having no knowledge of a risk or limitation that subsequently triggers a loss may reveal a deficiency in the diligence and reasonable basis of the research of the member or candidate but may not reveal a breach of Standard V(B).

Report Presentation

Once the analytical process has been completed, the member or candidate who prepares the report must include those elements that are important to the analysis and conclusions of the report so that the reader can follow and challenge the report's reasoning. A report writer who has done adequate investigation may emphasize certain areas, touch briefly on others, and omit certain aspects deemed unimportant. For instance, a report may dwell on a quarterly earnings release or new-product introduction and omit other matters as long as the analyst clearly stipulates the limits to the scope of the report.

Investment advice based on quantitative research and analysis must be supported by readily available reference material and should be applied in a manner consistent with previously applied methodology. If changes in methodology are made, they should be highlighted.

Distinction between Facts and Opinions in Reports

Standard V(B) requires that opinion be separated from fact. Violations often occur when reports fail to separate the past from the future by not indicating that earnings estimates, changes in the outlook for dividends, or future market price information are *opinions* subject to future circumstances.

In the case of complex quantitative analyses, members and candidates must clearly separate fact from statistical conjecture and should identify the known limitations of an analysis. Members and candidates may violate Standard V(B) by failing to identify the limits of statistically developed projections because such omission leaves readers unaware of the limits of the published projections.

Members and candidates should explicitly discuss with clients and prospective clients the assumptions used in the investment models and processes to generate the analysis. Caution should be used in promoting the perceived accuracy of any model or process to clients because the ultimate output is merely an estimate of future results and not a certainty.

49 STANDARD V(B): RECOMMENDED PROCEDURES

Because the selection of relevant factors is an analytical skill, determination of whether a member or candidate has used reasonable judgment in excluding and including information in research reports depends heavily on case-by-case review rather than a specific checklist.

Members and candidates should encourage their firms to have a rigorous methodology for reviewing research that is created for publication and dissemination to clients.

To assist in the after-the-fact review of a report, the member or candidate must maintain records indicating the nature of the research and should, if asked, be able to supply additional information to the client (or any user of the report) covering factors not included in the report.

50 STANDARD V(B): APPLICATION OF THE STANDARD

Example 1 (Costs of Services to Clients):

The nature of ABC Capital Private Equity Fund III's investments requires ABC Capital to routinely provide structuring advice to the companies in which the fund invests, for which ABC Capital charges a fee to those companies. It is the policy of ABC Capital to remit the fees it earns for restructuring advice to the fund if the investment in the underlying company decreases in value, but it retains the fees if the investment in the underlying company increases in value. The private placement memorandum does not disclose this arrangement because the firm's CEO, Alex Alphonso, views this as a common industry practice and that it provides a "win-win" for investors. ABC Capital's services contribute significantly to the returns enjoyed by investors in the ABC Capital Private Equity Fund III, and ABC Capital earns a substantial fee.

> *Comment*: Alphonso is in violation of Standard V(B) because the compensation received by ABC Capital has not been disclosed to clients who are investors in the fund. Alphonso may not rely on the sophistication of clients and their assumed understanding of the nature and details of the fee arrangements with underlying companies in which ABC Capital invests in as a reason for not providing the information required by this standard. This is true even though investors in ABC Private Equity Fund III benefit from the arrangement.

Example 2 (Costs of Services to Clients):

January James is an investment adviser tasked with completing a manager search for a client's portfolio. The search mandate is to identify a shortlist of investment managers who offer core fixed-income strategies managed to the benchmark identified in the client's investment policy statement. James begins her search with a set of criteria defined by her firm's manager research process policy. She identifies three candidates who fulfill these criteria but notices that her top-ranked manager has significantly higher fees than the other candidates on her list. Her firm's search criteria list fees as less important relative to the other criteria for ranking investment managers. To present investment performance for uniform comparison, James creates a fee comparison chart that lists each manager's performance on a gross-of-fee basis. She presents gross-of-fee performance over the same time periods and relative to the same benchmark. She also calculates the total amount of fees that would have been paid during each of the performance time periods presented. Finally, she lists each manager's fee schedule and any additional fees that may be charged outside the published fees. She explains to her client that prior to final selection, the investment managers will be required to present their final fee proposal.

> *Comment*: James's presentation of manager fees is appropriate because she provided a uniform comparison of manager services. Her presentation adheres to Standard V(B) Communication with Clients and Prospective Clients, which requires disclosure about the nature of services provided, along with information about the cost associated with those services.

Example 3 (Disclosure of Changed Fee Calculation Methodology):

Marc Maalouf works in a branch office for a large wealth management firm. The firm's fees are based on a percentage of the value of the assets managed in each client account. The firm has a standard method for valuing assets and calculating fees for all of its clients, which is disclosed to each client at the outset of the relationship. Maalouf becomes aware that, over time, the firm has transitioned to (1) using the market value of client assets at the end of the billing cycle instead of the average daily balance of the account and (2) including cash and cash equivalents in the fee calculation, which were previously excluded.

> *Comment*: Advisory fees are critical information that a client needs to know. Developing and maintaining clear, frequent, and thorough communication with clients about costs for the investment adviser's services allows them to make well-informed decisions about their investments, including about whether to engage or retain an investment adviser. Maalouf and his firm may change the advisory fee calculation methodology and policies over time for existing accounts, but Maalouf must make clients aware of any such changes. It is improper to change fee calculation methodology without disclosure, even if it results in lower fees.

Example 4 (Sufficient Disclosure of Investment System):

Sarah Williamson, director of marketing for Country Technicians, Inc., is convinced that she has found the perfect formula for increasing Country Technicians' income and diversifying its product base. Williamson plans to build on Country Technicians' reputation as a leading money manager by marketing an exclusive and expensive investment advice letter to high-net-worth individuals. One hitch in the plan is the complexity of Country Technicians' investment system—a combination of technical trading rules (based on historical price and volume fluctuations) and portfolio construction rules designed to minimize risk. To simplify the newsletter, she decides to include only each week's top five "buy" and "sell" recommendations and to leave out details of the valuation models and the portfolio structuring scheme.

Comment: Williamson's plans for the newsletter violate Standard V(B). Williamson need not describe the investment system in detail in order to implement the advice effectively, but she must inform clients of Country Technicians' basic process and logic. Without understanding the basis for a recommendation, clients cannot possibly understand its limitations or its inherent risks.

Example 5 (Providing Opinions as Facts):

Richard Dox is a mining analyst for East Bank Securities. He has just finished his report on Boisy Bay Minerals. Included in his report is his own assessment of the geological extent of mineral reserves likely to be found on the company's land. Dox completed this calculation on the basis of the core samples from the company's latest drilling. According to Dox's calculations, the company has more than 500,000 ounces of gold on the property. Dox concludes his research report as follows: "Based on the fact that the company has 500,000 ounces of gold to be mined, I recommend a strong *buy*."

Comment: If Dox issues the report as written, he will violate Standard V(B). His calculation of the total gold reserves for the property based on the company's recent sample drilling is a quantitative opinion, not a fact. Opinion must be distinguished from fact in research reports.

Example 6 (Proper Description of a Security):

Olivia Thomas, an analyst at Government Brokers, Inc., which is a brokerage firm specializing in government bond trading, has produced a report that describes an investment strategy designed to benefit from an expected decline in US interest rates. The firm's derivative products group has designed a structured product that will allow the firm's clients to benefit from this strategy. Thomas's report describing the strategy indicates that high returns are possible if various scenarios for declining interest rates are assumed. Citing the proprietary nature of the structured product underlying the strategy, the report does not describe in detail how the firm is able to offer such returns or the related risks in the scenarios, nor does the report address the likely returns of the strategy if, contrary to expectations, interest rates rise.

Comment: Thomas has violated Standard V(B) because her report fails to describe properly the basic characteristics of the actual and implied risks of the investment strategy, including how the structure was created and the degree to which leverage was embedded in the structure. The report should include a balanced discussion of how the strategy would perform in the case of rising as well as falling interest rates, preferably illustrating how the strategies might be expected to perform in the event of a reasonable variety of interest rate– and credit risk–spread scenarios. If liquidity issues are relevant with regard to the valuation of either the derivatives or the underlying securities, provisions the firm has made to address those risks should also be disclosed.

Example 7 (Notification of Fund Mandate Change):

May & Associates is an aggressive growth manager that has represented itself since its inception as a specialist at investing in small-cap US stocks. One of May's selection criteria is a maximum capitalization of US$250 million for any given company. After a string of successful years of superior performance relative to its peers, May has expanded its client base significantly, to the point at which assets under management now exceed US$3 billion. For liquidity purposes, May's chief investment officer (CIO) decides to lift the maximum permissible market-cap ceiling to US$500 million and change the firm's sales and marketing literature accordingly to inform prospective clients and third-party consultants.

> *Comment*: Although May's CIO is correct about informing potentially interested parties as to the change in investment process, he must also notify May's existing clients. Among the latter group might be a number of clients who not only retained May as a small-cap manager but also retained mid-cap and large-cap specialists in a multiple-manager approach. Such clients could regard May's change of criteria as a style change that distorts their overall asset allocations.

Example 8 (Notification of Fund Mandate Change):

Rather than lifting the ceiling for its universe from US$250 million to US$500 million, May & Associates extends its small-cap universe to include a number of non-US companies.

> *Comment*: Standard V(B) requires that May's CIO advise May's clients of this change because the firm may have been retained by some clients specifically for its prowess at investing in US small-cap stocks. Other changes that require client notification are introducing derivatives to emulate a certain market sector or relaxing various other constraints, such as portfolio beta. In all such cases, members and candidates must disclose changes to all interested parties.

Example 9 (Notification of Changes to the Investment Process):

RJZ Capital Management is an active value style equity manager that selects stocks by using a combination of four multifactor models. The firm has found favorable results when backtesting the most recent 10 years of available market data in a new dividend discount model (DDM) designed by the firm. This model is based on projected inflation rates, earnings growth rates, and interest rates. The president of RJZ decides to replace its simple model that uses price to trailing 12-month earnings with the new DDM.

> *Comment*: Because the introduction of a new and different valuation model represents a material change in the investment process, RJZ's president must communicate the change to the firm's clients. RJZ is moving away from a model based on hard data toward a new model that is at least partly dependent on the firm's forecasting skills. Clients would likely view such a model as a significant change rather than a mere refinement of RJZ's process.

Example 10 (Notification of Changes to the Investment Process):

RJZ Capital Management loses the chief architect of its multifactor valuation system. Without informing its clients, the president of RJZ decides to redirect the firm's talents and resources toward developing a product for passive equity management—a product that will emulate the performance of a major market index.

> *Comment*: By failing to disclose to clients a substantial change to its investment process, the president of RJZ has violated Standard V(B).

Example 11 (Notification of Changes to the Investment Process):

At Fundamental Asset Management, Inc., the responsibility for selecting stocks for addition to the firm's "approved" list has just shifted from individual security analysts to a committee consisting of the research director and three senior portfolio managers. Eleanor Morales, a portfolio manager with Fundamental Asset Management, thinks this change is not important enough to communicate to her clients.

> *Comment*: Morales must disclose the process change to all her clients. Some of Fundamental's clients might be concerned about the morale and motivation among the firm's best research analysts after such a change. Moreover, clients might challenge the stock-picking track record of the portfolio managers and might even want to monitor the situation closely.

Example 12 (Sufficient Disclosure of Investment System):

Amanda Chinn is the investment director for Diversified Asset Management, which manages the endowment of a charitable organization. Because of recent staff departures, Diversified has decided to limit its direct investment focus to large-cap securities and supplement the needs for small-cap and mid-cap management by hiring outside fund managers. In describing the planned strategy change to the charity, Chinn's update letter states, "As investment director, I will directly oversee the investment team managing the endowment's large-capitalization allocation. I will coordinate the selection and ongoing review of external managers responsible for allocations to classes." The letter also describes the reasons for the change and the characteristics external managers must have to be considered.

> *Comment*: Standard V(B) requires the disclosure of the investment process used to construct the portfolio of the fund. Changing the investment process from managing all classes of investments within the firm to the use of external managers is one example of information that needs to be communicated to clients. Chinn and her firm have embraced the principles of Standard V(B) by providing their client with relevant information. The charity can now make a reasonable decision about whether Diversified Asset Management remains the appropriate manager for its fund.

Example 13 (Notification of Changes to the Investment Process):

Michael Papis is the chief investment officer of his state's retirement fund. The fund has always used outside advisers for the real estate allocation, and this information is clearly presented in all fund communications. Thomas Nagle, a recognized sell-side research analyst and Papis's business school classmate, recently left the investment bank he worked for to start his own asset management firm, Accessible Real Estate. Nagle is trying to build his assets under management and contacts Papis about gaining some of the retirement fund's allocation. In the previous few years, the performance of the retirement fund's real estate investments was in line with the fund's benchmark but was not extraordinary. Papis decides to help out his old friend and also to seek better returns by moving the real estate allocation to Accessible. The only notice of the change in adviser appears in the next annual report in the listing of associated advisers.

Comment: Papis has violated Standard V(B). He attempted to hide the nature of his decision to change external managers by making only a limited disclosure. The plan recipients and the fund's trustees need to be aware when changes are made to ensure that operational procedures are being followed.

See also Standard IV(C) Responsibilities of Supervisors, Standard V(A) Diligence and Reasonable Basis, and Standard VI(A) Disclosure of Conflicts.

Example 14 (Notification of Errors):

Jérôme Dupont works for the credit research group of XYZ Asset Management, where he is in charge of developing and updating credit risk models. In order to perform accurately, his models need to be regularly updated with the latest market data.

Dupont does not interact with or manage money for any of the firm's clients. He is in contact with the firm's US corporate bond fund manager, John Smith, who has only very superficial knowledge of the model and who from time to time asks very basic questions regarding the output recommendations. Smith does not consult Dupont with respect to finalizing his clients' investment strategies.

Dupont's recently assigned objective is to develop a new emerging market corporate credit risk model. The firm is planning to expand into emerging credit, and the development of such a model is a critical step in this process. Because Smith seems to follow the model's recommendations without much concern for its quality as he develops his clients' investment strategies, Dupont decides to focus his time on the development of the new emerging market model and neglects to update the US model.

After several months without regular updates, Dupont's diagnostic statistics start to show alarming signs with respect to the quality of the US credit model. Instead of conducting the long and complicated data update, Dupont introduces new codes into his model with some limited new data as a quick "fix." He thinks this change will address the issue without needing to complete the full data update, so he continues working on the new emerging market model.

Several months following the quick "fix," another set of diagnostic statistics reveals nonsensical results and Dupont realizes that his earlier change contained an error. He quickly corrects the error and alerts Smith. Smith realizes that some of the prior trades he performed were due to erroneous model results. Smith rebalances the portfolio to remove the securities purchased based on the questionable results without reporting the issue to anyone else.

Comment: Smith violated V(B) by not disclosing a material error in the investment process. Clients should have been informed about the error and the corrective actions the firm was undertaking on their behalf.

See also Standard V(A) Diligence and Reasonable Basis.

Example 15 (Notification of Risks and Limitations):

Quantitative analyst Yuri Yakovlev has developed an investment strategy that selects small-cap stocks on the basis of quantitative signals. Yakovlev's strategy typically identifies only a small number of stocks (10–20) that tend to be illiquid, but according to his backtests, the strategy generates significant risk-adjusted returns. The partners at Yakovlev's firm, QSC Capital, are impressed by these results. After a thorough examination of the strategy's risks, stress testing, historical backtesting, and scenario analysis, QSC decides to seed the strategy with US$10 million of internal capital in order for Yakovlev to create a track record for the strategy.

After two years, the strategy has generated performance returns greater than the appropriate benchmark and the Sharpe ratio of the fund is close to 1.0. On the basis of these results, QSC decides to actively market the fund to large institutional investors. While creating the offering materials, Yakovlev informs the marketing team that the capacity of the strategy is limited. The extent of the limitation is difficult to ascertain with precision; it depends on market liquidity and other factors in his model that can evolve over time. Yakovlev indicates that given the current market conditions, investments in the fund beyond US$100 million of capital could become more difficult and negatively affect expected fund returns.

Alan Wellard, the manager of the marketing team, is a partner with 30 years of marketing experience and explains to Yakovlev that these are complex technical issues that will muddy the marketing message. According to Wellard, the offering material should focus solely on the great track record of the fund. Yakovlev does not object because the fund, with US$12 million of capital, is very far from the US$100 million threshold.

> *Comment*: Yakovlev and Wellard have not appropriately disclosed a significant limitation associated with the investment product. Yakovlev believes this limitation, once reached, will materially affect the returns of the fund. While the fund is currently far from the US$100 million mark, current and prospective investors must be made aware of this capacity issue. If significant limitations are complicated to grasp and clients do not have the technical background required to understand them, Yakovlev and Wellard should either educate the clients or ascertain whether the fund is suitable for each client.

Example 16 (Notification of Risks and Limitations):

Brickell Advisers offers investment advisory services mainly to South American clients. Julietta Ramon, a risk analyst at Brickell, describes to clients how the firm uses value at risk (VaR) analysis to track the risk of its strategies. Ramon assures clients that calculating a VaR at a 99% confidence level, using a 20-day holding period, and applying a methodology based on an *ex ante* Monte Carlo simulation is extremely effective. The firm has never had losses greater than those predicted by this VaR analysis.

> *Comment*: Ramon has not sufficiently communicated the risks associated with the investment process to satisfy the requirements of Standard V(B). The losses predicted by a VaR analysis depend greatly on the inputs used in the model. The size and probability of losses can differ significantly from what an individual model predicts. Ramon must disclose how the inputs were selected and the potential limitations and risks associated with the investment strategy.

Example 17 (Notification of Risks and Limitations):

Lily Smith attended an industry conference and noticed that John Baker, an investment manager with Baker Associates, attracted a great deal of attention from the conference participants. On the basis of her knowledge of Baker's reputation and the interest he received at the conference, Smith recommends adding Baker Associates to the approved manager platform. Her recommendation to the approval committee included the statement "John Baker is well respected in the industry, and his insights are consistently sought after by investors. Our clients are sure to benefit from investing with Baker Associates."

Comment: Smith is not appropriately separating facts from opinions in her recommendation to include the manager within the platform. Her actions conflict with the requirements of Standard V(B). Smith is relying on her opinions about Baker's reputation and the fact that many attendees were talking with him at the conference. Smith should also review the requirements of Standard V(A) regarding reasonable basis to determine the level of review necessary to recommend Baker Associates.

STANDARD V(C) RECORD RETENTION

51

- ☐ demonstrate the application of the Code of Ethics and Standards of Professional Conduct to situations involving issues of professional integrity
- ☐ recommend practices and procedures designed to prevent violations of the Code of Ethics and Standards of Professional Conduct
- ☐ identify conduct that conforms to the Code and Standards and conduct that violates the Code and Standards

Members and Candidates must develop and maintain appropriate records to support their investment analyses, recommendations, actions, and other investment-related communications with clients and prospective clients.

Guidance

Highlights:

- *New Media Records*
- *Records Are Property of the Firm*
- *Local Requirements*

Members and candidates must retain records that substantiate the scope of their research and reasons for their actions or conclusions. The retention requirement applies to decisions to buy or sell a security as well as reviews undertaken that do not lead to a change in position. Which records are required to support recommendations or investment actions depends on the role of the member or candidate in the investment decision-making process. Records may be maintained either in hard copy or electronic form.

Some examples of supporting documentation that assists the member or candidate in meeting the requirements for retention are as follows:

- personal notes from meetings with the covered company,
- press releases or presentations issued by the covered company,
- computer-based model outputs and analyses,
- computer-based model input parameters,
- risk analyses of securities' impacts on a portfolio,
- selection criteria for external advisers,

- notes from clients from meetings to review investment policy statements, and
- outside research reports.

New Media Records

The increased use of new and evolving technological formats (e.g., social media) for gathering and sharing information creates new challenges in maintaining the appropriate records and files. The nature or format of the information does not remove a member's or candidate's responsibility to maintain a record of information used in his or her analysis or communicated to clients.

Members and candidates should understand that although employers and local regulators are developing digital media retention policies, these policies may lag behind the advent of new communication channels. Such lag places greater responsibility on the individual for ensuring that all relevant information is retained. Examples of non-print media formats that should be retained include, but are not limited to,

- e-mails,
- text messages,
- blog posts, and
- social media posts.

Records Are Property of the Firm

As a general matter, records created as part of a member's or candidate's professional activity on behalf of his or her employer are the property of the firm. When a member or candidate leaves a firm to seek other employment, the member or candidate cannot take the property of the firm, including original forms or copies of supporting records of the member's or candidate's work, to the new employer without the express consent of the previous employer. The member or candidate cannot use historical recommendations or research reports created at the previous firm because the supporting documentation is unavailable. For future use, the member or candidate must re-create the supporting records at the new firm with information gathered through public sources or directly from the covered company and not from memory or sources obtained at the previous employer.

Local Requirements

Local regulators often impose requirements on members, candidates, and their firms related to record retention that must be followed. Firms may also implement policies detailing the applicable time frame for retaining research and client communication records. Fulfilling such regulatory and firm requirements satisfies the requirements of Standard V(C). In the absence of regulatory guidance or firm policies, CFA Institute recommends maintaining records for at least seven years.

52 STANDARD V(C): RECOMMENDED PROCEDURES

The responsibility to maintain records that support investment action generally falls with the firm rather than individuals. Members and candidates must, however, archive research notes and other documents, either electronically or in hard copy, that support their current investment-related communications. Doing so will assist their firms in complying with requirements for preservation of internal or external records.

STANDARD V(C): APPLICATION OF THE STANDARD 53

Example 1 (Record Retention and IPS Objectives and Recommendations):

One of Nikolas Lindstrom's clients is upset by the negative investment returns of his equity portfolio. The investment policy statement for the client requires that the portfolio manager follow a benchmark-oriented approach. The benchmark for the client includes a 35% investment allocation in the technology sector. The client acknowledges that this allocation was appropriate, but over the past three years, technology stocks have suffered severe losses. The client complains to the investment manager for allocating so much money to this sector.

> *Comment*: For Lindstrom, having appropriate records is important to show that over the past three years, the portion of technology stocks in the benchmark index was 35%, as called for in the IPS. Lindstrom should also have the client's IPS stating that the benchmark was appropriate for the client's investment objectives. He should also have records indicating that the investment has been explained appropriately to the client and that the IPS was updated on a regular basis. Taking these actions, Lindstrom would be in compliance with Standard V(C).

Example 2 (Record Retention and Research Process):

Malcolm Young is a research analyst who writes numerous reports rating companies in the luxury retail industry. His reports are based on a variety of sources, including interviews with company managers, manufacturers, and economists; on-site company visits; customer surveys; and secondary research from analysts covering related industries.

> *Comment*: Young must carefully document and keep copies of all the information that goes into his reports, including the secondary or third-party research of other analysts. Failure to maintain such files would violate Standard V(C).

Example 3 (Records as Firm, Not Employee, Property):

Martin Blank develops an analytical model while he is employed by Green Partners Investment Management, LLP (GPIM). While at the firm, he systematically documents the assumptions that make up the model as well as his reasoning behind the assumptions. As a result of the success of his model, Blank is hired to be the head of the research department of one of GPIM's competitors. Blank takes copies of the records supporting his model to his new firm.

> *Comment*: The records created by Blank supporting the research model he developed at GPIM are the records of GPIM. Taking the documents with him to his new employer without GPIM's permission violates Standard V(C). To use the model in the future, Blank must re-create the records supporting his model at the new firm.

54 STANDARD VI: CONFLICTS OF INTEREST

- [ ] demonstrate the application of the Code of Ethics and Standards of Professional Conduct to situations involving issues of professional integrity
- [ ] recommend practices and procedures designed to prevent violations of the Code of Ethics and Standards of Professional Conduct
- [ ] identify conduct that conforms to the Code and Standards and conduct that violates the Code and Standards

Standard VI(A) Avoid or Disclose Conflicts

Members and Candidates must avoid or make full and fair disclosure of all matters that could reasonably be expected to impair their independence and objectivity or interfere with respective duties to their clients, prospective clients, and employer. Members and Candidates must ensure that such disclosures are prominent, are delivered in plain language, and communicate the relevant information effectively.

Guidance

Highlights:

- *Disclosure of Conflicts to Employers*
- *Disclosure of Conflicts to Clients*
- *Cross-Departmental Conflicts*
- *Conflicts with Stock Ownership*
- *Conflicts as a Board Member or Director*

A conflict of interest is any matter that could reasonably be expected to impair independence and objectivity or raise a question about whether actions, judgment, or decision making is free from bias. Conflicts of interest occur when there is a personal or professional interest that may impair a member's or candidate's ability to perform his or her professional responsibilities in an independent and objective manner. Conflicts of interest often arise in the investment profession. Conflicts can occur between the interests of clients, the interests of employers, and the member's or candidate's own personal interests. Common sources for conflict are compensation structures, especially incentive and bonus structures that provide immediate returns for members and candidates with little or no consideration of long-term value creation. Identifying and managing conflicts of interest is critically important to engaging in ethical conduct.

Best practice is to avoid actual conflicts or the appearance of conflicts of interest. When it is not reasonable for members and candidates to avoid a conflict, clear and complete disclosure to mitigate the conflict is necessary.

Standard VI(A) protects investors and employers by requiring members and candidates to avoid or fully disclose to clients, potential clients, and employers all actual and potential conflicts of interest. When a member or candidate has made full disclosure of an unavoidable conflict, the member's or candidate's employer, clients, and prospective clients will have the information needed to evaluate the objectivity of the investment advice or action taken on their behalf.

To be effective, disclosures must be prominent and must be made in plain language and in a manner designed to effectively communicate the information. Members and candidates are responsible for determining how often, in what manner, and in what particular circumstances the disclosure of conflicts must be made. Best practice dictates updating disclosures when the nature of a conflict of interest changes materially—for example, if the nature of a conflict of interest worsens through the introduction of bonuses based on each quarter's profits as opposed to annual profits. In making and updating disclosures of conflicts of interest, members and candidates should err on the side of caution to ensure that conflicts are effectively communicated.

Disclosure of Conflicts to Employers

Disclosure of conflicts to employers may be appropriate in many instances. When reporting conflicts of interest to employers, members and candidates must give their employers enough information to assess the impact of the conflict. By complying with employer guidelines, members and candidates allow their employers to avoid potentially embarrassing and costly ethical or regulatory violations.

Reportable situations include conflicts that would interfere with rendering unbiased investment advice and conflicts that would cause a member or candidate to act not in the employer's best interest. The same circumstances that generate conflicts to be reported to clients and prospective clients also dictate reporting to employers. Ownership of stocks analyzed or recommended, participation on outside boards, and financial or other pressures that could influence a decision are to be promptly reported to the employer so that their impact can be assessed and a decision on how to resolve the conflict can be made.

The mere appearance of a conflict of interest may create problems for members, candidates, and their employers. Therefore, many of the conflicts previously mentioned may be explicitly prohibited by an employer in order to avoid those conflicts altogether. For example, many employers restrict personal trading, outside board membership, and related activities to prevent situations that might not normally be considered problematic from a conflict-of-interest point of view but that could give the appearance of a conflict of interest. Members and candidates must comply with these employer restrictions. Members and candidates should take reasonable steps to avoid conflicts. However, if the conflicts are not resolved, they must report conflicts promptly.

Standard VI(A) also deals with a member's or candidate's conflicts of interest that might be detrimental to the employer's business. Any potential conflict situation that could prevent clear judgment about or full commitment to the execution of a member's or candidate's duties to the employer should be avoided. If the member or candidate does not avoid the conflict, it must be reported to the member's or candidate's employer.

Disclosure of Conflicts to Clients

Members and candidates must maintain their objectivity when rendering investment advice or taking investment action. Investment advice or actions may be perceived to be tainted in numerous situations. For instance, a member or candidate may not be objective if he or she owns stock in the company that is the subject of an investment recommendation or if the member or candidate has a close personal relationship with the company managers. Requiring members and candidates to disclose all matters that reasonably could be expected to impair the member's or candidate's objectivity when a conflict exists mitigates the conflict and allows clients and prospective clients to judge motives and possible biases for themselves.

While avoiding conflicts altogether is preferred, often in the investment industry, a conflict or the perception of a conflict is not reasonably avoidable. The most obvious conflicts of interest, which must always be avoided or disclosed, are relationships between an issuer and the member, the candidate, or his or her firm (such as a directorship or consultancy by a member; investment banking, underwriting, and financial relationships; broker/dealer market-making activities; and material beneficial ownership of stock). For the purposes of Standard VI(A), members and candidates beneficially own securities or other investments if they have a direct or indirect pecuniary interest in the securities, have the power to vote or direct the voting of the shares of the securities or investments, or have the power to dispose or direct the disposition of the security or investment.

A member or candidate must take reasonable steps to determine whether a conflict of interest exists and disclose to clients any known conflicts of the member's or candidate's firm. As an example, disclosure of broker/dealer market-making activities alerts clients that a purchase or sale might be made from or to the firm's proprietary account and that the firm has a special interest in the price of the stock.

Additionally, disclosures must be made to clients regarding conflicts that may arise in fee arrangements, subadvisory agreements, or other situations involving nonstandard fee structures. Equally important is the disclosure of arrangements in which the firm benefits directly from investment recommendations. An obvious conflict of interest is the rebate of a portion of the service fee some classes of mutual funds charge to investors. Members and candidates must disclose such relationships so clients can fully understand such conflicts.

Cross-Departmental Conflicts

Other circumstances may give rise to actual or potential conflicts of interest. For instance, a sell-side analyst working for a broker/dealer may be encouraged, not only by members of her or his own firm but also by corporate issuers themselves, to write research reports about particular companies. The buy-side analyst is likely to be faced with similar conflicts as banks exercise their underwriting and security-dealing powers. The marketing division may ask an analyst to recommend the stock of a certain company in order to obtain business from that company.

The potential for conflicts of interest also exists with broker-sponsored limited partnerships formed to invest venture capital. Members and candidates may be expected not only to follow issues from these partnerships once they are offered to the public but also to promote the issues in the secondary market after public offerings. Members and candidates must resolve situations presenting potential conflicts of interest or disclose them in accordance with the principles set forth in Standard VI(A).

Conflicts with Stock Ownership

The most prevalent conflict requiring disclosure under Standard VI(A) is a member's or candidate's ownership of stock in companies that he or she recommends to clients or that clients hold. The simplest method for preventing a conflict is to avoid the conflict by prohibiting members and candidates from owning any such securities, but this approach may be overly burdensome and too restrictive. Members and candidates must disclose any beneficial ownership interest in a security or other investment that the member or candidate is recommending. Conflicts arising from personal investing are discussed more fully in the guidance for Standard VI(B).

Conflicts as a Board Member or Director

Service as a board member or director poses three basic conflicts of interest. First, a conflict may exist between the duties owed to clients and the duties owed to shareholders of the company. Second, investment personnel who serve as directors may receive securities or options to purchase securities of the company as compensation for serving on the board, which could raise questions about trading actions that might increase the value of those securities. Third, board service creates the opportunity to receive material nonpublic information involving the company. Even though the information is confidential, the perception could be that information not available to the public is being communicated to a director's firm—whether a broker, investment adviser, or other type of organization. When members or candidates providing investment services also serve as directors, they should be isolated from those making investment decisions by the use of firewalls or similar restrictions.

STANDARD VI(A): APPLICATION OF THE STANDARD

55

Example 1 (Conflict of Interest and Business Relationships):

Henry Weiss is a research analyst with Williamsburg Company, a broker and investment banking firm. Williamsburg's merger and acquisition department has represented Jimco, a conglomerate, in all of Jimco's acquisitions for 20 years. From time to time, Williamsburg officers sit on the boards of directors of various Jimco subsidiaries. Weiss is writing a research report on Jimco.

> *Comment*: Weiss must disclose in his research report Williamsburg's special relationship with Jimco. Broker/dealer management of and participation in public offerings must be disclosed in research reports. Because the position of underwriter to a company entails a special past and potential future relationship with a company that is the subject of investment advice, it threatens the independence and objectivity of the report writer and must be disclosed.

Example 2 (Conflict of Interest and Business Stock Ownership):

The investment management firm of Dover & Roe sells a 25% interest in its partnership to a multinational bank holding company, First of New York. Immediately after the sale, Roy Hobbs, president of Dover & Roe, changes her recommendation for First of New York's common stock from "sell" to "buy" and adds First of New York's commercial paper to Dover & Roe's approved list for purchase.

> *Comment*: Best practice would be for Hobbs to discontinue research coverage of First of New York because the new ownership interest in this company creates a conflict of interest. At minimum, Hobbs must disclose the new relationship with First of New York to all Dover & Roe clients. Hobbs must also require the ownership interest to be disclosed to clients by the firm's portfolio managers when they make specific investment recommendations or take investment actions with respect to First of New York's securities.

Example 3 (Conflict of Interest and Personal Stock Ownership):

Karl Fargmon, a research analyst who follows firms producing office equipment, has been recommending purchase of Kincaid Printing because of its innovative new line of copiers. After his initial report on the company, Fargmon's wife inherits from a distant relative US$3 million of Kincaid stock. One year after his initial report on the company, Fargmon is asked to write a follow-up report on Kincaid.

> *Comment*: At minimum, Fargmon must disclose his wife's ownership of the Kincaid stock to his employer and in his follow-up report. Best practice is to avoid the conflict by asking his employer to assign another analyst to draft the follow-up report.

Example 4 (Conflict of Interest and Personal Stock Ownership):

Julie Roberts is speculating in penny stocks for her own account and purchases 100,000 shares of Drew Mining, Inc., for US$0.30 a share. She intends to sell these shares at the sign of any substantial upward price movement of the stock. A week later, her employer asks her to write a report on penny stocks in the mining industry to be published in two weeks. Even without owning the Drew stock, Roberts would recommend it in her report as a "buy." A surge in the price of the stock to the US$2 range is likely to result once the report is issued.

> *Comment*: Roberts must disclose the conflict to her employer and should consider declining the research assignment on Drew Mining. If Roberts's employer has her write the report despite the conflict, Roberts must disclose the conflict in her report.

Example 5 (Conflict of Interest and Compensation Arrangements):

Sarah Snead, a portfolio manager for Thomas Investment Counsel, LLC, specializes in managing public retirement funds and defined benefit pension plan accounts, all of which have long-term investment objectives. A year ago, Snead's employer, in an attempt to motivate and retain key investment professionals, introduced a bonus compensation system that rewards portfolio managers on the basis of quarterly performance relative to their peers and to certain benchmark indexes. In an attempt to improve the short-term performance of her accounts, Snead changes her investment strategy and purchases several high-beta stocks for client portfolios. These purchases are seemingly contrary to the clients' investment policy statements (IPSs). No change in objective or strategy has been recommended by Snead during the year.

> *Comment*: Snead has violated Standard VI(A) by failing to inform her clients of the changes in her compensation arrangement with her employer, which created a conflict of interest between her compensation and her clients' IPSs. Firms may pay employees on the basis of performance, but pressure by Thomas Investment Counsel to achieve short-term performance goals conflicts with the requirement to take only investment actions that are consistent with the objectives of Snead's accounts.

Example 6 (Conflict of Interest and Compensation Arrangements):

Kevin Carter is a representative with Bengal International, a registered broker/dealer. Carter is approached by a stock promoter for Badger Company, who offers to pay Carter additional compensation for sales of Badger Company's stock to Carter's clients. Carter accepts the stock promoter's offer but does not disclose the arrangement to his clients or to his employer. Carter sells shares of the stock to his clients.

Comment: Carter has violated Standard VI(A) by failing to disclose to clients that he is receiving additional compensation for recommending and selling Badger stock. At minimum, Carter must disclose the arrangement with Badger to his clients so they may evaluate whether Carter's recommendations to buy Badger were affected by this arrangement. Best practice is for Carter to avoid this conflict of interest altogether by declining the offer of additional compensation from Badger Company.

Example 7 (Conflict of Interest and Requested Favors):

Henri Papis is the chief investment officer of his state's retirement fund. The fund has always used external managers for the real estate allocation, and this information is clearly presented in all fund communications. Eric Nagle, a recognized sell-side research analyst and Papis's business school classmate, recently left the investment bank he worked for to start his own asset management firm, Accessible Real Estate. Nagle is trying to build his assets under management, and he contacts Papis about gaining some of the retirement fund's real estate allocation. In the previous few years, the performance of the retirement fund's real estate investments was in line with the fund's benchmark but was not extraordinary. Papis decides to help out his old friend and also to seek better returns by moving the real estate allocation to Accessible. The only notice of the change in managers appears in the next annual report in the listing of external managers.

Comment: Papis has violated Standard VI(A) by not disclosing to his employer his personal relationship with Nagle. Disclosure of his past history with Nagle would allow his firm to determine whether the conflict may have impaired Papis's independence in deciding to change external managers.

STANDARD VI(B) PRIORITY OF TRANSACTIONS

56

- ☐ demonstrate the application of the Code of Ethics and Standards of Professional Conduct to situations involving issues of professional integrity
- ☐ recommend practices and procedures designed to prevent violations of the Code of Ethics and Standards of Professional Conduct
- ☐ identify conduct that conforms to the Code and Standards and conduct that violates the Code and Standards

Investment transactions for clients and employers must have priority over investment transactions in which a Member or Candidate is the beneficial owner.

Guidance

Highlights:

- *Avoiding Potential Conflicts*
- *Personal Trading Secondary to Trading for Clients*

- *Standards for Nonpublic Information*
- *Impact on All Accounts with Beneficial Ownership*

Standard VI(B) reinforces the responsibility of members and candidates to give the interests of their clients and employers priority over their personal financial interests. This standard is designed to prevent any potential conflict of interest or the appearance of a conflict of interest with respect to personal transactions. Client interests have priority. Client transactions must take precedence over transactions made on behalf of the member's or candidate's firm or personal transactions.

Avoiding Potential Conflicts

Conflicts between the client's interest and an investment professional's personal interest may occur. Although conflicts of interest exist, nothing is inherently unethical about individual managers, advisers, or mutual fund employees making money from personal investments as long as (1) the client is not disadvantaged by the trade, (2) the investment professional does not benefit personally from trades undertaken for clients, and (3) the investment professional complies with applicable regulatory requirements.

Some situations occur where a member or candidate may need to enter a personal transaction that runs counter to current recommendations or what the portfolio manager is doing for client portfolios. For example, a member or candidate may be required at some point to sell an asset to make a college tuition payment or a down payment on a home, to meet a margin call, or so on. The sale may be contrary to the long-term advice the member or candidate is currently providing to clients. In these situations, the same three criteria given in the preceding paragraph should be applied in the transaction so as to not violate Standard VI(B).

Personal Trading Secondary to Trading for Clients

Standard VI(B) states that transactions for clients and employers must have priority over transactions in securities or other investments for which a member or candidate is the beneficial owner. The objective of the standard is to prevent personal transactions from adversely affecting the interests of clients or employers. A member or candidate having the same investment positions or being co-invested with clients does not always create a conflict. Some clients in certain investment situations require members or candidates to have aligned interests. Personal investment positions or transactions of members or candidates or their firm should never, however, adversely affect client investments.

Standards for Nonpublic Information

Standard VI(B) covers the activities of members and candidates who have knowledge of pending transactions that may be made on behalf of their clients or employers, who have access to nonpublic information during the normal preparation of research recommendations, or who take investment actions. Members and candidates are prohibited from conveying nonpublic information to any person whose relationship to the member or candidate makes the member or candidate a beneficial owner of the person's securities. Members and candidates must not convey this information to any other person if the nonpublic information can be deemed material.

Impact on All Accounts with Beneficial Ownership

Members or candidates may undertake transactions in accounts for which they are a beneficial owner only after their clients and employers have had adequate opportunity to act on a recommendation. Personal transactions include those made for the member's or candidate's own account, for family (including spouse, children, and other immediate family members) accounts, and for accounts in which the member or candidate has a direct or indirect pecuniary interest, such as a trust or retirement account. Family accounts that are client accounts should be treated like any other firm account and should neither be given special treatment nor be disadvantaged because of the family relationship. If a member or candidate has a beneficial ownership in the account, however, the member or candidate may be subject to preclearance or reporting requirements of the employer or applicable law.

STANDARD VI(B): RECOMMENDED PROCEDURES

57

Policies and procedures designed to prevent potential conflicts of interest, and even the appearance of a conflict of interest, with respect to personal transactions are critical to establishing investor confidence in the securities industry. Therefore, members and candidates should urge their firms to establish such policies and procedures. Because investment firms vary greatly in assets under management, types of clients, number of employees, and so on, each firm should have policies regarding personal investing that are best suited to the firm. Members and candidates should then prominently disclose these policies to clients and prospective clients.

The specific provisions of each firm's standards will vary, but all firms should adopt certain basic procedures to address the conflict areas created by personal investing. These procedures include the following:

- *Limited participation in equity IPOs*: Some eagerly awaited IPOs rise significantly in value shortly after the issue is brought to market. Because the new issue may be highly attractive and sought after, the opportunity to participate in the IPO may be limited. Therefore, purchases of IPOs by investment personnel create conflicts of interest in two principal ways. First, participation in an IPO may have the appearance of taking away an attractive investment opportunity from clients for personal gain—a clear breach of the duty of loyalty to clients. Second, personal purchases in IPOs may have the appearance that the investment opportunity is being bestowed as an incentive to make future investment decisions for the benefit of the party providing the opportunity. Members and candidates can avoid these conflicts or appearances of conflicts of interest by not participating in IPOs.

  Reliable and systematic review procedures should be established to ensure that conflicts relating to IPOs are identified and appropriately dealt with by supervisors. Members and candidates should preclear their participation in IPOs, even in situations without any conflict of interest between a member's or candidate's participation in an IPO and the client's interests. Members and candidates should not benefit from the position that their clients occupy in the marketplace—through preferred trading, the allocation of limited offerings, or oversubscription.

- *Restrictions on private placements*: Strict limits should be placed on investment personnel acquiring securities in private placements, and appropriate supervisory and review procedures should be established to prevent noncompliance.

  Firms do not routinely use private placements for clients (e.g., venture capital deals) because of the high risk associated with them. Conflicts related to private placements are more significant to members and candidates who manage large pools of assets or act as plan sponsors because these managers may be offered special opportunities, such as private placements, as a reward or an enticement for continuing to do business with a particular broker.

Participation in private placements raises conflict-of-interest issues that are similar to issues surrounding IPOs. Investment personnel should not be involved in transactions, including (but not limited to) private placements, that could be perceived as favors or gifts that seem designed to influence future judgment or to reward past business deals.

Whether the venture eventually proves to be good or bad, managers have an immediate conflict concerning private placement opportunities. If and when the investments go public, participants in private placements have an incentive to recommend the investments to clients regardless of the suitability of the investments for their clients. Doing so increases the value of the participants' personal portfolios.

- *Establish blackout/restricted periods*: Investment personnel involved in the investment decision-making process should establish blackout periods prior to trades for clients so that managers cannot take advantage of their knowledge of client activity by "front-running" client trades (trading for one's personal account before trading for client accounts).

  Individual firms must decide who within the firm should be required to comply with the trading restrictions. At a minimum, all individuals who are involved in the investment decision-making process should be subject to the same restricted period. Each firm must determine specific requirements related to blackout and restricted periods that are most relevant to the firm while ensuring that the procedures are governed by the guiding principles set forth in the Code and Standards. Size of firm and type of securities purchased are relevant factors. For example, in a large firm, a blackout requirement is, in effect, a total trading ban because the firm is continually trading in most securities. In a small firm, the blackout period is more likely to prevent the investment manager from front-running.

- *Reporting requirements*: Supervisors should establish reporting procedures for investment personnel, including disclosure of personal holdings/beneficial ownerships, confirmations of trades to the firm and the employee, and preclearance procedures. Once trading restrictions are in place, they must be enforced. The best method for monitoring and enforcing procedures to eliminate conflicts of interest in personal trading is through reporting requirements, including the following:

  - *Disclosure of holdings in which the employee has a beneficial interest*: Disclosure by investment personnel to the firm should be made upon commencement of the employment relationship and at least annually thereafter. To address privacy considerations, disclosure of personal holdings should be handled in a confidential manner by the firm.
  - *Providing duplicate confirmations of transactions*: Investment personnel should be required to direct their brokers to supply to firms duplicate copies or confirmations of all their personal securities transactions and copies of periodic statements for all securities accounts. The duplicate confirmation requirement has two purposes: (1) The requirement sends a message that there is independent verification, which reduces the likelihood of unethical behavior, and (2) it enables verification of the accounting of the flow of personal investments that cannot be determined from merely looking at holdings.
  - *Preclearance procedures*: Investment personnel should examine all planned personal trades to identify possible conflicts prior to the execution of the trades. Preclearance procedures are designed to identify possible conflicts before a problem arises.

- *Disclosure of policies*: Members and candidates should fully disclose to investors their firm's policies regarding personal investing. The information about employees' personal investment activities and policies will foster an atmosphere of full and complete disclosure and calm the public's legitimate concerns about the conflicts of interest posed by investment personnel's personal trading. The disclosure must provide helpful information to investors; it should not be simply boilerplate language, such as "investment personnel are subject to policies and procedures regarding their personal trading."

STANDARD VI(B): APPLICATION OF THE STANDARD 58

Example 1 (Personal Trading):

Research analyst Marlon Long does not recommend purchase of a common stock for his employer's account because he wants to purchase the stock personally and does not want to wait until the recommendation is approved and the stock is purchased by his employer.

> *Comment*: Long has violated Standard VI(B) by taking advantage of his knowledge of the stock's value before allowing his employer to benefit from that information.

Example 2 (Trading for Family Member Account):

Carol Baker, the portfolio manager of an aggressive growth mutual fund, maintains an account in her husband's name at several brokerage firms with which the fund and a number of Baker's other individual clients do a substantial amount of business. Whenever a hot issue becomes available, she instructs the brokers to buy it for her husband's account. Because such issues normally are scarce, Baker often acquires shares in hot issues but her clients are not able to participate in them.

> *Comment*: To avoid violating Standard VI(B), Baker must acquire shares for her mutual fund first and acquire them for her husband's account only after doing so, even though she might miss out on participating in new issues via her husband's account. She also must disclose the trading for her husband's account to her employer because this activity creates a conflict between her personal interests and her employer's interests.

Example 3 (Family Accounts as Equals):

Erin Toffler, a portfolio manager at Esposito Investments, manages the retirement account established with the firm by her parents. Whenever IPOs become available, she first allocates shares to all her other clients for whom the investment is appropriate; only then does she place any remaining portion in her parents' account, if the issue is appropriate for them. She has adopted this procedure so that no one can accuse her of favoring her parents.

Comment: Toffler has violated Standard VI(B) by breaching her duty to her parents by treating them differently from her other accounts simply because of the family relationship. As fee-paying clients of Esposito Investments, Toffler's parents are entitled to the same treatment as any other client of the firm. If Toffler has beneficial ownership in the account, however, and Esposito Investments has preclearance and reporting requirements for personal transactions, she may have to preclear the trades and report the transactions to Esposito.

Example 4 (Personal Trading and Disclosure):

Gary Michaels is an entry-level employee who holds a low-paying job serving both the research department and the investment management department of an active investment management firm. He purchases a sports car and begins to wear expensive clothes after only a year of employment with the firm. The director of the investment management department, who has responsibility for monitoring the personal stock transactions of all employees, investigates and discovers that Michaels has made substantial investment gains by purchasing stocks just before they were put on the firm's recommended "buy" list. Michaels was regularly given the firm's quarterly personal transaction form but declined to complete it.

Comment: Michaels violated Standard VI(B) by placing personal transactions ahead of client transactions. In addition, his supervisor violated Standard IV(C) Responsibilities of Supervisors by permitting Michaels to continue to perform his assigned tasks without having signed the quarterly personal transaction form. Note also that if Michaels had communicated information about the firm's recommendations to a person who traded the security, that action would be a misappropriation of the information and a violation of Standard II(A) Material Nonpublic Information.

Example 5 (Trading Prior to Report Dissemination):

A brokerage's insurance analyst, Denise Wilson, makes a closed-circuit TV report to her firm's branches around the country. During the broadcast, she includes negative comments about a major company in the insurance industry. The following day, Wilson's report is printed and distributed to the sales force and public customers. The report recommends that both short-term traders and intermediate investors take profits by selling that insurance company's stock. Seven minutes after the broadcast, however, Ellen Riley, head of the firm's trading department, had closed out a long "call" position in the stock. Shortly thereafter, Riley established a sizable "put" position in the stock. When asked about her activities, Riley claimed she took the actions to facilitate anticipated sales by institutional clients.

Comment: Riley did not give customers an opportunity to buy or sell in the options market before the firm itself did. By taking action before the report was disseminated, Riley's firm may have depressed the price of the calls and increased the price of the puts. The firm could have avoided a conflict of interest if it had waited to trade for its own account until its clients had an opportunity to receive and assimilate Wilson's recommendations. As it is, Riley's actions violated Standard VI(B).

STANDARD VI(C) REFERRAL FEES

59

- ☐ demonstrate the application of the Code of Ethics and Standards of Professional Conduct to situations involving issues of professional integrity
- ☐ recommend practices and procedures designed to prevent violations of the Code of Ethics and Standards of Professional Conduct
- ☐ identify conduct that conforms to the Code and Standards and conduct that violates the Code and Standards

> Members and Candidates must disclose to their employer, clients, and prospective clients, as appropriate, any compensation, consideration, or benefit received from or paid to others for the recommendation of products or services.

Guidance

Standard VI(C) states the responsibility of members and candidates to inform their employer, clients, and prospective clients of any benefit received for referrals of customers and clients. Such disclosures allow clients or employers to evaluate (1) any partiality shown in any recommendation of services and (2) the full cost of the services. Members and candidates must disclose when they pay a fee or provide compensation to others who have referred prospective clients to the member or candidate.

Appropriate disclosure means that members and candidates must advise the client or prospective client, before entry into any formal agreement for services, of any benefit given or received for the recommendation of any services provided by the member or candidate. In addition, the member or candidate must disclose the nature of the consideration or benefit—for example, flat fee or percentage basis, one-time or continuing benefit, based on performance, benefit in the form of provision of research, or other noncash benefit—together with the estimated dollar value. Consideration includes all fees, whether paid in cash, in soft dollars, or in kind.

STANDARD VI(C): RECOMMENDED PROCEDURES

60

Members and candidates should encourage their employers to develop procedures related to referral fees. The firm may completely restrict such fees. If the firm does not adopt a strict prohibition of such fees, the procedures should indicate the appropriate steps for requesting approval.

Employers should have investment professionals provide to the clients notification of approved referral fee programs and provide the employer regular (at least quarterly) updates on the amount and nature of compensation received.

61 STANDARD VI(C): APPLICATION OF THE STANDARD

Example 1 (Disclosure of Referral Arrangements and Outside Parties):

Brady Securities, Inc., a broker/dealer, has established a referral arrangement with Lewis Brothers, Ltd., an investment counseling firm. In this arrangement, Brady Securities refers all prospective tax-exempt accounts, including pension, profit-sharing, and endowment accounts, to Lewis Brothers. In return, Lewis Brothers makes available to Brady Securities on a regular basis the security recommendations and reports of its research staff, which registered representatives of Brady Securities use in serving customers. In addition, Lewis Brothers conducts monthly economic and market reviews for Brady Securities personnel and directs all stock commission business generated by referral accounts to Brady Securities.

Willard White, a partner in Lewis Brothers, calculates that the incremental costs involved in functioning as the research department of Brady Securities are US$20,000 annually.

Referrals from Brady Securities last year resulted in fee income of US$200,000 for Lewis Brothers, and directing all stock trades through Brady Securities resulted in additional costs to Lewis Brothers' clients of US$10,000.

Diane Branch, the chief financial officer of Maxwell Inc., contacts White and says that she is seeking an investment manager for Maxwell's profit-sharing plan. She adds, "My friend Harold Hill at Brady Securities recommended your firm without qualification, and that's good enough for me. Do we have a deal?" White accepts the new account but does not disclose his firm's referral arrangement with Brady Securities.

> *Comment*: White has violated Standard VI(C) by failing to inform the prospective customer of the referral fee payable in services and commissions for an indefinite period to Brady Securities. Such disclosure could have caused Branch to reassess Hill's recommendation and make a more critical evaluation of Lewis Brothers' services.

Example 2 (Disclosure of Interdepartmental Referral Arrangements):

James Handley works for the trust department of Central Trust Bank. He receives compensation for each referral he makes to Central Trust's brokerage department and personal financial management department that results in a sale. He refers several of his clients to the personal financial management department but does not disclose the arrangement within Central Trust to his clients.

> *Comment*: Handley has violated Standard VI(C) by not disclosing the referral arrangement at Central Trust Bank to his clients. Standard VI(C) does not distinguish between referral payments paid by a third party for referring clients to the third party and internal payments paid within the firm to attract new business to a subsidiary. Members and candidates must disclose all such referral fees. Therefore, Handley is required to disclose, at the time of referral, any referral fee agreement in place among Central Trust Bank's departments. The disclosure should include the nature and the value of the benefit and should be made in writing.

Example 3 (Disclosure of Referral Arrangements and Informing Firm):

Katherine Roberts is a portfolio manager at Katama Investments, an advisory firm specializing in managing assets for high-net-worth individuals. Katama's trading desk uses a variety of brokerage houses to execute trades on behalf of its clients. Roberts asks the trading desk to direct a large portion of its commissions to Naushon, Inc., a small broker/dealer run by one of Roberts' business school classmates. Katama's traders have found that Naushon is not very competitive on pricing, and although Naushon generates some research for its trading clients, Katama's other analysts have found most of Naushon's research to be not especially useful. Nevertheless, the traders do as Roberts asks, and in return for receiving a large portion of Katama's business, Naushon recommends the investment services of Roberts and Katama to its wealthiest clients. This arrangement is not disclosed to either Katama or the clients referred by Naushon.

> *Comment*: Roberts is violating Standard VI(C) by failing to inform her employer of the referral arrangement.

Example 4 (Disclosure of Referral Arrangements and Outside Organizations):

Alex Burl is a portfolio manager at Helpful Investments, a local investment advisory firm. Burl is on the advisory board of his child's school, which is looking for ways to raise money to purchase new playground equipment for the school. Burl discusses a plan with his supervisor in which he will donate to the school a portion of his service fee from new clients referred by the parents of students at the school. Upon getting the approval from Helpful, Burl presents the idea to the school's advisory board and directors. The school agrees to announce the program at the next parent event and asks Burl to provide the appropriate written materials to be distributed. A week following the distribution of the flyers, Burl receives the first school-related referral. In establishing the client's investment policy statement, Burl clearly discusses the school's referral and outlines the plans for distributing the donation back to the school.

> *Comment*: Burl has not violated Standard VI(C) because he secured the permission of his employer, Helpful Investments, and the school prior to beginning the program and because he discussed the arrangement with the client at the time the investment policy statement was designed.

Example 5 (Disclosure of Referral Arrangements and Outside Parties):

The sponsor of a state employee pension is seeking to hire a firm to manage the pension plan's emerging market allocation. To assist in the review process, the sponsor has hired Thomas Arrow as a consultant to solicit proposals from various advisers. Arrow is contracted by the sponsor to represent its best interest in selecting the most appropriate new manager. The process runs smoothly, and Overseas Investments is selected as the new manager.

The following year, news breaks that Arrow is under investigation by the local regulator for accepting kickbacks from investment managers after they are awarded new pension allocations. Overseas Investments is included in the list of firms allegedly making these payments. Although the sponsor is happy with the performance of Overseas since it has been managing the pension plan's emerging market funds, the sponsor still decides to have an independent review of the proposals and the selection process to ensure that Overseas was the appropriate firm for its needs. This review confirms that, even though Arrow was being paid by both parties, the recommendation of Overseas appeared to be objective and appropriate.

Comment: Arrow has violated Standard VI(C) because he did not disclose the fee being paid by Overseas. Withholding this information raises the question of a potential lack of objectivity in the recommendation of Overseas by Arrow; this aspect is in addition to questions about the legality of having firms pay to be considered for an allocation.

Regulators and governmental agencies may adopt requirements concerning allowable consultant activities. Local regulations sometimes include having a consultant register with the regulatory agency's ethics board. Regulator policies may include a prohibition on acceptance of payments from investment managers receiving allocations and require regular reporting of contributions made to political organizations and candidates. Arrow would have to adhere to these requirements as well as the Code and Standards.

62 STANDARD VII: RESPONSIBILITIES AS A CFA INSTITUTE MEMBER OR CFA CANDIDATE

- ☐ demonstrate the application of the Code of Ethics and Standards of Professional Conduct to situations involving issues of professional integrity
- ☐ recommend practices and procedures designed to prevent violations of the Code of Ethics and Standards of Professional Conduct
- ☐ identify conduct that conforms to the Code and Standards and conduct that violates the Code and Standards

Standard VII(A) Conduct as Participants in CFA Institute Programs

> Members and Candidates must not engage in any conduct that compromises the reputation or integrity of CFA Institute or the CFA designation or the integrity, validity, or security of CFA Institute programs.

Guidance

Highlights:

- *Confidential Program Information*
- *Additional CFA Program Restrictions*
- *Expressing an Opinion*

Standard VII(A) covers the conduct of CFA Institute members and candidates involved with the CFA Program and prohibits any conduct that undermines the public's confidence that the CFA charter represents a level of achievement based on merit and ethical conduct. There is an array of CFA Institute programs beyond the CFA Program that provide additional educational and credentialing opportunities, including the Certificate in Investment Performance Measurement (CIPM®) Program and the CFA Institute Investment Foundations® Program. The standard's function is to hold members and candidates to a high ethical criterion while they are participating in or involved with any CFA Institute program. Conduct covered includes but is not limited to

- giving or receiving assistance (cheating) on any CFA Institute examinations;
- violating the rules, regulations, and testing policies of CFA Institute programs;
- providing confidential program or exam information to candidates or the public;
- disregarding or attempting to circumvent security measures established for any CFA Institute examinations;
- improperly using an association with CFA Institute to further personal or professional goals; and
- misrepresenting information on the Professional Conduct Statement or in the CFA Institute Continuing Education Program.

Confidential Program Information

CFA Institute is vigilant about protecting the integrity of CFA Institute programs' content and examination processes. CFA Institute program rules, regulations, and policies prohibit candidates from disclosing confidential material gained during the exam process.

Examples of information that cannot be disclosed by candidates sitting for an exam include but are not limited to

- specific details of questions appearing on the exam and
- broad topical areas and formulas tested or not tested on the exam.

All aspects of the exam, including questions, broad topical areas, and formulas, tested or not tested, are considered confidential until such time as CFA Institute elects to release them publicly. This confidentiality requirement allows CFA Institute to maintain the integrity and rigor of exams for future candidates. Standard VII(A) does not prohibit candidates from discussing nonconfidential information or curriculum material with others or in study groups in preparation for the exam.

Candidates increasingly use online forums and new technology as part of their exam preparations. CFA Institute actively polices blogs, forums, and related social networking groups for information considered confidential. The organization works with both individual candidates and the sponsors of online or offline services to promptly remove any and all violations. As noted in the discussion of Standard I(A) Knowledge of the Law, candidates, members, and the public are encouraged to report suspected violations to CFA Institute.

Additional CFA Program Restrictions

The CFA Program rules, regulations, and policies define additional allowed and disallowed actions concerning the exams. Violating any of the testing policies, such as the calculator policy, personal belongings policy, or the Candidate Pledge, constitutes a violation of Standard VII(A). Candidates will find all of these policies on the CFA

Program portion of the CFA Institute website (www.cfainstitute.org). Exhibit 2 provides the Candidate Pledge, which highlights the respect candidates must have for the integrity, validity, and security of the CFA exam.

Members may participate as volunteers in various aspects of the CFA Program. Standard VII(A) prohibits members from disclosing and/or soliciting confidential material gained prior to or during the exam and grading processes with those outside the CFA exam development process.

Examples of information that cannot be shared by members involved in developing, administering, or grading the exams include but are not limited to

- questions appearing on the exam or under consideration,
- deliberation related to the exam process, and
- information related to the scoring of questions.

Members may also be asked to offer assistance with other CFA Institute programs, including but not limited to the CIPM and Investment Foundations programs. Members participating in any CFA Institute program should do so with the same level of integrity and confidentiality as is required of participation in the CFA Program.

Expressing an Opinion

Standard VII(A) does *not* cover expressing opinions regarding CFA Institute, the CFA Program, or other CFA Institute programs. Members and candidates are free to disagree and express their disagreement with CFA Institute on its policies, its procedures, or any advocacy positions taken by the organization. When expressing a personal opinion, a candidate is prohibited from disclosing content-specific information, including any actual exam question and the information as to subject matter covered or not covered in the exam.

Exhibit 2: Sample of CFA Program Testing Policies

Candidate Pledge	As a candidate in the CFA Program, I am obligated to follow Standard VII(A) of the CFA Institute Standards of Professional Conduct, which states that members and candidates must not engage in any conduct that compromises the reputation or integrity of CFA Institute or the CFA designation or the integrity, validity, or security of the CFA exam. ▪ Prior to this exam, I have not given or received information regarding the content of this exam. During this exam, I will not give or receive any information regarding the content of this exam. ▪ After this exam, I will not disclose **ANY** portion of this exam and I will not remove **ANY** exam materials from the testing room in original or copied form. I understand that all exam materials, including my answers, are the property of CFA Institute and will not be returned to me in any form. ▪ I will follow **ALL** rules of the CFA Program as stated on the CFA Institute website and the back cover of the exam book. My violation of any rules of the CFA Program will result in CFA Institute voiding my exam results and may lead to suspension or termination of my candidacy in the CFA Program.

STANDARD VII(A): APPLICATION OF THE STANDARD

63

Example 1 (Sharing Exam Questions):

Travis Nero serves as a proctor for the administration of the CFA examination in his city. In the course of his service, he reviews a copy of the Level II CFA exam on the evening prior to the exam's administration and provides information concerning the exam questions to two candidates who use it to prepare for the exam.

> *Comment*: Nero and the two candidates have violated Standard VII(A). By giving information about the exam questions to two candidates, Nero provided an unfair advantage to the two candidates and undermined the integrity and validity of the Level II CFA exam as an accurate measure of the knowledge, skills, and abilities necessary to earn the right to use the CFA designation. By accepting the information, the candidates also compromised the integrity and validity of the Level II CFA exam and undermined the ethical framework that is a key part of the designation.

Example 2 (Bringing Written Material into Exam Room):

Loren Sullivan is enrolled to take the Level II CFA exam. He has been having difficulty remembering a particular formula, so prior to entering the exam room, he writes the formula on the palm of his hand. During the afternoon section of the exam, a proctor notices Sullivan looking at the palm of his hand. She asks to see his hand and finds the formula.

> *Comment*: Because Sullivan wrote down information from the Candidate Body of Knowledge (CBOK) and took that written information into the exam room, his conduct compromised the validity of his exam performance and violated Standard VII(A). Sullivan's conduct was also in direct contradiction with the rules and regulations of the CFA Program, the Candidate Pledge, and the CFA Institute Code and Standards.

Example 3 (Writing after Exam Period End):

At the conclusion of the morning section of the Level I CFA exam, the proctors announce, "Stop writing now." John Davis has not completed the exam, so he continues to randomly fill in ovals on his answer sheet. A proctor approaches Davis's desk and reminds him that he should stop writing immediately. Davis, however, continues to complete the answer sheet. After the proctor asks him to stop writing two additional times, Davis finally puts down his pencil.

> *Comment*: By continuing to complete his exam after time was called, Davis has violated Standard VII(A). By continuing to write, Davis took an unfair advantage over other candidates, and his conduct compromised the validity of his exam performance. Additionally, by not heeding the proctor's repeated instructions, Davis violated the rules and regulations of the CFA Program.

Example 4 (Sharing Exam Content):

After completing the Level II CFA exam, Annabelle Rossi posts on her blog about her experience. She posts the following: "Level II is complete! I think I did fairly well on the exam. It was really difficult, but fair. I think I did especially well on the derivatives questions. And there were tons of them! I think I counted 18! The ethics questions were really hard. I'm glad I spent so much time on the Code and Standards. I was surprised to see there were no questions at all about IPO allocations. I expected there to be a couple. Well, off to celebrate getting through it. See you tonight?"

> *Comment*: Rossi did not violate Standard VII(A) when she wrote about how difficult she found the exam or how well she thinks she may have done. By revealing portions of the CBOK covered on the exam and areas not covered, however, she did violate Standard VII(A) and the Candidate Pledge. Depending on the time frame in which the comments were posted, Rossi not only may have assisted future candidates but also may have provided an unfair advantage to candidates yet to sit for the same exam, thereby undermining the integrity and validity of the Level II exam.

Example 5 (Sharing Exam Content):

Level I candidate Etienne Gagne has been a frequent visitor to an internet forum designed specifically for CFA Program candidates. The week after completing the Level I CFA exam, Gagne and several others begin a discussion thread on the forum about the most challenging questions and attempt to determine the correct answers.

> *Comment*: Gagne has violated Standard VII(A) by providing and soliciting confidential exam information, which compromises the integrity of the exam process and violates the Candidate Pledge. In trying to determine correct answers to specific questions, the group's discussion included question-specific details considered to be confidential to the CFA Program.

Example 6 (Sharing Exam Content):

CFA4Sure is a company that produces test-preparation materials for CFA Program candidates. Many candidates register for and use the company's products. The day after the CFA exam, CFA4Sure sends an e-mail to all its customers asking them to share with the company the hardest questions from the exam so that CFA4Sure can better prepare its customers for the next exam administration. Marisol Pena e-mails a summary of the questions she found most difficult on the exam.

> *Comment*: Pena has violated Standard VII(A) by disclosing a portion of the exam questions. The information provided is considered confidential until publicly released by CFA Institute. CFA4Sure is likely to use such feedback to refine its review materials for future candidates. Pena's sharing of the specific questions undermines the integrity of the exam while potentially making the exam easier for future candidates.
>
> If the CFA4Sure employees who participated in the solicitation of confidential CFA Program information are CFA Institute members or candidates, they also have violated Standard VII(A).

Example 7 (Discussion of Exam Grading Guidelines and Results):

Prior to participating in grading CFA exams, Wesley Whitcomb is required to sign a CFA Institute Grader Agreement. As part of the Grader Agreement, Whitcomb agrees not to reveal or discuss the exam materials with anyone except CFA Institute staff or other graders. Several weeks after the conclusion of the CFA exam grading, Whitcomb tells several colleagues who are candidates in the CFA Program which question he graded. He also discusses the guideline answer and adds that few candidates scored well on the question.

> *Comment*: Whitcomb violated Standard VII(A) by breaking the Grader Agreement and disclosing information related to a specific question on the exam, which compromised the integrity of the exam process.

Example 8 (Compromising CFA Institute Integrity as a Volunteer):

Jose Ramirez is an investor-relations consultant for several small companies that are seeking greater exposure to investors. He is also the program chair for the CFA Institute society in the city where he works. Ramirez schedules only companies that are his clients to make presentations to the society and excludes other companies.

> *Comment*: Ramirez, by using his volunteer position at CFA Institute to benefit himself and his clients, compromises the reputation and integrity of CFA Institute and thus violates Standard VII(A).

Example 9 (Compromising CFA Institute Integrity as a Volunteer):

Marguerite Warrenski is a member of the CFA Institute GIPS Executive Committee, which oversees the creation, implementation, and revision of the GIPS standards. As a member of the Executive Committee, she has advance knowledge of confidential information regarding the GIPS standards, including any new or revised standards the committee is considering. She tells her clients that her Executive Committee membership will allow her to better assist her clients in keeping up with changes to the Standards and facilitating their compliance with the changes.

> *Comment*: Warrenski is using her association with the GIPS Executive Committee to promote her firm's services to clients and potential clients. In defining her volunteer position at CFA Institute as a strategic business advantage over competing firms and implying to clients that she would use confidential information to further their interests, Warrenski is compromising the reputation and integrity of CFA Institute and thus violating Standard VII(A). She may factually state her involvement with the Executive Committee but cannot infer any special advantage to her clients from such participation.

64 STANDARD VII(B) REFERENCE TO CFA INSTITUTE, THE CFA DESIGNATION, AND THE CFA PROGRAM

- ☐ demonstrate the application of the Code of Ethics and Standards of Professional Conduct to situations involving issues of professional integrity
- ☐ recommend practices and procedures designed to prevent violations of the Code of Ethics and Standards of Professional Conduct
- ☐ identify conduct that conforms to the Code and Standards and conduct that violates the Code and Standards

> When referring to CFA Institute, CFA Institute membership, the CFA designation, or candidacy in the CFA Program, Members and Candidates must not misrepresent or exaggerate the meaning or implications of membership in CFA Institute, holding the CFA designation, or candidacy in the CFA Program.

Guidance

Highlights:

- *CFA Institute Membership*
- *Using the CFA Designation*
- *Referring to Candidacy in the CFA Program*

Standard VII(B) is intended to prevent promotional efforts that make promises or guarantees that are tied to the CFA designation. Individuals must not exaggerate the meaning or implications of membership in CFA Institute, holding the CFA designation, or candidacy in the CFA Program.

Standard VII(B) is not intended to prohibit factual statements related to the positive benefit of earning the CFA designation. However, statements referring to CFA Institute, the CFA designation, or the CFA Program that overstate the competency of an individual or imply, either directly or indirectly, that superior performance can be expected from someone with the CFA designation are not allowed under the standard.

Statements that highlight or emphasize the commitment of CFA Institute members, CFA charterholders, and CFA candidates to ethical and professional conduct or mention the thoroughness and rigor of the CFA Program are appropriate. Members and candidates may make claims about the relative merits of CFA Institute, the CFA Program, or the Code and Standards as long as those statements are implicitly or explicitly stated as the opinion of the speaker. Statements that do not express opinions have to be supported by facts.

Standard VII(B) applies to any form of communication, including but not limited to communications made in electronic or written form (such as on firm letterhead, business cards, professional biographies, directory listings, printed advertising, firm brochures, or personal resumes) and oral statements made to the public, clients, or prospects.

CFA Institute Membership

The term "CFA Institute member" refers to "regular" and "affiliate" members of CFA Institute who have met the membership requirements as defined in the CFA Institute Bylaws. Once accepted as a CFA Institute member, the member must satisfy the following requirements to maintain his or her status:

- remit annually to CFA Institute a completed Professional Conduct Statement, which renews the commitment to abide by the requirements of the Code and Standards and the CFA Institute Professional Conduct Program, and
- pay applicable CFA Institute membership dues on an annual basis.

If a CFA Institute member fails to meet any of these requirements, the individual is no longer considered an active member. Until membership is reactivated, individuals must not present themselves to others as active members. They may state, however, that they were CFA Institute members in the past or refer to the years when their membership was active.

Using the CFA Designation

Those who have earned the right to use the Chartered Financial Analyst® designation are encouraged to do so but only in a manner that does not misrepresent or exaggerate the meaning or implications of the designation. The use of the designation may be accompanied by an accurate explanation of the requirements that have been met to earn the right to use the designation.

"CFA charterholders" are those individuals who have earned the right to use the CFA designation granted by CFA Institute. These people have satisfied certain requirements, including completion of the CFA Program and required years of acceptable work experience. Once granted the right to use the designation, individuals must also satisfy the CFA Institute membership requirements (see above) to maintain their right to use the designation.

If a CFA charterholder fails to meet any of the membership requirements, he or she forfeits the right to use the CFA designation. Until membership is reactivated, individuals must not present themselves to others as CFA charterholders. They may state, however, that they were charterholders in the past.

Given the growing popularity of social media, where individuals may anonymously express their opinions, pseudonyms or online profile names created to hide a member's identity should not be tagged with the CFA designation.

Use of the CFA designation by a CFA charterholder is governed by the terms and conditions of the annual Professional Conduct Statement Agreement, entered into between CFA Institute and its membership prior to commencement of use of the CFA designation and reaffirmed annually.

Referring to Candidacy in the CFA Program

Candidates in the CFA Program may refer to their participation in the CFA Program, but such references must clearly state that an individual is a *candidate* in the CFA Program and must not imply that the candidate has achieved any type of partial designation. A person is a candidate in the CFA Program if

- the person's application for registration in the CFA Program has been accepted by CFA Institute, as evidenced by issuance of a notice of acceptance, and the person is enrolled to sit for a specified examination or
- the registered person has sat for a specified exam but exam results have not yet been received.

If an individual is registered for the CFA Program but declines to sit for an exam or otherwise does not meet the definition of a candidate as described in the CFA Institute Bylaws, then that individual is no longer considered an active candidate. Once the person is enrolled to sit for a future examination, his or her CFA Program candidacy resumes.

CFA Program candidates must never state or imply that they have a partial designation as a result of passing one or more levels or cite an expected completion date of any level of the CFA Program. Final award of the charter is subject to meeting the CFA Program requirements and approval by the CFA Institute Board of Governors.

If a candidate passes each level of the exam in consecutive years and wants to state that he or she did so, that is not a violation of Standard VII(B) because it is a statement of fact. If the candidate then goes on to claim or imply superior ability by obtaining the designation in only three years, however, he or she is in violation of Standard VII(B).

Exhibit 3 provides examples of proper and improper references to the CFA designation.

Exhibit 3: Proper and Improper References to the CFA Designation

Proper References	Improper References
"Completion of the CFA Program has enhanced my portfolio management skills."	"CFA charterholders achieve better performance results."
"John Smith passed all three CFA Program exams in three consecutive years."	"John Smith is among the elite, having passed all three CFA exams in three consecutive attempts."
"The CFA designation is globally recognized and attests to a charterholder's success in a rigorous and comprehensive study program in the field of investment management and research analysis."	"As a CFA charterholder, I am the most qualified to manage client investments."
"The credibility that the CFA designation affords and the skills the CFA Program cultivates are key assets for my future career development."	"As a CFA charterholder, Jane White provides the best value in trade execution."
"I enrolled in the CFA Program to obtain the highest set of credentials in the global investment management industry."	"Enrolling as a candidate in the CFA Program ensures one of becoming better at valuing debt securities."
"I passed Level I of the CFA Program."	"CFA, Level II"
"I am a 2010 Level III candidate in the CFA Program."	"CFA, Expected 2011"
"I passed all three levels of the CFA Program and may be eligible for the CFA charter upon completion of the required work experience."	"CFA, Expected 2011" "John Smith, Charter Pending"

65 STANDARD VII(B): RECOMMENDED PROCEDURES

Misuse of a member's CFA designation or CFA candidacy or improper reference to it is common by those in a member's or candidate's firm who do not possess knowledge of the requirements of Standard VII(B). As an appropriate step to reduce this risk, members and candidates should disseminate written information about Standard VII(B) and the accompanying guidance to their firm's legal, compliance, public relations, and marketing departments (see www.cfainstitute.org).

For materials that refer to employees' affiliation with CFA Institute, members and candidates should encourage their firms to create templates that are approved by a central authority (such as the compliance department) as being consistent with Standard VII(B). This practice promotes consistency and accuracy in the firm of references to CFA Institute membership, the CFA designation, and CFA candidacy.

STANDARD VII(B): APPLICATION OF THE STANDARD

66

Example 1 (Passing Exams in Consecutive Years):

An advertisement for AZ Investment Advisors states that all the firm's principals are CFA charterholders and all passed the three exams on their first attempt. The advertisement prominently links this fact to the notion that AZ's mutual funds have achieved superior performance.

> *Comment*: AZ may state that all principals passed the three exams on the first try as long as this statement is true, but it must not be linked to performance or imply superior ability. Implying that (1) CFA charterholders achieve better investment results and (2) those who pass the exams on the first try may be more successful than those who do not violates Standard VII(B).

Example 2 (Right to Use CFA Designation):

Five years after receiving his CFA charter, Louis Vasseur resigns his position as an investment analyst and spends the next two years traveling abroad. Because he is not actively engaged in the investment profession, he does not file a completed Professional Conduct Statement with CFA Institute and does not pay his CFA Institute membership dues. At the conclusion of his travels, Vasseur becomes a self-employed analyst accepting assignments as an independent contractor. Without reinstating his CFA Institute membership by filing his Professional Conduct Statement and paying his dues, he prints business cards that display "CFA" after his name.

> *Comment*: Vasseur has violated Standard VII(B) because his right to use the CFA designation was suspended when he failed to file his Professional Conduct Statement and stopped paying dues. Therefore, he no longer is able to state or imply that he is an active CFA charterholder. When Vasseur files his Professional Conduct Statement, resumes paying CFA Institute dues to activate his membership, and completes the CFA Institute reinstatement procedures, he will be eligible to use the CFA designation.

Example 3 ("Retired" CFA Institute Membership Status):

After a 25-year career, James Simpson retires from his firm. Because he is not actively engaged in the investment profession, he does not file a completed Professional Conduct Statement with CFA Institute and does not pay his CFA Institute membership dues. Simpson designs a plain business card (without a corporate logo) to hand out to friends with his new contact details, and he continues to put "CFA" after his name.

> *Comment*: Simpson has violated Standard VII(B). Because he failed to file his Professional Conduct Statement and ceased paying dues, his membership has been suspended and he has given up the right to use the CFA designation. CFA Institute has procedures, however, for reclassifying a member and charterholder as "retired" and reducing the annual dues. If he wants to obtain retired status, he needs to file the appropriate paperwork with CFA Institute. When Simpson receives his notification from CFA Institute that his membership has been reclassified as retired and he resumes paying reduced dues, his membership will be reactivated and his right to use the CFA designation will be reinstated.

Example 4 (Stating Facts about CFA Designation and Program):

Rhonda Reese has been a CFA charterholder since 2000. In a conversation with a friend who is considering enrolling in the CFA Program, she states that she has learned a great deal from the CFA Program and that many firms require their employees to be CFA charterholders. She would recommend the CFA Program to anyone pursuing a career in investment management.

> *Comment*: Reese's comments comply with Standard VII(B). Her statements refer to facts: The CFA Program enhanced her knowledge, and many firms require the CFA designation for their investment professionals.

Example 5 (Order of Professional and Academic Designations):

Tatiana Prittima has earned both her CFA designation and a PhD in finance. She would like to cite both her accomplishments on her business card but is unsure of the proper method for doing so.

> *Comment*: The order of designations cited on such items as resumes and business cards is a matter of personal preference. Prittima is free to cite the CFA designation either before or after citing her PhD. Multiple designations must be separated by a comma.

Example 6 (Use of Fictitious Name):

Barry Glass is the lead quantitative analyst at CityCenter Hedge Fund. Glass is responsible for the development, maintenance, and enhancement of the proprietary models the fund uses to manage its investors' assets. Glass reads several high-level mathematical publications and blogs to stay informed on current developments. One blog, run by "Expert CFA," presents some intriguing research that may benefit one of CityCenter's current models. Glass is under pressure from firm executives to improve the model's predictive abilities, and he incorporates the factors discussed in the online research. The updated output recommends several new investments to the fund's portfolio managers.

Comment: "Expert CFA" has violated Standard VII(B) by using the CFA designation inappropriately. As with any research report, authorship of online comments must include the charterholder's full name along with any reference to the CFA designation.

See also Standard V(A), which Glass has violated for guidance on diligence and reasonable basis.

PRACTICE PROBLEMS

The following information relates to questions 1-39

Unless otherwise stated in the question, all individuals in the following questions are CFA Institute members or candidates in the CFA Program and, therefore, are subject to the CFA Institute Code of Ethics and Standards of Professional Conduct.

1. Smith, a research analyst with a brokerage firm, decides to change his recommendation for the common stock of Green Company, Inc., from a "buy" to a "sell." He mails this change in investment advice to all the firm's clients on Wednesday. The day after the mailing, a client calls with a buy order for 500 shares of Green Company. In this circumstance, Smith should:

   A. accept the order.

   B. advise the customer of the change in recommendation before accepting the order.

   C. not accept the order because it is contrary to the firm's recommendation.

2. Which statement about a manager's use of client brokerage commissions violates the Code and Standards?

   A. A client may direct a manager to use that client's brokerage commissions to purchase goods and services for that client.

   B. Client brokerage commissions should be used to benefit the client and should be commensurate with the value of the brokerage and research services received.

   C. Client brokerage commissions may be directed to pay for the investment manager's operating expenses.

3. Jamison is a junior research analyst with Howard & Howard, a brokerage and investment banking firm. Howard & Howard's mergers and acquisitions department has represented the Britland Company in all of its acquisitions for the past 20 years. Two of Howard & Howard's senior officers are directors of various Britland subsidiaries. Jamison has been asked to write a research report on Britland. What is the best course of action for her to follow?

   A. Jamison may write the report but must refrain from expressing any opinions because of the special relationships between the two companies.

   B. Jamison should not write the report because the two Howard & Howard officers serve as directors for subsidiaries of Britland.

   C. Jamison may write the report if she discloses the director relationship between the two companies.

4. Which of the following statements clearly *conflicts* with the recommended procedures for compliance presented in the CFA Institute *Standards of Practice*

Handbook?

A. Firms should disclose to clients the personal investing policies and procedures established for their employees.

B. Prior approval must be obtained for the personal investment transactions of all employees.

C. For confidentiality reasons, personal transactions and holdings should not be reported to employers unless mandated by regulatory organizations.

5. Bronson provides investment advice to the board of trustees of a private university endowment fund. The trustees have provided Bronson with the fund's financial information, including planned expenditures. Bronson receives a phone call on Friday afternoon from Murdock, a prominent alumnus, requesting that Bronson fax him comprehensive financial information about the fund. According to Murdock, he has a potential contributor but needs the information that day to close the deal and cannot contact any of the trustees. Based on the CFA Institute Standards, Bronson should:

   A. send Murdock the information because disclosure would benefit the client.

   B. not send Murdock the information, to preserve confidentiality.

   C. send Murdock the information, provided Bronson promptly notifies the trustees.

6. Willier is the research analyst responsible for following Company X. All the information he has accumulated and documented suggests that the outlook for the company's new products is poor, so the stock should be rated a weak "hold." During lunch, however, Willier overhears a financial analyst from another firm whom he respects offer opinions that conflict with Willier's forecasts and expectations. Upon returning to his office, Willier releases a strong "buy" recommendation to the public. Willier:

   A. violated the Standards by failing to distinguish between facts and opinions in his recommendation.

   B. violated the Standards because he did not have a reasonable and adequate basis for his recommendation.

   C. was in full compliance with the Standards.

7. An investment management firm has been hired by ETV Corporation to work on an additional public offering for the company. The firm's brokerage unit now has a "sell" recommendation on ETV, but the head of the investment banking department has asked the head of the brokerage unit to change the recommendation from "sell" to "buy." According to the Standards, the head of the brokerage unit would be permitted to:

   A. increase the recommendation by no more than one increment (in this case, to a "hold" recommendation).

   B. place the company on a restricted list and give only factual information about the company.

   C. assign a new analyst to decide whether the stock deserves a higher rating.

8. Albert and Tye, who recently started their own investment advisory business,

have registered to take the Level III CFA exam. Albert's business card reads, "Judy Albert, CFA Level II." Tye has not put anything about the CFA designation on his business card, but promotional material that he designed for the business describes the CFA requirements and indicates that Tye participates in the CFA Program and has completed Levels I and II. According to the Standards:

A. Albert has violated the Standards, but Tye has not.

B. Tye has violated the Standards, but Albert has not.

C. both Albert and Tye have violated the Standards.

9. Scott works for a regional brokerage firm. He estimates that Walkton Industries will increase its dividend by US$1.50 a share during the next year. He realizes that this increase is contingent on pending legislation that would, if enacted, give Walkton a substantial tax break. The US representative for Walkton's home district has told Scott that, although she is lobbying hard for the bill and prospects for its passage are favorable, concern of the US Congress over the federal deficit could cause the tax bill to be voted down. Walkton Industries has not made any statements about a change in dividend policy. Scott writes in his research report, "We expect Walkton's stock price to rise by at least US$8.00 a share by the end of the year because the dividend will increase by US$1.50 a share. Investors buying the stock at the current time should expect to realize a total return of at least 15% on the stock." According to the Standards:

A. Scott violated the Standards because he used material inside information.

B. Scott violated the Standards because he failed to separate opinion from fact.

C. Scott violated the Standards by basing his research on uncertain predictions of future government action.

10. Which one of the following actions will help ensure the fair treatment of brokerage firm clients when a new investment recommendation is made?

A. Informing all people in the firm in advance that a recommendation is to be disseminated

B. Distributing recommendations to institutional clients prior to individual accounts

C. Minimizing the time between the decision and the dissemination of a recommendation

11. The mosaic theory holds that an analyst:

A. violates the Code and Standards if the analyst fails to have knowledge of and comply with applicable laws.

B. can use material public information and nonmaterial nonpublic information in the analyst's analysis.

C. should use all available and relevant information in support of an investment recommendation.

12. Jurgen is a portfolio manager. One of her firm's clients has told Jurgen that he will compensate her beyond the compensation provided by her firm on the basis of

the capital appreciation of his portfolio each year. Jurgen should:

A. turn down the additional compensation because it will result in conflicts with the interests of other clients' accounts.

B. turn down the additional compensation because it will create undue pressure on her to achieve strong short-term performance.

C. obtain permission from her employer prior to accepting the compensation arrangement.

13. One of the discretionary accounts managed by Farnsworth is the Jones Corporation employee profit-sharing plan. Jones, the company president, recently asked Farnsworth to vote the shares in the profit-sharing plan in favor of the slate of directors nominated by Jones Corporation and against the directors sponsored by a dissident stockholder group. Farnsworth does not want to lose this account, because he directs all the account's trades to a brokerage firm that provides Farnsworth with useful information about tax-free investments. Although this information is not of value in managing the Jones Corporation account, it does help in managing several other accounts. The brokerage firm providing this information also offers the lowest commissions for trades and provides best execution. Farnsworth investigates the director issue, concludes that the management-nominated slate is better for the long-run performance of the company than the dissident group's slate, and votes accordingly. Farnsworth:

A. violated the Standards in voting the shares in the manner requested by Jones but not in directing trades to the brokerage firm.

B. did not violate the Standards in voting the shares in the manner requested by Jones or in directing trades to the brokerage firm.

C. violated the Standards in directing trades to the brokerage firm but not in voting the shares as requested by Jones.

14. Brown works for an investment counseling firm. Green, a new client of the firm, is meeting with Brown for the first time. Green used another counseling firm for financial advice for years, but she has switched her account to Brown's firm. After spending a few minutes getting acquainted, Brown explains to Green that she has discovered a highly undervalued stock that offers large potential gains. She recommends that Green purchase the stock. Brown has committed a violation of the Standards. What should she have done differently?

A. Brown should have determined Green's needs, objectives, and tolerance for risk before making a recommendation of any type of security.

B. Brown should have thoroughly explained the characteristics of the company to Green, including the characteristics of the industry in which the company operates.

C. Brown should have explained her qualifications, including her education, training, and experience and the meaning of the CFA designation.

15. Grey recommends the purchase of a mutual fund that invests solely in long-term US Treasury bonds. He makes the following statements to his clients:

I. "The payment of the bonds is guaranteed by the US government; therefore, the default risk of the bonds is virtually zero."

II. "If you invest in the mutual fund, you will earn a 10% rate of return each year

for the next several years based on historical performance of the market."
Did Grey's statements violate the CFA Institute Code and Standards?

A. Neither statement violated the Code and Standards.

B. Only statement I violated the Code and Standards.

C. Only statement II violated the Code and Standards.

16. Anderb, a portfolio manager for XYZ Investment Management Company—a registered investment organization that advises investment firms and private accounts—was promoted to that position three years ago. Bates, her supervisor, is responsible for reviewing Anderb's portfolio account transactions and her required monthly reports of personal stock transactions. Anderb has been using Jonelli, a broker, almost exclusively for brokerage transactions for the portfolio account. For securities in which Jonelli's firm makes a market, Jonelli has been giving Anderb lower prices for personal purchases and higher prices for personal sales than Jonelli gives to Anderb's portfolio accounts and other investors. Anderb has been filing monthly reports with Bates only for those months in which she has no personal transactions, which is about every fourth month. Which of the following is *most likely* to be a violation of the Code and Standards?

A. Anderb failed to disclose to her employer her personal transactions.

B. Anderb owned the same securities as those of her clients.

C. Bates allowed Anderb to use Jonelli as her broker for personal trades.

17. Which of the following is a correct statement of a member's or candidate's duty under the Code and Standards?

A. In the absence of specific applicable law or other regulatory requirements, the Code and Standards govern the member's or candidate's actions.

B. A member or candidate is required to comply only with applicable local laws, rules, regulations, or customs, even though the Code and Standards may impose a higher degree of responsibility or a higher duty on the member or candidate.

C. A member or candidate who trades securities in a securities market where no applicable local laws or stock exchange rules regulate the use of material nonpublic information may take investment action based on material nonpublic information.

18. Ward is scheduled to visit the corporate headquarters of Evans Industries. Ward expects to use the information he obtains there to complete his research report on Evans stock. Ward learns that Evans plans to pay all of Ward's expenses for the trip, including the costs of meals, his hotel room, and air transportation. Which of the following actions would be the *best* course for Ward to take under the Code and Standards?

A. Accept the expense-paid trip, and write an objective report.

B. Pay for all travel expenses, including the costs of meals and incidental items.

C. Accept the expense-paid trip, but disclose the value of the services accepted in the report.

19. Which of the following statements is *correct* under the Code and Standards?

A. CFA Institute members and candidates are prohibited from undertaking independent practice in competition with their employer.

B. Written consent from the employer is necessary to permit independent practice that could result in compensation or other benefits in competition with a member's or candidate's employer.

C. Members and candidates are prohibited from making arrangements or preparations to go into a competitive business before terminating their relationship with their employer.

20. Smith is a financial analyst with XYZ Brokerage Firm. She is preparing a purchase recommendation on JNI Corporation. Which of the following situations is *most likely* to represent a conflict of interest for Smith that would have to be avoided or disclosed?

A. Smith frequently purchases items produced by JNI.

B. XYZ holds for its own account a substantial common stock position in JNI.

C. Smith's brother-in-law is a supplier to JNI.

21. Michelieu tells a prospective client, "I may not have a long-term track record yet, but I'm sure that you'll be very pleased with my recommendations and service. In the three years that I've been in the business, my equity-oriented clients have averaged a total return of more than 26% a year." The statement is true, but Michelieu only has a few clients, and one of his clients took a large position in a penny stock (against Michelieu's advice) and realized a huge gain. This large return caused the average of all of Michelieu's clients to exceed 26% a year. Without this one investment, the average gain would have been 8% a year. Has Michelieu violated the Standards?

A. No, because Michelieu is not promising that he can earn a 26% return in the future.

B. No, because the statement is a true and accurate description of Michelieu's track record.

C. Yes, because the statement misrepresents Michelieu's track record.

22. An investment banking department of a brokerage firm often receives material nonpublic information that could have considerable value if used in advising the firm's brokerage clients. In order to conform to the Code and Standards, which one of the following is the best policy for the brokerage firm?

A. Permanently prohibit both "buy" and "sell" recommendations of the stocks of clients of the investment banking department.

B. Establish physical and informational barriers within the firm to prevent the exchange of information between the investment banking and brokerage operations.

C. Monitor the exchange of information between the investment banking department and the brokerage operation.

23. Stewart has been hired by Goodner Industries, Inc., to manage its pension fund.

Stewart's duty of loyalty, prudence, and care is owed to:

A. the management of Goodner.

B. the participants and beneficiaries of Goodner's pension plan.

C. the shareholders of Goodner.

24. Which of the following statements is a stated purpose of disclosure in Standard VI(C) Referral Fees?

A. Disclosure will allow the client to request discounted service fees.

B. Disclosure will help the client evaluate any possible partiality shown in the recommendation of services.

C. Disclosure means advising a prospective client about the referral arrangement once a formal client relationship has been established.

25. Rose, a portfolio manager for a local investment advisory firm, is planning to sell a portion of his personal investment portfolio to cover the costs of his child's academic tuition. Rose wants to sell a portion of his holdings in Household Products, but his firm recently upgraded the stock to "strong buy." Which of the following describes Rose's options under the Code and Standards?

A. Based on his firm's "buy" recommendation, Rose cannot sell the shares because he would be improperly prospering from the inflated recommendation.

B. Rose is free to sell his personal holdings once his firm is properly informed of his intentions.

C. Rose can sell his personal holdings but only when a client of the firm places an order to buy shares of Household.

26. A former hedge fund manager, Jackman, has decided to launch a new private wealth management firm. From his prior experiences, he believes the new firm needs to achieve US$1 million in assets under management in the first year. Jackman offers a US$10,000 incentive to any adviser who joins his firm with the minimum of US$200,000 in committed investments. Jackman places notice of the opening on several industry web portals and career search sites. Which of the following is *correct* according to the Code and Standards?

A. A member or candidate is eligible for the new position and incentive if he or she can arrange for enough current clients to switch to the new firm and if the member or candidate discloses the incentive fee.

B. A member or candidate may not accept employment with the new firm, because Jackman's incentive offer violates the Code and Standards.

C. A member or candidate is not eligible for the new position unless he or she is currently unemployed, because soliciting the clients of the member's or candidate's current employer is prohibited.

27. Carter works for Invest Today, a local asset management firm. A broker that provides Carter with proprietary research through client brokerage arrangements is offering a new trading service. The broker is offering low-fee, execution-only trades to complement its traditional full-service execution-and-research trades. To entice Carter and other asset managers to send additional business its way, the

broker will apply the commissions paid on the new service toward satisfying the brokerage commitment of the prior full-service arrangements. Carter has always been satisfied with the execution provided on the full-service trades, and the fees of the new low-fee trades are comparable to those of other brokers currently used for the accounts that prohibit soft dollar arrangements.

A. Carter can trade for his accounts that prohibit soft dollar arrangements under the new low-fee trading scheme.

B. Carter cannot use the new trading scheme because the commissions are prohibited by the soft dollar restrictions of the accounts.

C. Carter should trade only through the new low-fee scheme and should increase his trading volume to meet his required commission commitment.

28. Rule has worked as a portfolio manager for a large investment management firm for the past 10 years. Rule earned his CFA charter last year and has decided to open his own investment management firm. After leaving his current employer, Rule creates some marketing material for his new firm. He states in the material, "In earning the CFA charter, a highly regarded credential in the investment management industry, I further enhanced the portfolio management skills learned during my professional career. While completing the examination process in three consecutive years, I consistently received the highest possible scores on the topics of Ethics, Alternative Investments, and Portfolio Management." Has Rule violated Standard VII(B) Reference to CFA Institute, the CFA Designation, and the CFA Program in his marketing material?

A. Rule violated Standard VII(B) in stating that he completed the exams in three consecutive years.

B. Rule violated Standard VII(B) in stating that he received the highest scores in the topics of Ethics, Alternative Investments, and Portfolio Management.

C. Rule did not violate Standard VII(B).

29. Stafford is a portfolio manager for a specialized real estate mutual fund. Her firm clearly describes in the fund's prospectus its soft dollar policies. Stafford decides that entering the CFA Program will enhance her investment decision-making skill and decides to use the fund's soft dollar account to pay the registration and exam fees for the CFA Program. Which of the following statements is *most likely* correct?

A. Stafford did not violate the Code and Standards because the prospectus informed investors of the fund's soft dollar policies.

B. Stafford violated the Code and Standards because improving her investment skills is not a reasonable use of the soft dollar account.

C. Stafford violated the Code and Standards because the CFA Program does not meet the definition of research allowed to be purchased with brokerage commissions.

30. Long has been asked to be the keynote speaker at an upcoming investment conference. The event is being hosted by one of the third-party investment managers currently used by his pension fund. The manager offers to cover all conference and travel costs for Long and make the conference registrations free for three additional members of his investment management team. To ensure that the conference obtains the best speakers, the host firm has arranged for an exclusive

golf outing for the day following the conference on a local championship-caliber course. Which of the following is *least likely* to violate Standard I(B)?

A. Long may accept only the offer to have his conference-related expenses paid by the host firm.

B. Long may accept the offer to have his conference-related expenses paid and may attend the exclusive golf outing at the expense of the hosting firm.

C. Long may accept the entire package of incentives offered to speak at this conference.

31. Andrews, a private wealth manager, is conducting interviews for a new research analyst for his firm. One of the candidates is Wright, an analyst with a local investment bank. During the interview, while Wright is describing his analytical skills, he mentions a current merger in which his firm is acting as the adviser. Andrews has heard rumors of a possible merger between the two companies, but no releases have been made by the companies concerned. Which of the following actions by Andrews is *least likely* a violation of the Code and Standards?

A. Waiting until the next day before trading on the information to allow time for it to become public

B. Notifying all investment managers in his firm of the new information so none of their clients are disadvantaged

C. Placing the securities mentioned as part of the merger on the firm's restricted trading list

32. Pietro, president of Local Bank, has hired the bank's market maker, Vogt, to seek a merger partner. Local is currently listed on a stock exchange and has not reported that it is seeking strategic alternatives. Vogt has discussed the possibility of a merger with several firms, but they have all decided to wait until after the next period's financial data are available. The potential buyers believe the results will be worse than the results of prior periods and will allow them to pay less for Local Bank. Pietro wants to increase the likelihood of structuring a merger deal quickly. Which of the following actions would *most likely* be a violation of the Code and Standards?

A. Pietro could instruct Local Bank to issue a press release announcing that it has retained Vogt to find a merger partner.

B. Pietro could place a buy order for 2,000 shares (or four times the average weekly volume) through Vogt for his personal account.

C. After confirming with Local's chief financial officer, Pietro could instruct Local to issue a press release reaffirming the firm's prior announced earnings guidance for the full fiscal year.

33. ABC Investment Management acquires a new, very large account with two concentrated positions. The firm's current policy is to add new accounts for the purpose of performance calculation after the first full month of management. Cupp is responsible for calculating the firm's performance returns. Before the end of the initial month, Cupp notices that one of the significant holdings of the new accounts is acquired by another company, causing the value of the investment to double. Because of this holding, Cupp decides to account for the new portfolio as of the date of transfer, thereby allowing ABC Investment to reap the positive im-

pact of that month's portfolio return. Which of the following statements is true?

A. Cupp did not violate the Code and Standards, because the GIPS standards allow composites to be updated on the date of large external cash flows.

B. Cupp did not violate the Code and Standards, because companies are allowed to determine when to incorporate new accounts into their composite calculation.

C. Cupp violated the Code and Standards because the inclusion of the new account produces an inaccurate calculation of the monthly results according to the firm's stated policies.

34. Cannan has been working from home on weekends and occasionally saves correspondence with clients and completed reports on her home computer. Because of worsening market conditions, Cannan is one of several employees released by her firm. While Cannan is looking for a new job, she uses the files she saved at home to request letters of recommendation from former clients. She also provides to prospective clients some of the reports as examples of her abilities. Which of the following statements is true?

A. Cannan violated the Code and Standards because she did not receive permission from her former employer to keep or use the files after her employment ended.

B. Cannan did not violate the Code and Standards, because the files were created and saved on her own time and computer.

C. Cannan violated the Code and Standards because she is prohibited from saving files on her home computer.

35. Quinn sat for the Level III CFA exam this past weekend. He updates his resume with the following statement: "In finishing the CFA Program, I improved my skills related to researching investments and managing portfolios. I will be eligible for the CFA charter upon completion of the required work experience." Which of the following statements is true?

A. Quinn violated the Code and Standards by claiming he improved his skills through the CFA Program.

B. Quinn violated the Code and Standards by incorrectly stating that he is eligible for the CFA charter.

C. Quinn did not violate the Code and Standards with his resume update.

36. During a round of golf, Rodriguez, chief financial officer of Mega Retail, mentions to Hart, a local investment adviser and long-time personal friend, that Mega is having an exceptional sales quarter. Rodriguez expects the results to be almost 10% above the current estimates. The next day, Hart initiates the purchase of a large stake in the local exchange-traded retail fund for her personal account.

A. Hart violated the Code and Standards by investing in the exchange-traded fund that included Mega Retail.

B. Hart did not violate the Code and Standards, because she did not invest directly in securities of Mega Retail.

C. Rodriguez did not violate the Code and Standards, because the comments made to Hart were not intended to solicit an investment in Mega Retail.

37. Park is very frustrated after taking the Level II CFA exam. While she was studying for the exam, to supplement the curriculum provided, she ordered and used study material from a third-party provider. Park believes the additional material focused her attention on specific topic areas that were not tested while ignoring other areas. She posts the following statement on the provider's discussion board: "I am very dissatisfied with your firm's CFA Program Level II material. I found the exam extremely difficult and myself unprepared for specific questions after using your product. How could your service provide such limited instructional resources on the analysis of inventories and taxes when the exam had multiple questions about them? I will not recommend your products to other candidates." Which of the following statements is true?

A. Park violated the Code and Standards by purchasing third-party review material.

B. Park violated the Code and Standards by providing her opinion on the difficulty of the exam.

C. Park violated the Code and Standards by providing specific information on topics tested on the exam.

38. Paper was recently terminated as one of a team of five managers of an equity fund. The fund had two value-focused managers and terminated one of them to reduce costs. In a letter sent to prospective employers, Paper presents, with written permission of the firm, the performance history of the fund to demonstrate his past success. Which of the following statements is true?

A. Paper did not violate the Code and Standards.

B. Paper violated the Code and Standards by claiming the performance of the entire fund as his own.

C. Paper violated the Code and Standards by including the historical results of his prior employer.

39. Townsend was recently appointed to the board of directors of a youth golf program that is the local chapter of a national not-for-profit organization. The program is beginning a new fund-raising campaign to expand the number of annual scholarships it provides. Townsend believes many of her clients make annual donations to charity. The next week in her regular newsletter to all clients, she includes a small section discussing the fund-raising campaign and her position on the organization's board. Which of the following statements is true?

A. Townsend did not violate the Code and Standards.

B. Townsend violated the Code and Standards by soliciting donations from her clients through the newsletter.

C. Townsend violated the Code and Standards by not getting approval of the organization before soliciting her clients.

SOLUTIONS

1. The correct answer is B. This question involves Standard III(B) Fair Dealing. Smith disseminated a change in the stock recommendation to his clients but then received a request contrary to that recommendation from a client who probably had not yet received the recommendation. Prior to executing the order, Smith should take additional steps to ensure that the customer has received the change of recommendation. Answer A is incorrect because the client placed the order prior to receiving the recommendation and, therefore, does not have the benefit of Smith's most recent recommendation. Answer C is also incorrect; simply because the client request is contrary to the firm's recommendation does not mean a member can override a direct request by a client. After Smith contacts the client to ensure that the client has received the changed recommendation, if the client still wants to place a buy order for the shares, Smith is obligated to comply with the client's directive.

2. The correct answer is C. This question involves Standard III(A) Loyalty, Prudence, and Care and the specific topic of soft dollars or soft commissions. Answer C is the correct choice because client brokerage commissions may not be directed to pay for the investment manager's operating expenses. Answer B describes how members and candidates should determine how to use brokerage commissions—that is, if the use is in the best interests of clients and is commensurate with the value of the services provided. Answer A describes a practice that is commonly referred to as "directed brokerage." Because brokerage is an asset of the client and is used to benefit the client, not the manager, such practice does not violate a duty of loyalty to the client. Members and candidates are obligated in all situations to disclose to clients their practices in the use of client brokerage commissions.

3. The correct answer is B. This question involves Standard VI(A) Avoid or Disclose Conflicts. The question establishes a conflict of interest in which an analyst, Jamison, is asked to write a research report on a company that is a client of her employer. In addition, two directors of the company are senior officers of Jamison's employer. Best practice would be to avoid the conflicts of interest by not providing a research report on companies that are clients of or have a director relationship with Howard & Howard. If the conflicts are not avoided, both the client relationship and director relationship must be disclosed by Jamison in her research report. Answer C is incorrect because Jamison would be disclosing only one of the conflicts. Answer A is incorrect because whether Jamison expresses any opinions in the report is irrelevant to her duty to disclose all conflicts of interest. Not expressing opinions does not relieve the analyst of the responsibility to disclose the special relationships between the two companies.

4. The correct answer is C. This question asks about compliance procedures relating to personal investments of members and candidates. The statement in answer C clearly conflicts with the recommended procedures in the *Standards of Practice Handbook*. Employers should compare personal transactions of employees with those of clients on a regular basis regardless of the existence of a requirement by any regulatory organization. Such comparisons ensure that employees' personal trades do not conflict with their duty to their clients, and the comparisons can be conducted in a confidential manner. The statement in answer A does not conflict with the procedures in the *Handbook*. Disclosure of such policies will give full information to clients regarding potential conflicts of interest on the part of those entrusted to manage their money. Answer B is incorrect because firms are

encouraged to establish policies whereby employees clear their personal holdings and transactions with their employers.

5. The correct answer is B. This question relates to Standard III(A) Loyalty, Prudence, and Care and Standard III(E) Preservation of Confidentiality. In this case, the member manages funds of a private endowment. Clients—in this case, the trustees of the fund—must place some trust in members and candidates. Bronson cannot disclose confidential financial information to anyone without the permission of the fund, regardless of whether the disclosure may benefit the fund. Therefore, answer A is incorrect. Answer C is incorrect because Bronson must notify the fund and obtain the fund's permission before publicizing the information.

6. The correct answer is B. This question relates to Standard V(A) Diligence and Reasonable Basis. The opinion of another financial analyst is not an adequate basis for Willier's action in changing the recommendation. Answer C is thus incorrect. Answer A is incorrect because, although it is true that members and candidates must distinguish between facts and opinions in recommendations, the question does not illustrate a violation of that nature. If the opinion overheard by Willier had sparked him to conduct additional research and investigation that justified a change of opinion, then a changed recommendation would be appropriate.

7. The correct answer is B. This question relates to Standard I(B) Independence and Objectivity. When asked to change a recommendation on a company stock to gain business for the firm, the head of the brokerage unit must refuse in order to maintain his independence and objectivity in making recommendations. He must not yield to pressure by the firm's investment banking department. To avoid the appearance of a conflict of interest, the firm should discontinue issuing recommendations about the company. Answer A is incorrect; changing the recommendation in any manner that is contrary to the analyst's opinion violates the duty to maintain independence and objectivity. Answer C is incorrect because merely assigning a new analyst to decide whether the stock deserves a higher rating will not address the conflict of interest.

8. The correct answer is A. Standard VII(B) Reference to CFA Institute, the CFA Designation, and the CFA Program is the subject of this question. The reference on Albert's business card implies that there is a "CFA Level II" designation; Tye merely indicates in promotional material that he is participating in the CFA Program and has completed Levels I and II. Candidates may not imply that there is some sort of partial designation earned after passing a level of the CFA exam. Therefore, Albert has violated Standard VII(B). Candidates may communicate that they are participating in the CFA Program, however, and may state the levels that they have completed. Therefore, Tye has not violated Standard VII(B).

9. The correct answer is B. This question relates to Standard V(B) Communication with Clients and Prospective Clients. Scott has issued a research report stating that he expects the price of Walkton Industries stock to rise by US$8 a share "because the dividend will increase" by US$1.50 per share. He has made this statement knowing that the dividend will increase only if Congress enacts certain legislation, an uncertain prospect. By stating that the dividend will increase, Scott failed to separate fact from opinion. The information regarding passage of legislation is not material nonpublic information because it is conjecture, and the question does not state whether the US representative gave Scott her opinion on the passage of the legislation in confidence. She could have been offering this opinion to anyone who asked. Therefore, answer A is incorrect. It may be acceptable to base a recommendation, in part, on an expectation of future events, even though

they may be uncertain. Therefore, answer C is incorrect.

10. The correct answer is C. This question, which relates to Standard III(B) Fair Dealing, tests the knowledge of the procedures that will assist members and candidates in treating clients fairly when making investment recommendations. The step listed in C will help ensure the fair treatment of clients. Answer A may have negative effects on the fair treatment of clients. The more people who know about a pending change, the greater the chance that someone will inform some clients before the information's release. The firm should establish policies that limit the number of people who are aware in advance that a recommendation is to be disseminated. Answer B, distributing recommendations to institutional clients before distributing them to individual accounts, discriminates among clients on the basis of size and class of assets and is a violation of Standard III(B).

11. The correct answer is B. This question deals with Standard II(A) Material Nonpublic Information. The mosaic theory states that an analyst may use material public information and nonmaterial nonpublic information in creating a larger picture than shown by any individual piece of information and the conclusions the analyst reaches become material only after the pieces are assembled. Answers A and C are accurate statements relating to the Code and Standards but do not describe the mosaic theory.

12. The correct answer is C. This question involves Standard IV(B) Additional Compensation Arrangements. The arrangement described in the question—whereby Jurgen would be compensated beyond the compensation provided by her firm, on the basis of an account's performance—is not a violation of the Standards as long as Jurgen discloses the arrangement in writing to her employer and obtains permission from her employer prior to entering into the arrangement. Answers A and B are incorrect; although the private compensation arrangement could conflict with the interests of other clients and lead to short-term performance pressures, members and candidates may enter into such agreements as long as they have disclosed the arrangements to their employer and obtained permission for the arrangement from their employer.

13. The correct answer is B. This question relates to Standard III(A) Loyalty, Prudence, and Care—specifically, a member's or candidate's responsibility for voting proxies and the use of client brokerage. According to the facts stated in the question, Farnsworth did not violate Standard III(A). Although the company president asked Farnsworth to vote the shares of the Jones Corporation profit-sharing plan a certain way, Farnsworth investigated the issue and concluded, independently, the best way to vote. Therefore, even though his decision coincided with the wishes of the company president, Farnsworth is not in violation of his responsibility to be loyal and to provide care to his clients. In this case, the participants and the beneficiaries of the profit-sharing plan are the clients, not the company's management. Had Farnsworth not investigated the issue or had he yielded to the president's wishes and voted for a slate of directors that he had determined was not in the best interest of the company, Farnsworth would have violated his responsibilities to the beneficiaries of the plan. In addition, because the brokerage firm provides the lowest commissions and best execution for securities transactions, Farnsworth has met his obligations to the client in using this brokerage firm. It does not matter that the brokerage firm also provides research information that is not useful for the account generating the commission, because Farnsworth is not paying extra money of the client for that information.

14. The correct answer is A. In this question, Brown is providing investment recommendations before making inquiries about the client's financial situation, investment experience, or investment objectives. Brown is thus violating Standard

III(C) Suitability. Answers B and C provide examples of information members and candidates should discuss with their clients at the outset of the relationship, but these answers do not constitute a complete list of those factors. Answer A is the best answer.

15. The correct answer is C. This question involves Standard I(C) Misrepresentation. Statement I is a factual statement that discloses to clients and prospects accurate information about the terms of the investment instrument. Statement II, which guarantees a specific rate of return for a mutual fund, is an opinion stated as a fact and, therefore, violates Standard I(C). If statement II were rephrased to include a qualifying statement, such as "in my opinion, investors may earn . . . ," it would not be in violation of the Standards.

16. The correct answer is A. This question involves three of the Standards. Anderb, the portfolio manager, has been obtaining more favorable prices for her personal securities transactions than she gets for her clients, which is a breach of Standard III(A) Loyalty, Prudence, and Care. In addition, she violated Standard I(D) Misconduct by failing to adhere to company policy and by hiding her personal transactions from her firm. Anderb's supervisor, Bates, violated Standard IV(C) Responsibilities of Supervisors; although the company had requirements for reporting personal trading, Bates failed to adequately enforce those requirements. Answer B does not represent a violation because Standard VI(B) Priority of Transactions requires that personal trading in a security be conducted after the trading in that security of clients and the employer. The Code and Standards do not prohibit owning such investments, although firms may establish policies that limit the investment opportunities of members and candidates. Answer C does not represent a violation, because the Code and Standards do not contain a prohibition against employees using the same broker for their personal accounts that they use for their client accounts. This arrangement should be disclosed to the employer so that the employer may determine whether a conflict of interest exists.

17. The correct answer is A because this question relates to Standard I(A) Knowledge of the Law—specifically, global application of the Code and Standards. Members and candidates who practice in multiple jurisdictions may be subject to various securities laws and regulations. If applicable law is more strict than the requirements of the Code and Standards, members and candidates must adhere to applicable law; otherwise, members and candidates must adhere to the Code and Standards. Therefore, answer A is correct. Answer B is incorrect because members and candidates must adhere to the higher standard set by the Code and Standards if local applicable law is less strict. Answer C is incorrect because when no applicable law exists, members and candidates are required to adhere to the Code and Standards, and the Code and Standards prohibit the use of material nonpublic information.

18. The correct answer is B. The best course of action under Standard I(B) Independence and Objectivity is to avoid a conflict of interest whenever possible. Therefore, for Ward to pay for all his expenses is the correct answer. Answer C details a course of action in which the conflict would be disclosed, but the solution is not as appropriate as avoiding the conflict of interest. Answer A would not be the best course because it would not remove the appearance of a conflict of interest; even though the report would not be affected by the reimbursement of expenses, it could appear to be.

19. The correct answer is B. Under Standard IV(A) Loyalty, members and candidates may undertake independent practice that may result in compensation or other benefit in competition with their employer as long as they obtain consent

from their employer. Answer C is not consistent with the Standards because the Standards allow members and candidates to make arrangements or preparations to go into competitive business as long as those arrangements do not interfere with their duty to their current employer. Answer A is not consistent with the Standards because the Standards do not include a complete prohibition against undertaking independent practice.

20. The correct answer is B. This question involves Standard VI(A) Avoid or Disclose Conflicts—specifically, the holdings of an analyst's employer in company stock. XYZ ownership of the stock of the company that is the subject of the research report creates a conflict of interest that must be disclosed in the research report. XYZ could avoid the conflict by not having Smith prepare a recommendation for JNI or any other company in which XYZ has an ownership interest. Answers A and C do not describe conflicts of interest that Smith would have to avoid or disclose. Answer A describes the use of a firm's products, which would not be a required disclosure because it will likely not create a conflict of interest. In answer C, the relationship between the analyst and the company through a relative is so tangential that it does not create a conflict of interest necessitating disclosure.

21. The correct answer is C. This question relates to Standard I(C) Misrepresentation. Although Michelieu's statement about the total return of his clients' accounts on average may be technically true, it is misleading because the majority of the gain resulted from one client's large position taken against Michelieu's advice. Therefore, this statement misrepresents the investment performance the member is responsible for. He has not taken steps to present a fair, accurate, and complete presentation of performance. Answer B is thus incorrect. Answer A is incorrect because although Michelieu is not guaranteeing future results, his words are still a misrepresentation of his performance history.

22. The correct answer is B. The best policy to prevent violation of Standard II(A) Material Nonpublic Information is the establishment of firewalls in a firm to prevent the exchange of insider information. The physical and informational barrier of a firewall between the investment banking department and the brokerage operation prevents the investment banking department from providing information to analysts on the brokerage side who may be writing recommendations on a company stock. Prohibiting recommendations of the stock of companies that are clients of the investment banking department is an alternative, but answer A states that this prohibition would be permanent, which is not the best answer. Once an offering is complete and the material nonpublic information obtained by the investment banking department becomes public, resuming publishing recommendations on the stock is not a violation of the Code and Standards, because the information of the investment banking department no longer gives the brokerage operation an advantage in writing the report. Answer C is incorrect because no exchange of information should be occurring between the investment banking department and the brokerage operation, so monitoring of such exchanges is not an effective compliance procedure for preventing the use of material nonpublic information.

23. The correct answer is B. Under Standard III(A) Loyalty, Prudence, and Care, members and candidates who manage a company's pension fund owe these duties to the participants and beneficiaries of the pension plan, not the management of the company or the company's shareholders.

24. The correct answer is B. Answer B gives one of the two primary reasons listed in the *Handbook* for disclosing referral fees to clients under Standard VI(C) Referral Fees. (The other is to allow clients and employers to evaluate the full cost of the services.) Answer A is incorrect because Standard VI(C) does not require mem-

bers or candidates to discount their fees when they receive referral fees. Answer C is inconsistent with Standard VI(C) because disclosure of referral fees, to be effective, should be made to prospective clients before entering into a formal client relationship with them.

25. The correct answer is B. Standard VI(B) Priority of Transactions does not limit transactions of company employees that differ from current recommendations as long as the sale does not disadvantage current clients. Thus, answer A is incorrect. Answer C is incorrect because the Standard does not require the matching of personal and client trades.

26. Answer C is correct. Standard IV(A) Loyalty discusses activities permissible to members and candidates when they are leaving their current employer; soliciting clients is strictly prohibited. Thus, answer A is inconsistent with the Code and Standards even with the required disclosure. Answer B is incorrect because the offer does not directly violate the Code and Standards. There may be out-of-work members and candidates who can arrange the necessary commitments without violating the Code and Standards.

27. Answer A is correct. The question relates to Standard III(A) Loyalty, Prudence, and Care. Carter believes the broker offers effective execution at a fee that is comparable with those of other brokers, so he is free to use the broker for all accounts. Answer B is incorrect because the accounts that prohibit soft dollar arrangements do not want to fund the purchase of research by Carter. The new trading scheme does not incur additional commissions from clients, so it would not go against the prohibitions. Answer C is incorrect because Carter should not incur unnecessary or excessive "churning" of the portfolios (excessive trading) for the purpose of meeting the brokerage commitments of soft dollar arrangements.

28. Answer B is correct, according to Standard VII(B) Reference to CFA Institute, the CFA Designation, and the CFA Program. CFA Program candidates do not receive their actual scores on the exam. Topic and subtopic results are grouped into three broad categories, and the exam is graded only as "pass" or "fail." Although a candidate may have achieved a topical score of "above 70%," she or he cannot factually state that she or he received the highest possible score because that information is not reported. Thus, answer C is incorrect. Answer A is incorrect as long as the member or candidate actually completed the exams consecutively. Standard VII(B) does not prohibit the communication of factual information about completing the CFA Program in three consecutive years.

29. Answer C is correct. According to Standard III(A) Loyalty, Prudence, and Care, the CFA Program would be considered a personal or firm expense and should not be paid for with the fund's brokerage commissions. Soft dollar accounts should be used only to purchase research services that directly assist the investment manager in the investment decision-making process, not to assist the management of the firm or to further education. Thus, answer A is incorrect. Answer B is incorrect because the reasonableness of how the money is used is not an issue; the issue is that educational expense is not research.

30. Answer A is correct. Standard I(B) Independence and Objectivity emphasizes the need for members and candidates to maintain their independence and objectivity. Best practices dictate that firms adopt a strict policy not to accept compensation for travel arrangements. At times, however, accepting paid travel would not compromise one's independence and objectivity. Answers B and C are incorrect because the added benefits—free conference admission for additional staff members and an exclusive golf retreat for the speaker—could be viewed as inducements related to the firm's working arrangements and not solely related

to the speaking engagement. Should Long wish to bring other team members or participate in the golf outing, he or his firm should be responsible for the associated fees.

31. Answer C is correct. The guidance to Standard II(A) Material Nonpublic Information recommends adding securities to the firm's restricted list when the firm has or may have material nonpublic information. By adding these securities to this list, Andrews would uphold this standard. Because waiting until the next day will not ensure that news of the merger is made public, answer A is incorrect. Negotiations between the two companies may take much longer, and the merger may never happen. Andrews must wait until the information is disseminated to the market before he trades on that information. Answer B is incorrect because Andrews should not disclose the information to other managers; no trading is allowed on material nonpublic information.

32. Answer B is correct. Through placing a personal purchase order that is significantly greater than the average volume, Pietro is violating Standard II(B) Market Manipulation. He is attempting to manipulate an increase in the share price and thus bring a buyer to the negotiating table. The news of a possible merger and confirmation of the firm's earnings guidance may also have positive effects on the price of Local Bank, but Pietro's actions in instructing the release of the information does not represent a violation through market manipulation. Announcements of this nature are common and practical to keep investors informed. Thus, answers A and C are incorrect.

33. Answer C is correct. Cupp violated Standard III(D) Performance Presentations when he deviated from the firm's stated policies solely to capture the gain from the holding being acquired. Answer A is incorrect because the firm does not claim GIPS compliance and the GIPS standards require external cash flows to be treated in a manner consistent with the firm's documented policies. Answer B is incorrect because the firm does not state that it is updating its composite policies. If such a change were to occur, all cash flows for the month would have to be reviewed to ensure their consistent treatment under the new policy.

34. Answer A is correct. According to Standard V(C) Record Retention, Cannan needed the permission of her employer to maintain the files at home after her employment ended. Without that permission, she should have deleted the files. All files created as part of a member's or candidate's professional activity are the property of the firm, even those created outside normal work hours. Thus, answer B is incorrect. Answer C is incorrect because the Code and Standards do not prohibit using one's personal computer to complete work for one's employer.

35. Answer B is correct. According to Standard VII(B) Reference to CFA Institute, the CFA Designation, and the CFA Program, Quinn cannot claim to have finished the CFA Program or be eligible for the CFA charter until he officially learns that he has passed the Level III CFA exam. Until the results for the most recent exam are released, those who sat for the exam should continue to refer to themselves as "candidates." Thus, answer C is incorrect. Answer A is incorrect because members and candidates may discuss areas of practice in which they believe the CFA Program improved their personal skills.

36. Answer A is correct. Hart's decision to invest in the retail fund appears directly correlated with Rodriguez's statement about the successful quarter of Mega Retail and thus violates Standard II(A) Material Nonpublic Information. Rodriguez's information would be considered material because it would influence the share price of Mega Retail and probably influence the price of the entire exchange-traded retail fund. Thus, answer B is incorrect. Answer C is also incor-

rect because Rodriguez shared information that was both material and nonpublic. Company officers regularly have such knowledge about their firms, which is not a violation. The sharing of such information, however, even in a conversation between friends, does violate Standard II(A).

37. Answer C is correct. Standard VII(A) Conduct as Members and Candidates in the CFA Program prohibits providing information to candidates or the public that is considered confidential to the CFA Program. In revealing that questions related to the analysis of inventories and analysis of taxes were on the exam, Park has violated this standard. Answer B is incorrect because the guidance for the standard explicitly acknowledges that members and candidates are allowed to offer their opinions about the CFA Program. Answer A is incorrect because candidates are not prohibited from using outside resources.

38. Answer B is correct. Paper has violated Standard III(D) Performance Presentation by not disclosing that he was part of a team of managers that achieved the results shown. If he had also included the return of the portion he directly managed, he would not have violated the standard. Thus, answer A is incorrect. Answer C is incorrect because Paper received written permission from his prior employer to include the results.

39. Answer A is correct. Townsend has not provided any information about her clients to the leaders or managers of the golf program; thus, she has not violated Standard III(E) Preservation of Confidentiality. Providing contact information about her clients for a direct-mail solicitation would have been a violation. Answer B is incorrect because the notice in the newsletter does not violate Standard III(E). Answer C is incorrect because the golf program's fund-raising campaign had already begun, so discussing the opportunity to donate was appropriate.

LEARNING MODULE

4

Introduction to the Global Investment Performance Standards (GIPS)

LEARNING OUTCOMES	
Mastery	*The candidate should be able to:*
☐	explain why the GIPS standards were created, who can claim compliance, and who benefits from compliance
☐	describe the key concepts of the GIPS Standards for Firms
☐	explain the purpose of composites in performance reporting
☐	describe the fundamentals of compliance, including the recommendations of the GIPS standards with respect to the definition of the firm and the firm's definition of discretion
☐	describe the concept of independent verification

INTRODUCTION

1

The objective of this reading is to provide candidates with an orientation to the GIPS standards. It explains why the GIPS standards were created, who can claim compliance, and who benefits from compliance. It also covers key concepts of the GIPS standards—composites, the definition of the firm, and the definition of investment discretion. Finally, the reading briefly discusses the purpose and benefits of verification. Upon completion of this reading, candidates should appreciate the benefits of an industry-wide set of standards for calculating and presenting investment performance based on the principles of fair representation and full disclosure.

The 2020 edition of the GIPS standards has three chapters:

1. GIPS Standards for Firms
2. GIPS Standards for Asset Owners
3. GIPS Standards for Verifiers

Organizations that compete for business must comply with the GIPS Standards for Firms.

Candidates are also responsible for reading the sections of the GIPS Standards for Firms specifically referenced in this reading. A complete copy of the 2020 GIPS Standards for Firms can be found here: https://www.cfainstitute.org/en/ethics/codes/gips-standards/firms.

2 WHY WERE THE GIPS STANDARDS CREATED, WHO CAN CLAIM COMPLIANCE, & WHO BENEFITS FROM COMPLIANCE?

- ☐ explain why the GIPS standards were created, who can claim compliance, and who benefits from compliance
- ☐ describe the key concepts of the GIPS Standards for Firms

The mission of the GIPS standards is to promote ethics and integrity and instill trust through the use of the GIPS standards by achieving universal demand for compliance by asset owners, adoption by asset managers, and support from regulators for the ultimate benefit of the global investment community.

Institutions and individuals are constantly scrutinizing past investment performance returns in search of the best manager to achieve their investment objectives.

In the past, the investment community had great difficulty making meaningful comparisons on the basis of accurate investment performance data. Several performance measurement practices hindered the comparability of performance returns from one firm to another, while others called into question the accuracy and credibility of performance reporting overall. Misleading practices included:

- *Representative Accounts*: Selecting a top-performing portfolio to represent the firm's overall investment results for a specific mandate.
- *Survivorship Bias*: Presenting an "average" performance history that *excludes* portfolios whose poor performance was weak enough to result in termination of the firm.
- *Varying Time Periods*: Presenting performance for a selected time period during which the mandate produced excellent returns or out-performed its benchmark—making comparison with other firms' results difficult or impossible.

Making a valid comparison of investment performance among even the most ethical investment management firms was problematic. For example, a pension fund seeking to hire an investment management firm might receive proposals from several firms, possibly from different countries, all using different methodologies for calculating their results.

The GIPS standards are a practitioner-driven set of ethical principles that establish a standardized, industry-wide approach for investment firms to follow in calculating and presenting their historical investment results to prospective clients. The GIPS standards ensure fair representation and full disclosure of investment performance. In other words, the GIPS standards lead investment management firms to avoid misrepresentations of performance and to communicate all relevant information that prospective clients and investors should know in order to evaluate past results.

The objectives of the GIPS standards are as follows:

- Promote investor interests and instill investor confidence.

- Ensure accurate and consistent data.
- Obtain worldwide acceptance of a single standard for calculating and presenting performance.
- Promote fair, global competition among investment firms.
- Promote industry self-regulation on a global basis.

Who Can Claim Compliance?

Any firm that *manages actual assets* may choose to comply with the GIPS standards. Consultants cannot make a claim of compliance unless they actually manage the assets for which they are making a claim of compliance. They can claim to endorse the GIPS standards and/or require that their investment managers comply with the GIPS standards. Similarly, software (and the vendors who supply software) cannot be "compliant." Software can assist firms in achieving compliance with the GIPS standards (e.g., by calculating performance in a manner consistent with the calculation requirements of the GIPS standards), but only a firm managing assets can claim compliance once the firm has satisfied all applicable requirements of the GIPS standards.

Asset owners may comply with the GIPS standards in the same way as firms if they compete for business. If they don't compete for business but report their performance to an oversight body, asset owners may choose to comply with the GIPS Standards for Asset Owners.

Compliance is a firm-wide process that cannot be achieved on a single product or composite. A firm has only two options with regard to compliance with the GIPS standards:

1. fully comply with *all* requirements of the GIPS standards and claim compliance through the use of the GIPS Compliance Statement; or

2. not comply with all requirements of the GIPS standards and not claim compliance with, or make any reference to, the GIPS standards.

Complying with the GIPS standards is voluntary. Compliance with the GIPS standards is not typically required by legal or regulatory authorities.

Who Benefits from Compliance?

The GIPS standards benefit firms and their prospective clients and investors, as well as asset owners and their oversight bodies.

- By choosing to comply with the GIPS standards, firms assure prospective clients and investors that the historical track record they report is both complete and fairly presented. Compliance enables the GIPS-compliant firm to participate in competitive bids against other compliant firms throughout the world. Achieving and maintaining compliance may also strengthen the firm's internal controls over performance-related policies and procedures.
- Prospective clients and investors have a greater level of confidence in the integrity of performance presentations of a GIPS-compliant firm and can more easily compare performance presentations from different investment management firms. The GIPS standards certainly do not eliminate the need for in-depth due diligence on the part of the client or investor, but compliance with the Standards enhances the credibility of investment management firms that have chosen to undertake this responsibility.
- Asset owners provide performance information to their oversight bodies that allows them to make investment decisions and evaluate the performance of the funds under their supervision. Particularly where asset owners require their external managers to comply with the GIPS standards,

reporting to the oversight body using the same principles facilitates the understanding of the sources of risk and excess return in the funds under supervision.

- **Key Concepts**
- Key concepts of the GIPS standards that apply to firms include the following:
- The GIPS standards are ethical standards for investment performance presentation to ensure fair representation and full disclosure of investment performance.
- Meeting the objectives of fair representation and full disclosure is likely to require more than simply adhering to the minimum requirements of the GIPS standards. Firms should also adhere to the recommendations to achieve best practice in the calculation and presentation of performance.
- Firms must comply with all applicable requirements of the GIPS standards, including any Guidance Statements, interpretations, and Questions & Answers (Q&As) published by CFA Institute and the GIPS standards governing bodies.
- The GIPS standards do not address every aspect of performance measurement and will continue to evolve over time to address additional areas of investment performance.
- The GIPS standards require firms to create and maintain composites for all strategies for which the firm manages segregated accounts or markets to segregated accounts. Firms must include all actual, fee-paying, discretionary segregated accounts in at least one composite defined by investment mandate, objective, or strategy. Pooled funds must also be included in any composite for which the pooled fund meets the composite definition. Firms must maintain and make available information about all of the strategies they manage using composites or pooled funds. These requirements prevent firms from cherry-picking their best performance.
- The GIPS standards rely on the integrity of input data, the quality of which is critical to creating accurate performance presentations. The underlying valuations of portfolio holdings drive performance. It is essential for these and other inputs to be accurate. The GIPS standards require firms to adhere to certain calculation methodologies to allow for comparability across firms.

Please read the Preface and the Introduction to the Global Investment Performance Standards for Firms for additional insight into the history and purpose of the GIPS standards.

3 COMPOSITES

☐ explain the purpose of composites in performance reporting

One of the key concepts of the GIPS standards is the required use of composites. A composite is an aggregation of one or more portfolios managed according to a similar investment mandate, objective, or strategy. The requirement to create, use, and maintain composites is designed to prevent firms from cherry-picking—using the best-performing accounts to represent the performance of an investment strategy. A composite must include all actual, fee-paying, discretionary portfolios managed in accordance with the same investment mandate, objective, or strategy. For example, if a GIPS-compliant firm presents its track record for a Global Equity Composite (the Composite), the Composite must include all fee-paying portfolios that are managed, or have historically been managed, in the firm's Global Equity strategy. The firm may not subjectively select which Global Equity portfolios will be included in or excluded from the calculation and presentation of the Global Equity Composite. The determination of which portfolios to include in the Composite should be done according to pre-established criteria (i.e., on an *ex ante* basis), not after the fact. This prevents a firm from including only their best-performing portfolios in the Composite.

A firm that claims compliance must include all fee-paying, discretionary segregated accounts in at least one composite. A firm must also include all fee-paying discretionary pooled funds in any composite for which the pooled funds meet the composite definition.

Please read Section 3.A. of the GIPS Standards for Firms on composites.

FUNDAMENTALS OF COMPLIANCE 4

☐ describe the fundamentals of compliance, including the recommendations of the GIPS standards with respect to the definition of the firm and the firm's definition of discretion

Several core principles create the foundation for the GIPS standards, including properly defining the firm, providing GIPS Reports to all prospective clients and certain pooled fund prospective investors, adhering to applicable laws and regulations, and ensuring that information presented is not false or misleading. Two important issues that a firm must consider when becoming compliant with the GIPS standards are the definition of the firm and the firm's definition of discretion. The definition of the firm is the foundation for firm-wide compliance and creates defined boundaries whereby total firm assets can be determined.

The GIPS standards state "The firm should adopt the broadest, most meaningful definition of the firm. The scope of this definition should include all geographical (country, regional, etc.) offices operating under the same brand name, regardless of the actual name of the individual investment management company."

The firm's definition of discretion establishes criteria to judge which portfolios must be included in a composite and is based on the firm's ability to implement its investment strategies. If documented client-imposed restrictions interfere with the implementation of the intended strategy to the extent that the portfolio is no longer representative of the strategy, the firm may determine that the portfolio is non-discretionary. Non-discretionary portfolios must not be included in a firm's composites.

Section 1 of the 2020 GIPS Standards for Firms addresses the fundamentals of compliance in more detail.

VERIFICATION 5

☐ describe the concept of independent verification

Firms that claim compliance with the GIPS standards are responsible for their claim of compliance and for maintaining that compliance. That is, firms self-regulate their claim of compliance. Once a firm claims compliance with the GIPS standards, it may voluntarily hire an independent third party to perform a verification in order to increase confidence in the firm's claim of compliance. Verification may also increase the knowledge of the firm's performance measurement team and improve the consistency and quality of the firm's GIPS standards-related performance information.

Verification is a process by which an independent verification firm (verifier) conducts testing of a firm on a firm-wide basis in accordance with the required verification procedures of the GIPS standards. Verification provides assurance on whether the firm's policies and procedures related to composite and pooled fund maintenance, as well as the calculation, presentation, and distribution of performance, have been designed in compliance with the GIPS standards and have been implemented on a firm-wide basis.

Verification is performed with respect to an entire firm, not on specific composites or pooled funds. Verification does not ensure the accuracy of any specific performance report.

Verification must be performed by an independent third party. A firm cannot perform its own verification.

Third-party verification brings additional credibility to a firm's claim of compliance. A verified firm may provide existing and prospective clients and investors with greater assurance about its claim of compliance with the GIPS standards. Verification may also provide improved internal processes and procedures as well as marketing advantages to the firm.

PRACTICE PROBLEMS

1. A firm that does not adopt the GIPS standards could mischaracterize its overall performance by presenting a performance history:

   A. that includes terminated portfolios.

   B. composed of a single top-performing portfolio.

   C. for an investment mandate over all periods since the firm's inception.

2. Which of the following statements regarding GIPS compliance is correct?

   A. Asset owners that manage assets can claim compliance with the GIPS standards.

   B. Software that calculates performance in a manner consistent with the GIPS standards can claim compliance with the GIPS standards.

   C. Firms can comply with the GIPS standards by limiting their compliance claims to the provisions they have chosen to follow.

3. Each composite of a GIPS-compliant firm must consist of:

   A. multiple portfolios.

   B. portfolios selected on an *ex post* basis.

   C. portfolios managed according to a similar investment mandate, objective, or strategy.

4. Verification:

   A. must be performed on a firm-wide basis.

   B. may be provided by the firm's compliance department.

   C. ensures the accuracy of a specific composite presentation.

5. Which of the following *cannot* claim compliance with the GIPS standards?

   A. Investment management firms

   B. Software vendors

   C. Private pension funds

6. Which of the following is an abusive practice that the GIPS standards were designed to avoid?

   A. Presenting performance results that include terminated portfolios

   B. Comparing performance results with an appropriate benchmark

   C. Presenting performance results for select time periods

7. The process of testing a firm or asset owner that claims compliance with the

GIPS standards is referred to as a:

A. verification.

B. validation.

C. certification.

8. Firms that claim compliance with the GIPS standards are required to receive a verification:

   A. before the firm can initially claim compliance.

   B. after the firm has claimed compliance for 12 months.

   C. never; verification is not required.

9. Which of the following is not a commonly perceived benefit of the GIPS standards?

   A. Comparability of results across managers that claim compliance

   B. Adherence to regulatory requirements

   C. Increased confidence by investors and beneficiaries

10. When defining the firm, the GIPS standards recommend that firms should:

    A. adopt the narrowest, most relevant definition of the firm.

    B. adopt the broadest, most meaningful definition of the firm.

    C. exclude offices operating under different brand names.

11. A composite return reflects the performance of:

    A. all portfolios managed by the firm, regardless of investment strategy.

    B. all discretionary portfolios that meet the composite definition.

    C. all discretionary and non-discretionary portfolios that meet the composite definition.

SOLUTIONS

1. B is correct. Selecting a top-performing portfolio to represent a firm's overall investment results for a specific mandate, also known as using representative accounts, is a misleading practice that is not allowed under the GIPS standards. A is incorrect because including terminated portfolios is consistent with the GIPS standards. If the firm instead presented a performance history that excludes terminated portfolios, however, such a practice would be misleading and not allowed under the GIPS standards. C is incorrect because presenting performance for its mandate covering all periods since the firm's inception is consistent with the GIPS standards. If the firm instead presented performance for a selected period during which it produced excellent returns or outperformed its benchmark, however, such a practice would be misleading and not allowed under the GIPS standards.

2. A is correct. Asset owners can claim compliance if they manage actual assets for which they are making a claim of compliance. B is incorrect because software (and the vendors that supply software) cannot be GIPS compliant. Software can assist firms in achieving compliance with the GIPS standards, but only a firm that manages actual assets can claim compliance. C is incorrect because a firm has only two options regarding compliance with the GIPS standards: fully comply with all applicable requirements of the GIPS standards and claim compliance through the use of the GIPS Compliance Statement; or not comply with all requirements of the GIPS standards and not claim compliance with, or make any reference to, the GIPS standards.

3. C is correct. A composite is an aggregation of one or more portfolios managed according to a similar investment mandate, objective, or strategy. For example, if a GIPS-compliant firm presents performance for a global equity composite (the composite), the composite must include portfolios that are managed, or have historically been managed, according to the firm's global equity strategy. A is incorrect because a composite is an aggregation of one or more portfolios managed according to a similar investment mandate, objective, or strategy. A composite may consist of a single portfolio when it is the only portfolio managed according to a particular investment mandate. B is incorrect because the determination of which portfolio(s) to include in a composite should be done according to pre-established criteria (*ex ante* basis), not after the fact (*ex post* basis).

4. A is correct. Verification is performed with respect to an entire firm, not on specific composites. B is incorrect because verification must be performed by an independent third party. C is incorrect because verification provides assurance on whether the firm's policies and procedures related to composite and pooled fund maintenance, as well as the calculation, presentation, and distribution of performance, have been designed in compliance with the GIPS standards and have been implemented on a firm-wide basis; it does not ensure the accuracy of a specific composite presentation.

5. B is correct. Only investment management firms and asset owners (including pension funds, whether public or private) that manage actual assets may claim compliance with the GIPS standards. Software vendors and other intermediaries cannot claim compliance.

6. C is correct. The GIPS standards require performance to be presented for consistent, standardized time periods.

7. A is correct. Verification is the process of testing a firm or asset owner that claims compliance with the GIPS standards, in accordance with the required verification procedures of the GIPS standards.

8. C is correct. Firms are not required to be verified in order to claim compliance with the GIPS standards, although verification is recommended and viewed as best practice.

9. B is correct. Compliance with the GIPS standards is not typically required by regulators, nor are the GIPS standards intended to cover all regulatory requirements.

10. B is correct. Firms are encouraged to adopt the broadest, most meaningful definition possible of the firm.

11. B is correct. Composites must be defined based on investment mandate, objective, or strategy. Composites can include only discretionary portfolios.

LEARNING MODULE

5

Ethics Application

LEARNING OUTCOMES	
Mastery	***The candidate should be able to:***
☐	evaluate practices, policies, and conduct relative to the CFA Institute Code of Ethics and Standards of Professional Conduct
☐	explain how the practices, policies, and conduct do or do not violate the CFA Institute Code of Ethics and Standards of Professional Conduct

INTRODUCTION

1

This reading presents a number of short vignettes, or scenarios, inspired by real-world situations and events.[1] After reading the facts of each scenario, use your knowledge of the CFA Institute Code of Ethics and Standards of Professional Conduct to choose the best response to the multiple-choice question. After making your choice, be sure to review the correct response and case analysis, which discusses the rationale for why or why not a violation of the Code and Standards might have taken place and conduct that would comply with the Code and Standards.

PROFESSIONALISM

2

☐	evaluate practices, policies, and conduct relative to the CFA Institute Code of Ethics and Standards of Professional Conduct
☐	explain how the practices, policies, and conduct do or do not violate the CFA Institute Code of Ethics and Standards of Professional Conduct

1 Based on cases from CFA Institute, "Ethics in Practice: Ethics in Investment Management Casebook" (2019). www.cfainstitute.org/-/media/documents/ethics-in-practice/ethics-in-practice-casebook-2nd-edition-web.pdf.

Knowledge of the Law

> Members and Candidates must understand and comply with all applicable laws, rules, and regulations (including the CFA Institute Code of Ethics and Standards of Professional Conduct) of any government, regulatory organization, licensing agency, or professional association governing their professional activities. In the event of conflict, Members and Candidates must comply with the more strict law, rule, or regulation. Members and Candidates must not knowingly participate or assist in and must dissociate from any violation of such laws, rules, or regulations.

Mandracken

SBS Bank (SBS) serves as a custody bank for a wide range of clients. SBS offers a variety of services to its clients, including custody, clearing, payment, settlement, and record keeping. SBS charges its clients an asset-based fee for these services. Pursuant to the bank's client agreement, custody clients agree to reimburse the bank for out-of-pocket expenses for items paid by the custodian on their behalf. The majority of these expenses are for messages sent via the Society for Worldwide Interbank Financial Telecommunication (SWIFT), a secure messaging network used by banks and other financial institutions. Although SBS charges custody clients an established rate for SWIFT messages, the rate is greater than the actual cost of providing this service.

Mandracken, CFA, a vice president at SBS who oversees client service responsibilities, recognizes this discrepancy and brings it to the attention of his supervisor. In an email, Mandracken states that "although disclosure of charging for SWIFT fees is noted in the clients' fee schedules, the fees have always included an increase over actual cost, so the charge to clients is not a true pass-through because we add a margin." Mandracken's supervisor instructs him to reduce the SWIFT fee rate for new clients and to revisit the rate for existing clients when their contracts are renewed.

To meet his obligations under the CFA Institute Code and Standards, Mandracken should

A. implement the corrective procedures as directed by his supervisor.

B. implement the corrective procedures as directed by his supervisor but report his objections to the bank's board of directors.

C. refuse to participate in any client interactions using the fee schedule until the bank revises the SWIFT rate to reflect the actual cost of the service.

Analysis

C is correct. This case involves how to appropriately address the misconduct of others in carrying out your professional responsibilities. Standard I(A) Knowledge of the Law prohibits CFA Institute members and candidates from knowingly participating or assisting in legal or ethical violations and requires them to dissociate from any such activity. SBS is misrepresenting its reimbursable expenses to its custody clients and overcharging them. Although Mandracken brings the issue to the attention of his supervisor, his supervisor's corrective measures are inadequate because they (1) address the issue only for new clients, (2) do not immediately address the issue for existing clients, and (3) do not address the misrepresentation and overcharges to past clients. Mandracken must thus refuse to participate in any client interactions that use the fee schedule until the bank revises the SWIFT fees charged to custody clients to reflect actual out-of-pocket costs.

A is incorrect. Under the Code and Standards, Mandracken cannot continue to participate in or be associated with this misconduct. Inaction by a member and continuing association with those involved in illegal or unethical conduct might be viewed as participation or assistance in the illegal or unethical conduct.

B is incorrect. Mandracken might need to take drastic measures to dissociate from the activity and to protect client interests, such as leaving the bank or reporting the misconduct to the bank's board of directors or regulators. Several interim steps should be considered before this action, such as talking to his supervisor or the bank's compliance department about the inadequacy of the proposed corrective measures, but Mandracken cannot continue to interact with clients using a fraudulent fee schedule.

Pellie

Pellie, CFA, is CEO of Kwaume Investment Group (KIG), an investment adviser that is a wholly owned subsidiary of Kwaume Bank. A longtime bank customer that Pellie and some of the bank's board members know personally recently opened an investment account at KIG with a stated investment objective of earning income. The client made a few investments over the course of the next year, but most of the activity in the account involved several hundred bank transactions that totaled $90 million in deposits and $84 million in withdrawals.

The transactions included electronic transfers to and from individuals and entities located in bank secrecy havens and countries identified by the government as at risk for money-laundering activity. Pellie knew that the client was engaged in international business pursuits involving transactions with a higher risk potential for corruption and bribery. Given the client's longstanding relationship with the bank, Pellie assumes the transactions have a legitimate business purpose and accepts vague descriptions, such as "for services provided," "consulting fees," and "commissions." When he receives the daily anti-money-laundering (AML) reports, which are required by law when transactions trigger red flags of potentially suspicious activity, he approves them without further inquiry.

Pellie's actions are

A. a violation of the CFA Institute Code and Standards.

B. appropriate because Pellie is protecting the confidentiality of client information.

C. appropriate because Pellie can rely on the account's clearing firm to report suspicious activity for the account.

Analysis

A is correct. Pellie's actions violate Standard I(A) Knowledge of the Law, which states that CFA Institute members and candidates "must understand and comply with all applicable laws, rules, and regulations . . . governing their professional activities." The facts presented should have raised questions regarding the legitimacy of the client's account. The high volume of deposits and withdrawals combined with the low number of investment transactions is inconsistent with an investment account having a stated objective of earning income. The transactions in the account appeared to be high-risk transactions for money-laundering activity and should have received a greater level of scrutiny by Pellie. But rather than investigate as required by law, Pellie did not inquire further because of the client's longstanding relationship with the bank and its board members. Pellie's failure to comply with AML requirements imposed by law violates Standard I(A).

B is incorrect. The duty of loyalty to clients and the preservation of confidentiality of client information cannot be used as justification to allow clients to violate the law or otherwise damage the integrity or viability of global capital markets.

C is incorrect. Pellie cannot rely on the clearing firm to meet KIG's obligation to review the transactions for suspicious activity because that is his responsibility.

Mwangi

Mwangi, CFA, works for a firm that sells insurance products. Three of Mwangi's clients purchase one type of product (Class A) but later change their minds and ask to switch to another, lower-priced product (Class B). For Mwangi to complete the transaction, the law requires that she have her clients sign new sale and purchase documents for the Class B product. Given that not all the documents are ready for signing at the time of the clients' request, Mwangi advises her clients to wait to sign until the complete set of documents has been prepared. When the full set of documents is ready, Mwangi tries unsuccessfully to reach her clients for their signatures. Because of the missing signatures, Mwangi's manager threatens to cancel the exchange, which, because of other investment purchases, would place the clients' accounts into an overdraft position. Under the firm's policies, account shortfalls are covered by selling account assets once the shortfall has been outstanding for two weeks. To prevent this from happening, Mwangi signs the necessary documents on behalf of her clients.

Mwangi's actions are

A. a violation of the CFA Institute Code and Standards.

B. acceptable because her clients had already given their permission for the exchange to be made.

C. acceptable if the clients gave Mwangi explicit permission to sign the documents on their behalf.

Analysis

A is correct. This case involves Standard I(A) Knowledge of the Law, which requires CFA Institute members and candidates to "comply with all applicable laws, rules, and regulations . . . governing their professional activities." To complete the exchange from the Class A to the Class B product, Mwangi's clients were legally required to sign the new sale and purchase documents, which did not happen. By signing the documents on behalf of the clients, Mwangi forged their signatures. This violation of the law constitutes a violation of Standard I(A).

B is incorrect. General approval, written or verbal, of the transaction by the clients is insufficient to meet the legal requirement for client signatures.

C is incorrect. Even if the clients fully understand what is required to make the switch and explicitly give Mwangi permission to sign the forms on their behalf, the law requires that the genuine signatures of the clients be on the documents. Although the intent of the law is to protect the clients and the clients would be waiving their rights, Mwangi is still not permitted to circumvent the legal requirements.

Independence and Objectivity

> Members and Candidates must use reasonable care and judgment to achieve and maintain independence and objectivity in their professional activities. Members and Candidates must not offer, solicit, or accept any gift, benefit, compensation, or consideration that reasonably could be expected to compromise their own or another's independence and objectivity.

Myers

Myers, CFA, is a partner at Corboba, a $3 billion hedge fund that focuses on environmental, social, and governance investments. To support upcoming public office elections, Myers wants to personally donate $10,000 to one of the candidates, DeFrietas. As a passionate climate advocate and an avid proponent of responsible investment, Myers supports DeFrietas's backing of environmental policies to reduce air pollution and mitigate the effects of climate change. Myers believes his political contribution might also be beneficial for Corboba because DeFrietas is running for a position that can influence which hedge funds receive investments from the state's pension plans.

Myers's best course of action is to

A. refrain from donating to DeFrietas.

B. donate to DeFrietas because he is using personal funds in an amount that is insignificant relative to the size of the hedge fund.

C. donate to DeFrietas because he will be supporting a candidate whose environmental policies align with his beliefs.

Analysis

A is correct. If Myers makes the donation to DeFrietas's campaign, his actions would potentially violate Standard I(B) Independence and Objectivity, which states that CFA Institute members and candidates "must not offer . . . any gift, benefit, compensation, or consideration that reasonably could be expected to compromise . . . another's independence and objectivity." Although Myers has a legitimate reason for donating to DeFrietas, the facts clearly indicate that he believes the donation might also influence DeFrietas to choose Corboba to manage money for the state's pension plans. Standard I(B) prohibits CFA Institute members and candidates from attempting to gain lucrative allocations from government-sponsored pension funds by making donations to the political campaigns of individuals directly responsible for the manager hiring decisions.

B is incorrect. The source and the amount of the funds are irrelevant if the donation is meant to influence DeFrietas. In addition, the sum of $10,000 might be significant in the context of the campaign and thus important to DeFrietas. The critical issue is whether the donation is reasonably designed to improperly affect DeFrietas's independence and objectivity and benefit Myers or Corboba directly. Many factors would go into this determination, including the size of the donation, Myers's intent in making the donation, and how influential DeFrietas's position would be in making the hiring decision. The facts state that one of the reasons for Myers's donation is to have influence over receiving investment management business from the state.

C is incorrect. Myers seems to have both proper and improper motivations for making a political contribution to DeFrietas. Myers supports DeFrietas's positions on protecting the environment and wants to further those goals. Standard I(B) is not meant to prevent investment professionals from participating in the political process through financial or other support for candidates. But Myers recognizes that financial support of DeFrietas could benefit Corboba by gaining favor with someone who might be in a position to determine whether to invest in Corboba's fund. Therefore, Myers' actions could be perceived as inappropriate, so the best course of action would be to avoid any potential conflict by not donating to DeFrietas's campaign and finding other ways to support environmental protection policies.

Misrepresentation

> Members and Candidates must not knowingly make any misrepresentations relating to investment analysis, recommendations, actions, or other professional activities.

Lee

Lee, CFA, is a financial planner for AKC. AKC compensates its planners based on the number of AKC products they sell. Lee advises a married couple to transfer their retirement funds totaling $125,000 into a single AKC investment fund that follows a large-cap equity strategy. Lee discloses to the couple that they will have to pay a penalty totaling $30,000 for closing their retirement accounts but claims they will make up the loss with better investment returns from the AKC product.

Lee's actions are

A. acceptable if the AKC product is suitable for the couple.

B. a violation of the CFA Institute Code and Standards because she is promising a specific rate of return.

C. acceptable because she fully discloses the negative consequences of closing their retirement accounts.

Analysis

B is correct. This case involves Standard I(C) Misrepresentation, which states that CFA Institute members and candidates must not knowingly make any misrepresentation related to investment analysis, recommendations, or actions. This standard prohibits members and candidates from making any statements that promise or guarantee a specific rate of return on volatile investments. Because the equity-based investment is inherently volatile and the future return is unpredictable, Lee's promises about future returns making up for the penalty of withdrawing the funds violates Standard I(C). Trust is the foundation of the investment profession. Investment professionals who make false or misleading statements not only harm investors but also reduce the level of investor confidence in the investment profession and threaten the integrity of the capital markets.

A is incorrect. Even if the AKC product is suitable for the couple, it is an equity-based investment that is inherently volatile. Any statements that the investment will provide a certain rate of return or be worth a certain amount in the future is a misrepresentation. This case also raises questions about whether advising the couple to take such a significant loss in their retirement savings would be in their best interest and whether Lee's independence and objectivity are compromised because her recommendation is influenced by the compensation scheme of her employer.

C is incorrect. Although Lee fully discloses the negative consequences of transferring the couple's assets to the AKC product, that disclosure does not mitigate her inappropriate and misleading statement about future expected returns.

Andersen

Andersen, CFA, is the CEO of an asset management firm. Andersen and other senior investment managers at his firm make an in-person proposal to manage the investments of a large pension plan. In response to a request from the pension plan, Andersen provides a list of the key personnel who would manage the account. While waiting for the outcome of the evaluation, one of the key personnel that Andersen identified and who was part of the team that made the in-person presentation leaves the firm.

Andersen should

A. do nothing because the pension plan is hiring the firm, not an individual.

B. immediately inform the pension plan that one of the key personnel has left the firm.

C. hire a competent replacement for the person who left and then inform the pension plan of the change.

Analysis

B is correct. This case relates to Standard I(C) Misrepresentation, which prohibits members and candidates from knowingly misrepresenting anything relating to their professional activities. After the proposal is submitted to the pension plan for its investment management business, a staff member leaves Andersen's team. Andersen has identified the person leaving as a key member of the team that made the initial presentation. Given the pension plan asked for a list of individuals who would be handling the account, this information is clearly important in their decision to hire Andersen's firm. Withholding the information about the person leaving would be a misrepresentation by omission.

A is incorrect. Andersen obviously has confidence in the firm as a whole and will likely replace the person leaving with a competent professional with similar experience and talent so that the transition in service is seamless for clients. The pension plan is clearly concerned about the specific personnel involved in managing its assets because it asked for that information. If this were a junior employee, a staff member who had limited effect on the investment decision-making process, or someone who was not listed as a key employee or who had not been part of the team making the presentation, then Andersen might not need to provide an update to the pension plan. However, given the information in the case, to avoid a misrepresentation, Andersen must tell the pension plan about the departure of the key staff member.

C is incorrect. Waiting until a replacement is found is too late because knowing who the managers are on the team is clearly important to the pension plan's hiring decision.

Brodeur

Brodeur, CFA, is CEO of LeTour, a global company that makes electric cars. Brodeur and LeTour disclose to the public and regulators that the company will use Brodeur's personal social media account to disseminate information to LeTour investors and the investing public. After the media reports that the company is having difficulty producing cars and delivering them to buyers, Brodeur posts on his social media that the company is "considering taking LeTour private at $420 a share. Funding is secure."

Previously, Brodeur had met with a large sovereign wealth fund (SWF) that expressed general interest in investing in the company and taking the company private. But Brodeur and the SWF had not reached any agreement or determined a share purchase price. Brodeur was also in discussions with investment banks but had not yet retained any advisers to assist with taking the company private. After the post, LeTour's stock price increased more than 6% on significantly increased volume and closed at $380 per share, 10% higher than on the previous day. When asked about the specific stock price in the post, Brodeur admitted that he had not discussed pricing with any potential investor but chose the price as a joke. Brodeur's actions are

- **A.** inappropriate because the post was a misrepresentation of the facts.
- **B.** inappropriate because not all investors use social media, so Brodeur is selectively disclosing information and putting some investors at a disadvantage.
- **C.** appropriate because his post said only that he was "considering" taking the company private and thus contained only speculative, nonmaterial information.

Analysis

A is correct. This case relates to Standard I(C) Misrepresentation, which states that CFA Institute members and candidates must not knowingly make any misrepresentation relating to professional or investment activities. Brodeur's post was based on assumptions and contrary to the facts. Among other things, he (1) had not reached any agreement with the SWF, (2) had never discussed a share price of $420, (3) had set the price as a joke, and (4) had not formally retained any legal or financial advisers to assist with taking the company private. Unlike market participants reading his post, Brodeur knew that his supposed "secure" funding was based on a general conversation regarding a potential investment of an unspecified amount in the context of an undefined transaction structure. Because of the uncertainties that would need to be resolved before going private could be possible, Brodeur knew or should have known that his statements were false and misleading. The online or interactive aspects of social media do not remove the need to be open and honest about the information being distributed.

B is incorrect. Disseminating information to investors using social media might be appropriate and ethical under certain conditions. Distribution channels to make information public do not need to be guaranteed to reach all investors, but they must be designed to effectively make the information public. As long as the information shared reaches all clients or is available to the investing public, social media platforms would be comparable with other, traditional forms of communication, such as press releases or email communication. But because the information was misleading, Brodeur's use of social media was not appropriate.

C is incorrect. The post can be considered "material" information and not speculative because (1) the source of the post was the company's CEO, (2) the subject matter was dramatic and elemental, and (3) investors would want to know the information before making an investment decision.

Misconduct

> Members and Candidates must not engage in any professional conduct involving dishonesty, fraud, or deceit or commit any act that reflects adversely on their professional reputation, integrity, or competence.

Hanse

Hanse, CFA, is a portfolio manager employed by a global investment bank. She manages an environmental, social, and governance (ESG) investment fund. In her free time, Hanse participates in civil disobedience demonstrations organized by the Extinction Rebellion, a sociopolitical movement that uses nonviolent resistance to protest climate breakdown, biodiversity loss, and ecological collapse. At several demonstrations held in the financial district, Hanse is arrested on charges of unlawful assembly, obstructing public transit, and disorderly conduct. She is ultimately convicted of several minor criminal offenses. Hanse has signed a standard employment contract with the bank that allows it to terminate any employee who is convicted of a criminal offense.

Under the CFA Institute Code and Standards, Hanse's actions

A. do not violate the Code and Standards.

B. violate the Code and Standards because she has violated her employment contract with the bank.

C. violate the Code and Standards because she is arrested for misconduct in the financial district.

Analysis

A is correct. This case relates to what constitutes professional misconduct. Standard I(D) Misconduct prohibits CFA Institute members and candidates from engaging "in any professional conduct involving dishonesty, fraud, or deceit" or from committing "any act that reflects adversely on their professional reputation, integrity, or competence."

Generally, Standard I(D) is not meant to cover legal transgressions resulting from acts of civil disobedience in support of personal beliefs, because such conduct does not reflect adversely on the member's professional reputation, integrity, or competence.

B is incorrect. Hanse's arrest is not likely an automatic violation of bank policies. Although Hanse's employment contract gives the bank the option to fire her for criminal activity, the bank can apparently use discretion in retaining employees depending on the nature and circumstances of the conviction. Further, the Code and Standards are not automatically violated with every violation of an employer's employment contract unless the violations relate to conduct addressed in the Code and Standards.

C is incorrect. The fact that Hanse is arrested in the financial district is not a sufficient link to her professional activities to make her actions a violation of the Code and Standards. The acts of civil disobedience by Hanse reflect her personal beliefs, which would generally not be considered an act involving fraud, dishonesty, or deceit or an act that reflects poorly on her professional reputation, integrity, or competence.

Mang

Mang, CFA, is an investment adviser for a regional bank that has a number of discretionary, fee-based accounts for high-net-worth individuals. The bank's policies permit trade error corrections up to 30 days following a failure to place a trade when an adviser forgets to send an order to the trading desk. To rectify the error, the adviser is permitted to buy or sell a security at the current market price, with the price differential charged to the adviser personally through an internal error account.

On many occasions, Mang uses the trade error correction policy to benefit clients who are unhappy with their account's performance. Mang identifies a security whose price has increased in the past 30 days. He then tells the trade desk he mistakenly failed to buy that particular security some days before, when the price was substantially lower than the current market price. Once the request is approved, the trade desk purchases the security and charges the price differential to Mang personally through the error account. Shortly after that trade, Mang sends an order to sell the security and net a profit for the client. Mang then tells the client that he has given them a "gift" or "no-risk" trade.

Mang's actions

A. violate the CFA Institute Code and Standards.

B. are appropriate because Mang is acting for the benefit of the client.

C. are appropriate because the bank is not harmed by Mang's actions.

Analysis

A is correct. Mang is violating Standard I(D) Misconduct, which prohibits CFA Institute members and candidates from engaging in professional conduct involving dishonesty, fraud, or deceit. He is engaging in a misleading, fraudulent, and deceptive practice and misusing the bank's policies to enhance the performance of his clients' accounts when no legitimate error was made. He personally compensates clients as a means to mislead them about his ability as an investment adviser as well as the actual performance of their accounts.

B is incorrect. Although the trades benefit his clients, Mang is engaging in professional misconduct by misleading his clients with fraudulent and deceptive conduct.

C is incorrect. The fact that these practices did not cause financial losses for the bank does not make Mang's conduct any less deceptive, fraudulent, or misleading.

Competence

> Members and Candidates must act with and maintain the competence necessary to fulfill their professional responsibilities.

Mahajan

Mahajan, CFA, is a successful research analyst for a large, global investment firm, working as part of a research team covering the renewable energy sector. To further his career, Mahajan applies for a new position and is hired by a boutique investment research firm focusing on ESG factors and ratings. As part of the new position, Mahajan will be supervising a team of several junior analysts. Although he worked with other analysts at his prior positions, he has not previously had supervisory responsibility. His team's remit includes the renewable energy sector, as well as transportation and construction. To prepare for his new job, Mahajan enrolls in the CFA Institute Certificate in ESG Investing program, attends several webinars focusing on environmentally friendly practices in the construction industry, engages in extensive outside reading on developments in electric transportation, and joins a trade organization for ESG-focused analysts.

With regard to meeting his responsibilities to comply with the Code and Standards, Mahajan's actions

A. are sufficient to comply with all his responsibilities under the Code and Standards.

B. fail to meet the requirements of the Code and Standards because he is not enrolled in a formal continuing education program.

C. fail to meet the requirements of the Code and Standards because he has not undertaken activities to obtain the skills and knowledge needed for fulfilling his new role as supervisor.

Analysis

C is correct. This case relates to Standard I(E) Competence, which requires members and candidates to act with and maintain the competence necessary to fulfill their professional responsibilities. Mahajan's professional responsibilities changed when he took the new position that requires competence in other skills, abilities, and knowledge beyond those needed for his previous position. He will have supervisory responsibility for the first time, and the industry sectors that he will be covering have expanded. Standard I(E) requires Mahajan to extend his competence to cover all responsibilities of his new role. Through education and self-study, Mahajan endeavors to develop competence for his widening responsibility for research and analysis. However, he does not take steps to obtain the skills and knowledge needed for fulfilling his supervisory responsibility over the other analysts. To do this, he could have taken such steps as attending conferences or taking professional development courses on management, earning compliance credentials, and undergoing internal training from his firm on supervisory responsibility.

A is incorrect. While he focuses on improving his competence on the new industries he will be covering as part of his new position, Mahajan does not take steps to obtain the skills and knowledge needed for fulfilling his new supervisory responsibility of the other analysts, as required by Standard I(E).

B is incorrect. Standard I(B) does not require members and candidates to participate in formal continuing education or a professional development program to comply with Standard I(E), although doing so would be one method of developing and maintaining competence.

INTEGRITY OF CAPITAL MARKETS

3

- ☐ evaluate practices, policies, and conduct relative to the CFA Institute Code of Ethics and Standards of Professional Conduct
- ☐ explain how the practices, policies, and conduct do or do not violate the CFA Institute Code of Ethics and Standards of Professional Conduct

Material Nonpublic Information

> Members and Candidates who possess material nonpublic information that could affect the value of an investment must not act or cause others to act on the information.

Khatri

Khatri, a candidate in the CFA Program, plays on a local cricket team with his friends, including Patel, his brother-in-law and an attorney, and Ahuja, owner of a software development company called ZeroPower (ZP). Patel handles the legal work for ZP. Khatri, Patel, and many other friends in their circle have invested in ZP. Recently, a large global information technology company (GIT) made an offer to buy ZP at a substantial premium over the company's current share price. Patel is working with lawyers from GIT to assist in their due diligence.

One weekend, during a particularly intense period of negotiations, Khatri, Patel, and Ahuja are playing in a cricket tournament. Between matches, Khatri overhears Patel speaking with representatives of GIT on his cell phone. Although mention of a ZP acquisition is not made, Khatri hears Patel repeatedly reference the name "GIT." Khatri guesses that the acquisition of ZP is happening soon after seeing Patel and Ahuja huddled in private conversation several times over the course of the weekend. On Monday, Khatri calls his broker and increases his investment in ZP by 5,000 shares. One week later, ZP announces its acquisition by GIT and its share price increases 30%.

Khatri's actions are

A. a violation of the CFA Institute Code and Standards.

B. acceptable because Khatri's investment was based on his own speculation.

C. acceptable because Khatri received the information in a public environment.

Analysis

A is correct. Khatri comes into possession of material nonpublic information by overhearing confidential information from Patel's phone calls and witnessing Patel's interactions with Ahuja that were prompted by those calls. Standard II(A) Material Nonpublic Information prohibits CFA Institute members and candidates from taking investment action based on material nonpublic information in their possession. Patel should have been more careful to keep his phone conversations private, but his failure to do so does not allow Khatri to use material nonpublic information received from overhearing those conversations.

B is incorrect. Although information about the acquisition of ZP was not explicitly stated and Khatri was required to make some degree of deduction, he knew or should have known that this information was confidential, nonpublic, and material. His actions are different from mosaic theory, in which investment analysts combine nonmaterial and nonpublic information with public information in their analysis to derive insights.

C is incorrect. Although Patel's phone calls and interactions with Ahuja take place in a public environment, that does not mean the information is public.

Kwame

Kwame, CFA, is the chief financial officer of PH3D, a biotech firm that researches, develops, and commercializes pharmaceutical drugs for women's health. PH3D submits a drug application to the government regulator for a promising new drug. The regulator postpones two scheduled meetings with PH3D when unspecified deficiencies with the drug arise. The public announcement of the postponements results in a 10% drop in the company's stock price.

When the meeting between the regulator and PH3D finally takes place, PH3D presents unpublished preliminary test data with favorable indicators for the drug. The regulator reacts positively and gives PH3D provisional regulatory approval, contingent on further studies. Afterward, some of the sell-side research analysts covering PH3D ask Kwame about the meeting. Kwame responds by email, indicating that he believes the meeting with the regulator was "very positive and productive" and that the company was "pleasantly surprised" by the regulator's reaction. Kwame does not share the favorable preliminary test data. After Kwame's emails to the analysts, the company's stock price increases 19%.

Kwame's actions

A. violate the CFA Institute Code and Standards.

B. are appropriate because he does not share the unpublished preliminary test data with the analysts and restricts his comments to the general tenor of the meeting.

C. are appropriate because he responds to questions from research analysts covering the company.

Analysis

A is correct. This case relates to selective disclosure of material nonpublic information. Standard II(A) Material Nonpublic Information prohibits CFA Institute members and candidates from causing others to act on material nonpublic information. Information is material if its disclosure would affect the price of a security or if reasonable investors would want to know the information before making an investment decision. Information is "nonpublic" until it has been disseminated or made available to the marketplace in general, and Kwame's response to select sell-side analysts inquiring about PH3D's meeting with the regulator would not be considered public dissemination of the information. In this case, both the drug's positive preliminary test results and the regulator's positive reaction to the new drug is information that would have an impact on the price of the security in addition to information that reasonable investors would want to know.

B is incorrect. Although Kwame does not share the test results with the analysts, he shares that the meeting with the regulator was "very positive and productive." This is information that reasonable investors would want to know.

C is incorrect. Kwame shares this information with a select group of analysts who regularly cover PH3D and not the general investing public. The fact that Kwame is only responding to questions is irrelevant. Kwame and PH3D should have issued a public announcement about the meeting with the regulator before or at the same time that information was disclosed to analysts.

Market Manipulation

Members and Candidates must not engage in practices that distort prices or artificially inflate trading volume with the intent to mislead market participants.

Abbha

Abbha, CFA, is a securities contractor working to assist Superior Energy (SE) with listing its shares on the Regional Security Exchange (RSX). SE files a prospectus for an offer of up to 5 million shares at $2 each to raise $10 million. The RSX current applicable listing rule requires that entities seeking admission to the RSX meet a "minimum spread requirement" of at least 300 shareholders with a minimum value holding to qualify for listing. In their listing application, representatives of SE inform RSX that the minimum spread requirement of 300 shareholders has been met. These disclosures include as shareholders 31 people or companies arranged by Abbha, though none are actual buyers of SE securities. Abbha provides false names and addresses for the 31 shareholders. The SE share offer raises more than $3.5 million, with more than 1.75 million shares issued. SE is admitted to the official list of the RSX, with its shares quoted on the exchange. Over time, the price of SE shares steadily increases, the company attracts hundreds of investors and shareholders, and early investors achieve an excellent investment return.

Abbha's actions

A. violate the CFA Institute Code and Standards.

B. are acceptable because SE proved to be a strong company with excellent performance.

C. are acceptable because no investors were harmed by the technical violation of RSX rules.

Analysis

A is correct. Abbha engaged in information-based manipulation by inflating the number of initial shareholders in SE securities to create the impression that its shares would have sufficient liquidity and to give new investors comfort in buying them. Standard II(B) Market Manipulation prohibits CFA Institute members and candidates from engaging in practices that artificially inflate trading volume to mislead market participants. To circumvent regulatory requirements and drive investor interest, Abbha's misrepresentations overstated initial interest in SE securities, thereby creating false pretenses under which the company was listed.

B is incorrect. The fact that SE ultimately proved to be a bona fide and well-performing investment does not mitigate Abbha's unethical, misleading, and deceitful conduct.

C is incorrect. The purpose of the minimum spread requirement for RSX security listings is to demonstrate that investor interest in a company is sufficient to justify the company's listing. Th minimum spread requirement ensures some level of liquidity at the time a company is listed and prevents lower-quality applicants that are unable to attract sufficient investor interest from being listed. Falsifying the number of initial investors goes beyond a technical violation of RSX rules and has substantial consequences.

4 DUTIES TO CLIENTS

- ☐ evaluate practices, policies, and conduct relative to the CFA Institute Code of Ethics and Standards of Professional Conduct
- ☐ explain how the practices, policies, and conduct do or do not violate the CFA Institute Code of Ethics and Standards of Professional Conduct

Loyalty, Prudence, and Care

Members and Candidates have a duty of loyalty to their clients and must act with reasonable care and exercise prudent judgment. Members and Candidates must act for the benefit of their clients and place their clients' interests before their employer's or their own interests.

Maste

Maste, CFA, is the sole director of Dov Services (Dov), a firm that sells financial products and advice. Maste directs Dov's authorized representatives to incorporate the Dov Client Protection Policy into their contracts with clients. The protection policy, which sets forth the terms for providing financial advice, states that it "contains a number of client protections designed to ensure that you (the client) receive the best possible advice and the maximum protection available under the law." The protection policy's terms (1) excuse Dov and its authorized representatives from various liabilities arising from their failure to act in a client's best interest, (2) relieve Dov and its authorized representatives of their duty to conduct suitability analyses of clients and investments, and (3) lead clients to believe that they cannot make claims against Dov or its representatives for violating securities law.

Maste's actions

A. violate the CFA Institute Code and Standards.

B. are appropriate because Dov and Maste fully disclose the terms of the Dov Client Protection Policy to clients.

C. are appropriate because Dov and Maste are free to negotiate the terms of advisory agreements with clients.

Analysis

A is correct. The terms of the Dov Client Protection Policy improperly attempt to use disclosure to relieve Dov and Maste of their fundamental ethical (and very likely legal) obligations to clients by limiting liability for failures to act in the client's best interests or to provide appropriate advice. Standard III(A) Loyalty, Prudence, and Care sets forth a duty of loyalty on the part of CFA Institute members and candidates to their clients and requires them to act for the benefit of their clients and to place their clients' interests before their own. In addition, Standard V(A) Diligence and Reasonable Basis requires members and candidates to provide diligent, independent, and thorough advice and to have a reasonable and adequate basis for investment action; Standard III(B) Fair Dealing requires members and candidates to conduct a suitability analysis for any investment recommendation to their clients; and Standard I(C) Misrepresentation says that members and candidates cannot make any misrepresentations relating to investment services. These components of the CFA Institute Code and Standards define the fundamental principles applicable to investment professionals and detail the conduct investors should expect from their financial advisers.

B is incorrect. Disclosure cannot be used to relieve advisers of their fundamental ethical obligations to clients. The Dov Client Protection Policy is also deceptive because it misrepresents the client's right to bring legal action for ethical and regulatory violations and appears to give the false impression that a client would benefit from its terms.

C is incorrect. Although in general, clients and advisers are free to negotiate the terms of advisory agreements, for advisers to use the client agreement to create a significant imbalance between the rights and obligations of the adviser and the client or to limit the fundamental ethical obligations of loyalty, prudence, and care to the client is improper.

Gaini

Gaini, CFA, is a commodities trader with a number of retail clients, including Laube, who opens a self-directed foreign exchange retail account for which Gaini does not advise on any trades. Laube signs Gaini's standard customer agreement, which contains provisions relating to margin requirements and liquidation in the event of margin deficits. The agreement authorizes Gaini, at his discretion, "to liquidate, without notice, any or all open positions in an account with insufficient margin."

Laube initially purchases two 100,000 US dollar/Swiss franc (USD/CHF) contracts and sets her margin requirement to $4,000. Laube then places two additional 100,000 USD/CHF "pending limit" orders that will execute if the contract trading prices reach a specified level. Each order has a different limit price, so one will execute before the other. Shortly after placing the orders, Laube goes on an extended vacation. While she is away, execution on the first limit order occurs, and the margin requirement increases to $6,000. Then, the next limit price is reached, and the second order executes, increasing the margin requirement to $8,000. After the trades, while Laube is still on vacation, her account balance drops to $6,900. Without notice, Gaini liquidates all positions in Laube's account, realizing a loss of $37,000 from the liquidation.

Gaini's actions

A. are appropriate because Gaini followed the policy and procedures set forth in Laube's client agreement.

B. violate the CFA Institute Code and Standards because Gaini has a duty to act in the best interest of Laube by protecting her financial position.

C. are inappropriate because Gaini could have met the margin requirement by liquidating only one foreign exchange contract position.

Analysis

A is correct. This case relates to Standard III(A) Loyalty, Prudence, and Care, which imposes on CFA Institute members and candidates a duty to act with loyalty, prudence, and care in their clients' best interests and in relation to other clients and the markets. However, the conduct that fulfills this responsibility depends on the nature of the relationship with the client. Laube self-directs her trades, which are executed by Gaini, who does not provide investment advice. Additionally, Laube freely contracts with Gaini regarding the consequences of insufficient margins in her account, and these policies and procedures are clearly set forth in her client agreement. Nothing indicates that Gaini misled Laube about the margin requirements or the liquidation procedures. Although the contractual provision authorizing liquidation without notice does not waive Laube's right to be dealt with in good faith, the margin and liquidation provisions are not an attempt by Gaini to waive his duty of loyalty, prudence, and care. They simply set forth the parameters of the relationship, which Gaini and Laube are free to negotiate. Although Laube suffered significant trading losses, Gaini liquidated Laube's open positions in accordance with the terms of the customer agreement, serving to protect the integrity of the market.

B is incorrect. Given the facts of this case, Gaini's responsibility to protect his own financial position and that of his other customers supersedes any duties he owes to Laube when she defaults on the margin requirements. Because of the limited nature of the relationship between Laube and Gaini, Gaini is not obligated to actively monitor Laube's account to protect her financial interests. Doing so would require Gaini to continuously monitor a potentially deteriorating market or to take on additional risk management measures that he has not agreed to and that Laube has not contracted for.

C is incorrect. Gaini is not obligated to use a less drastic alternative by closing only one foreign exchange contract position and does not breach a duty to Laube by liquidating all open positions when the parties have contractually agreed that total liquidation to meet a margin deficit may be done at Gaini's discretion without notice.

Braung

A regional government hires Braung, CFA, and his firm to serve as its financial adviser for issuing general obligation bonds. The municipality conducts several bond offerings over the years for constructing municipal facilities, including a maximum-security detention facility and two school buildings. In connection with the bond issues, Braung makes a number of trips to New York City to meet with ratings agencies. The trips are typically planned for a Monday or Friday because the costs for weekend travel are less. Braung's wife accompanies him on the trips, and they typically spend the weekend either before or after the meetings in New York City to enjoy sporting events, theater performances, and museums. Braung often makes a number of train and hotel changes after a trip is booked to accommodate meetings with other clients. Braung submits his travel expenses to his supervisor, who deducts costs she believes are unrelated to the business purpose of the trip and submits the bills to the municipality for reimbursement.

Which of the following expenses can most likely be billed to the government entity issuing the bonds?

A. Braung's accommodation and meal expenses for the weekend days because the travel rates are less expensive over a weekend

B. Tickets to the sporting and theater events, as long as they do not exceed a reasonable amount for business entertainment

C. Flight and hotel change fees that result from the regular course of Braung's business activities

Analysis

A is correct. This case relates to Standard III(A) Loyalty, Prudence, and Care, which states that CFA Institute members and candidates have a duty of loyalty to their clients, must act for their clients' benefit, and must place client interests before their own. Under this standard, investment professionals, including municipal security dealers, must not engage in any deceptive, dishonest, or unfair practice when handling client accounts. The savings in travel fees for booking a weekend travel schedule could be greater than the additional accommodation and meal expenses for Braung to stay the extra days in New York City, making the cost to the client lower. Under these circumstances, Braung would be meeting his duty of loyalty to the client by choosing the most inexpensive travel schedule overall, thus limiting costs to the client. Charging personal theater and sporting event tickets or travel change fees associated with seeing unrelated clients would not qualify as chargeable expenses to the client. The best scenario would be to detail in writing at the outset of the engagement which expenses would be considered reimbursable.

B is incorrect. In the context of conflicts of interest, the CFA Institute Code and Standards allow members and candidates to accept or provide modest gifts and entertainment in the ordinary course of business (a gift basket at the holidays from a vendor or to a client, for example). But that "ordinary course of business" does not allow investment professionals to charge clients for obviously extraneous entertainment expenses not connected to a business meeting. Charging excessive or lavish expenses for the personal benefit of the investment professional at the expense of the client can constitute a deceptive, dishonest, or unfair practice that violates Standard III(A).

C is incorrect. Although busy investment professionals might be forced by other priorities to change travel arrangements when a client trip has already been scheduled, additional expenses resulting from the change most likely must be borne by the investment professional (Braung) as an overhead cost, not charged to the client. (Under some limited circumstances, those expenses might be charged to the client who necessitates the travel changes.)

Fair Dealing

> Members and Candidates must deal fairly and objectively with all clients when providing investment analysis, making investment recommendations, taking investment action, or engaging in other professional activities.

Scherzer

Scherzer, CFA, is the head of research at a large investment management firm. She publishes monthly "Recommendation Update Reports" to communicate to clients any investment recommendation changes her firm has made. The reports are sent to clients via email on the first Friday of the month and posted on the firm's website the following Monday. The firm's internal policy is that a change in recommendation can only be made once a month through this report. Scherzer also publishes weekly reports with information gathered by analysts that might implicitly signal a future change in recommendation or lead a reader to infer that a recommendation will be changing. Although the monthly "Recommendation Update Reports" are sent to all clients, clients who wish to receive the weekly publication must pay an annual fee of $1,000. This option is available to any client and is fully disclosed as part of every client agreement.

To comply with the CFA Institute Code and Standards, Scherzer is required to

A. do nothing because her actions comply with the Code and Standards.

B. publish the monthly report on the firm's website at the same time it is sent to clients.

C. send the weekly reports to all clients at no additional charge.

Analysis

A is correct. Standard III(B) Fair Dealing requires CFA Institute members and candidates to deal fairly and objectively with all clients when providing investment analysis and making investment recommendations. It also requires that information about investment recommendations be disseminated in such a manner that all clients have a fair opportunity to act on the information. Scherzer distributes the recommendation update reports to all clients simultaneously via email, giving each an opportunity to act on the information. Scherzer is also not limited by the Code and Standards in communicating with clients about investments only when an investment recommendation is provided and can provide updated or clarifying information to clients as appropriate. In addition, Scherzer does not violate the Code and Standards by providing weekly reports to clients who pay a subscription fee for the service as long as (1) all clients are eligible to purchase the service, (2) the different levels of service are disclosed to clients, and (3) no change in recommendations is made that would disadvantage existing clients who receive only the monthly report.

B is incorrect. The Code and Standards do not require Scherzer to publish the reports to the public on the firm's website.

C is incorrect. The Code and Standards allow CFA Institute members and candidates to provide more personal, specialized, or in-depth service to clients who are willing to pay for premium services through additional fees as long as (1) those services do not disadvantage other clients who do not pay additional fees, (2) the differing levels of service are disclosed to clients, and (3) the services are made available to all.

Suitability

1. When Members and Candidates are in an advisory relationship with a client, they must:

   a. Make a reasonable inquiry into a client's or prospective client's investment experience, risk and return objectives, and financial constraints prior to making any investment recommendation or taking investment action and must reassess and update this information regularly.

   b. Determine that an investment is suitable to the client's financial situation and consistent with the client's written objectives, mandates, and constraints before making an investment recommendation or taking investment action.

   c. Judge the suitability of investments in the context of the client's total portfolio.

2. When Members and Candidates are responsible for managing a portfolio to a specific mandate, strategy, or style, they must make only investment recommendations or take only investment actions that are consistent with the stated objectives and constraints of the portfolio.

Marte

Marte, CFA, is an asset manager in Puerto Rico, a US territory. Residents of Puerto Rico receive significant tax advantages when they invest in local securities. To capitalize on this advantage, Marte's firm offers its clients shares in a closed-end investment fund, organized under Puerto Rico's financial laws and regulations, that holds at least 67% local securities and is permitted to borrow against up to 50% of its assets. The fund is usually leveraged to the extent legally permitted. Many of Marte's clients have a modest net worth and conservative or moderate investment objectives. Marte convinces them to invest 85% or more of their assets in shares of the closed-end fund.

Marte's actions

A. violate the CFA Institute Code and Standards.

B. are appropriate because they take advantage of the fund's unique tax benefits for his clients.

C. are appropriate as long as Marte fully discloses the risks and benefits of the fund to his clients.

Analysis

A is correct. Standard III(C) Suitability states that CFA Institute members and candidates in an advisory relationship with clients must "determine that an investment is suitable to the client's financial situation and consistent with the client's written objectives, mandates, and constraints before making an investment recommendation or taking investment action." Given the financial circumstances and conservative investment objectives of his clients, the high concentration of the fund's shares in his clients' accounts, combined with the leverage, makes the large investment in the fund unsuitable because greater portfolio diversification is needed. Despite the tax advantages, highly concentrated investments carry an increased risk that a single market event affecting the value of the fund's shares would significantly decrease the total account value. This risk is exacerbated by the fact that the closed-end fund is internally leveraged, which could magnify the fund's loss during a market event that causes share values to drop steeply.

B is incorrect. Given the favorable tax advantages of the investment vehicle, investment in shares of the closed-end fund might be suitable and appropriate for his clients at some level. But given the financial circumstances and investment objectives of his clients, the high concentration, combined with the leverage, makes the large investment in the fund unsuitable.

C is incorrect. Although Marte should always fully disclose the risks and benefits of his recommendations to his clients, doing so does not take away the need for the investment to be suitable for the clients' financial circumstances, risk tolerance, and investment goals.

Duri

Duri, CFA, is a registered account representative providing financial advice to retail clients. She is also a principal partner of Tabak Accountants. Duri assists a number of advisory clients who want to move their retirement assets from existing superannuation (pension) accounts to self-managed superannuation funds (SMSFs) that have the goal of investing in direct residential property. When clients express interest in these types of SMSFs, Duri accepts their reasons for wanting to invest in direct property and assumes that they have the time and expertise to manage their superannuation affairs. She reclassifies their investment objectives as "growth" to match the new investment strategy. Duri charges her clients for establishing the SMSFs and recommends that her firm, Tabak Accountants, prepare the clients' annual accounts and tax returns.

Duri's actions

A. violate the CFA Institute Code and Standards.

B. are acceptable because she is following the directives of her clients.

C. are acceptable if the services provided by Tabak Accountants are reasonable and the costs of services are competitive.

Analysis

A is correct. Standard III(C) Suitability requires CFA Institute members and candidates in an advisory relationship to make a reasonable inquiry into a client's investment experience, risk and return objectives, and financial constraints to determine whether an investment is suitable for the client's financial situation and consistent with the client's objectives and mandates before taking investment action. When Duri's clients want to move their retirement assets into an SMSF that invests in direct residential property, Duri appears to accept their reasoning without conducting a suitability analysis. The case does not indicate whether Duri did any of the following:

- Assess the reasons a client wants to invest in direct property
- Consider the client's financial goals

- Compare the benefits, risks, and costs associated with establishing an SMSF or owning rental property to existing superannuation account investment alternatives
- Consider asset diversification
- Determine whether the client intends to draw a pension from the SMSF once the individual reaches retirement or how the client will do that with an illiquid asset, such as investment property
- Evaluate whether the client has the time and expertise to manage his or her superannuation affairs, including managing a rental property
- Consider whether the SMSF investment strategy will remain viable if the client's income is reduced or the property is unoccupied for a period of time

Without analyzing these and other factors, for Duri to move her clients to the SMSFs would be inappropriate.

B is incorrect. If her clients request a change in their investment strategy, Duri has a responsibility as their investment adviser to conduct an analysis to ensure that the new direction is suitable and appropriate. Duri appears to have classified all clients as growth investors to superficially justify their investment in an SMSF vehicle without analyzing whether this classification was an accurate assessment.

C is incorrect. Duri appears to be recommending that her firm provide clients with accounting services for the SMSF investments to create additional income for herself. But Standard III(A) Loyalty, Prudence, and Care requires members and candidates to act for the benefit of their clients and to place their clients' interests before their own. At a minimum, Duri's relationship with Tabak must be fully disclosed to clients as a potential conflict of interest.

Performance Presentation

> When communicating investment performance information, Members and Candidates must make reasonable efforts to ensure that it is fair, accurate, and complete.

Jergenn

Jergenn, CFA, is the portfolio manager for the Volare Investment Management (VIM) fund, a registered collective investment scheme (CIS) organized under the laws of South Africa. VIM's 2022 regulatory disclosure and marketing material for the fund, produced by Jergenn, presents annual investment performance data for the 2014–20 period that is accurate and calculated correctly. The performance history is that of a composite of separate accounts that followed the strategy used by the VIM fund before the assets were moved over to the CIS environment in 2021.

In presenting the fund's performance history, Jergenn's actions

A. violate the CFA Institute Code and Standards.

B. are appropriate because the investment performance is accurate.

C. are appropriate as long as the performance calculations are net of fees.

Analysis

A is correct. Standard III(D) Performance Presentation states that CFA Institute members and candidates must make a reasonable effort to ensure that investment performance information is fair, accurate, and complete. Although the performance information presented by Jergenn is calculated correctly and includes technically accurate data, Jergenn's failure to indicate clearly that the performance data applied to a period before the VIM fund was registered as a CIS has the potential to mislead investors into believing that the CIS fund had a long track record. To meet the "fair, accurate, and complete" requirement of the standard, Jergenn should disclose that the 2014–20 performance history was for a prior but similar entity with the same investment strategy and objectives and that the VIM fund, as a CIS, has been in existence only since 2021.

B is incorrect. Although the performance is accurate and correctly calculated, the lack of disclosure about the nature of the accounts makes the presentation misleading.

C is incorrect. Performance can be presented either net or gross of fees as long as investors are sufficiently informed about how the performance is calculated and what effect fees might have on the returns.

Preservation of Confidentiality

Members and Candidates must keep information about current, former, and prospective clients confidential unless:

1. The information concerns illegal activities on the part of the client or prospective client,
2. Disclosure is required by law, or
3. The client or prospective client permits disclosure of the information.

Giddings and Marsh

Giddings, CFA, is responsible for compliance at GWH, a large broker/dealer and investment adviser. In connection with GWH's wealth management business, the company maintains personally identifiable information (names, addresses, phone numbers, account numbers, balances, and holdings) of its clients. Giddings adopts a number of policies and restrictions, including a Code of Conduct, that address employees' access to and handling of this confidential information. Marsh, CFA, who works for GWH as a client services associate, decides to download client data to his personal server located at his residence to facilitate his telecommuting. Marsh's server is hacked, and portions of the personal client information Marsh downloaded are posted for sale on the internet.

Did either Marsh or Giddings violate the CFA Institute Code and Standards?

A. Marsh violated the Code and Standards.
B. Giddings violated the Code and Standards.
C. Both Marsh and Giddings violated the Code and Standards.

Analysis

C is correct. Standard III(E) Preservation of Confidentiality requires that CFA Institute members and candidates keep information about current, former, and prospective clients confidential unless the information concerns illegal activities, disclosure is required by law, or the client permits disclosure. Although the standard does not require investment professionals to be information security experts, they must make reasonable efforts to prevent the accidental distribution of confidential information by following compliance procedures. Assuming Marsh did not have permission to download client data to his personal server, his misappropriation of client information for his own purposes is a violation of Standard III(E). And although he was not responsible for the distribution of the information, his misconduct facilitated the publication of the information. Marsh needed to understand and follow the firm's electronic information communication and storage procedures.

As the compliance officer, Giddings is responsible for implementing sufficient compliance policies and procedures reasonably designed to protect client information. He is responsible for ensuring the confidentiality of customer information, protecting against any potential threats to the security or integrity of the records, and preventing unauthorized access or use of client information that could harm GWH clients. Although GWH has policies restricting access to and handling of client information, the extent of those safeguards was apparently insufficient because Marsh was able to download company files to his personal computer. The fact that client information was accessed and published makes the effectiveness of Giddings's compliance efforts questionable. Even if the policies were sufficient, nothing indicates that Giddings audited and/or tested the effectiveness of the safeguards meant to keep client information confidential.

A is incorrect. Both Marsh and Giddings violated the Code and Standards.

B is incorrect. Both Marsh and Giddings violated the Code and Standards.

5 DUTIES TO EMPLOYERS

- ☐ evaluate practices, policies, and conduct relative to the CFA Institute Code of Ethics and Standards of Professional Conduct
- ☐ explain how the practices, policies, and conduct do or do not violate the CFA Institute Code of Ethics and Standards of Professional Conduct

Loyalty

> In matters related to their employment, Members and Candidates must act for the benefit of their employer and not deprive their employer of the advantage of their skills and abilities, divulge confidential information, or otherwise cause harm to their employer.

Nickoli

Nickoli, CFA, is an investment counselor with HHI Capital Management (HHI). A colleague at her local society encourages Nickoli to leave HHI and join her at Vesuvius Asset Advisers. Nickoli eventually agrees and decides to leave at the beginning of the new year. In the weeks before submitting her resignation, she tells her clients that they will likely be working with a new investment counselor because she is leaving HHI. Her clients express surprise, and when asked for details about why she is leaving, Nickoli shares that she is frustrated by the firm's structure, disagrees with the direction the firm is going, lacks confidence in the current leadership, doubts the firm will be able to attract and retain good people, and believes other HHI employees have been mistreated and will also be leaving soon. Several of Nickoli's HHI clients indicate that they would like information about Vesuvius and might be interested in switching their accounts. After submitting her resignation, Nickoli immediately shares the names of the interested clients with Vesuvius, and after the first of the year, she begins soliciting them to transfer their accounts from HHI to her new firm.

Nickoli's conduct is

A. a violation of the Code and Standards.

B. acceptable because she did not solicit clients until after she left HHI.

C. acceptable because she is looking out for her clients' best interests and believes Vesuvius provides better service.

Analysis

A is correct. Standard IV(A) Loyalty states that CFA Institute members and candidates "must act for the benefit of their employer and not . . . otherwise cause harm to their employer." Although a departing employee is generally free to make arrangements or preparations to change firms before terminating the relationship, those preparations must not conflict with the employee's continued duty to act in the best interests of the current employer and not otherwise undermine, disparage, or cause harm to that employer. In this case, Nickoli decides to leave HHI and join Vesuvius weeks before she notifies the firm and submits her resignation. During that time, Standard IV(A) obligates her to continue to act in her current employer's best interests and not engage in any activities that would conflict with this duty until her resignation becomes effective. Nickoli violates her duty of loyalty to HHI by making disparaging and harmful statements about the firm to its clients in the weeks before she submits her resignation and by promoting Vesuvius to HHI clients while she is still employed by HHI.

B is incorrect. Although she did not make actual solicitations until after she left HHI, Nickoli used the final weeks of her employment with HHI to determine which of the firm's clients might be interested in receiving information about Vesuvius and possibly transferring their accounts from HHI and then contacted them after her move to Vesuvius.

C is incorrect. Although investment professionals should protect their clients' best interests, even if Nickoli believes the clients will be better off with her at Vesuvius, the clients' relationship is with HHI. She is a representative of HHI, so she must not act in a manner harmful to the firm while still employed there.

Kuznetsov

Kuznetsov, CFA, is a portfolio manager for a medium-sized investment firm that encourages its employees to sell proprietary investment products to their clients. Kuznetsov begins selling these investment products, and within a year, he becomes the firm's top seller of the products. He receives glowing performance reviews and a large bonus. However, Kuznetsov begins to realize that the firm's investment products are underperforming and are more expensive than other, external investment options that are suitable for his clients and present stronger growth opportunities. He stops selling the firm's investment products to his clients. Although his supervisor puts increasing pressure on him to resume selling the firm's products, Kuznetsov refuses. He complains several times to management that he is being pressured to place the firm's interests above his clients. He secretly records several conversations with his supervisor and makes copies of client records that document what he considers inappropriate conduct by his supervisor. When management ignores his complaints and Kuznetsov's supervisor begins giving him poor performance reviews, he files a complaint with the local regulator against his supervisor and his firm, providing the recordings and copies of client files as evidence. After the firm becomes aware of Kuznetsov's actions, he is fired.

Kuznetsov's actions are

A. appropriate because he is protecting his clients' interests.

B. a violation of the CFA Institute Code and Standards because he fails to keep client information confidential.

C. a violation of the CFA Institute Code and Standards because he violates his duty of loyalty to his employer by taking his dispute with his supervisor to the regulator and exposing the employer to financial and reputational harm.

Analysis

A is correct. Standard IV(A) Loyalty states that CFA Institute members and candidates "must act for the benefit of their employer and not . . . divulge confidential information, or otherwise cause harm to their employer." But occasionally, circumstances might arise in which investment professionals need to engage in conduct contrary to their employer's interests to protect clients' interests. In pressuring Kuznetsov to sell more expensive, suboptimal investment products to his clients, the employer is acting in its own interests and not in the clients' best interests. Kuznetsov is clearly acting in the best interests of the clients by notifying the regulators of his employer's unethical practices.

B is incorrect. Copying client records to give to the regulator is a justifiable step for Kuznetsov to take to protect his clients' interests.

C is incorrect. In general, Kuznetsov's decision to record conversations with his supervisor and report the employer to the regulator is justified because he is attempting to protect his clients' interests by calling out his employer's unethical (and possibly illegal) conduct. However, certain jurisdictions might have laws against recording conversations without the other party's consent. Under these circumstances, his "whistle-blowing" activity is not a violation of the Code and Standards.

Clemence

Clemence, CFA, is a wealth management adviser for DeLaurier Strategic Advisers, where she is responsible for financial planning and wealth management for more than 400 retail clients. She met many of her clients through her spouse, who is a well-known attorney, and her sister, who is a physician. Clemence decides to leave DeLaurier to take a position at another firm, where she will not be expected to generate new advisory clients but will take on more research and investment management responsibilities. She leaves DeLaurier on good terms, providing her supervisor with all the background and information to seamlessly transition her clients to a new account manager. Not all of Clemence's clients have sufficient assets under management to become clients at her new firm. On the day Clemence leaves DeLaurier, she downloads a spreadsheet of DeLaurier's clients, prospects, and former clients and sends it to her personal email. The list includes names, assets under management, addresses, and phone numbers. Clemence intends to contact her clients as a courtesy to inform them of her new position, thank them for being clients, and express her confidence that DeLaurier will continue to provide them with competent and professional service even though she has left the firm.

Clemence's actions are

A. a violation of the CFA Institute Code and Standards.

B. appropriate because she is protecting the interests of her clients.

C. appropriate as long as she contacts only those clients who are personal friends to inform them of her new position.

Analysis

A is correct. Standard IV(A) Loyalty requires that CFA Institute members and candidates "act for the benefit of their employer and not . . . divulge confidential information, or otherwise cause harm to their employer." Clemence has violated her duty of loyalty to her employer by downloading the client list and taking it with her for use after she leaves DeLaurier. The client list is DeLaurier's property. The list also contains proprietary confidential information about DeLaurier clients that Clemence is improperly using for her own purposes, no matter how well intentioned those purposes might be. Clemence could have asked her employer's permission to send a "thank you" note to her clients immediately before leaving DeLaurier, thus eliminating the need to take client information with her.

B is incorrect. Clemence is clearly not motivated to use the client list and information to benefit her new firm but appears rather to be working for DeLaurier to protect the interests of her former clients and make them feel comfortable in continuing to use DeLaurier as their financial adviser. But in obtaining information about her clients, Clemence goes too far and also takes more information than perhaps intended. In addition to information about her clients she has also obtained information about the firm's former, current, and prospective clients.

C is incorrect. Clemence may contact her former clients who are friends through personal channels, such as social media or a personal contact, but she cannot use DeLaurier's property to facilitate this communication. As an alternative, she could ask DeLaurier's permission to take her clients' contact information so she can send them a final "thank you" correspondence.

Additional Compensation Arrangements

> Members and Candidates must not accept gifts, benefits, compensation, or consideration that competes with or might reasonably be expected to create a conflict of interest with their employer's interest unless they obtain written consent from all parties involved.

Estevez

Estevez, CFA, is a senior research analyst at BIR, a boutique investment research firm covering micro- and small-cap companies that hire BIR to provide research coverage (called issuer-paid research) to promote their stock to investors. Because of BIR's stellar reputation, its research services are in high demand among both investors and companies seeking potential investors. Estevez helps BIR select the companies it covers and oversees a team of junior research analysts. Some companies encourage Estevez to select their company for BIR research coverage by giving her a separate bonus if they are included in the BIR research universe. Estevez's actions are

A. a violation of the CFA Institute Code and Standards because her independence and objectivity in conducting the research are compromised.

B. acceptable as long as Estevez does not use material nonpublic information from the company.

C. acceptable as long as her company approves in writing the payments offered by covered companies.

Analysis

C is correct. Standard IV(B) Additional Compensation Arrangements requires members and candidates to obtain written consent from their employer before they accept any gift, benefit, or compensation that "might reasonably be expected to create a conflict of interest with their employer's interest." Estevez receives a benefit from companies that BIR selects to receive research coverage. Estevez's involvement in the process of choosing the companies that BIR agrees to research presents a conflict of interest because she might favor those companies that pay her the bonus. Estevez would have to disclose to her company that she is receiving the benefit from the selected company, and BIR would have to disclose to the users of the report that the company paid Estevez the bonus and is paying for the research coverage.

A is incorrect. Issuer-paid research itself is not automatically unethical nor does it automatically compromise an analyst's independence and objectivity. However, this area is filled with potential conflicts, so important safeguards must be observed. BIR must adopt strict procedures to protect the analyst's objectivity from being influenced by the company. Such safeguards must also include full disclosure of any conflicts of interest on the part of the analyst conducting the research; full disclosure of any compensation arrangements, including the source of the payment for the research; and policies that separate the research recommendations from the level or nature of the payment.

B is incorrect. Even if she is not using material nonpublic information from the company, this does not alleviate Estevez's need for full disclosure and employer consent regarding her bonuses from companies.

Responsibilities of Supervisors

> Members and Candidates must make reasonable efforts to ensure that anyone subject to their supervision or authority complies with applicable laws, rules, regulations, and the Code and Standards.

Duhih

RC Group (RCG) is a registered futures commission merchant with several branch offices, including one in Memphis, Tennessee (USA). Duhih, CFA, is hired to be the branch manager of the Memphis office, supervising several employees, including Lewes, CFA. Duhih allows Lewes to work from home, so Lewes does not have a physical workspace in the Memphis office or even access to the building, and Duhih only occasionally checks in with Lewes regarding work. Unknown to either Duhih or RCG, Lewes also works for another futures commission merchant, called AFCM. Lewes arranges swap agreements for AFCM, including orders with several cattle feed yard clients. Working with another employee at RCG, Lewes opens new futures accounts for the feed yard clients that RCG represents. Although the other RCG employee receives all the commissions for the accounts, she secretly splits them with Lewes. Duhih is unaware of Lewes' participation in this commission-sharing arrangement.

Duhih's actions as a supervisor are

A. a violation of the CFA Institute Code and Standards.

B. acceptable if the RCG headquarters conducts regular audits of the Memphis branch.

C. acceptable if RCG did not develop adequate policies and procedures for the detection and deterrence of possible employee misconduct.

Analysis

A is correct. Standard IV(C) Responsibilities of Supervisors states that members and candidates "must make reasonable efforts to ensure that anyone subject to their supervision or authority complies with applicable laws, rules, regulations, and the Code and Standards." At a minimum, supervisors must make reasonable efforts to detect and prevent legal, regulatory, and policy violations by ensuring that effective compliance systems have been established. Although the case does not clearly present what steps Duhih took to diligently exercise supervisory responsibility, the fact that Lewes works from home and did not have access to the branch office suggests that Duhih's supervision is minimal at best and noticeably ineffective. In addition, Duhih should support his company by encouraging it to adopt a code of ethics, have clearly written compliance policies and procedures, and conduct employee training on appropriate ethical behavior.

B is not correct. A regular audit of the Memphis branch by compliance personnel from RCG headquarters could be an excellent way to ensure that branch employees are complying with applicable law, regulations, and RCG policies. However, it would not be a substitute for effective and regular supervision by Duhih, the onsite branch manager.

C is incorrect. Supervisors must understand what constitutes an adequate compliance system and make reasonable efforts to ensure that appropriate compliance procedures are established, documented, communicated to covered personnel, and followed. If Duhih knew that RCG did not have adequate policies and procedures for detecting and deterring potential employee misconduct, he was obligated to tell management about the shortcoming, help develop adequate compliance policies, or decline supervisory responsibility. A lack of adequate policies is not an excuse for failing to detect potential misconduct by RCG employees, including Lewes. Duhih should not have accepted supervisory responsibility until he understood not only RCG's policies and procedures but also the company's expectations of him with regard to maintaining his subordinates' compliance with them.

Denikin & Denikin

Sasha Denikin, CFA, began his investment career as a research analyst for Galak Investment Partners, a company founded and controlled by his father, Franz Denikin, CFA. After several years, Franz transfers ownership of Galak to Sasha, who becomes a director of the company. Franz tells the firm's clients that he retains management of all client accounts. When the longtime chief compliance officer (CCO) announces her retirement, Sasha is promoted to CCO. While Sasha has no previous compliance experience, the plan is for the prior CCO to retain compliance responsibilities as a consultant while mentoring and training Sasha. Despite his title, Sasha has no actual authority to supervise his father's conduct, and Franz continues to exert absolute control over Galak. Sasha also does not have permission to contact clients or review Galak communications with clients because his father insists that all client contact go through him. During his tenure as CCO, Sasha raises multiple compliance issues with his father regarding his father's actions, but Sasha is powerless to enforce company policies and procedures concerning his father's conduct. After continuing to serve as Galak CCO for a time, Sasha finally resigns in frustration.

Sasha Denikin's actions are

A. a violation of the CFA Institute Code and Standards.

B. acceptable because Franz holds the actual power and client responsibilities at the firm and thus cannot be under the supervision of a subordinate.

C. acceptable because Sasha resigns as CCO when he is frustrated by his inability to exercise his compliance responsibilities.

Analysis

A is correct. Standard IV(C) Responsibilities of Supervisors requires CFA Institute members and candidates to "make reasonable efforts to ensure that anyone subject to their supervision or authority complies with applicable laws, rules, regulations, and the Code and Standards." Members and candidates with supervisory responsibility must make reasonable efforts to prevent and detect violations by ensuring that effective compliance systems are established. If they cannot carry out their supervisory responsibilities because of an inadequate compliance system, they should decline in writing to accept the supervisory responsibility until the firm adopts reasonable procedures to allow for the adequate exercise of that supervisory responsibility. Sasha knows that he is not qualified to serve as CCO of Galak but still accepts the role. As CCO, Sasha has supervisory responsibility for all firm employees in compliance matters. However, Sasha has difficulty performing his CCO duties because the firm's structure gives him no real authority over his father to ensure that his father's conduct complies with internal policies and regulatory rules. Sasha knows that his father is ignoring firm rules, but despite being CCO and a director of the company, Sasha has no real authority or ability to supervise and influence Franz's conduct.

B is incorrect. Franz's status as the founder and the one truly controlling the company does not exempt him from oversight by the CCO.

C is incorrect. If Sasha is unable to fulfill his responsibilities because of an inadequate compliance system or a lack of experience, he should refuse the CCO role until he has been fully trained and Galak adopts procedures allowing him to effectively exercise supervisory responsibility over his father. For example, Sasha could work with the outgoing CCO to establish a compliance program that includes a code of ethics, compliance policies and procedures, education and training programs, an incentive structure rewarding ethical behavior, and firmwide best practice standards to help meet his supervisory obligations. However, Sasha chooses to quit the CCO job and resign from the firm only after a significant period during which he fails to adequately meet his supervisory responsibilities and, likely, the best interests of the firm's clients.

6 INVESTMENT ANALYSIS, RECOMMENDATIONS, AND ACTIONS

- ☐ evaluate practices, policies, and conduct relative to the CFA Institute Code of Ethics and Standards of Professional Conduct
- ☐ explain how the practices, policies, and conduct do or do not violate the CFA Institute Code of Ethics and Standards of Professional Conduct

Diligence and Reasonable Basis

Members and Candidates must:

1. Exercise diligence, independence, and thoroughness in analyzing investments, making investment recommendations, and taking investment actions.

2. Have a reasonable and adequate basis, supported by appropriate research and investigation, for any investment analysis, recommendation, or action.

Harrel and Chong

Corix Bioscience is a startup company in the manufacturing and distribution of cannabidiol (CBD) products. To promote the company, the Corix CEO hires Harrel, an independent research analyst and CFA Program candidate, to write and distribute a research report on the company. The CEO tells Harrel the following:

- Corix has an agreement with indigenous tribes that allows it to access tribal lands for commercial hemp and cannabis farming and to sell hemp and cannabis products in retail outlets on tribal lands.
- Corix has a certificate of compliance from the national regulator that permits the company to transport, process, and export industrial hemp products.
- The prior year's harvest of hemp exceeded expectations in both quality and quantity, resulting in a substantial inventory of product.

Harrel includes all this information in a research report and provides a positive analysis of the company. However, Corix does not have agreements with indigenous tribes, nor does it have regulatory approval—the certificate of compliance is a forgery—and Corix never cultivated or harvested significant quantities of commercial hemp.

Chong, a CFA charterholder and research analyst at Nature's Harvest Investment Management (NHIM), incorporates the information and conclusions from Harrel's research report into his own research on Corix and includes a "buy" recommendation on the company. Chong's report is distributed to portfolio managers at NHIM. Corix is ultimately shown to be a fake operation, leading to substantial losses for NHIM's clients.

Which individual(s) most likely violated the CFA Institute Code and Standards?

A. Harrel only

B. Chong only

C. Both Harrel and Chong

Analysis

C is correct. Standard V(A) Diligence and Reasonable Basis states that CFA Institute members and candidates must exercise diligence and thoroughness in analyzing investments and must have a reasonable and adequate basis that is supported by appropriate research and investigation for any investment recommendation. Harrel and Chong do not meet the requirements of this standard. By relying on the statements given by Corix and not conducting an independent investigation into the accuracy of the information, Harrel did not exercise diligence and thoroughness in analyzing the company. Chong seemingly relied on Harrel's research to formulate his "buy" recommendation without conducting his own independent research. Investment professionals who rely on third-party research must make reasonable and diligent efforts to determine whether that research is correct. The facts do not indicate that Chong independently verified the information, critically assessed Harrel's research, or had reason to rely on Harrel's report based on past experience and familiarity with the quality of Harrel's work. In addition, Harrel works as an independent researcher and thus has no management structure that could enforce due diligence standards, which should raise concerns about the quality of Harrel's due diligence. Chong also did not recognize that Harrel's work was issuer-paid research and thus subject to increased scrutiny. NHIM should have had clear due diligence policies and procedures in place that Chong would need to follow before completing and disseminating research on behalf of the firm.

A is incorrect. Both Harrel and Chong violated the Code and Standards.

B is incorrect. Both Harrel and Chong violated the Code and Standards.

Communication with Clients and Prospective Clients

Members and Candidates must:

1. Disclose to clients and prospective clients the nature of the services provided, along with information about the costs to the client associated with those services.

2. Disclose to clients and prospective clients the basic format and general principles of the investment processes they use to analyze investments, select securities, and construct portfolios and must promptly disclose any changes that might materially affect those processes.

3. Disclose to clients and prospective clients significant limitations and risks associated with the investment process.

4. Use reasonable judgment in identifying which factors are important to their investment analyses, recommendations, or actions and include those factors in communications with clients and prospective clients.

5. Distinguish between fact and opinion in the presentation of investment analysis and recommendations.

Dukis

Dukis, CFA, is a managing director at a global credit ratings service. She is responsible for the group that assigns new issue and surveillance credit ratings to commercial mortgage-backed securities (CMBSs). To determine the ratings, Dukis and her group calculate the debt service coverage ratio (DSCR) of each security, a key quantitative metric used to rate CMBSs. Shortly after the global financial crisis, the ratings agency changes its methodology for calculating the DSCR for certain securities so that it more accurately reflects risk. Dukis's group publishes subsequent credit ratings without disclosing the change. When the new methodology is used, the securities receive higher credit ratings than they would have received if the original methodology had been used.

Dukis's actions are

A. appropriate because the new methodology more accurately reflects risk.

B. a violation of the CFA Institute Code and Standards because she did not disclose the change in methodology to the investing public.

C. appropriate because no disclosure is necessary, given that calculating DSCR is only one element in determining the overall rating of the security.

Analysis

B is correct. Standard V(B) Communication with Clients and Prospective Clients requires CFA Institute members and candidates to disclose to investors the basic format and general principles of the investment process they use to analyze investments, as well as any changes that might materially affect those processes. Ratings agencies' consistency and transparency are important to investors. If rating methodologies are not applied consistently, ratings might not be easily comparable. Similarly, without transparency, investors cannot assess the methodologies used by the credit ratings agency or the application of those methodologies, which means they cannot determine how much weight to give the rating. Dukis should have disclosed to investors the change in methodology for calculating the DSCR.

A is incorrect. Even if the new methodology does more accurately reflect risk, the change must still be communicated to investors.

C is incorrect. The DSCR is clearly a key quantitative metric used to rate the securities because the change in methodology materially affected the credit ratings by rating them higher than the original method. A change in such a key factor must be disclosed.

Record Retention

Members and Candidates must develop and maintain appropriate records to support their investment analyses, recommendations, actions, and other investment-related communications with clients and prospective clients.

Duermott

Duermott, CFA, is president of Enhanced Investment Strategies (EIS), a small investment firm. Most clients of EIS are longtime associates of Duermott who have had their investment portfolios with the firm for decades. Because of his close personal relationship with his clients, Duermott is very familiar with their investment profile, income and retirement requirements, and risk tolerance. He keeps up with all his clients' life-changing events—such as health issues, real estate purchases, children's university expenses, and retirement—and adjusts the clients' portfolios accordingly. Duermott regularly meets with his clients at EIS's offices, and he also sees them on numerous occasions outside the office, which gives him additional opportunities to update them on their investments. EIS clients complete a client agreement and risk profile when opening their account, and those profiles are updated whenever Duermott finds the time to do so.

Duermott's business practices are

A. a violation of the CFA Institute Code and Standards.

B. acceptable because he regularly communicates with clients about their investments.

C. acceptable because he adjusts clients' investments to ensure that they are suitable for the clients' needs given their changing income and risk profile.

Analysis

A is correct. Standard V(C) Record Retention states that CFA Institute members and candidates must "develop and maintain appropriate records to support their investment analyses, recommendations, actions, and other investment-related communications with clients and prospective clients." In this case, Duermott is personally close to his clients, but he updates client records only when he "finds the time to do so," which does not appear to be promptly or regularly. Duermott has a responsibility as his clients' adviser and as the president of his company to maintain appropriate records when client circumstances change. Without necessary, relevant, and up-to-date know-your-client information, Duermott would have difficulty establishing and proving that EIS has identified the needs and circumstances of its clients and has taken them into account in recommending investments. When client circumstances, investment goals, risk tolerances, or income needs change, records should be promptly updated, and they should be reviewed regularly to document these changes.

B is incorrect. Although Duermott is fulfilling his ethical obligations as an investment manager by communicating regularly with his clients, he is not keeping regular, up-to-date client records.

C is incorrect. Although Duermott is reviewing and adjusting client portfolios on a timely basis to meet clients' changing financial circumstances, he is not keeping regular, up-to-date client records.

CONFLICTS OF INTEREST 7

- ☐ evaluate practices, policies, and conduct relative to the CFA Institute Code of Ethics and Standards of Professional Conduct
- ☐ explain how the practices, policies, and conduct do or do not violate the CFA Institute Code of Ethics and Standards of Professional Conduct

Avoid or Disclose Conflicts

> Members and Candidates must avoid or make full and fair disclosure of all matters that could reasonably be expected to impair their independence and objectivity or interfere with respective duties to their clients, prospective clients, and employer. Members and Candidates must ensure that such disclosures are prominent, are delivered in plain language, and communicate the relevant information effectively.

Reebh

Reebh, CFA, is the CEO and founding partner of Lux Asset Management (Lux). Reebh provides asset management and allocation services for high-net-worth individuals and several small institutional clients. His services include investing client funds with third-party subadvisers who have a specialty in a particular asset class. Reebh's clients are aware and approve of Lux's allocation of their assets to subadvisers. The third-party subadvisers make payments to Lux based on the total value of a client's assets placed or invested in the subadvisers' funds.

Reebh's actions are

A. appropriate because Reebh has disclosed the use of subadvisers.

B. inappropriate because the payments are an improper referral fee.

C. inappropriate unless Reebh discloses the financial arrangement he has with the subadvisers to his clients.

Analysis

C is correct. Standard VI(A) Avoid or Disclose Conflicts requires CFA Institute members and candidates to "avoid or make full and fair disclosure of all matters that could reasonably be expected to impair their independence and objectivity or interfere with respective duties to their clients." The payments subadvisers make to Lux based on the value of the client assets Lux places with the subadvisers creates a potential conflict of interest because Reebh is thereby incentivized to hire subadvisers who pay the fee but who might not necessarily be the best subadvisers for his clients. Reebh can avoid this conflict by not agreeing to this compensation structure. If Reebh continues to accept payment in this manner, Reebh must disclose the financial arrangement to clients.

A is incorrect. Reebh has disclosed Lux's use of subadvisers, but he has not disclosed the financial arrangement for Lux to use those subadvisers.

B is incorrect. Although referral arrangements might be acceptable with full disclosure to clients, Reebh is not referring clients to the subadvisers but is hiring them directly on his clients' behalf.

Priority of Transactions

> Investment transactions for clients and employers must have priority over investment transactions in which a Member or Candidate is the beneficial owner.

Yang

Yang, CFA, is a research analyst at Dacco, a registered broker/dealer and investment adviser. While employed with Dacco, Yang establishes Prestige Trade Investments Limited (Prestige) and acts as investment adviser for the firm's clients. Yang is responsible for formulating Prestige's investment strategy and directs all trades on behalf of

Prestige. Over several days, Yang purchases 50,000 shares of Zhongpin stock and 1,978 Zhongpin call options for his personal account at Dacco. Shortly after, Yang uses $29.8 million of Prestige's funds to purchase more than 3 million shares of Zhongpin stock.

Yang's actions are

A. a violation of the CFA Institute Code and Standards.

B. acceptable because Yang's personal investments are not in conflict with the investment advice being given to his clients at Prestige.

C. acceptable as long as Prestige clients are not negatively affected by Yang's prior purchase of Zhongpin securities through his account at Dacco.

Analysis

A is correct. Standard VI(B) Priority of Transactions states that "investment transactions for clients . . . must have priority over investment transactions in which a [CFA Institute] Member or Candidate is the beneficial owner." Yang is "front-running" his Prestige clients' trades. Front-running involves trading for one's personal account before trading for client accounts. Yang purchases Zhongpin stock and call options in his personal account at Dacco before directing the Zhongpin trades for clients at Prestige. The $29.8 million of Prestige funds invested in Zhongpin stock could have a material upward effect on the price of the stock and options Yang holds. Even the perception that Yang could profit by using Prestige's funds will diminish investors' trust in Yang and the capital markets.

B is incorrect. Yang's personal investments are tracking with his client investments, so no conflict exists between his personal trading and the investment actions/advice for clients. However, the timing of the trades is the issue in this case because Yang is "front-running" his clients' trades.

C is incorrect. The fact that Prestige clients are not harmed by Yang's earlier trades for his personal accounts does not make his actions acceptable.

Kapadia

Kapadia, CFA, is a trader for an asset management company that manages several large global mutual funds. Kapadia executes the equity buy-and-sell orders for the portfolio managers of one of the company's mutual funds. He has the discretion to execute the orders at any time during the day, depending on market conditions. Before executing the orders, Kapadia contacts several close friends and relatives to give them information on which securities the mutual fund will be trading. In turn, these friends and relatives make trades that mirror the imminent trades to be executed by Kapadia on behalf of the mutual fund.

Kapadia's actions are

A. a violation of the CFA Institute Code and Standards.

B. inappropriate only if the client is harmed financially by the conduct.

C. appropriate because he does not share confidential information about individual clients.

Analysis

A is correct. Standard VI(B) Priority of Transactions states that "investment transactions for clients must have priority over investment transactions" for a member or candidate's personal benefit. Kapadia is facilitating front-running by his friends and relatives on the trades of his employer's mutual fund. Front-running is the unethical and often illegal practice of trading on advance information for one's personal account before trading for client accounts to gain an economic advantage. Although Kapadia might not directly benefit financially, he benefits personally by providing the information to those with whom he has close relationships.

B is incorrect. Kapadia's engagement in the practice of front-running, which involves trading in personal accounts before trading for client accounts, is unethical and inappropriate even if the trades of Kapadia's friends and relatives do not disadvantage the mutual fund by moving the price of the security or causing the fund to lose the price advantage or any profit from its own trades.

C is incorrect. Although Kapadia does not share the confidential information of individual clients or individual investors in the fund, he does share confidential information about the fund itself.

Perrkins

Perrkins, CFA, is the chief investment officer of GT Financial (GTF). Perrkins's wife is GTF's compliance officer. GTF has several dozen retail clients and total assets under management of $70 million. All client assets are managed on a discretionary basis. Perrkins frequently makes trades for his clients using an omnibus trading account through a broker/dealer, which allows Perrkins to buy and sell securities in a block trade on behalf of multiple clients simultaneously. Perrkins regularly allocates the securities purchases to individual client accounts after the market closes. Over one six-month period, Perrkins allocates 75% of the profitable trades to nine accounts that Perrkins and his wife own or control. At the same time, he allocates 82% of the unprofitable trades to the account of the three largest GTF clients.

Perrkins's actions are

A. a violation of the CFA Institute Code and Standards.

B. acceptable as long as he discloses the trade allocation practices to his clients.

C. acceptable as long as he reverses his trade allocation practices to favor the larger clients so that they are not harmed over the long term.

Analysis

A is correct. Standard VI(B) Priority of Transactions states that investment transactions for clients have priority over personal transactions. By trading in the firm's omnibus account and then delaying the allocation of trades to a specific account until he has an opportunity to observe the security's intraday performance, Perrkins can pick the winning trades for accounts in which he has a beneficial interest. This practice is a violation of Standard VI(B). He then allocates the losing trades to clients' accounts that are large enough to absorb incremental trading losses without arousing suspicion that the losses are due to fraud. Perrkins's actions are also likely a violation of Standard III(B) Fair Dealing, which states that members and candidates "must deal fairly and objectively with all clients when . . . taking investment action or engaging in other professional activities."

B is incorrect. Disclosure to his clients as to how he is allocating the trades does not make Perrkins's unethical, fraudulent behavior acceptable.

C is incorrect. Perrkins cannot temporarily favor his personal interests over his clients' interests with the intent of rectifying the situation for his clients in the future. Ethical conduct is not subject to a ledger-keeping exercise. CFA Institute members and candidates must comply with the ethical principles and requirements of the Code and Standards at all times.

Referral Fees

> Members and Candidates must disclose to their employer, clients, and prospective clients, as appropriate, any compensation, consideration, or benefit received from or paid to others for the recommendation of products or services.

Kiang

Kiang, CFA, is a successful investment adviser with several high-net-worth clients who are very happy with his services. Many of Kiang's clients recommend his advisory services to their friends and family, and Kiang encourages these recommendations to build his business. Each year, Kiang hosts an elaborate party for clients who have referred new clients to his advisory firm. At the party, Kiang distributes nominal gift cards to attendees. In some cases, Kiang offers discounts on advisory fees to clients who sent him referrals that proved particularly lucrative. Many of the clients attending these celebrations were referred to Kiang by other clients, and they, in turn, continue the cycle of recommending Kiang to a wider circle of friends and family.

Kiang's actions most likely are

A. acceptable as a reward for client loyalty.

B. acceptable because he treats all clients fairly.

C. a violation of the CFA Institute Code and Standards.

Analysis

C is correct. Standard VI(C) Referral Fees states that members and candidates "must disclose to their employer, clients, and prospective clients, as appropriate, any compensation, consideration, or benefit . . . paid to others for the recommendation of . . . services." In this case, Kiang hosts an elaborate party, distributes gift cards, and, in some cases, offers discounted advisory fees to clients who have referred particularly lucrative clients. Under the standard, these benefits would be considered referral fees that must be disclosed. The facts do not indicate that Kiang makes any disclosure to potential clients. The fact that some prospects, upon becoming clients, become aware that he pays for referrals when they receive discounted fees is insufficient disclosure. It would be acceptable if Kiang were to host a party or give gift cards to all his clients to reward their loyalty, regardless of whether they provided referrals.

A is incorrect. The party, gift cards, and discounted advisory fees are more than a reward for client loyalty and would be considered referral fees that are provided only to existing clients for recommending Kiang's services.

B is incorrect. Arguably, Kiang treats his clients fairly because he offers all of his clients the opportunity to receive these benefits and fee discounts as long as they refer others to his business, and whether the clients access these benefits by making referrals is up to them. However regardless of whether Kiang is treating all clients fairly, he is violating Standard VI(C) by not disclosing the benefits and compensation he awards for referrals.

RESPONSIBILITIES AS A CFA INSTITUTE MEMBER OR CFA CANDIDATE — 8

- ☐ evaluate practices, policies, and conduct relative to the CFA Institute Code of Ethics and Standards of Professional Conduct
- ☐ explain how the practices, policies, and conduct do or do not violate the CFA Institute Code of Ethics and Standards of Professional Conduct

Conduct as Participants in CFA Institute Programs

> Members and Candidates must not engage in any conduct that compromises the reputation or integrity of CFA Institute or the CFA designation or the integrity, validity, or security of the CFA Institute programs.

Taveras

Taveras, CFA, leads an exam preparation course sponsored by his local society. The society hosts a celebration for the students after the exam is over. During the celebration, several of Taveras's students describe their experience of taking the exam. Most give their opinion on the relative difficulty of the exam compared to their expectations, and some describe their surprise about areas of the curriculum that were not tested. Taveras asks his students for their opinions on the most difficult exam questions.

Under the CFA Institute Code and Standards, Taveras is most likely

A. prohibited from discussing the exam with students after it is over.

B. free to pass along information about the exam to candidates in future prep courses to help prepare them for the exam.

C. allowed to share the opinions of his students about the difficulty of the exam with candidates in future prep courses to emphasize the need to thoroughly prepare.

Analysis

B is correct. Standard VII(A) Conduct as Participants in CFA Institute Programs states that candidates "must not engage in any conduct that compromises . . . the integrity, validity, or security of CFA Institute programs." For Taveras to share with future prep course participants the opinions of his previous students who found the CFA exam more difficult than expected is acceptable as a way to encourage future students to study the curriculum thoroughly and prepare as much as possible. However, Tavares should not solicit or pass on information regarding the specifics of the exam.

A is incorrect. A group of candidates who collectively completed the rigorous process of studying for and taking the CFA exam will naturally want to celebrate the accomplishment and discuss the exam after it is over. Candidates are allowed to discuss their exam experience with Taveras in general terms, but they cannot provide specific information about the exam regarding the questions or the general areas tested.

C is incorrect. Taveras cannot pass along specific information to future candidates and should not be soliciting information about specific questions; doing so would be a violation of Standard VII(A), which is designed to protect the integrity and security of future exams.

Reference to CFA Institute, the CFA Designation, and the CFA Program

> When referring to CFA Institute, CFA Institute membership, the CFA designation, or candidacy in the CFA Program, Members and Candidates must not misrepresent or exaggerate the meaning or implications of membership in CFA Institute, holding the CFA designation, or candidacy in the CFA program.

Ahmed

Ahmed recently earned his CFA designation and joined a medium-sized hedge fund as a senior analyst. His supervisor, Bennett, the firm's founder, earned her CFA designation 10 years ago and proudly uses the CFA designation on her business card and on all marketing materials for the fund. Bennett shares with Ahmed that she has not paid her CFA Institute membership dues for the past four years and no longer participates in the organization's continuing education program. When Ahmed asks Bennett about her use of the designation, she states that by passing the CFA exam, she earned the CFA charter and that the credential is like a university degree that cannot be taken away. Later, during a marketing meeting the two have with a potential investor, the investor notes that he narrowed his manager search to only firms that employ CFA charterholders in senior positions. When he asks Bennett if everyone in the firm on the investment side is a CFA charterholder, she responds, "Yes, that is correct." Ahmed does not respond.

Did either Ahmed or Bennett violate the CFA Institute Code and Standards?

A. Ahmed violated the Code and Standards, but Bennett did not.

B. Bennett violated the Code and Standards, but Ahmed did not.

C. Both Ahmed and Bennett violated the Code and Standards.

Analysis

C is correct. Standard VII(B) Reference to CFA Institute, the CFA Designation, and the CFA Program states that when referring to the CFA designation, members and candidates "must not misrepresent . . . holding the CFA designation." The CFA designation is not like a degree from a university, because once individuals have been granted the right to use the designation, they must also satisfy CFA Institute membership requirements, which include paying dues, to maintain the right to refer to themselves as CFA charterholders. Participation in the CFA Institute Professional Learning program is not mandatory for members to maintain their designation, but it is encouraged as a way to meet the CFA Institute Code of Ethics provision that members maintain and improve their professional competence. Bennett's membership is considered lapsed because she has not been paying dues to CFA Institute. Until she reactivates her membership, Bennett is violating Standard VII(B) by continuing to use the CFA designation and representing herself as a charterholder to a potential client. Ahmed knows that Bennett's CFA Institute membership has lapsed. Standard I(A) Knowledge of the Law prohibits members and candidates from knowingly participating or assisting in the violations of others and requires members and candidates to dissociate from any unethical or illegal conduct. By staying silent in a sales meeting in which he knows false information is being given to a potential investor that could cause harm to that investor, Ahmed would be seen as assisting Bennett in providing that false information, even though Ahmed is not actively engaging in the misconduct himself. Best practice would be for Ahmed to address Bennett directly about her conduct and ask her to reinstate her membership or correct the statement she made to the potential investor. If Bennett refuses to take corrective action, Ahmed should report her conduct to the fund's compliance department for it to address and should dissociate himself from the activity by not participating in any additional sales meetings with Bennett.

A is not correct, because both Ahmed and Bennett violated the Code and Standards.

B is not correct, because both Ahmed and Bennett violated the Code and Standards.

Glossary

Abandonment option The option to terminate an investment at some future time if the financial results are disappointing.

Abnormal return The amount by which a security's actual return differs from its expected return, given the security's risk and the market's return.

Absolute dispersion The amount of variability present without comparison to any reference point or benchmark.

Accelerated book build An offering of securities by an investment bank acting as principal that is accomplished in only one or two days.

Accounting profit Income as reported on the income statement, in accordance with prevailing accounting standards, before the provisions for income tax expense. Also called *income before taxes* or *pretax income*.

Accredited investors Investors that meet certain minimum regulatory net worth or other requirements in order to invest in certain types of alternative assets.

Accrued interest The amount of interest in currency or par value terms of a fixed-income instrument that accumulates from the last coupon payment until the trade settlement date. The amount is paid by the buyer to the seller.

Action lag Delay from policy decisions to implementation.

Active investment An approach to investing in which the investor seeks to outperform a given benchmark.

Active return The return on a portfolio minus the return on the portfolio's benchmark.

Activist Short for "activist shareholder." Managers secure sufficient equity holdings to allow them to seek a position in a company's board and influence corporate policies or direction.

Activity ratios Ratios that measure how well a company is managing key current assets and working capital over time.

Ad hoc committee A small group of lenders or bondholders who negotiate with an issuer on debt restructuring and refinancing before the issuer submits a final proposal to the wider group of all lenders and bondholders.

Add-on pricing A pricing approach based on high-margin optional features, customizations, and additional content.

Add-on rate A yield or pricing convention for money market instrument quotations. It is the interest earned on an instrument, derived from the difference between the price and face value, expressed as a percentage of the price and multiplied by the periodicity of the annual rate.

Agency costs Direct and indirect costs borne by the principal in a principal-agent relationship owing primarily to information asymmetries. Agency costs include the costs of monitoring and assessing the agent as well as missed opportunities.

Agency RMBS Securities created by the pooling of residential mortgage-backed securities in the United States by either the Federal National Mortgage Association (Fannie Mae) or the Federal Home Loan Mortgage Corporation (Freddie Mac). These RMBS carry the full faith and credit of the government, essentially a guarantee with respect to timely payment of interest and repayment of principal.

All-or-nothing (AON) orders An order that includes the instruction to trade only if the trade fills the entire quantity (size) specified.

Allocationally efficient A characteristic of a market, a financial system, or an economy that promotes the allocation of resources to their highest value uses.

Altcoin A cryptocurrency other than Bitcoin.

Alternative data Data that are generated from non-traditional sources, such as social media and sensor networks.

Alternative hypothesis The hypothesis that is accepted if the null hypothesis is rejected.

Alternative investment markets Market for investments other than traditional securities investments (i.e., traditional common and preferred shares and traditional fixed income instruments). The term usually encompasses direct and indirect investment in real estate (including timberland and farmland) and commodities (including precious metals); hedge funds, private equity, and other investments requiring specialized due diligence.

Alternative trading systems Trading venues that function like exchanges but that do not exercise regulatory authority over their subscribers except with respect to the conduct of the subscribers' trading in their trading systems. Also called *electronic communications networks* or *multilateral trading facilities*.

American depository receipt A US dollar-denominated security that trades like a common share on US exchanges.

American depository share The underlying shares on which American depository receipts are based. They trade in the issuing company's domestic market.

American options Options that may be exercised at any time from contract inception until maturity.

American-style Type of option contract that can be exercised at any time up to the option's expiration date.

Amortization The process of allocating the cost of intangible long-term assets having a finite useful life to accounting periods; the allocation of the amount of a bond premium or discount to the periods remaining until bond maturity.

Amortizing debt A loan or bond with a payment schedule that calls for the complete repayment of principal over the instrument's time to maturity.

Analysis of variance (ANOVA) A table that presents the sums of squares, degrees of freedom, mean squares, and F-statistic for a regression model.

Analytical duration Estimates of duration using mathematical formulas. Estimates of the impact of yield changes on bond prices using analytical duration implicitly assume that benchmark yields and spreads are independent variables and are uncorrelated.

Anchoring and adjustment bias An information-processing bias in which the use of a psychological heuristic influences the way people estimate probabilities.

Annual general meeting (AGM) A yearly meeting of the corporate board of directors and shareholders, typically held in person and digitally, during which votes on directors, compensation plans, shareholder resolutions, and any other matters properly brought forward at the meeting are held. Issuer management may also make presentations and hold events.

Anomalies Apparent deviations from market efficiency.

Antidilutive With reference to a transaction or a security, one that would increase earnings per share (EPS) or result in EPS higher than the company's basic EPS—antidilutive securities are not included in the calculation of diluted EPS.

Arbitrage (1) The simultaneous purchase of an undervalued asset or portfolio and sale of an overvalued but equivalent asset or portfolio in order to obtain a riskless profit on the price differential. Taking advantage of a market inefficiency in a risk-free manner. (2) The condition in a financial market in which equivalent assets or combinations of assets sell for two different prices, creating an opportunity to profit at no risk with no commitment of money. In a well-functioning financial market, few arbitrage opportunities are possible. (3) A risk-free operation that earns an expected positive net profit but requires no net investment of money.

Arbitrageurs Traders who engage in arbitrage. See *arbitrage*.

Arithmetic mean The sum of the observations divided by the number of observations.

Artificial intelligence (AI) Computer systems that are capable of performing tasks that previously required human intelligence. AI methods are sometimes better suited to identify complex, non-linear relationships than are traditional quantitative and statistical methods.

Ask The price at which a dealer or trader is willing to sell an asset, typically qualified by a maximum quantity (ask size). See *offer*.

Ask size The maximum quantity of an asset that pertains to a specific ask price from a trader. For example, if the ask for a share issue is $30 for a size of 1,000 shares, the trader is offering to sell at $30 up to 1,000 shares.

Asset allocation The process of determining how investment funds should be distributed among asset classes.

Asset class A group of assets that have similar characteristics, attributes, and risk–return relationships.

Asset utilization ratios Ratios that measure how efficiently a company performs day-to-day tasks, such as the collection of receivables and management of inventory.

Asset-backed commercial paper Secured form of commercial paper issuance. Loans or receivables are sold to a special purpose entity that issues the ABCP and makes interest and principal payments to investors from asset cash flows.

Asset-backed securities (ABS) A type of bond issued by a legal entity called a special purpose entity created solely to own assets such as loans, receivables, and mortgages and to distribute cash flows to ABS investors. Generally, ABS backed by mortgages are known as mortgage-backed securities (MBS) while ABS refer to non-mortgage ABS.

Asset-backed token A token that represents the ownership of a physical asset that does not exist on the blockchain and whose value is based on the underlying asset.

Asset-based valuation models Valuation based on estimates of the market value of a company's assets.

Asymmetric information Also known as *information asymmetry*; the differential of information between corporate insiders and outsiders regarding the company's performance and prospects. Managers typically have more information about the company's performance and prospects than owners and creditors.

At-the-money Describes a unique situation in which the price of the underlying is equal to an option's exercise price. Like an out-of-the-money option, the intrinsic value is zero.

Auction/reverse auction models Pricing models that establish prices through bidding (by sellers in the case of reverse auctions).

Autarky Countries seeking political self-sufficiency with little or no external trade or finance. State-owned enterprises control strategic domestic industries.

Automatic stabilizer A countercyclical factor that automatically comes into play as an economy slows and unemployment rises.

Availability bias An information-processing bias in which people take a heuristic approach to estimating the probability of an outcome based on how easily the outcome comes to mind.

Available-for-sale Under US GAAP, debt securities not classified as either held-to-maturity or held-for-trading securities. The investor is willing to sell but not actively planning to sell. In general, available-for-sale debt securities are reported at fair value on the balance sheet, with unrealized gains included as a component of other comprehensive income.

Average revenue (AR) Total revenue divided by quantity sold.

Backfill Bias A problem whereby certain surviving hedge funds may be added to databases and various hedge fund indexes only after they are initially successful and start to report their returns. Also see *survivorship bias*.

Backup line of credit A type of credit enhancement provided by a bank to an issuer of commercial paper to ensure that the issuer will have access to sufficient liquidity to repay maturing commercial paper if issuing new paper is not a viable option.

Backwardation A downward-sloping, or inverted, forward curve in a futures market.

Balance sheet ratios Financial ratios involving balance sheet items only.

Balanced With respect to a government budget, one in which spending and revenues (taxes) are equal.

Balloon payment A large payment required at maturity to retire a bond's outstanding principal amount.

Base rates The reference rate on which a bank bases lending rates to all other customers.

Base-rate neglect A type of representativeness bias in which the base rate or probability of the categorization is not adequately considered.

Basic EPS Net earnings available to common shareholders (i.e., net income minus preferred dividends) divided by the weighted average number of common shares outstanding.

Basis risk The possibility that the expected value of a derivative differs unexpectedly from that of the underlying.

Basket of listed depository receipts (BLDR) An exchange-traded fund (ETF) that represents a portfolio of depository receipts.

Bayes' formula The rule for updating the probability of an event of interest—given a set of prior probabilities for the event, information, and information given the event—if you receive new information.

Bearer bonds Bonds for which ownership is not recorded; only the clearing system knows who the bond owner is.

Behavioral finance A field of finance that examines the psychological variables that affect and often distort the investment decision making of investors, analysts, and portfolio managers.

Behind the market Said of prices specified in orders that are worse than the best current price; e.g., for a limit buy order, a limit price below the best bid.

Benchmark A bond used to compare against another bond to discern attributes, often a government bond with the same or similar time-to-maturity as the bond under analysis.

Benchmark spread The difference in yield-to-maturity between a bond and that of a benchmark bond.

Best bid The highest bid in the market.

Best effort offering An offering of a security using an investment bank in which the investment bank, as agent for the issuer, promises to use its best efforts to sell the offering but does not guarantee that a specific amount will be sold.

Best offer The lowest offer (ask price) in the market.

Best-in-class An ESG implementation approach that seeks to identify the most favorable companies and sectors based on ESG considerations. Also called *positive screening*.

Beta A measure of the sensitivity of a given investment or portfolio to movements in the overall market.

Bid The price at which a dealer or trader is willing to buy an asset, typically qualified by a maximum quantity.

Bid size The maximum quantity of an asset that pertains to a specific bid price from a trader.

Big data The vast amount of information being generated by both traditional sources—for example, stock exchanges, companies, governments—and non-traditional sources—for example, electronic devices, social media, sensor networks, and company exhaust.

Bilateralism The conduct of political, economic, financial, or cultural cooperation between two countries. Countries engaging in bilateralism may have relations with many different countries but in one-at-a-time agreements without multiple partners. Typically, countries exist on a spectrum between bilateralism and multilateralism.

Bimodal A distribution that has two most frequently occurring values.

Bitcoin A cryptocurrency using blockchain technology that was created in 2009.

Bivariate correlation Also known as Pearson correlation. A parametric measure of the relationship between two variables.

Black swan risk An event that is rare and difficult to predict but has an important impact.

Block brokers A broker (agent) that provides brokerage services for large-size trades.

Blockchain A type of digital ledger in which information is recorded sequentially and then linked together and secured using cryptographic methods.

Blue chip Widely held large market capitalization companies that are considered financially sound and are leaders in their respective industry or local stock market.

Board of directors A body or individual selected by a limited company's member(s) or shareholder(s), in a manner determined by the company's charter, that manages the company. Typically, for larger companies, boards of directors appoint and oversee executive management.

Bond equivalent yield A money market interest rate quoted on a 365-day add-on rate basis.

Bond indenture A legal document between a bond issuer and investors that governs each party's rights and responsibilities.

Bond market vigilantes Bond market participants who might reduce their demand for long-term bonds, thus pushing up their yields.

Bondholders Investors in an entity's securitized debt claims, such as commercial paper, notes, and bonds. Common types of bondholders include investment funds and institutional investors.

Bonds Contractual agreements between an issuer and bondholders.

Bonus issue of shares A type of dividend in which a company distributes additional shares of its common stock to shareholders instead of cash.

Book building Investment bankers' process of compiling a "book" or list of indications of interest to buy part of an offering.

Book value Shareholders' equity (total assets minus total liabilities) minus the value of preferred stock; common shareholders' equity.

Boom An expansionary phase characterized by economic growth "testing the limits" of the economy.

Bootstrap A resampling method that repeatedly draws samples with replacement of the selected elements from the original observed sample. Bootstrap is usually conducted by using computer simulation and is often used to find standard error or construct confidence intervals of population parameters.

Bottom-up analysis An investment selection approach that focuses on company-specific circumstances rather than emphasizing economic cycles or industry analysis.

Box and whisker plot A graphic for visualizing the dispersion of data across quartiles. It consists of a box with "whiskers" connected to the box.

Breakeven point Represents the price of the underlying in a derivative contract in which the profit to both counterparties would be zero.

Bridge financing Interim financing that provides funds until permanent financing can be arranged.

Broker An agent who executes orders to buy or sell securities on behalf of a client in exchange for a commission.

Brokered market A market in which brokers arrange trades among their clients.

Broker–dealer A financial intermediary (often a company) that may function as a principal (dealer) or as an agent (broker) depending on the type of trade.

Brownfield investments The third stage of development of an infrastructure asset. Brownfield investments involve expanding existing facilities and may involve privatization of public assets or a sale leaseback of completed greenfield projects. They are characterized by a shorter investment period with immediate cash flows and an operating history.

Budget surplus/deficit The difference between government revenue and expenditure for a stated fixed period of time.

Bullet bond A bond whose principal repayment is made entirely at maturity.

Bundling A pricing approach that refers to combining multiple products or services so that customers are incentivized or required to buy them together.

Business cycles Are recurrent expansions and contractions in economic activity affecting broad segments of the economy.

Business model A concise description of how a business works and makes revenues and profits, including its customers, products or services, channels for reaching customers, and pricing.

Businesses Organization entities formed and managed for the purpose of providing a return or economic benefits to its investors and owners.

Buy-side firm An investment management company or other investor that uses the services of brokers or dealers (i.e., the client of the sell side firms).

Buyback A transaction in which a company buys back its own shares. Unlike stock dividends and stock splits, share repurchases use corporate cash.

Cabotage The right to transport passengers or goods within a country by a foreign firm. Many countries—including those with multilateral trade agreements—impose restrictions on cabotage across transportation subsectors, meaning that shippers, airlines, and truck drivers are not allowed to transport goods and services within another country's borders.

Call market A market in which trades occur only at a particular time and place (i.e., when the market is called).

Call money rate The interest rate that buyers pay for their margin loan.

Call option The right to buy an underlying.

Call period The time during which the issuer of a callable bond can exercise the call option.

Call price The price at which the issuer of a callable bond has the right to purchase the bond from investors.

Call protection period The time during which the issuer of a callable bond is not allowed to exercise the call option.

Call risk The uncertain maturity and limited price appreciation associated with callable bonds.

Callable bond A bond containing an embedded call option that gives the issuer the right to buy the bond back from the investor at specified prices on predetermined dates.

Cannibalization A transfer of sales or market share from one product to another product owned by the same company. It tends to occur when the two products are actual or perceived substitutes.

Capacity The ability of the borrower to make its debt payments on time.

Capital Other company resources available that reduce reliance on debt.

Capital allocation The process that companies use for decision making on capital investments—those projects with a life of one year or longer.

Capital allocation line (CAL) A graph line that describes the combinations of expected return and standard deviation of return available to an investor from combining the optimal portfolio of risky assets with the risk-free asset.

Capital asset pricing model (CAPM) An equation describing the expected return on any asset (or portfolio) as a linear function of its beta relative to the market portfolio.

Capital expenditure Expenditure on physical capital (fixed assets).

Capital investments An expenditure for an asset or resource with a useful life of more than one year.

Capital market expectations (CME) Expectations concerning the risk and return prospects of asset classes.

Capital market line (CML) The line with an intercept point equal to the risk-free rate that is tangent to the efficient frontier of risky assets; represents the efficient frontier when a risk-free asset is available for investment.

Capital market securities Fixed-income securities with original maturities greater than one year.

Capital markets Financial markets that trade securities of longer duration, such as bonds and equities.

Capital restrictions Controls placed on foreigners' ability to own domestic assets and/or domestic residents' ability to own foreign assets.

Capital structure The mix of debt and equity that a company uses to finance its business; a company's specific mix of long-term financing.

Capital-indexed bond A type of index-linked bond for which changes in the index are captured with adjustments to the principal. A common example is Treasury Inflation Protected Securities (TIPS) issued by the United States government.

Capital-intensive businesses Companies or business activities that are characterized by a relatively low fixed asset turnover, a high percentage of capital expenditures to sales, or a high net-working-capital-to-sales ratio.

Capital-light businesses Also known as *asset light businesses,* companies or business activities characterized by relatively high fixed asset turnover, a low percentage of capital expenditures to sales, or a low net-working-capital-to-sales ratio.

Carried interest A performance fee (also referred to as an incentive fee, or carry) that is applied based on excess returns above a hurdle rate.

Carrying Investing and holding an asset for a period of time.

Carrying amount The amount at which an asset or liability is valued according to accounting principles.

Carrying value Of a fixed-income instrument is the purchase price plus (minus) the amortized amount of the discount (premium) if the bond is purchased at a price below (above) par value.

Cartel Participants in collusive agreements that are made openly and formally.

Cash conversion cycle The amount of time between an issuer paying its suppliers in cash and receiving cash from its customers.

Cash flow additivity principle The principle that dollar amounts indexed at the same point in time are additive.

Cash flow from operations A cash profit measure over a period for an issuer's primary business activities. It includes cash from customers as well as interest and dividends received from financial investments, less cash paid to employees and suppliers as well as taxes paid to governments and interest paid to lenders.

Cash flow hedge Refers to a specific **hedge accounting** classification in which a derivative is designated as absorbing the variable cash flow of a floating-rate asset or liability, such as foreign exchange, interest rates, or commodities.

Cash markets Markets in which specific assets are exchanged at current prices. Cash markets are often referred to as **spot markets**.

Cash prices The current prices prevailing in **cash markets**.

Cash ratio A measure of liquidity that is the ratio of cash and marketable securities to current liabilities.

Catch-up clause A clause in an agreement that favors the GP. For a GP who earns a 20% performance fee, a catch-up clause allows the GP to receive 100% of the distributions above the hurdle rate *until* she receives 20% of the profits generated, and then every excess dollar is split 80/20 between the LPs and GP.

CDS credit spread Reflects the credit spread of a credit default swap (CDS) derivative contract. As with cash bonds, CDS credit spreads depend on the probability of default (POD) and the loss given default (LGD).

Central bank digital currencies (CBDCs) A tokenized version of the currency issued by the central bank, such as a digital bank note or coin, and a digital liability of the central bank.

Central bank funds market The market in which deposit-taking banks that have an excess reserve with their national central bank can lend money to banks that need funds for maturities ranging from overnight to one year. Called the federal or fed funds market in the United States.

Central bank funds rate The interest rate at which central bank funds are bought (borrowed) and sold (lent) for maturities ranging from overnight to one year. Called federal or fed funds rate in the United States.

Central clearing mandate A requirement instituted by global regulatory authorities following the 2008 global financial crisis that most **over-the-counter (OTC)** derivatives be **cleared** by a **central counterparty (CCP)**.

Central counterparty (CCP) An economic entity that assumes the **counterparty credit risk** between derivative **counterparties**, one of which is typically a financial intermediary. CCPs provide **clearing** and **settlement** for most **derivative contracts**.

Central limit theorem The theorem that states the sum (and the mean) of a set of independent, identically distributed random variables with finite variances is normally distributed, whatever distribution the random variables follow.

Certificate of deposit (CD) An instrument that represents a specified amount of funds on deposit with a bank for a specified maturity and interest rate. CDs are issued in various denominations and can be negotiable or non-negotiable.

Channels Venues where a company markets and/or delivers its products and services.

Character The quality of a debt issuer's management.

Checking accounts Bank deposits with no stated maturity available for transactional purposes that pay little or no interest. Also known as a *demand deposit*.

Circuit breaker A pause in intraday trading for a brief period if a price limit is reached.

Classical cycle Refers to fluctuations in the level of economic activity when measured by GDP in volume terms.

Clawback A requirement that the general partner return any funds distributed as incentive fees until the limited partners have received their initial investment and a percentage of the total profit.

Clearing An exchange's process of verifying the execution of a transaction, exchange of payments, and recording of participants.

Clearing instructions Instructions that indicate how to arrange the final settlement ("clearing") of a trade.

Clearinghouse An entity associated with a futures market that acts as middleman between the contracting parties and guarantees to each party the performance of the other.

Closed-end fund A mutual fund in which no new investment money is accepted. New investors invest by buying existing shares, and investors in the fund liquidate by selling their shares to other investors.

Cluster sampling A procedure that divides a population into subpopulation groups (clusters) representative of the population and then randomly draws certain clusters to form a sample.

Co-investing In co-investing, the investor invests in assets *indirectly* through the fund but also possesses rights (known as co-investment rights) to invest *directly* in the same assets. Through co-investing, an investor is able to make an investment *alongside* a fund when the fund identifies deals.

Code of ethics An established guide that communicates an organization's values and overall expectations regarding member behavior. A code of ethics serves as a general guide for how community members should act.

Coefficient of determination (R^2) The percentage of the variation of the dependent variable that is explained by the independent variable. It is a measure of goodness of fit of a regression model.

Coefficient of variation The ratio of a set of observations' standard deviation to the observations' mean value.

Cognitive cost The effort involved in processing new information and updating beliefs.

Cognitive dissonance The mental discomfort that occurs when new information conflicts with previously held beliefs or cognitions.

Cognitive errors Behavioral biases resulting from faulty reasoning; cognitive errors stem from basic statistical, information-processing, or memory errors.

Coincident economic indicators Turning points that are usually close to those of the overall economy; they are believed to have value for identifying the economy's present state.

Collateral Assets or financial guarantees underlying a debt obligation that are above and beyond the issuer's promise to pay.

Collateral manager Buys and sells debt obligations for and from the CDO's collateral pool to generate sufficient cash flows to meet the obligations to the CDO bondholders.

Collateralized bond obligations (CBOs) CDOs backed by high-yield corporate and emerging market bonds.

Collateralized debt obligations (CDOs) Securities backed by a diversified pool of one or more debt obligations. CDOs can be backed by a broad range of debt.

Collateralized loan obligations (CLOs) Investment vehicle with exposure to a portfolio of leveraged loans separated into tranches with different cash flow claims and exposure to losses based on a waterfall.

Collateralized mortgage obligations Securitize mortgage pass-through securities or multiple pools of loans. CMOs are structured to redistribute the cash flows to different bond classes or tranches and create securities that have different exposures to prepayment risk.

Commercial paper (CP) Short-term, negotiable, unsecured promissory note that represents a debt obligation of the issuer.

Committed (regular) lines of credit Bank commitments to extend credit; the commitment is considered a short-term liability and is usually in effect for 364 days (one day short of a full year).

Committed capital The amount that the limited partners have agreed to provide to the private equity fund.

Commodities A product or service from a firm that is indistinguishable from products or services of competing firms, usually conforming to a common standard or grade imposed by convention or regulation.

Commoditization A process by which competing products become less differentiated over time and become interchangeable "commodities" in the eyes of customers. This process is typically associated with declining profitability for the selling firms.

Commodity producers A firm that makes and/or sells commodities.

Commodity swap A type of swap involving the exchange of payments over multiple dates as determined by specified reference prices or indexes relating to commodities.

Common market Level of economic integration that incorporates all aspects of the customs union and extends it by allowing free movement of factors of production among members.

Common shares A type of security that represents an ownership interest in a company. Also called *common stock*.

Common stock A type of security that represents an ownership interest in a company. Also called *common shares*.

Common-size analysis The restatement of financial statement items using a common denominator or reference item that allows one to identify trends and major differences; an example is an income statement in which all items are expressed as a percent of revenue.

Companies Organization entities formed and managed for the purpose of providing a return or economic benefits to its investors and owners.

Company research report A document that presents an analyst's investment recommendation on an issuer and its securities, supported by financial modeling, industry overviews and competitive analyses, valuation scenarios, ESG considerations, and investment risks.

Complete markets Informally, markets in which the variety of distinct securities traded is so broad that any desired payoff in a future state-of-the-world is achievable.

Concession agreement A contractual arrangement under which an entity (also known as a grantor) establishes terms and conditions with a developer or operator (referred to as a concessionaire) to plan, build, operate, finance, and maintain an infrastructure asset for a specific period.

Conditional expected value The expected value of a stated event given that another event has occurred.

Conditional pass-through covered bonds Convert to pass-through securities after the original maturity date if all bond payments have not yet been made.

Conditional variances The variance of one variable, given the outcome of another.

Conditions The general economic, competitive, and business environment faced by all borrowers that may affect their ability to service or refinance debt.

Confidence level The complement of the level of significance.

Confirmation bias A type of cognitive bias that makes individuals view information that confirms beliefs they already hold as more salient.

Consensus protocol A set of rules governing how blocks can join the blockchain that is designed to resist attempts at malicious manipulation up to a certain level of security; it can be either a proof of work or a proof of stake.

Conservatism bias A belief perseverance bias in which people maintain their prior views or forecasts by inadequately incorporating new information.

Constant yield-price trajectory A graphical depiction of the relationship between time to maturity and a bond price, assuming no default, that shows that a bond price approaches par as time passes.

Constituent securities With respect to an index, the individual securities within an index.

Contango Refers to spot price below forward price in a futures market.

Contingency provision Clause in a legal document that allows for some action if a specific event or circumstance occurs.

Contingency table A table of the frequency distribution of observations classified on the basis of two discrete variables.

Contingent claim A type of derivative in which one of the *counterparties* determines whether and when the trade will settle. An *option* is a common type of contingent claim.

Contingent convertible bonds Bonds that automatically convert to equity if a specific event or circumstance occurs, such as the issuer's equity capital falling below the minimum requirement set by regulators.

Continuous trading market A market in which trades can be arranged and executed any time the market is open.

Continuously compounded return The natural logarithm of 1 plus the holding period return, or equivalently, the natural logarithm of the ending price over the beginning price.

Contract manufacturers Companies that make products for other companies that meet specific terms and specifications.

Contract size Amount(s) used for calculation to price and value the derivative. The contract size is often referred to as "notional amount or notional principal."

Contraction The period of a business cycle after the peak and before the trough; often called a *recession* or, if exceptionally severe, called a *depression*.

Contraction risk The risk of earlier repayment of a mortgage-backed security than expected.

Contractionary Tending to cause the real economy to contract.

Contractionary fiscal policy A fiscal policy that has the objective to make the real economy contract.

Contribution margin A profitability measure using variable costs: unit price less unit variable cost. It can also be expressed as a percentage of price or sales.

Controlling shareholder An individual or entity that owns a majority of the voting rights in a corporation.

Convenience sampling A procedure of selecting an element from a population on the basis of whether or not it is accessible to a researcher or how easy it is for a researcher to access the element.

Convenience yield A non-cash benefit of holding a physical commodity versus a derivative.

Conversion price Predetermined share price at which convertible debt may be fully exchanged for common shares during the conversion period.

Conversion ratio The number of common shares a convertible bond or noteholder may receive in exchange for a specific bond par value.

Conversion value The current contingency feature value derived by comparing a convertible bond's price with its value if a bondholder were to exchange bonds for shares.

Convertible bond A bond that gives the bondholder the right to exchange the bond for a specified number of common shares in the issuing company.

Convertible debt A fixed-income instrument which combines the features of debt with equity via a contingent feature, allowing debtholders to exchange their claim for common shares at a predetermined fixed price in the future.

Convertible preference shares A type of equity security that entitles shareholders to convert their shares into a specified number of common shares.

Convexity The second order, usually a positive change in the price of a bond for a given change in yield, which can be negative for a callable bond such as a high-yield bond.

Convexity adjustment A measure that is used to complement modified duration to capture the second-order effect of yield changes on a bond's price. It is equal to the annual convexity statistic times one-half times the given change in the yield-to-maturity squared.

Convexity bias Refers to the difference in price changes for a given change in yield between interest rate futures and interest rate forward contracts. That is, interest rate forwards exhibit a non-linear or convex relationship between price and yield, while the price–yield relationship is linear for interest rate futures.

Cooperation The process by which countries work together toward some shared goal or purpose. These goals may, and often do, vary widely—from strategic or military concerns, to economic influence, to cultural preferences.

Cooperative country A country that engages and reciprocates in rules standardization; harmonization of tariffs; international agreements on trade, immigration, or regulation; and allowing the free flow of information, including technology transfer.

Core real estate strategies Strategies with exposure to well-leased, high-quality commercial and residential real estate in the best markets, generally offered by open-end funds. Investors expect core real estate to deliver stable returns, primarily from income from the property.

Core-plus real estate strategies Value-add investments that require modest redevelopment or upgrades to lease any vacant space together with possible alternative use of the underlying properties. Compared to core real estate strategies, these may be appealing for investors seeking higher returns and willing to accept additional risks from development, redevelopment, repositioning, and leasing.

Corporate issuers Limited companies or corporations that seek financing in financial markets by, for example, issuing debt or equity securities.

Corporations Another term for limited companies, though often used to refer to public limited companies. See *limited company*, *private limited company*, and *public limited company*.

Correlation A measure of the linear relationship between two random variables.

Correlation coefficient A number between −1 and +1 that measures the consistency or tendency for two investments to act in a similar way. It is used to determine the effect on portfolio risk when two assets are combined.

Cost averaging The periodic investment of a fixed amount of money.

Cost of capital The cost of financing for a company; the rate of return that suppliers of capital require as compensation for their contribution of capital (also called *opportunity cost of funds*).

Cost of carry The net of the costs and benefits related to owning an underlying asset for a specific period.

Cost of debt The required return on debt financing for a company, such as when it issues a bond, takes out a bank loan, or leases an asset through a finance lease.

Cost of equity The return required by equity investors to compensate for both the time value of money and the risk. Also referred to as the required rate of return on common stock or the required return on equity.

Counterparty Legal entities entering a **derivative contract**.

Counterparty credit risk The likelihood that a **counterparty** is unable to meet its financial obligations under the contract.

Counterparty risk The risk that the other party to a contract will fail to honor the terms of the contract.

Country The geopolitical environment as well as the legal and political system faced by all issuers in a jurisdiction that may affect debt payment.

Coupon Periodic interest payments paid by a bond issuer to investors, typically expressed as a percentage of par on an annual basis.

Cournot assumption Assumption in which each firm determines its profit-maximizing production level assuming that the other firms' output will not change.

Covariance A measure of the co-movement (linear association) between two random variables.

Covenants The terms and conditions of lending agreements that the issuer must comply with; they specify the actions that an issuer is obligated to perform (affirmative covenant) or prohibited from performing (negative covenant).

Credit default swap (CDS) A type of credit derivative in which one party, the credit protection buyer who is seeking credit protection against a third party, makes a series of regularly scheduled payments to the other party, the credit protection seller. The seller makes no payments until a credit event occurs.

Credit enhancements Provisions or methods that allow a borrower improve their creditworthiness in a structured transaction.

Credit event An occurrence that triggers the settlement of a CDS contract, including failure to make a debt payment, debt restructuring, or a bankruptcy filing.

Credit facilities Loan agreements with pre-specified terms and limits but with fluctuating balances based on borrower-specific needs at different points in time, analogous to a credit card.

Credit migration risk The risk that a bond issuer's creditworthiness deteriorates, or migrates lower, leading investors to believe the risk of default is higher. Also called **downgrade risk**.

Credit rating Letter-grade, qualitative measures of an issuer's ability to meet its debt obligations based on both the probability of default and the expected loss under a default scenario.

Credit rating agencies Institutions that issue and maintain credit ratings. The three largest are Standard & Poor's, Moody's, and Fitch Ratings.

Credit risk The expected economic loss under a potential borrower default over the life of the contract.

Credit spread The compensation for the risk of default in a debt security, typically measured by the yield-to-maturity difference between a bond and a comparable government benchmark security.

Credit spread risk The risk of greater expected loss due to changes in credit conditions as a result of macroeconomic, market, and/or issuer-related factors.

Credit tranching Internal credit enhancement where cash flows into a senior/subordinate structure.

Credit-linked notes Bonds whose coupon changes when the bonds' credit rating changes.

Critical values Values of the test statistic at which the decision changes from fail to reject the null hypothesis to reject the null hypothesis.

Cross-default clause Covenant or contract clause that specifies borrowers are considered in default if they default on another debt obligation.

Cross-sectional analysis Analysis over a group as of a given time.

Crossing networks Trading systems that match buyers and sellers who are willing to trade at prices obtained from other markets.

Crowdsourcing A business model that enables users to contribute directly to a product, service, or online content.

Cryptocurrency An electronic medium of exchange that lacks physical form.

Cryptocurrency wallet A storage unit for public and/or private keys for cryptocurrency transactions. These wallets may be a physical device, program, or service.

Cryptography An algorithmic process to encrypt data, making the data unusable if received by unauthorized parties.

Cumulative preference shares Preference shares for which any dividends that are not paid accrue and must be paid in full before dividends on common shares can be paid.

Cumulative voting A voting process whereby shareholders can accumulate and vote all their shares for a single candidate in an election, as opposed to having to allocate their voting rights evenly among all candidates.

Currencies Monies issued by national monetary authorities.

Currency Money issued by national monetary authorities.

Currency swap A swap in which each party makes interest payments to the other in different currencies.

Current government spending With respect to government expenditures, spending on goods and services that are provided on a regular, recurring basis including health, education, and defense.

Current ratio A measure of liquidity that is the ratio of current assets to current liabilities.

Current yield The sum of the coupon payments received over the year divided by the flat price. Also called the income, interest yield, or running yield.

Customs union Extends the free trade area (FTA) by not only allowing free movement of goods and services among members, but also creating a common trade policy against nonmembers.

CVaR Conditional VaR, a tail loss measure. The weighted average of all loss outcomes in the statistical distribution that exceed the VaR loss.

Daily settlement A specific process of *mark-to-market* by a central clearing party in which the profits and losses of all counterparties to derivatives contracts are determined using settlement prices for each contract.

Dark pools Alternative trading systems that do not display the orders that their clients send to them.

Data mining The practice of determining a model by extensive searching through a dataset for statistically significant patterns. Also called *data snooping*.

Data science An interdisciplinary field that harnesses advances in computer science, statistics, and other disciplines for the purpose of extracting information from big data (or data in general).

Data snooping The subconscious or conscious manipulation of data in a way that produces a statistically significant result (i.e., the p-value is sufficiently small or the t-statistic sufficiently large to indicate statistical significance), such as by running multiple simulations and naively accepting the best result. Also known as p-hacking.

Day order An order that is good for the day on which it is submitted. If it has not been filled by the close of business, the order expires unfilled.

Days of inventory on hand (DOH) The average number of days it would take to sell the amount of inventory on hand. It is calculated as either the ending or average balance of inventories divided by (cost of goods sold/days in the period).

Days payable outstanding (DPO) The average number of days it takes a company to pay its suppliers. It is calculated as either the ending or average balance of accounts payable divided by (cost of goods sold/days in the period).

Days sales outstanding (DSO) The average number of days it takes for a company to receive payment from customers who purchase goods or services on credit. It is calculated as either the ending or average balance of accounts receivable divided by (revenues/days in the period).

Dealers Financial intermediaries, such as commercial banks or investment banks, who transact as **counterparties** with derivative end users.

Debt A claim against an entity to receive cash, stock, or other assets at a future date. From the perspective of the debtor or borrower, an obligation to pay cash, stock, or other assets at a future date. Generally, debt claims are unconditional and are senior to equity claims.

Debt service coverage ratio A key indicator of credit performance equal to the ratio of net operating income to debt service.

Debt tax shield The tax benefit from interest paid on debt being tax deductible from income, equal to the marginal tax rate multiplied by the value of the debt.

Debt-to-assets ratio A solvency ratio calculated as total debt divided by total assets.

Debt-to-capital ratio A solvency ratio calculated as total debt divided by total debt plus total shareholders' equity.

Debt-to-equity ratio A solvency ratio calculated as total debt divided by total shareholders' equity.

Debt-to-income ratio (DTI) Residential lending metric that compares an individual's monthly debt payments to their monthly pre-tax, gross income.

Debut issuer An issuer approaching the bond market for the first time.

Deciles Values that divide a distribution ranked smallest to largest into 10 equal parts.

Declaration date The day that the corporation issues a statement declaring a specific dividend.

Decreasing returns to scale When a production process leads to increases in output that are proportionately smaller than the increase in inputs.

Deductible temporary differences Temporary differences that result in a reduction of or deduction from taxable income in a future period when the balance sheet item is recovered or settled.

Deep learning An area of artificial intelligence in which a system uses neural networks to perform multistage, non-linear data processing to identify patterns. Also called *deep learning nets*.

Deep learning nets See *Deep learning*.

Deep-in-the-money option An option that is highly likely to be exercised.

Deep-out-of-the-money option An option that is highly unlikely to be exercised.

Default When a borrower on a mortgage loan fails to meet the obligations of the loan.

Default risk premium An extra return that compensates investors for the possibility that the borrower will fail to make a promised payment at the contracted time and in the contracted amount.

Defeasance Mechanism that allows prepayment on mortgage, but the borrower must purchase a portfolio of government securities that fully replicates the cash flows of the remaining scheduled principal and interest payments, including the balloon loan balance, on the loan.

Defensive interval ratio A liquidity ratio that estimates the number of days that an entity could meet cash needs from liquid assets; calculated as (cash + short-term marketable investments + receivables) divided by daily cash expenditures.

Deferred coupon bonds Bonds that pay no coupons for their first few years but then pay a higher coupon than they otherwise normally would for the remainder of their life. Also called *split coupon bonds.*

Deferred tax assets A balance sheet asset that arises when an excess amount is paid for income taxes relative to accounting profit. The taxable income is higher than accounting profit and income tax payable exceeds tax expense. The company expects to recover the difference during the course of future operations when tax expense exceeds income tax payable.

Deferred tax liabilities A balance sheet liability that arises when a deficit amount is paid for income taxes relative to accounting profit. The taxable income is less than the accounting profit and income tax payable is less than tax expense. The company expects to eliminate the liability over the course of future operations when income tax payable exceeds tax expense.

Defined benefit pension plans (DB plans) Plans in which the company promises to pay a certain annual amount (defined benefit) to the employee after retirement. The company bears the investment risk of the plan assets.

Defined contribution pension plans Individual accounts to which an employee and typically the employer makes contributions during their working years and expect to draw on the accumulated funds at retirement. The employee bears the investment and inflation risk of the plan assets.

Deflation Negative inflation.

Degree of financial leverage The ratio of percentage change in net income to percentage change in operating income over a period. It is a measure of how sensitive net income is to changes in operating income, driven by the firm's use of debt in its capital structure.

Degree of operating leverage The ratio of percentage change in operating income to percentage change in sales over a period. It is a measure of how sensitive operating income is to changes in sales, driven by the fixed and variable cost composition of operating expenses.

Delta The sensitivity of the derivative price to a small change in the value of the underlying asset.

Demand shock A typically unexpected disturbance to demand, such as an unexpected interruption in trade or transportation.

Dependent variable The variable that is explained by a regression model.

Depository bank A bank that raises funds from depositors and other investors and lends it to borrowers.

Depository institutions Commercial banks, savings and loan banks, credit unions, and similar institutions that raise funds from depositors and other investors and lend it to borrowers.

Depository receipt A security that trades like an ordinary share on a local exchange and represents an economic interest in a foreign company.

Depreciation The process of systematically allocating the cost of long-lived (tangible) assets to the periods during which the assets are expected to provide economic benefits.

Derivative A financial instrument that derives its value from the performance of an underlying asset or factor (e.g., stock price, interest rate, or exchange rate).

Derivative contract A legal agreement between counterparties with a specific **maturity**, or length of time, until the closing of the transaction, or **settlement**.

Derivative pricing rule A pricing rule used by crossing networks in which a price is taken (derived) from the price that is current in the asset's primary market.

Differentiated products A product or service from a firm that is distinguishable or distinct from those of competing firms. It is customers who determine and value whether a product is differentiated.

Diffuse prior The assumption of equal prior probabilities.

Diffusion index Reflects the proportion of the index's components that are moving in a pattern consistent with the overall index.

Digital assets The umbrella term covering assets that can be created, stored, and transmitted electronically and have associated ownership or use rights. Digital assets include a variety of assets, such as cryptocurrencies, tokens (security and utility), and digital collectables.

Diluted EPS The EPS that would result if all dilutive securities were converted into common shares.

Dilution An increase in the number of shares outstanding from share issuance that decreases the percentage of shares owned by existing shareholders.

Direct investing Occurs when an investor makes a direct investment in an asset without the use of an intermediary.

Direct lending Providing capital directly from private debt investors.

Direct listing Where the equity of a security is floated on the public markets directly, without underwriters, reducing the complexity and cost of the transaction.

Direct sales Marketing and/or delivering products and services to customers without an intermediary or third party between the customer and seller.

Direct taxes Taxes levied directly on income, wealth, and corporate profits.

Discount factor The price equivalent of a zero rate. Also may be stated as the present value of a currency unit on a future date.

Discount rate A yield or pricing convention for money market instrument quotations. It is the interest earned on an instrument, derived from the difference between the price and face value, expressed as a percentage of the face value and multiplied by the periodicity of the annual rate.

Discounted cash flow models Valuation models that estimate the intrinsic value of a security as the present value of the future benefits expected to be received from the security.

Discriminatory pricing rule A pricing rule used in continuous markets in which the limit price of the order or quote that first arrived determines the trade price.

Diseconomies of scale Increase in cost per unit resulting from increased production.

Dispersion The variability of a population or sample of observations around the central tendency.

Display size The size of an order displayed to public view.

Disposition effect A type of cognitive bias that makes individuals unwilling to sell their possessions at a loss.

Distressed debt Debt of mature companies in financial difficulty, in bankruptcy, or likely to default on debt.

Distressed/restructuring These strategies focus on securities of companies either in or perceived to be near bankruptcy. In one approach, hedge funds simply purchase fixed-income securities trading at a significant discount to par but that are still senior enough to be backed by sufficient corporate assets.

Distributed ledger A type of database that can be shared among entities in a network.

Distributed ledger technology (DLT) Technology based on a distributed ledger.

Diversification ratio The ratio of the standard deviation of an equally weighted portfolio to the standard deviation of a randomly selected security.

Dividend discount model (DDM) The model of the value of stock that is the present value of all future dividends, discounted at the required return on equity.

Dividend payout ratio The ratio of cash dividends paid to earnings for a period.

Dividends Distributions of profits and/or net assets from a corporation to its shareholders. While often in cash, dividends can be also be paid in stock or assets, such as property.

Divisor A number (denominator) used to determine the value of a price return index. It is initially chosen at the inception of an index and subsequently adjusted by the index provider, as necessary, to avoid changes in the index value that are unrelated to changes in the prices of its constituent securities.

Domestic bonds A type of bond for which the issuer's domicile and jurisdiction of issuance are the same.

Domestic content provisions Stipulate that some percentage of the value added or components used in production should be of domestic origin.

Double taxation Income is taxed twice.

Downside risk The potential for loss.

Drag on liquidity An action or event that reduces available funds or delays cash inflows.

Drivers Causative factors that explain the level of and changes in an output variable.

DSC ratio A property's annual net operating income (NOI) divided by the debt service.

Dual-class structure A capital structure that includes at least two classes of equity shares with unequal voting rights.

Dupont analysis An approach to decomposing return on investment, e.g., return on equity, as the product of other financial ratios.

Duration The first-order, linear change in a bond's price for a given yield change in yield, which is a negative or inverse relationship.

Duration gap the difference between a bond's Macaulay duration and its investor's investment horizon.

Dynamic pricing A pricing approach that charges different prices at different times. Specific examples include off-peak pricing, "surge" pricing, and "congestion" pricing.

Early repayment option May entitle the borrower to prepay all or part of the outstanding mortgage principal prior to maturity. This creates a risk from the lender's or investor's viewpoint because the cash flow amounts and timing cannot be known with certainty.

Earnings surprise The difference between reported EPS and expected EPS. Also referred to as *unexpected earnings*.

Economic indicators Economic statistics provided by government and established private organizations that contain information on an economy's recent past activity or its current or future position in the business cycle.

Economic infrastructure investments A category of infrastructure investments that support economic activity through transportation assets, information and communication technology assets, and utility and energy assets.

Economic stabilization Reduction of the magnitude of economic fluctuations.

Economic union Incorporates all aspects of a common market and in addition requires common economic institutions and coordination of economic policies among members.

Economies of scale A decline in costs per unit as output grows, generally resulting from having fixed costs in the cost structure that are spread over more units of output.

Economies of scope A decline in costs per unit as the number of product or business lines increases, generally resulting from having shared costs between the product lines.

Effective annual rate An interest rate with a periodicity of one.

Effective convexity An interest rate risk statistic that measures the non-linear/second-order effect of changes in the benchmark yield curve on a bond's price.

Effective duration The sensitivity of the bond's price to an instantaneous parallel shift in a benchmark yield curve—for example, the government par curve.

Efficient market A market in which asset prices reflect new information quickly and rationally. See also, *informationally efficient market.*

Either/or fee A custom fee arrangement whereby major investors are offered a structure where managers agree to charge *either* a lower management fee *or* a higher incentive fee, whichever is greater.

Electronic communications networks (ECNs) See *alternative trading systems* and *multilateral trading facilities.*

Embedded derivative A derivative within an underlying, such as a callable, putable, or convertible bond.

Embedded options Contingency provisions found in a bond's indenture representing rights that enable their holders to take advantage of interest rate movements. They can be exercised by the issuer, by the bondholder, or automatically depending on the course of interest rates.

Emotional biases Behavioral biases resulting from reasoning influenced by feelings; emotional biases stem from impulse or intuition.

Empirical duration Estimation of the price–yield relationship using historical bond market data in statistical models.

Employee stock ownership plan (ESOP) A type of employee benefit plan in which a company sets up a trust fund to receive contributions of newly issued shares or cash to buy existing shares. Contributions are tax deductible up to certain limits. Shares in the trust fund are allocated to individual employees based on relative pay or a formula.

Endowment bias An emotional bias in which people value an asset more when they hold rights to it than when they do not.

Enterprise risk management An overall assessment of a company's risk position. A centralized approach to risk management sometimes called firmwide risk management.

Enterprise value A measure of a company's total market value from which the value of cash and short-term investments have been subtracted.

Equal weighting An index weighting method in which an equal weight is assigned to each constituent security at inception.

Equity Ownership interest in an entity. A residual claim on the assets of an entity after more senior claims, such as debt, have been satisfied. Also known as *net assets*.

Equity swap A swap transaction in which at least one cash flow is tied to the return to an equity portfolio position, often an equity index.

Error term Represents the difference between the observed value of the independent variable and that expected from the true underlying population relation between the dependent and independent variable.

Estimated parameters In a simple linear regression, the estimated parameters are the intercept and slope of the fitted line.

Ether A programmable cryptocurrency created on the Ethereum blockchain in 2015 that allows for the execution of smart contracts.

Ethical principles Beliefs regarding what is good, acceptable, or obligatory behavior and what is bad, unacceptable, or forbidden behavior.

Ethics The study of moral principles or of making good choices. Ethics encompasses a set of moral principles and rules of conduct that provide guidance for our behavior.

Eurobonds A type of bond issued internationally, outside the jurisdiction of the country in whose currency the bond is denominated.

European options Options that may be exercised only at contract maturity.

European-style Said of an option contract that can only be exercised on the option's expiration date.

Event risk Risk that evolves around set dates, such as elections, new legislation, or other date-driven milestones, such as holidays or political anniversaries, known in advance. Example: Brexit referendum.

Ex-dividend date The first date that a share trades without (i.e., "ex") the right to receive the declared dividend for the period.

Excess kurtosis Degree of kurtosis (fatness of tails) relative to the kurtosis of the normal distribution.

Excess spread Surplus difference of yield remaining after payments to bondholders are made after expenses are made and losses are covered.

Exchange A rules-based, open access market venue where financial instruments are traded, with price and volume transparency accessible by issuers, investors, and their intermediaries.

Exchange-traded derivative (ETD) Futures, options, and other financial contracts available on exchanges.

Execution instructions Instructions that indicate how to fill an order.

Exercise The decision to transact the underlying by an option holder.

Exercise date The day that an option is exercised by its holder. For a call option, the day the strike price is paid and underlying is purchased. For a put option, when the strike price is received and the underlying is sold.

Exercise price The pre-agreed execution price specified in an option contract. Sometimes, this price is referred to as the strike price.

Exogenous risk A sudden or unanticipated risk that impacts either a country's cooperative stance, the ability of non-state actors to globalize, or both. Examples include sudden uprisings, invasions, or the aftermath of natural disasters.

Expansion The period of a business cycle after its lowest point and before its highest point.

Expansionary Tending to cause the real economy to grow.

Expansionary fiscal policy Fiscal policy aimed at achieving real economic growth.

Expected exposure (EE) The size of the investor's claim at the time of default.

Expected loss (EL) Default probability times loss severity given default.

Expected return on the portfolio Denoted as ($E(R_p)$). The weighted average of the expected returns (R_1 to R_n) on the component securities using their respective weights (w_1 to w_n).

Expected value of a random variable The probability-weighted average of the possible outcomes of a random variable.

Expert system A type of computer programming, often based on "if–then" rules, that attempts to simulate the knowledge base and analytical abilities of human experts in specific problem-solving contexts.

Export subsidy Paid by the government to the firm when it exports a unit of a good that is being subsidized.

Exposure at default (EAD) The size of the investor's claim at the time of default.

Extension risk The risk of later repayment of a mortgage-backed security than expected.

External credit enhancements Provisions or methods from a third party that allow a borrower improve their creditworthiness in a structured transaction.

External debt Sovereign debt owed to foreign creditors.

Extra dividend A dividend paid by a company that does not pay dividends on a regular schedule, or a dividend that supplements regular cash dividends with an extra payment.

Extraordinary general meetings (EGMs) Meetings besides an AGM of the corporate board and shareholders, typically held to deliberate and vote on urgent matters. Corporate charters and bylaws specify who can call an EGM and under what conditions.

Extreme value theory A branch of statistics that focuses primarily on extreme outcomes.

Face value The amount of principal on a bond, also known as par value.

Factoring arrangement When a company sells its accounts receivable to a lender (known as a factor) that assumes responsibility for the credit-granting and collection process.

Fair value A market-based measure of an investment based on observable or derived assumptions to determine a price that market participants would use to exchange an asset or liability in an orderly transaction at a specific time.

Fair value hedge Refers to a specific **hedge accounting** designation that applies when a derivative is deemed to offset the fluctuation in fair value of an asset or liability.

Fallen angels Formerly investment-grade-rated issuers whose bonds are downgraded to high yield due to credit deterioration.

Fat-Tailed Describes a distribution that has fatter tails than a normal distribution (also called leptokurtic).

Fed funds rate The US interbank lending rate on overnight borrowings of reserves.

Federal funds rate The US interbank lending rate on overnight borrowings of reserves. Also known as *Fed Funds rate*.

Fiat money Money that is not convertible into any other commodity.

Fiduciary call A combination of a purchased call option and investment in a risk-free bond with face value of the option's exercise price.

Fill or kill See *immediate or cancel order*.

Finance lease A type of lease which is more akin to the purchase or sale of the underlying asset.

Financial leverage The use of debt in the capital structure. Measured using ratios such as operating income to operating income less interest expense, total assets to total equity, or debt to equity.

Financial leverage ratio A measure of financial leverage calculated as average total assets divided by average total equity.

Financial risk The risk arising from a company's capital structure and, specifically, from the level of debt and debt-like obligations.

Fintech Technological innovation in the financial services industry, specifically with the design and delivery of financial services and products. It may also refer more broadly to companies involved in developing the new technologies and their applications, as well as the business sector that includes such companies.

Firm commitment A pre-determined amount (price and quantity) is agreed to be exchanged at settlement. Examples of firm commitments include forward contracts, futures contracts, and swaps.

First lien Also known as a priority lien, this investor protection grants a lender the right to take possession of property from a borrower which fails to repay debt.

First lien debt Debt secured by a pledge of certain assets that could include buildings, but it may also include property and equipment, licenses, patents, brands, etc.

First mortgage debt Debt secured by a pledge of a specific property.

Fiscal multiplier The ratio of a change in national income to a change in government spending.

Fiscal policy The use of taxes and government spending to affect the level of aggregate expenditures.

Fixed charge coverage A solvency ratio measuring the number of times interest and lease payments are covered by operating income, calculated as (EBIT + lease payments) divided by (interest payments + lease payments).

Fixed charge coverage ratio A measure of how well a company's earnings covers its fixed expenses, which may include debt payments, interest expense, and lease costs.

Fixed-income instruments Debt instruments such as loans or bonds.

Fixed-income securities Fixed-income instruments designed to be more easily tradeable than a loan, such as a bond.

Fixed-price call A contingency provision that grants an issuer the right to buy back a bond at a predetermined price in the future.

Fixed-rate payer The counterparty paying fixed cash flows in a swap contract. May also be referred to as the floating-rate receiver.

Flat price The full price of a bond minus accrued interest. Flat prices are usually quoted by bond dealers.

Float-adjusted market-capitalization weighting An index weighting method in which the weight assigned to each constituent security is determined by adjusting its market capitalization for its market float.

Floating-rate notes Notes on which interest payments are not fixed but instead vary from period to period depending on the current level of a reference interest rate. Also known as *floaters*.

Floating-rate payer The counterparty paying the variable cash flows in a swap contract. May also be referred to as the fixed-rate receiver.

Forecast object A variable on or related to an issuer's financial statements that an analyst makes a projection for. Examples include drivers of financial statements, financial statement lines, and summary measures like EBITDA.

Foreclosure Allows a lender to take possession of the property and ultimately sell the property to recover funds toward satisfying the outstanding debt obligation.

Foreign bonds A type of bond for which the issuer's domicile and jurisdiction of issuance are different.

Foreign currency reserves Holding by the central bank of non-domestic currency deposits and non-domestic bonds.

Foreign direct investments (FDI) Long-term investments in the productive capacity of a foreign country.

Foreign exchange gains (or losses) Gains (or losses) that occur when the exchange rate changes between the investor's currency and the currency that foreign securities are denominated in.

Forward contract A **derivative contract** for the future exchange of an **underlying** at a fixed price set at contract signing.

Forward price Represents the price agreed upon in a forward contract to be exchanged at the contract's maturity date, T. This price is shown in equations as $F_0(T)$.

Forward price-to-earnings ratio A P/E calculated on the basis of a forecast of EPS; a stock's current price divided by next year's expected earnings.

Forward rate agreement (FRA) An OTC derivatives contract in which counterparties agree to apply a specific interest rate to a future time period.

Founders class shares A way to entice early participation in startup funds whereby managers offer incentives that entitle investors to a lower fee structure and/or other favorable terms.

Framing bias An information-processing bias in which a person answers a question differently based on the way in which it is asked (framed).

Franchising A situation where an owner of an asset and associated intellectual property divests the asset and licenses intellectual property to a third-party operator (franchisee) in exchange for royalties. Franchisees operate under the constraints of a franchise agreement.

Free cash flow The actual cash that would be available to the company's investors after making all investments necessary to maintain the company as an ongoing enterprise (also referred to as free cash flow to the firm); the internally generated funds that can be distributed to the company's investors (e.g., shareholders and bondholders) without impairing the value of the company.

Free cash flow hypothesis The hypothesis that higher debt levels discipline managers by forcing them to make fixed debt service payments and by reducing the company's free cash flow.

Free float The portion of a listed company's equity securities that are not held by insiders, strategic investors, sponsors, founders, and so on, that are more freely available for trading.

Free trade areas One of the most prevalent forms of regional integration, in which all barriers to the flow of goods and services among members have been eliminated.

Free-cash-flow-to-equity models Valuation models based on discounting expected future free cash flow to equity.

Freemium business model A pricing approach that allows customers a certain level of usage or functionality at no charge. Those who wish to use more must pay.

Frequency table A representation of the frequency of occurrence of two discrete variables.

Full price The price of a bond including any accrued interest owed to the seller. It is the flat price plus accrued interest.

Fully amortizing loan A loan or bond with a payment schedule that calls for the complete repayment of principal over the instrument's time to maturity.

Fund investing In fund investing, the investor invests in assets indirectly by contributing capital to a fund as part of a group of investors. Fund investing is available for all major alternative investment types.

Fund of funds Funds that hold a portfolio of hedge funds; also called *funds of hedge funds.*

Fundamental analysis The examination of publicly available information and the formulation of forecasts to estimate the intrinsic value of assets.

Fundamental growth These strategies use fundamental analysis to identify companies expected to exhibit high growth and capital appreciation.

Fundamental long/short In this strategy, the hedge fund takes a long position in companies that are trading at inexpensive levels compared to their potential intrinsic value and shorts those that trade in the other direction, with the intention of reversing this trade to obtain alpha.

Fundamental value These strategies use fundamental analysis to identify undervalued and unloved companies for which there is a possibility that a corporate turnaround, with future revenue and cash flow growth, will result in higher valuations.

Fundamental weighting An index weighting method in which the weight assigned to each constituent security is based on its underlying company's size. It attempts to address the disadvantages of market-capitalization weighting by using measures that are independent of the constituent security's price.

Fungible Freely exchangeable, interchangeable, or substitutable with other things of the same type. Money and commodities are the most common examples.

Futures contract A variation of a forward contract that has essentially the same basic definition but with some additional features, such as a clearinghouse guarantee against credit losses, a daily settlement of gains and losses, and an organized electronic or floor trading facility.

Futures contract basis point value (BPV) The change in price of a futures contract given a 1 basis point (0.01%) change in yield.

Futures margin account An account held by an exchange clearinghouse for each derivatives counterparty. The funds in such an account are used to ensure that counterparties do not default on their contract obligation.

Futures price The pre-agreed price at which a futures contract buyer (seller) agrees to pay (receive) for the underlying at the maturity date of the futures contract.

FX swap The combination of a spot and a forward FX transaction.

G-spread Yield spread in basis points between a bond's yield-to-maturity and that of an actual or interpolated government bond. It represents the return for bearing risks relative to the government bond.

Game theory The set of tools decision makers use to incorporate responses by rival decision makers into their strategies.

Gamma A numerical measure of how sensitive an option's delta (the sensitivity of the derivative's price) is to a change in the value of the underlying.

Gate A provision that when implemented limits or restricts redemptions for a period of time.

General collateral repo Rather than involving a specific security, a repo that instead references a specific group of securities as eligible collateral (such as government bonds of a specific maturity).

General collateral repo rate The interest rate on a general collateral repo.

General obligation (GO) bonds Unsecured bonds issued by a non-sovereign government which are backed by the taxing authority of the issuer.

General obligation bonds Also known as GO bonds. Bonds issued by non-sovereign governments for general purposes and repaid from tax cash flows.

General partners (GPs) Private fund managers responsible for sourcing and deploying capital from limited partner investors over an investment life cycle and distributing returns to those investors over a finite investment holding period.

General partnership A business organizational form owned entirely by general partners.

Geophysical resource endowment Includes such factors as livable geography and climate as well as access to food and water, which are necessary for sustainable growth. Geophysical resource endowment is highly unequal among countries.

Geopolitics The study of how geography affects politics and international relations. These relations matter for investments because they contribute to important drivers of investment performance, including economic growth, business performance, market volatility, and transaction costs.

Gilts Bonds issued by the UK government.

Global depository receipt (GDR) A depository receipt that is issued outside of the company's home country and outside of the United States.

Global minimum-variance portfolio The portfolio on the minimum-variance frontier with the smallest variance of return.

Global registered share (GRS) A common share that is traded on different stock exchanges around the world in different currencies.

Globalization The process of interaction and integration among people, companies, and governments worldwide. It is marked by the spread of products, information, jobs, and culture across borders.

Gold standard With respect to a currency, if a currency is on the gold standard a given amount can be converted into a prespecified amount of gold.

Good-on-close An execution instruction specifying that an order can only be filled at the close of trading. Also called *market-on-close.*

Good-on-open An execution instruction specifying that an order can only be filled at the opening of trading.

Good-till-cancelled order An order specifying that it is valid until the entity placing the order has cancelled it (or, commonly, until some specified amount of time such as 60 days has elapsed, whichever comes sooner).

Goodwill An intangible asset that represents the excess of the purchase price of an acquired company over the value of the net identifiable assets acquired.

Governance tokens In permissionless networks, governance tokens serve as votes to determine how the particular network is run.

Government debt management Government policies that relate to the issuance of debt securities, typically handled by a treasurer or finance ministry.

Government equivalent yield Measures quoted using actual/actual day counts.

Grant date The day that terms of compensation are communicated by an issuer and accepted by an employee recipient.

Green bonds Bonds used to specifically finance environmental-related projects.

Greenfield investments New, "to-be-built" infrastructure projects and assets created to provide a specific essential service or to supply a public good.

Gross profit margin The ratio of gross profit to revenues.

Groupthink A behavioral bias that occurs when a team minimizes conflict and dissent in reaching and maintaining a consensus.

Growth cycle Refers to fluctuations in economic activity around the long-term potential trend growth level, focusing on how much actual economic activity is below or above trend growth in economic activity.

Growth option The option to make additional investments in a project at some future time if the financial results are strong. Also called an *expansion option*.

Growth rate cycle Refers to fluctuations in the growth rate of economic activity.

Haircut The difference between the market value of the security used as collateral and the value of the loan. Also called *repo margin*.

Halo effect An emotional bias that extends a favorable evaluation of some characteristics to other characteristics.

Hard commodities Traded natural resources, such as crude oil and metals, with markets often involving the physical delivery of the underlying upon settlement.

Hard hurdle rate Hurdle ratewhere the manager earns fees on annual returns in excess of the hurdle rate

Hard-bullet covered bonds Type of security where if payments do not occur according to the original schedule of a covered bond, a bond default is triggered and bond payments are accelerated.

Harmonic mean A type of weighted mean computed as the reciprocal of the arithmetic average of the reciprocals.

Hedge The **derivative contract** used in **hedging** an exposure.

Hedge accounting Accounting standard(s) that allow an issuer to offset a hedging instrument (usually a derivative) against a hedged transaction or balance sheet item to reduce financial statement volatility.

Hedge funds Private investment vehicles that may invest in public equities or publicly traded fixed-income assets, private capital, and/or real assets, but they are distinguished by their investment *approach* rather than by the investments themselves.

Hedge ratio The proportion of an underlying that will offset the risk associated with a derivative position.

Hedging The use of a derivative contract to offset or neutralize existing or anticipated exposure to an **underlying**.

Hegemony Countries that are regional or even global leaders and use their political or economic influence of others to control resources.

Held-to-maturity Debt (fixed-income) securities that a company intends to hold to maturity; these are presented at their original cost, updated for any amortisation of discounts or premiums.

Herding Clustered trading that may or may not be based on information.

Herfindahl-Hirschman Index (HHI) A measure of market concentration, calculated as the sum of the squares of competitor market shares. Antitrust regulators in some countries consider markets with an HHI between 1,500 and 2,500 moderately concentrated and consider markets with an HHI over 2,500 highly concentrated.

Heteroskedasticity Non-constant variance across all observations.

Hidden order An order that is exposed not to the public but only to the brokers or exchanges that receive it.

Hidden revenue business model Business models that provide services to users at no charge and generate revenues elsewhere.

High yield Bond issuers and issues rated BB+ (Ba1 on Moody's scale) or lower. Also known as speculative grade and junk.

High-water mark The highest value, net of fees, that a fund has reached in history. It reflects the highest cumulative return used to calculate an incentive fee.

Hindsight bias A type of cognitive bias that makes individuals misremember the past in ways that make them appear to have made better and more well-informed choices.

Holder-of-record date The date that a shareholder listed on the corporation's books will be deemed to have ownership of the shares for purposes of receiving an upcoming dividend.

Holding period return The single-period internal rate of return for a real estate property that includes property income and the change in property value over the period.

Home bias A preference for securities listed on the exchanges of one's home country.

Homogeneity of expectations The assumption that all investors have the same economic expectations and thus have the same expectations of prices, cash flows, and other investment characteristics.

Homoskedasticity Constant variance across all observations.

Horizon yield An investor's total rate of return on a fixed income instrument over their holding period, including reinvested coupon payments. It is an internal rate of return expressed as an annualized rate.

Hostile takeover When a potential acquirer seeks to acquire a company (the target) against the wishes of the target's board of directors. Typically, a tender offer is used to carry out the hostile takeover, against which a board might use a poison pill in its defense.

Household A person or a group of people living in the same residence, taken as a basic unit in economic analysis.

Human capital The present value of an individual's future expected labor income.

Hurdle rate Also called "preferred return." The minimum rate of return on investment that a fund must reach before a GP receives carried interest.

Hypothesis A proposed explanation or theory that can be tested.

Hypothesis testing The process of testing of hypotheses about one or more populations using statistical inference.

I-spread also known as interpolated spread, it is the yield spread for a bond over the standard swap rate in that currency of the same tenor.

Iceberg order An order in which the display size is less than the order's full size.

If-converted method A method for accounting for the effect of convertible securities on earnings per share (EPS) that specifies what EPS would have been if the convertible securities had been converted at the beginning of the period, taking account of the effects of conversion on net income and the weighted average number of shares outstanding.

Illusion of control bias A bias in which people tend to believe that they can control or influence outcomes when, in fact, they cannot.

Immediate or cancel order An order that is valid only upon receipt by the broker or exchange. If such an order cannot be filled in part or in whole upon receipt, it cancels immediately. Also called *fill or kill*.

Impact lag The lag associated with the result of actions affecting the economy with delay.

Implied forward rate An interest rate or yield over a future period implied by the current term structure of interest rates.

Import license Specifies the quantity of a good that can be imported into a country.

In-the-money Describes an option with a positive intrinsic value.

Income tax paid The actual amount paid for income taxes in the period; not a provision, but the actual cash outflow.

Income tax payable The income tax owed by the company on the basis of taxable income.

Increasing returns to scale When a production process leads to increases in output that are proportionately larger than the increase in inputs.

Incurrence test A financial ratio or other measurement taken prior to an action such as debt issuance, usually on a pro forma basis taking the action into account. Satisfaction of the test (e.g., leverage ratio below a certain value) is linked to covenants between the issuer and investors.

Indenture A written contract between a lender and borrower that specifies the terms of the loan, such as interest rate, interest payment schedule, or maturity.

Independent With reference to events, the property that the occurrence of one event does not affect the probability of another event occurring. With reference to two random variables X and Y, they are independent if and only if $P(X,Y) = P(X)P(Y)$.

Independent directors Members of a corporation's board of directors who do not have an employment or familial relationship with the company, nor do they have a relationship that would impair their independence such as an economic interest in a vendor or competitor of the company.

Independent variable An explanatory variable in a regression model.

Independently and identically distributed With respect to random variables, the property of random variables that are independent of each other but follow the identical probability distribution.

Index-linked bonds A bond whose coupon payments or principal repayment is linked to a specified index.

Indexing An investment strategy in which an investor constructs a portfolio to mirror the performance of a specified index.

Indicator variable A variable that takes on only one of two values, 0 or 1, based on a condition. In simple linear regression, the slope is the difference in the dependent variable for the two conditions. Also referred to as a *dummy variable*.

Indifference curve A curve representing all the combinations of two goods or attributes such that the consumer is entirely indifferent among them.

Indirect taxes Taxes such as taxes on spending, as opposed to direct taxes.

Inflation premium An extra return that compensates investors for expected inflation.

Inflation reports A type of economic publication put out by many central banks.

Inflation-linked bonds Debt instruments that link the principal and interest to inflation.

Information cascade The transmission of information from those participants who act first and whose decisions influence the decisions of others.

Information-motivated traders Traders that trade to profit from information that they believe allows them to predict future prices.

Informationally efficient market A market in which asset prices reflect new information quickly and rationally.

Infrastructure A type of real asset that is intended for public use and provides essential services. These assets are typically long-lived fixed assets, such as bridges and toll roads.

Initial coin offering (ICO) An unregulated process whereby companies raise capital by selling crypto-tokens to investors in exchange for fiat money or another agreed-upon cryptocurrency.

Initial margin The ratio of the price of collateral to the value of cash exchanged in a repo; a value over 1.0 or 100% indicates overcollateralization.

Initial margin requirement The margin requirement on the first day of a transaction as well as on any day in which additional margin funds must be deposited.

Initial public offering (IPO) The first issuance of common shares to the public by a formerly private corporation.

Inside directors Members of a corporation's board of directors who are not independent. Typically, inside directors are employees or founders (and their family) of the company.

Insolvency A situation in which an issuer's total liabilities exceed the market value of its assets.

Institution An established organization or practice in a society or culture. An institution can be a formal structure, such as a university, organization, or process backed by law; or it can be informal, such as a custom or behavioral pattern important to society. Institutions can, but need not be, formed by national governments. Examples of institutions include non-governmental organizations, charities, religious customs, family units, the media, political parties, and educational practice.

Intangible assets Assets without a physical form, such as patents and trademarks.

Interbank market The market of loans and deposits between banks for maturities ranging from overnight to one year.

Intercept The estimated value of the dependent variable when the independent variable is zero.

Interest coverage A solvency ratio calculated as EBIT divided by interest payments.

Interest coverage ratio A measure of an issuer's ability to service its debt, typically the ratio of operating income or EBIT to interest expense.

Interest rate A rate of return that reflects the relationship between differently dated cash flows; a discount rate.

Interest rate swap A swap in which the underlying is an interest rate. Can be viewed as a currency swap in which both currencies are the same and can be created as a combination of currency swaps.

Interest-indexed bond A type of index-linked bond for which changes in the index are captured with adjustments to interest payments.

Internal credit enhancements Provisions or methods a borrower initiates to improve their creditworthiness in a structured transaction, such as overcollateralization or excess spread.

internal rate of return The discount rate that makes net present value equal 0; the discount rate that makes the present value of an investment's costs (outflows) equal to the present value of the investment's benefits (inflows).

Internal rate of return (IRR) The uniform discount rate for a series of cash flows over *n* periods that returns a net present value of zero.

Internet of things The vast array of physical devices, home appliances, smart buildings, vehicles, and other items that are embedded with electronics, sensors, software, and network connections that enable the objects in the system to interact and share information.

Interquartile range The difference between the third and first quartiles of a dataset.

Intrinsic value The amount gained (per unit) by an option buyer if an option is exercised at any given point in time. May be referred to as the exercise value of the option.

Investment banks Financial intermediaries that provide advice to their mostly corporate clients and help them arrange transactions such as initial and seasoned securities offerings.

Investment grade Bond issuers and issues rated BBB- (Baa3 on Moody's scale).

Investment policy statement (IPS) A written planning document that describes a client's investment objectives and risk tolerance over a relevant time horizon, along with constraints that apply to the client's portfolio.

Issue rating A rating which seeks to capture the probability of default or expected loss of the issuer's senior unsecured bonds.

Issuer rating A rating which seeks to capture the credit risk of a specific financial obligation of an issuer which takes such factors as seniority into account.

J-curve effect Net income over a multiyear private investment holding period characterized by negative returns in an initial phase, followed by cash flow and income growth toward the end of the holding period.

Jackknife A resampling method that repeatedly draws samples by taking the original observed data sample and leaving out one observation at a time (without replacement) from the set.

January effect Calendar anomaly that stock market returns in January are significantly higher compared to the rest of the months of the year, with most of the abnormal returns reported during the first five trading days in January. Also called *turn-of-the-year effect*.

Joint probability function A function giving the probability of joint occurrences of values of stated random variables.

Judgmental sampling A procedure of selectively handpicking elements from the population based on a researcher's knowledge and professional judgment.

Junior debt Debt obligation with lower priority of payment than senior debt obligations.

Key rate duration Also known as partial duration, is a measure of a bond's sensitivity to a change in the benchmark yield at a specific maturity.

Keynesians Economists who believe that fiscal policy can have powerful effects on aggregate demand, output, and employment when there is substantial spare capacity in an economy.

Kurtosis The statistical measure that indicates the combined weight of the tails of a distribution relative to the rest of the distribution.

Lagging economic indicators Turning points that take place later than those of the overall economy; they are believed to have value in identifying the economy's past condition.

Law of one price A principle that states that if two investments have the same or equivalent future cash flows regardless of what will happen in the future, then these two investments should have the same current price.

Lead underwriter The lead investment bank in a syndicate of investment banks and broker–dealers involved in a securities underwriting.

Leading economic indicators Turning points that usually precede those of the overall economy; they are believed to have value for predicting the economy's future state, usually near-term.

Legal tender Something that must be accepted when offered in exchange for goods and services.

Lender of last resort An entity willing to lend money when no other entity is ready to do so.

Leptokurtic Describes a distribution that has fatter tails than a normal distribution (also called fat-tailed).

Lessee Tenant or property user that enters a lease with a property owner or lessor.

Lessor Property owner or manager that leases a property to a tenant or property user.

Level of significance The probability of a Type I error in testing a hypothesis.

Leverage A measure for identifying a potentially influential high-leverage point.

Leveraged buyout (LBO) A transaction in which a private acquiror uses equity and a high proportion of debt to acquire a public or private company in order to make changes to increase value over an investment period.

Leveraged loan Where private debt investor firms borrow money to make a direct loan to a borrower.

Leveraged loans Loans made to a borrower or issuer with relatively lower credit quality and/or higher leverage.

Liability-driven investing An investment industry term that generally encompasses asset allocation that is focused on funding an investor's liabilities in institutional contexts.

Licensing arrangements Rights to produce a product or have access to intangible assets using someone else's brand name in return for a royalty (often a percentage of revenues).

Lien A legal right or claim to property by a creditor.

Likelihood The probability of an observation, given a particular set of conditions.

Limit order Instructions to a broker or exchange to obtain the best price immediately available when filling an order, but in no event accept a price higher than a specified (limit) price when buying or accept a price lower than a specified (limit) price when selling.

Limit order book The book or list of limit orders to buy and sell that pertains to a security.

Limited company A business organizational form owned by shareholders or members with limited liability who elect a board of directors to appoint management. Generally, limited companies have indefinite life and easier transfer of ownership interests than limited partnerships.

Limited liability partnership (LLP) A business organizational form available in some jurisdictions owned entirely by limited partners with limited liability.

Limited partners (LPs) Outside investors in a private market fund who own a fractional interest in a limited, closed-end partnership managed by a general partner based on the investment commitment and other terms set out in a limited partner agreement.

Limited partnership Closed-end form of ownership frequently used in private market funds in which private market fund investors, or limited partners, commit capital that is invested, managed, and distributed by a private market fund manager, or general partner, over an investment holding period.

Limited partnership agreement (LPA) A legal document that outlines the rules of the partnership and establishes the framework that ultimately guides the fund's operations throughout its life.

lin-log model A functional form for transforming regression model data in which the dependent variable is linear but the independent variable is logarithmic.

Linear derivatives Firm commitment derivative contracts in which the contract's payoff/profit function is linear with respect to the price of the underlying.

Liquid market Said of a market in which traders can buy or sell with low total transaction costs when they want to trade.

Liquidity The extent to which a company is able to meet its short-term obligations using cash flows and those assets that can be readily transformed into cash.

Liquidity premium The compensation for liquidity risk that increases in proportion to the investment's illiquidity.

Liquidity ratios Financial ratios measuring the company's ability to meet its short-term obligations to creditors as they come due.

Liquidity risk The risk that an investment may not be readily sold at its true value.

Liquidity trap A condition in which the demand for money becomes infinitely elastic (horizontal demand curve) so that injections of money into the economy will not lower interest rates or affect real activity.

Load fund A mutual fund in which, in addition to the annual fee, a percentage fee is charged to invest in the fund and/or for redemptions from the fund.

Loan-to-value ratio (LTV) Ratio of the amount of the mortgage to the property's value. The lower the LTV, the higher the borrower's equity. From the lender's perspective, the higher the borrower's equity, the less likely the borrower is to default.

Loans Debt instruments agreed to between a borrower and lender, typically a bank.

Lockout or revolving period For an ABS with a non-amortizing collateral pool, such as credit card debt, is the period in which the cash proceeds from principal repayments are reinvested in additional loans with a principal equal to the principal repaid. During this period, there is no prepayment risk and potential default risk is generally limited. When the lockout period is over, principal repayments are used to pay off the outstanding principal on the ABS. Lockout period and revolving period are interchangeable.

Lockup period The minimum holding period before investors are allowed to make withdrawals or redeem shares from a fund. Its purpose is to allow the hedge fund manager the required time to implement and potentially realize a strategy's expected results.

log-lin model A functional form for transforming regression model data in which the dependent variable is logarithmic but the independent variable is linear.

log-log model A functional form for transforming regression model data in which both the dependent and independent variables are in logarithmic form.

Long A trading position in a **derivative contract** that gains value as the price of the **underlying** moves higher.

Long position A position in an asset or contract in which one owns the asset or has an exercisable right under the contract.

Long-run average total cost The curve describing average total cost when no costs are considered fixed.

Loss aversion The tendency of people to dislike losses more than they like comparable gains.

Loss given default (LGD) The amount a debtholder fails to recover if a default occurs, usually expressed as a percentage of par value.

Loss severity Portion of a bond's value (including unpaid interest) an investor loses in the event of default.

Loss-aversion bias A bias in which people tend to strongly prefer avoiding losses as opposed to achieving gains.

Low-cost producer A firm with lower production costs than its industry competitors.

M^2 A measure of what a portfolio would have returned if it had taken on the same total risk as the market index.

M^2 alpha Difference between the risk-adjusted performance of the portfolio and the performance of the benchmark.

Macaulay duration the present-value weighted average time to receipt of cash flows for fixed-income instrument, also the holding period needed to balance coupon reinvestment risk and price risk for a one-time instantaneous "parallel" shift in the yield curve once the bond purchase is settled. It is named after Frederick Macaulay, the Canadian economist who introduced the concept in 1938.

Machine learning (ML) Involves computer-based techniques that seek to extract knowledge from large amounts of data without making any assumptions about the data's underlying probability distribution. The goal of ML algorithms is to automate decision-making processes by generalizing, or "learning," from known examples to determine an underlying structure in the data.

Maintenance capital expenditures Investments in assets to keep them in operation or increase their efficiency without extending their useful lives.

Maintenance margin Minimum balance set below the initial margin that each contract buyer and seller must hold in the futures margin account from trade initiation until final settlement at maturity.

Maintenance margin requirement The margin requirement on any day other than the first day of a transaction.

Management buy-in A type of leveraged buyout where the current management team is replaced with the acquiring team involved in managing the company.

Management buyout A private sale to a strategic buyer that includes a company's existing management. The management team commits their own equity capital along with other investors as an incentive to grow the firm's cash flows and value.

Management guidance Management of public companies may publicly provide targets for earnings, revenues, and other measures (e.g., capital expenditures) for the next quarter, year, or longer term. Guidance can be detailed or rather directional and is often updated throughout the year. Initial guidance for next fiscal year might be provided during the fourth-quarter earnings call and updated for completed quarters, and new information provided at the first-, second-, and third-quarter earnings calls. Also known simply as *guidance*.

Margin call Request to a derivatives contract counterparty to immediately deposit funds to return the futures margin account balance to the initial margin.

Margin financing A financing arrangement whereby the prime broker lends shares, bonds, or derivatives and the hedge fund (or investment manager) deposits cash or other collateral into a margin account at the prime broker based on certain fractions of the investment positions.

Margin loan Money borrowed from a broker to purchase securities.

Marginal propensity to consume The proportion of an additional unit of disposable income that is consumed or spent; the change in consumption for a small change in income.

Marginal propensity to save The proportion of an additional unit of disposable income that is saved (not spent).

Mark to market (MTM) The practice in which a central clearing party assigns profits and losses to counterparties to derivative contracts. In exchange-traded markets, this practice takes place daily and is often referred to as daily settlement.

Market anomaly Change in the price or return of a security that cannot directly be linked to current relevant information known in the market or to the release of new information into the market.

Market bid–ask spread The difference between the best bid and the best offer.

Market discount rate The rate of return required by investors given the risk of the bond investment, also known as the required yield or required rate of return.

Market float The number of shares that are available to the investing public.

Market makers **Over-the-counter (OTC) dealers** who typically enter into offsetting bilateral transactions with one another to transfer risk to other parties.

Market model A regression model with the return on a stock as the dependent variable and the returns on a market index as the independent variable.

Market multiple models Valuation models based on share price multiples or enterprise value multiples.

Market neutral These strategies use quantitative, fundamental, and technical analysis to identify under- and overvalued equity securities. The hedge fund takes long positions in undervalued securities and short positions in overvalued securities, while seeking to maintain a market-neutral net position.

Market order Instructions to a broker or exchange to obtain the best price immediately available when filling an order.

Market reference rate (MRR) The interest rate underlying used in interest rate swaps. These rates typically match those of loans or other short-term obligations. Survey-based Libor rates used as reference rates in the past have been replaced by rates based on a daily average of observed market transaction rates. For example, the Secured Overnight Financing Rate (SOFR) is an overnight cash borrowing rate collateralized by US Treasuries. Other MRRs include the euro short-term rate (€STR) and the Sterling Overnight Index Average (SONIA).

Market risk Risk related to market movements, e.g., unexpected changes in share prices, interest rates, currency exchange rates, and commodity prices.

Market share A company's or product's revenue expressed as a percentage of its market size.

Market size Total sales for a good or service, which can be calculated on a global or more regional basis.

Market value The price at which an asset or security can currently be bought or sold in an open market.

Market-capitalization weighting An index weighting method in which the weight assigned to each constituent security is determined by dividing its market capitalization by the total market capitalization (sum of the market capitalization) of all securities in the index. Also called *value weighting*.

Market-on-close An execution instruction specifying that an order can only be filled at the close of trading.

Marketable limit order A buy limit order in which the limit price is placed above the best offer, or a sell limit order in which the limit price is placed below the best bid. Such orders generally will partially or completely fill right away.

Markowitz efficient frontier The graph of the set of portfolios offering the maximum expected return for their level of risk (standard deviation of return).

Master limited partnership (MLP) Has similar features to limited partnerships but is usually a more liquid investment that is often publicly traded.

Master repurchase agreement A legal document governing all repo trades between two parties.

Match funding Financing an asset with a source, such as a loan or bond, that is aligned with certain attributes of the asset, such as duration and the respective streams of income and financing costs.

Material (materiality) Refers to information that is decision-useful for a reasonable investor.

Matrix pricing An estimation process for financial instruments based on the prices of comparable instruments.

Maturity The date of a fixed-income instrument's final payment to investors.

Maturity premium An extra return that compensates investors for the increased sensitivity of the market value of debt to a change in market interest rates as maturity is extended.

Maturity structure of interest rates Also known as the term structure of interest rates, refers to the difference in interest rates or benchmark yields by time-to-maturity.

Mean absolute deviation With reference to a sample, the mean of the absolute values of deviations from the sample mean.

Mean square error (MSE) Calculated as the sum of squares error (SSE) divided by the degrees of freedom, which are the number of observations minus the number of independent variables minus one. Since simple linear regression has just one independent variable, the degrees of freedom calculation is the number of observations minus 2.

Mean square regression (MSR) Calculated as the sum of squares regression (SSR) divided by the number of independent variables in the regression model. In simple linear regression, there is only one independent variable, so MSR equals SSR.

Mean–variance analysis An approach to portfolio analysis using expected means, variances, and covariances of asset returns.

Measure of central tendency A quantitative measure that specifies where data are centered.

Measures of location Quantitative measures that describe the location or distribution of data. They include not only measures of central tendency but also other measures, such as percentiles.

Median The "middlemost" observation; i.e., in a set of observations that has been ranked from highest to lowest, the median will lie in the middle.

Meme coin A type of altcoin that is often inspired by a joke.

Mental accounting bias An information-processing bias in which people treat one sum of money differently from another equal-sized sum based on which mental account the money is assigned to.

Merger arbitrage Special situations investments related to business combinations in which investors seek to capitalize on price discrepancies of securities issued by the target company.

Mesokurtic Describes a distribution with kurtosis equal to that of the normal distribution, namely, kurtosis equal to three.

Mezzanine debt Refers to private credit subordinated to senior secured debt but senior to equity in the borrower's capital structure.

Mezzanine-stage financing Mezzanine venture capital that prepares a company to go public as it continues to expand capacity and enhance its growth trajectory. It represents the bridge financing needed to fund a private firm until it can execute an IPO or be sold.

Miner A validator of transactions on the blockchain that locks blocks of transactions into the blockchain and receives compensation for this process in the form of a digital asset.

Minimum efficient scale The smallest output that a firm can produce such that its long-run average total cost is minimized.

Minimum-variance portfolio The portfolio with the minimum variance for each given level of expected return.

Minority shareholder An individual or entity that owns less than a majority of the voting rights in a corporation.

Mode The most frequently occurring value in a distribution.

Modern portfolio theory (MPT) The analysis of rational portfolio choices based on the efficient use of risk.

Modified duration The first derivative of a bond's price with respect to its yield, this statistic is a measure of interest rate risk used to estimate the percentage price change for a given change in yield-to-maturity.

Monetarists Economists who believe that the rate of growth of the money supply is the primary determinant of the rate of inflation.

Monetary policy Actions taken by a nation's central bank to affect aggregate output and prices through changes in bank reserves, reserve requirements, or its target interest rate.

Monetary transmission mechanism The process whereby a central bank's interest rate gets transmitted through the economy and ultimately affects the rate of increase of prices.

Monetary union An economic union in which the members adopt a common currency.

Money convexity A measure that is used to complement modified duration to capture the second-order effect of yield changes on a bond's price, expressed in currency terms.

Money duration A measure of the price change of a fixed-income instrument in currency units from a change in yield-to-maturity. The money duration can be stated per 100 of par value or in terms of the actual position size. In the United States, money duration is commonly called "dollar duration."

Money market The market for short-term debt instruments (one-year maturity or less).

Money market securities Fixed-income securities with original maturities of one year or less.

Money-weighted return The internal rate of return on a portfolio, taking account of all cash flows.

Moneyness Expresses the relationship between an option's value and its exercise price across the full range of possible underlying prices.

Monopolistic competition Highly competitive form of imperfect competition; the competitive characteristic is a notably large number of firms, while the monopoly aspect is the result of product differentiation.

Monopoly In pure monopoly markets, there are no substitutes for the given product or service. There is a single seller, which exercises considerable power over pricing and output decisions.

Monte Carlo simulation A technique that uses the inverse transformation method for converting a randomly generated uniformly distributed number into a simulated value of a random variable of a desired distribution. Each key decision variable in a Monte Carlo simulation requires an assumed statistical distribution; this assumption facilitates incorporating non-normality, fat tails, and tail dependence as well as solving high-dimensionality problems.

Moral principles Beliefs regarding what is good, acceptable, or obligatory behavior and what is bad, unacceptable, or forbidden behavior.

Mortgage loan Agreement to finance real estate by the collateral of a specified property that obliges the borrower to make a predetermined series of payments to the lender.

Mortgage pass-through security Security created when mortgage lenders pool mortgages together and sell securities to investors. The cash flow from the mortgage pool--monthly payments of principal, interest, and prepayments--are "passed through" to the security holders.

Mortgage-backed securities (MBS) Debt obligations that represent claims to the cash flows from pools of mortgage loans, most commonly on residential property.

Multi-factor model A model that explains a variable in terms of the values of a set of factors.

Multi-market indexes Comprised of indexes from different countries, designed to represent multiple security markets.

Multilateral trading facilities See *alternative trading systems*.

Multilateralism The conduct of countries who participate in mutually beneficial trade relationships and extensive rules harmonization. Private firms are fully integrated into global supply chains with multiple trade partners. Examples of multilateral countries include Germany and Singapore.

Multiple of invested capital (MOIC) Also referred to as the multiple of money or total value to paid-in, this private market performance measure incorporates both the cumulative distributions received and the net asset value of a fund as a proportion of invested capital.

Multiple-price auction A debt securities auction in which bidders receive distinct prices based on their bids.

Multiplier models Valuation models based on share price multiples or enterprise value multiples.

Mutual fund A comingled investment pool in which investors in the fund each have a pro-rata claim on the income and value of the fund.

Nash equilibrium When two or more participants in a non-coop-erative game have no incentive to deviate from their respective equilibrium strategies given their opponent's strategies.

Nationalism The promotion of a country's own economic interests to the exclusion or detriment of the interests of other nations. Nationalism is marked by limited economic and financial cooperation. These actors may focus on national production and sales, limited cross-border investment and capital flows, and restricted currency exchange.

Natural language processing (NLP) A field of research within the field of text analytics and at the intersection of computer science, AI, and linguistics that focuses on developing computer programs to analyze and interpret human language.

Natural resources These include commodities (hard and soft), agricultural land (farmland), and timberland.

Negative externalities A cost to a third party because of the production or consumption of a good or service.

Negative pledge clause Limitations on investments, the disposal of assets, or issuance of debt senior to existing obligations. Negative covenants seek to ensure that an issuer maintains the ability to make interest and principal payments.

Net cash An issuer's total debt less cash and marketable securities. When the balance is negative it is referred to as net cash.

Net debt An issuer's total debt less cash and marketable securities. When the balance is positive it is referred to as net debt.

Net investment hedge Refers to a specific **hedge accounting** designation that applies when either a foreign currency bond or a derivative, such as an FX swap or forward, is used to offset the exchange rate risk of the equity of a foreign operation.

Net present value (NPV) The present value of an investment's cash inflows (benefits) minus the present value of its cash outflows (costs).

Net profit margin An indicator of profitability, calculated as net income divided by revenue; indicates how much of each dollar of revenues is left after all costs and expenses. Also called *profit margin* or *return on sales*.

Net tax rate The tax rate net of transfer payments.

Net working capital Working capital excluding short-term items unrelated to business operations, such as cash, marketable securities, and short-term debt.

Network effects A business model that enables users to contribute directly to a product, service, or online content.

Neural networks A type of computer program design based on how the human brain learns and processes information.

Neutral rate of interest The rate of interest that neither spurs on nor slows down the underlying economy.

No-load fund A mutual fund in which there is no fee for investing in the fund or for redeeming fund shares, although there is an annual fee based on a percentage of the fund's net asset value.

Node Each value on a binomial tree from which successive moves or outcomes branch.

Non-agency RMBS MBS backed by residential mortgages that are issued by private entities and not guaranteed by a federal agency or a GSE.

Non-amortizing loans Type of debt where there are no scheduled principal repayments.

Non-cooperative country A country with inconsistent and even arbitrary rules; restricted movement of goods, services, people, and capital across borders; retaliation; and limited technology exchange.

Non-cumulative preference shares Preference shares for which dividends that are not paid in the current or subsequent periods are forfeited permanently (instead of being accrued and paid at a later date).

Non-financial risks Risks that arise from sources other than changes in the external financial markets, such as changes in accounting rules, legal environment, or tax rates.

Non-fungible token (NFT) A unique cryptographic token on the blockchain that cannot be replicated and is used to represent ownership of physical assets, such as artwork, real estate, or other assets.

Non-linear derivatives Derivatives, such as options or other contingent claims, with payoff/profit profiles that are non-linear (asymmetric) with respect to the price of the underlying.

Non-participating preference shares Preference shares that do not entitle shareholders to share in the profits of the company. Instead, shareholders are only entitled to receive a fixed dividend payment and the par value of the shares in the event of liquidation.

Non-probability sampling A sampling plan dependent on factors other than probability considerations, such as a sampler's judgment or the convenience to access data.

Non-recourse loan Loan in which the lender does not have a claim against the borrower and thus can look only to the property to recover the outstanding mortgage balance.

Non-state actors Those that participate in global political, economic, or financial affairs but do not directly control national security or country resources. Examples of non-state actors are non-governmental organizations (NGOs), multinational companies, charities, and even influential individuals, such as business leaders or cultural icons.

Nonparametric test A test that is not concerned with a parameter or that makes minimal assumptions about the population from which a sample comes.

Nonsystematic risk Unique risk that is local or limited to a particular asset or industry that need not affect assets outside of that asset class.

Normal distribution A continuous, symmetric probability distribution that is completely described by its mean and its variance.

Normalized earnings The expected level of mid-cycle earnings for a company in the absence of any unusual or temporary factors that affect profitability (either positively or negatively).

Notching Ratings adjustment methodology where specific issues from the same borrower may be assigned different credit ratings.

Notice period The length of time (typically 30–90 days) in advance that investors may be required to notify a fund of their intent to redeem some or all of their investment. This allows a fund manager to liquidate a position in an orderly fashion without magnifying losses.

Novation process A process that substitutes the initial **swap execution facility (SEF)** contract with identical trades facing the **central counterparty (CCP)**. The CCP serves as **counterparty** for both financial intermediaries, eliminating bilateral **counterparty credit risk** and providing **clearing** and **settlement** services.

Null hypothesis The hypothesis that is tested.

Off-the-run Seasoned government bonds that are often less liquid.

Off-the-run securities Sovereign debt securities outstanding other than on-the-sun securities. Off-the-run securities are less liquid than on-the-run securities.

Offer The price at which a dealer or trader is willing to sell an asset, typically qualified by a maximum quantity (ask size).

Official interest rate An interest rate that a central bank sets and announces publicly; normally the rate at which it is willing to lend money to the commercial banks. Also called *official policy rate* or *policy rate.*

Official policy rate An interest rate that a central bank sets and announces publicly; normally the rate at which it is willing to lend money to the commercial banks.

Oligopoly Market structure with a relatively small number of firms supplying the market.

Omnichannel Refers to a company selling its products or services in multiple channels, such as in store and online.

On-the-run Most recently issued, and liquid, government bonds.

On-the-run securities The most recently issued and liquid sovereign debt securities.

Open interest The number of outstanding contracts.

Open market operations The purchase or sale of bonds by the national central bank to implement monetary policy. The bonds traded are usually sovereign bonds issued by the national government.

Open-end fund A mutual fund that accepts new investment money and issues additional shares at a value equal to the net asset value of the fund at the time of investment.

Operating cycle The length of time between a company's acquisition of goods or raw materials and the collection of cash from sales to customers.

Operating efficiency ratios Ratios that measure how efficiently a company performs day-to-day tasks, such as the collection of receivables and management of inventory.

Operating leases A type of lease which is more akin to the rental of the underlying asset.

Operating leverage The sensitivity of a firm's operating profit to a change in revenues, determined by the composition of fixed and variable operating costs.

Operating profit margin A profitability ratio calculated as operating income (i.e., income before interest and taxes) divided by revenue. Also called *operating margin.*

Operational deposits Bank deposits generated by clearing, custody, and cash management activities.

Operational independence A bank's ability to execute monetary policy and set interest rates in the way it thought would best meet the inflation target.

Operational risk The risk that arises from inadequate or failed people, systems, and internal policies, procedures, and processes, as well as from external events that are beyond the control of the organization but that affect its operations.

Operationally efficient Said of a market, a financial system, or an economy that has relatively low transaction costs.

Opportunistic real estate strategies Include major redevelopment, repurposing of assets, taking on large vacancies, or speculating on significant improvement in market conditions. These may be appealing for investors seeking higher returns and willing to accept additional risks from development, redevelopment, repositioning, and leasing.

Opportunity cost Reflects the foregone opportunity of investing in a different asset. It is typically denoted by the risk-free rate of interest, *r*.

Optimal capital structure The capital structure at which the value of the company is maximized.

Option A primary example of a **contingent claim**. A **derivative contract** that provides the buyer the right, but not the obligation, to buy or sell an **underlying**.

Option contract See *option.*

Option premium An amount that is paid upfront from the option buyer to the option seller. Reflects the value of the option buyer's right to exercise in the future.

Option-adjusted price The sum of a bond's flat price and value of an embedded option.

Option-adjusted spread or OAS for a bond is its Z-spread adjusted for the value of an embedded option.

Option-adjusted yield A yield measure for a bond adjusted for embedded options.

Order A specification of what instrument to trade, how much to trade, and whether to buy or sell.

Order precedence hierarchy With respect to the execution of orders to trade, a set of rules that determines which orders execute before other orders.

Order-driven markets A market (generally an auction market) that uses rules to arrange trades based on the orders that traders submit; in their pure form, such markets do not make use of dealers.

Ordinary shares Equity shares that are subordinate to all other types of equity (e.g., preferred equity). Also called *common stock* or *common shares.*

Organizational form A legal and tax classification of a business, specific to a jurisdiction, that determines the organization's legal identity, owner–manager relationship, owner liability, taxation, and access to financing.

Out-of-the-money Describes an option with zero intrinsic value because the option buyer would not rationally exercise the option. An example of such would be the case in which the price of the underlying is less than the option's exercise price for a call option.

Over-the-counter (OTC) Refers to derivative markets in which **derivative contracts** are created and traded between derivatives end users and **dealers**, or financial intermediaries, such as commercial banks or investment banks.

Overcollateralization Credit enhancement technique where collateral underlying the transaction exceeds the face value of the issued bonds.

Overconfidence bias A bias in which people demonstrate unwarranted faith in their own intuitive reasoning, judgments, and/or cognitive abilities.

Overfitting When a machine learning model learns the input and target dataset too precisely, making the system more likely to discover false relationships or unsubstantiated patterns that will lead to prediction errors.

P-value The smallest level of significance at which the null hypothesis can be rejected.

Par rate A yield-to-maturity that makes the present value of a bond's cash flows equal to par.

Par swap rate The fixed swap rate that equates the present value of all future expected floating cash flows to the present value of fixed cash flows.

Par value The amount of principal on a bond, also known as face value.

Parallel shift When all maturities along a yield curve increase or decrease in yield in the same direction by the same magnitude. A parallel shift in the yield curve is implicitly assumed in analytical duration and convexity.

Parameter A descriptive measure computed from or used to describe a population of data, conventionally represented by Greek letters.

Parametric test Any test (or procedure) concerned with parameters or whose validity depends on assumptions concerning the population generating the sample.

Pari passu clause A covenant or contract clause that ensures a debt obligation is treated the same as the borrower's other senior debt instruments and is not subordinated to similar obligations.

Partially amortizing bond A loan or bond with a payment schedule that calls for partial repayment of principle over the life of the bond, with the remaining principal paid at maturity.

Participating preference shares Preference shares that entitle shareholders to receive the standard preferred dividend plus the opportunity to receive an additional dividend if the company's profits exceed a pre-specified level.

Pass-through businesses Businesses that, by virtue of their organizational form and/or other legal and regulatory attributes, do not pay entity-level taxes on income or loss; income or loss is passed through to owners, who pay personal taxes.

Pass-through rate The coupon rate of a mortgage pass-through security that is received by the investor after administrative charges. It is lower than the weighted average mortgage rate earned on the underlying pool of mortgages because of administrative charges. The pass-through rate that the investor receives is said to be "net interest" or "net coupon."

Passive investment A buy-and-hold approach in which an investor does not make portfolio changes based on short-term expectations of changing market or security performance.

Payable date The day that the company actually mails out (or electronically transfers) a dividend payment.

Payment date The day that the company actually mails out (or electronically transfers) a dividend payment.

Payment-in-kind A bond feature whereby coupon payments can be fully or partially paid in the form of additional issuance or added to the principal amount.

Payments system The system for the transfer of money.

Pearson correlation A parametric measure of the relationship between two variables.

Pecking order theory The theory that managers consider how their actions might be interpreted by outsiders and thereby order their preferences for various forms of corporate financing. Forms of financing that are least visible to outsiders (e.g., internally generated funds) are most preferable to managers, and those that are most visible (e.g., equity issuance) are least preferable.

Penetration pricing A discount pricing approach used when a firm willingly sacrifices margins in order to build scale and market share.

Percentiles Values that divide a distribution into 100 equal parts.

Perfect competition A market structure in which the individual firm has virtually no impact on market price, because it is assumed to be a very small seller among a very large number of firms selling essentially identical products.

Performance evaluation The measurement and assessment of the outcomes of investment management decisions.

Performance fee Fee paid to the general partner from the limited partner(s) based on realized net profits.

Period costs Costs (e.g., executives' salaries) that cannot be directly matched with the timing of revenues and which are thus expensed immediately.

Periodicity Number of periods in a year, used for compound interest. The periodicity of a fixed-income instrument usually matches the frequency of its coupon payments.

Permanent differences Differences between tax and financial reporting of revenue (expenses) that will not be reversed at some future date. These result in a difference between the company's effective tax rate and statutory tax rate and do not result in a deferred tax item.

Permissioned networks Networks that are fully open only to select participants on a DLT network.

Permissionless networks Networks that are fully open to any user on a DLT network.

Perpetual bonds Bonds with no stated maturity date.

Perpetuity A perpetual annuity, or a set of never-ending level sequential cash flows, with the first cash flow occurring one period from now.

PESTLE analysis A framework for analyzing factors that influence an industry's economic outcomes.

Pet projects A capital investment that is pursued by management but is not economically justifiable by a disinterested party. Motivations for pet projects include self-dealing and vanity.

Physical risks Economic and financial losses from the increase in the severity and frequency of extreme weather due to climate change—for example, the loss of coastal real estate from a storm.

PIPE (private investment in public equity) A private offering to select investors with fewer disclosures and lower transaction costs that allows the issuer to raise capital more quickly and cost effectively.

Platykurtic Describes a distribution that has relatively less weight in the tails than the normal distribution (also called thin-tailed).

Pledge A legal right or claim to property by a creditor. Also called a lien.

Poison pill Officially known as a shareholder rights plan, a poison pill is a hostile-takeover defense adopted by boards of directors according to rules specified in the corporate charter. There are several types of poison pills. Generally, they allow shareholders, *excluding* the shareholder making the hostile bid and their affiliates, to buy newly issued shares at a discounted price. The share issuance would dilute the bidder's ownership percentage, rendering it impossible for the bidder to attain control.

Policy rate An interest rate that a central bank sets and announces publicly; normally the rate at which it is willing to lend money to the commercial banks.

Portfolio companies The individual companies owned by a private equity firm.

Portfolio investment flows Short-term investments in foreign assets, such as stocks or bonds.

Portfolio planning The process of creating a plan for building a portfolio that is expected to satisfy a client's investment objectives.

Position The quantity of an asset that an entity owns or owes.

Posterior probability An updated probability that reflects or comes after new information.

Power of a test The probability of correctly rejecting the null—that is, rejecting the null hypothesis when it is false.

Pre-funding period Allows the trust to acquire during a certain period of time after the close of the transaction.

Preference shares A type of equity interest which ranks above common shares with respect to the payment of dividends and the distribution of the company's net assets upon liquidation. They have characteristics of both debt and equity securities. Also called *preferred stock*.

Preferred stock See *preference shares*.

Premium In the case of bonds, premium refers to the amount by which a bond is priced above its face (par) value. In the case of an option, the amount paid for the option contract.

Prepayment option May entitle the borrower to prepay all or part of the outstanding mortgage principal prior to maturity. This creates a risk from the lender's or investor's viewpoint because the cash flow amounts and timing cannot be known with certainty.

Prepayment risk The risk that the some or all of a mortgage-backed security's principal is repaid at a different speed than expected, either in the form of contraction risk (or earlier repayment than expected) or extension risk (later repayment).

Present value models Valuation models that estimate the intrinsic value of a security as the present value of the future benefits expected to be received from the security. Also called *discounted cash flow models*.

Pretax margin A profitability ratio calculated as earnings before taxes divided by revenue.

Price discrimination A pricing approach that charges different prices to different customers based on their willingness to pay.

Price index Represents the average prices of a basket of goods and services.

Price limits Establish a band relative to the previous day's settlement price within which all trades must occur.

Price multiple A ratio that compares the share price with some sort of monetary flow or value to allow evaluation of the relative worth of a company's stock.

Price priority The principle that the highest priced buy orders and the lowest priced sell orders execute first.

Price return Measures *only* the price appreciation or percentage change in price of the securities in an index or portfolio.

Price return index An index that reflects *only* the price appreciation or percentage change in price of the constituent securities. Also called *price index*.

Price stability In economics, refers to an inflation rate that is low on average and not subject to wide fluctuation.

Price takers Producers that must accept whatever price the market dictates.

Price value of a basis point (PVBP) An estimate of the change in the full price of a bond given a 1 bp change in its yield-to-maturity. The PVBP is also called the "PV01," standing for the "price value of an 01" or "present value of an 01," where "01" means 1 bp. In the United States, it is commonly called the "DV01" for the "dollar value" of 1 bp.

Price weighting An index weighting method in which the weight assigned to each constituent security is determined by dividing its price by the sum of all the prices of the constituent securities.

Price-setting option The option to adjust prices when demand or supply varies from what is forecast.

Price-to-earnings ratio (P/E) The ratio of share price to earnings per share.

Pricing power A company's ability to set prices and other economic terms with customers without affecting its sales volumes.

Primary bond markets Fixed-income markets comprised of issuers issuing bonds to investors to raise capital, often intermediated by a third-party such as an investment bank.

Primary capital markets (primary markets) The market where securities are first sold and the issuers receive the proceeds.

Primary dealer Financial institution that is authorized to deal in new issues of sovereign bonds and that serves primarily as a trading counterparty of the office responsible for issuing sovereign bonds.

Primary market The market where securities are first sold and the issuers receive the proceeds.

Prime broker A broker that provides services that commonly include custody, administration, lending, short borrowing, and trading.

Prime loans Lending made to borrowers of high credit quality with strong employment and credit histories, a low DTI, substantial equity in the underlying property, and a first lien on the mortgaged property serving as the collateral for the loan.

Principal The amount that an issuer agrees to repay the debtholders on the maturity date.

Principal-agent relationship An arrangement in which one party (the agent) has authority to act for or on behalf of another party (the principal). Such an arrangement imposes a duty on the agent to act in the principal's best interest.

Prior probabilities Probabilities reflecting beliefs prior to the arrival of new information.

Priority of claims Priority of payment, with the most senior or highest ranking debt having the first claim on the cash flows and assets of the issuer.

Private capital Funding provided to companies that is not sourced from the public markets.

Private company A company, typically a limited company, that does not list its equity securities on an exchange.

Private debt Capital extended to companies through a loan or other form of debt.

Private debtholders Investors in an entity's non-securitized debt claims, such as a loan or lease. The most common type of private debtholder is a bank.

Private equity Equity investment capital raised from sources other than public markets and traditional institutions.

Private equity fund A hedge fund that seeks to buy, optimize, and ultimately sell portfolio companies to generate profits. See *venture capital fund*.

Private equity securities Securities that are not listed on public exchanges and have no active secondary market. They are issued primarily to institutional investors via non-public offerings, such as private placements.

Private investment in public equity (PIPE) An investment in the equity of a publicly traded firm that is made at a discount to the market value of the firm's shares.

Private limited company A type of limited company in many jurisdictions with pass-through taxation but restrictions on the number of shareholders or members and on the transfer of ownership interest.

Private placement A sale of debt or equity securities to a small group of investors on an unregulated basis. The terms of the offering are negotiated by the issuer and investors.

Probability of default (POD) The likelihood that a borrower fails to make full and timely payments of principal and interest according to debt terms, usually expressed in annual percentage terms.

Probability sampling A sampling plan that allows every member of the population to have an equal chance of being selected.

Probability tree diagram A diagram with branches emanating from nodes representing either mutually exclusive chance events or mutually exclusive decisions.

Production flexibility option The option to alter production when demand varies from what is forecast.

Profession An occupational group that has specific education, expert knowledge, and a framework of practice and behavior that underpins community trust, respect, and recognition.

Profit margin An indicator of profitability, calculated as net income divided by revenue; indicates how much of each dollar of revenues is left after all costs and expenses.

Profitability ratios Ratios that measure a company's ability to generate profitable sales from its resources (assets).

Prospectus Legal document in securitization that describes the structure of the transaction, including the priority and amount of payments to be made to the servicer, administrators, and the ABS holders, as well as the credit enhancements used in the securitization.

Protective put A strategy of purchasing an underlying asset and purchasing a put on the same asset.

Proxy contest When a shareholder or group of shareholders campaigns for certain matters they have submitted to a shareholder vote, often a slate of directors who oppose the incumbent board and management. The incumbent board and management simultaneously campaign for their side.

Proxy voting A form of casting a ballot in an election in which a voter authorizes a representative to vote on their behalf according to instructions. In corporate elections, proxy ballots are cast by shareholders that direct a representative, typically the corporate secretary, to enter their votes as instructed.

Public (listed) company A company with its equity securities traded on an exchange.

Public limited companies A type of limited company in many jurisdictions with entity-level taxation but no restrictions on the number of shareholders or transferability of ownership interest; the most suitable organizational form for a company that seeks to go public.

Public–private partnership A long-term contractual relationship between the public and private sectors for the purpose of having the private sector deliver a project or service traditionally provided by the public sector. Infrastructure is increasingly being financed privately through public–private partnerships by local, regional, and national governments.

Public–private partnership (PPP) An agreement between the public sector and the private sector to finance, build, and operate public infrastructure, such as hospitals and toll roads.

Pull on liquidity An action or event that accelerates cash outflows.

Purchase agreement Legal document in a securitization transaction that outlines the representations and warranties that the seller makes about the assets sold.

Pure discount bonds Bonds that do not pay interest during their life. They are issued at a discount to par value and redeemed at par. Also called zero-coupon bonds.

Put An option that gives the holder the right to sell an underlying asset to another party at a fixed price over a specific period of time.

Put option The right to sell an underlying.

Putable bonds Bonds that give the bondholder the right to sell the bond back to the issuer at a predetermined price on specified dates.

Put–call forward parity Describes the no-arbitrage condition in which at $t = 0$ the present value of the price of a long forward commitment plus the price of the long put must equal the price of the long call plus the price of the risk-free asset (with face value of the exercise price of both the call and the put).

Put–call parity Describes the no-arbitrage condition in which at $t = 0$ the price of the long underlying asset plus the price of the long put must equal the price of the long call plus the price of the risk-free asset (with face value of the exercise price of both the call and the put).

Quantile A value at or below which a stated fraction of the data lies. Also referred to as a fractile.

Quantitative easing An expansionary monetary policy based on aggressive open market purchase operations.

Quartiles Quantiles that divide a distribution into four equal parts.

Quick ratio A measure of liquidity that is the ratio of cash, marketable securities, and receivables to current liabilities.

Quintiles Quantiles that divide a distribution into five equal parts.

Quota rents Profits that foreign producers can earn by raising the price of their goods higher than they would without a quota.

Quotas Government policies that restrict the quantity of a good that can be imported into a country, generally for a specified period of time.

Quote-driven market A market in which dealers acting as principals facilitate trading.

Quoted margin Specified spread of a floating rate instrument over a market reference rate or benchmark.

Range The difference between the maximum and minimum values in a dataset.

Rapid amortization provisions Provisions in receivable ABS that may require early principal amortization if specific events occur. Such provisions are referred to as early amortization and are included to safeguard the credit quality of the issue, particularly during the revolving period.

Razor, razorblade pricing A pricing approach that combines a low price on a piece of equipment and high-margin pricing on repeat-purchase consumables.

Real assets Generally, these are tangible physical assets, such as real estate, infrastructure, and natural resources, but they also include such intangibles as patents, intellectual property, and goodwill. Real assets generate current or expected future cash flows and/or are considered a store of value.

Real estate Includes borrowed or ownership capital in buildings or land. Developed land includes commercial and industrial real estate, residential real estate, and infrastructure.

Real option A right, but not an obligation, for management to make a decision with respect to a capital investment that alters future cash flows from the original forecasted scenario.

Real risk-free interest rate The single-period interest rate for a completely risk-free security if no inflation were expected.

Rebalancing Adjusting the weights of the constituent securities in an index.

Rebalancing policy The set of rules that guide the process of restoring a portfolio's asset class weights to those specified in the strategic asset allocation.

Recapitalization Recapitalization via private equity describes the steps a firm takes to increase or introduce leverage to its portfolio company and pay itself a dividend out of the new capital structure.

Recognition lag The lag in government response to an economic problem resulting from the delay in confirming a change in the state of the economy.

Recourse loan Loan in which the lender has a claim against the borrower for the shortfall (deficiency) between the amount of the outstanding mortgage balance and the proceeds received from the sale of the property.

Recovery rate (RR) The percentage of an outstanding debt claim recovered when an issuer defaults

Redemption fee A fee charged to discourage redemptions and to offset the transaction costs for remaining investors in the fund.

Refinancing rate A type of central bank policy rate.

Regionalism In between the two extremes of bilateralism and multilateralism. In regionalism, a group of countries cooperate with one another. Both bilateralism and regionalism can be conducted at the exclusion of other groups. For example, regional blocs may agree to provide trade benefits to one another and increase barriers for those outside of that group.

Registered bonds Bonds for which ownership is recorded by either name or serial number.

Regression analysis Allows us to test hypotheses about the relationship between two variables, by quantifying the strength of the relationship between the two variables, and to use one variable to make predictions about the other variable.

Regression coefficients The collective term for the intercept and slope coefficients in the regression model.

Regret The feeling that an opportunity has been missed; typically, an expression of *hindsight bias.*

Regret-aversion bias An emotional bias in which people tend to avoid making decisions that will result in action out of fear that the decision will turn out poorly.

Relative dispersion The amount of dispersion relative to a reference value or benchmark.

Reopening Issuing bonds by increasing the size of an existing bond issue with a price significantly different from par.

Replication A strategy in which a derivative's cash flow stream may be recreated using a combination of long or short positions in an underlying asset and borrowing or lending cash.

Repo rate The interest rate on a repurchase agreement.

Representativeness bias A belief perseverance bias in which people tend to classify new information based on past experiences and classifications.

Repurchase agreement (Repo) A form of collateralized loan involving the sale of a security with a simultaneous agreement by the seller to buy back the same security from the purchaser at an agreed-on price and future date. The party who sells the security at the inception of the repurchase agreement and buys it back at maturity is borrowing money from the other party, and the security sold and subsequently repurchased represents the collateral.

Repurchase date The date when the party who sold the security at the inception of a repurchase agreement buys back the security from the cash lending counterparty.

Repurchase price The price at which the party who sold the security at the inception of the repurchase agreement buys back the security from the cash lending counterparty.

Required margin Also known as discount margin. The market-determined yield spread over or under the market reference rate such that a floating-rate loan is priced at par on a rate reset date following issuance.

Required rate of return The rate of return required by investors given the risk of the bond investment, also known as the market discount rate or required yield.

Required yield The rate of return required by investors given the risk of the bond investment, also known as the market discount rate of required rate of return.

Required yield spread The difference in yield-to-maturity between a bond and that of a government benchmark bond with the same or similar time-to-maturity.

Resampling A statistical method that repeatedly draws samples from the original observed data sample for the statistical inference of population parameters.

Reserve currency A currency held by global central banks in significant quantities and widely used to conduct international trade and financial transactions.

Reserve requirement The requirement for banks to hold reserves in proportion to the size of deposits.

Residual The amount of deviation of an observed value of the dependent variable from its estimated value based on the fitted regression line.

Restricted domestic currency A currency with limited convertibility into other currencies due to illiquidity.

Return on assets (ROA) A profitability ratio calculated as net income divided by average total assets; indicates a company's net profit generated per dollar invested in total assets.

Return on equity (ROE) A profitability ratio calculated as net income divided by average shareholders' equity.

Return on invested capital (ROIC) A measure of the profitability of a company relative to the amount of capital invested by the equityholders and debtholders.

Return on sales An indicator of profitability, calculated as net income divided by revenue; indicates how much of each dollar of revenues is left after all costs and expenses. Also referred to as *net profit margin.*

Return-generating model A model that can provide an estimate of the expected return of a security given certain parameters and estimates of the values of the independent variables in the model.

Revenue bonds Bonds issued by non-sovereign governments related to a government sponsored project expected to generate future cash flow as a primary source of repayment.

Reverse repurchase agreement A repurchase agreement viewed from the perspective of the cash lending counterparty.

Reverse stock split A reduction in the number of shares outstanding with a corresponding increase in share price but no change to the company's underlying fundamentals.

Revolving credit agreements The most reliable form of short-term bank borrowing facilities; they are in effect for multiple years (e.g., three to five years) and can have optional medium-term loan features. Also known as *revolvers.*

Rho The change in a given derivative instrument for a given small change in the risk-free interest rate, holding everything else constant. Rho measures the sensitivity of the option to the risk-free interest rate.

Ricardian equivalence An economic theory that implies that it makes no difference whether a government finances a deficit by increasing taxes or issuing debt.

Risk Exposure to uncertainty. The chance of a loss or adverse outcome as a result of an action, inaction, or external event.

Risk averse The assumption that an investor will choose the least risky alternative.

Risk aversion The dislike for risk such that compensation is required in terms of higher expected returns for assuming higher risk.

Risk budgeting The establishment of objectives for individuals, groups, or divisions of an organization that takes into account the allocation of an acceptable level of risk.

Risk exposure The state of being exposed or vulnerable to a risk. The extent to which an organization is sensitive to underlying risks.

Risk governance The top-down process and guidance that directs risk management activities to align with and support the overall enterprise.

Risk management The process of identifying the level of risk an organization wants, measuring the level of risk the organization currently has, taking actions that bring the actual level of risk to the desired level of risk, and monitoring the new actual level of risk so that it continues to be aligned with the desired level of risk.

Risk management framework The infrastructure, process, and analytics needed to support effective risk management in an organization.

Risk premium An extra return expected by investors for bearing some specified risk.

Risk shifting Actions to change the distribution of risk outcomes.

Risk tolerance The level of risk an investor is willing and able to bear.

Risk transfer Strategies implemented to mitigate the impact of specific risks by transferring them to an insurance company.

Risk-neutral pricing A no-arbitrage derivative value established separately from investor views on risk that uses underlying asset volatility and the risk-free rate to calculate the present value of future cash flows.

Risk-neutral probability The computed probability used in binomial option pricing by which the discounted weighted sum of expected values of the underlying equal the current option price. Specifically, this probability is computed using the risk-free rate and assumed up gross return and down gross return of the underlying.

Rollover risk The likelihood that a property owner will lose an existing tenant and forgo income until a new one is found.

Safety-first rules Rules for portfolio selection that focus on the risk that portfolio value or portfolio return will fall below some minimum acceptable level over some time horizon.

Sample correlation coefficient A standardized measure of how two variables in a sample move together. It is the ratio of the sample covariance to the product of the two variables' standard deviations.

Sample covariance A measure of how two variables in a sample move together.

Sample excess kurtosis A sample measure of the degree of a distribution's kurtosis in excess of the normal distribution's kurtosis.

Sample mean The sum of the sample observations divided by the sample size.

Sample skewness A sample measure of the degree of asymmetry of a distribution.

Sample standard deviation The positive square root of the sample variance.

Sample variance The sum of squared deviations around the mean divided by the degrees of freedom.

Sample-size neglect A type of representativeness bias in which financial market participants incorrectly assume that small sample sizes are representative of populations (or "real" data).

Sampling distribution The distribution of all distinct possible values that a statistic can assume when computed from samples of the same size randomly drawn from the same population.

Sampling error The difference between the observed value of a statistic and the estimate resulting from using subsets of the population.

Sampling plan The set of rules used to select a sample.

Saving deposits Bank deposits typically held for non-transactional purposes that often have a stated term.

Scatter plot A two-dimensional graphical plot of paired observations of values for the independent and dependent variables in a simple linear regression.

Scenario analysis A variation of the valuation process combining a base case with alternative outcomes, allowing the incorporation of more favorable or adverse scenarios in the valuation process.

Scraping An automated, large-scale, algorithm-driven approach that retrieves otherwise unstructured data available on websites and creates data in a more structured format.

Seasoned offering An offering in which an issuer sells additional units of a previously issued security.

Secondary bond markets Fixed-income markets comprised of investors trading existing bonds amongst themselves.

Secondary market The market where securities are traded among investors.

Secondary precedence rules Rules that determine how to rank orders placed at the same time.

Secondary sale Sale of a private company stake to another private equity firm or group of financial buyers.

Secondary-stage investments The second stage of development of an infrastructure asset. Secondary-stage investments involve existing infrastructure facilities or fully operational assets that do not require further investment or development over the investment horizon. These assets generate immediate cash flow and returns expected over the investment period.

Sector indexes Indexes that represent and track different economic sectors—such as consumer goods, energy, finance, health care, and technology—on either a national, regional, or global basis.

Secured With collateral; secured debt is backed by the cash flows of the issuer and the collateral as a secondary source of repayment.

Secured loans Loans collateralized by an asset of the borrower.

Security Evidence of equity or debt interest or in an entity or a related right, such as a derivative. Often standardized to conform to security exchange requirements.

Security characteristic line A plot of the excess return of a security on the excess return of the market.

Security market index A portfolio of securities representing a given security market, market segment, or asset class.

Security market line The graphical representation of the CAPM formula, showing the relationship between expected return and beta.

Security selection The process of selecting individual securities; typically, security selection has the objective of generating superior risk-adjusted returns relative to a portfolio's benchmark.

Security tokens Digitizes the ownership rights associated with publicly traded securities.

Segmenting A process of identifying and grouping customers by decision-useful attributes.

Self-attribution bias A bias in which people take too much credit for successes (*self-enhancing*) and assign responsibility to others for failures (*self-protecting*).

Self-control bias A bias in which people fail to act in pursuit of their long-term, overarching goals because of a lack of self-discipline.

Self-investment limits With respect to investment limitations applying to pension plans, restrictions on the percentage of assets that can be invested in securities issued by the pension plan sponsor.

Sell-side firm A broker/dealer that sells securities and provides independent investment research and recommendations to their clients (i.e., buy-side firms).

Semi-strong-form efficient market A market in which security prices reflect all publicly known and available information.

Semiannual bond basis yield Also known as a semiannual bond equivalent yield, it is an annualized interest rate with a periodicity of two.

Semiannual bond equivalent yield Also known as a semiannual bond basis yield, it is an annualized interest rate with a periodicity of two.

Senior debt A debt obligation with higher priority of payment than junior debt obligations.

Senior unsecured debt The highest-ranked debt in an issuer's capital structure which is a general obligation of the borrower.

Seniority Priority of payment of various debt obligations.

Sensitivity analysis A form of analysis used to determine the impact of a change in one or more key variables affecting investment returns or valuation.

Separately managed account (SMA) An investment portfolio managed exclusively for the benefit of an individual or institution.

Service period The time between the grant and vesting dates for an employee share-based award, usually measured in years.

Settlement The closing date at which the counterparties of a derivative contract exchange payment for the underlying as required by the contract.

Settlement price The price determined by an exchange's clearinghouse in the daily settlement of the mark-to-market process. The price reflects an average of the final futures trades of the day.

Share class Types of equity securities that have different voting rights—for example, an issuer may issue Class A shares that carry one vote per share and Class B shares that carry ten votes per share.

Share repurchase A transaction in which a company buys back its own shares. Unlike stock dividends and stock splits, share repurchases use corporate cash.

Shareholder activism A range of actions by a corporation's shareholders that are intended to result in some change in the corporation, typically a change in the board of directors, management, or business strategy.

Shareholder derivative lawsuit A legal action by a shareholder on behalf of a company, not the shareholder personally, against a third party. Often, the third party is a director or manager who the shareholder believes has harmed the company.

Shareholder engagement Shareholder engagement reflects active ownership by investors in which the investor seeks to influence a corporation's decisions on ESG matters, either through dialogue with corporate officers or votes at a shareholder assembly (in the case of equity).

Shareholder theory of corporate governance Espoused by Milton Friedman in his famous 1970 essay, the shareholder theory holds that the objective of a business is to increase profits and shareholder value.

Shareholders Hold a direct equity position in a firm, and both individual persons and financial institutions can be shareholders. The term comes from the individual or investment firm literally having a share of the company. It is most commonly used when talking about the rights and responsibilities that come with being an "owner" of a company, such as stewardship, voting, and engagement. This differentiates it from a situation where an individual or an investment firm lends money or invests in a bond (in other words, they are not an equityholder of a company). Because bond investors do not have a share and are not owners of a company, they cannot vote. Nonetheless, expectations around engagement are increasing for those who invest in loans and bonds as well, making the difference between the two terms more subtle.

Shares Units of ownership interest in a limited company.

Sharpe ratio The ratio of mean excess return to standard deviation (excess return).

Shelf registration A type of public offering that allows the issuer to file a single, all-encompassing offering circular that covers a series of bond issues.

Short A trading position in a **derivative contract** that gains value as the price of the **underlying** moves lower.

Short biased These strategies use quantitative, technical, and fundamental analysis to short overvalued equity securities with limited or no long-side exposures.

Short position A position in an asset or contract in which one has sold an asset one does not own, or in which a right under a contract can be exercised against oneself.

Short selling A transaction in which borrowed securities are sold with the intention to repurchase them at a lower price at a later date and return them to the lender.

Short-run average total cost The curve describing average total cost when some costs are considered fixed.

Shortfall risk The risk that portfolio value or portfolio return will fall below some minimum acceptable level over some time horizon.

Shutdown point The point at which average revenue is equal to the firm's average variable cost.

Side letter A side agreement created between the GP and specific LPs. These agreements exist *outside* the LPA. These agreements provide additional terms and conditions related to the investment agreement.

Signpost An indicator, market level, data piece, or event that signals a risk is becoming more or less likely. An analyst can think of signposts like a traffic light.

Simple linear regression (SLR) An approach for estimating the linear relationship between a dependent variable and a single independent variable by minimizing the sum of the squared deviations between the fitted line and the observed values.

Simple random sample A subset of a larger population created in such a way that each element of the population has an equal probability of being selected to the subset.

Simple random sampling The procedure of drawing a sample to satisfy the definition of a simple random sample.

Simple yield The sum of the coupon payments plus the straight-line amortized share of the gain or loss divided by the bond's flat price. Simple yields are used mostly to quote JGBs.

Simulation A technique for exploring how a target variable (e.g. portfolio returns) would perform in a hypothetical environment specified by the user, rather than a historical setting.

Simulation trial A complete pass through the steps of a simulation.

Single-price auction A debt securities auction in which all bidders pay the same price.

Sinking fund Provisions that reduce the credit risk of a bond issue by requiring the issuer to retire a portion of the bond's principal outstanding each year.

Situational influences External factors, such as environmental or cultural elements, that shape our behavior.

Skewed Not symmetrical.

Skewness A quantitative measure of skew (lack of symmetry); a synonym of skew. It is computed as the average cubed deviation from the mean standardized by dividing by the standard deviation cubed.

Slope coefficient The change in the estimated value of the dependent variable for a one-unit change in the value of the independent variable.

Small country A country that is a price taker in the world market for a product and cannot influence the world market price.

Smart beta Involves the use of simple, transparent, rules-based strategies as a basis for investment decisions.

Smart contracts Computer programs that are designed to self-execute on the basis of pre-specified terms and conditions agreed to by parties to a contract.

Social infrastructure investments A category of infrastructure investments that are directed toward human activities and include such assets as educational, health care, social housing, and correctional facilities, with the focus on providing, operating, and maintaining the asset infrastructure.

Soft commodities Standardized agricultural products, such as cattle and corn, with markets often involving the physical delivery of the underlying upon settlement.

Soft hurdle rate Hurdle rate where the fee is calculated on the entire return when the hurdle is exceeded. With a soft hurdle, GPs are able to catch up performance fees once the hurdle threshold is exceeded.

Soft power A means of influencing another country's decisions without force or coercion. Soft power can be built over time through actions, such as cultural programs, advertisement, travel grants, and university exchange.

Soft-bullet covered bonds Delay the bond default and payment acceleration of bond cash flows until a new final maturity date, which is usually up to a year after the original maturity date.

Solvency Refers to the condition in which firm value exceeds the face value of debt used to finance the firm's assets.

Solvency ratios Ratios that measure a company's ability to meet its long-term obligations.

Solvency risk The risk that an organization does not survive or succeed because it runs out of cash, even though it might otherwise be solvent.

Sophisticated investors Individuals or entities that are permitted in a jurisdiction to trade unregistered or, generally, less regulated securities, including shares of privately held companies; also called *accredited investors*.

Sovereign immunity A principle that limits legal recourse of lenders from forcing a sovereign borrower to declare bankruptcy or liquidate its assets to settle debt claims.

Spearman rank correlation coefficient A measure of correlation applied to ranked data.

Special dividend A dividend paid by a company that does not pay dividends on a regular schedule, or a dividend that supplements regular cash dividends with an extra payment.

Special purpose acquisition company A "blank check" company that exists solely for the purpose of acquiring an unspecified private company within a predetermined period or return capital to investors.

Special purpose entity (SPE) Also referred to as a special purpose vehicle (SPV), this legal entity is created for a specific economic purpose. In the case of a project SPV, the entity's sole purpose is to facilitate the construction, operation, and financing of an infrastructure asset over its contractual life.

Special purpose vehicle See *special purpose entity*.

Special situations An area of private capital investment which targets return by investing in stressed, distressed, or event-driven opportunities.

Split ratings Complex risks viewed very differently by rating agencies

Sponsored A type of depository receipt in which the foreign company whose shares are held by the depository has a direct involvement in the issuance of the receipts.

Spot curve Yields-to-maturity on a series of default-risk-free zero-coupon bonds.

Spot markets Markets in which specific assets are exchanged at current prices. Spot markets are often referred to as **cash markets**.

Spot prices The current prices prevailing in **spot markets**.

Spot rates Yields-to-maturity on default-risk-free zero-coupon bonds.

Spread The difference in yield-to-maturity between a bond and that of a another bond.

Spread risk Bond price risk arising from changes in the yield spread on credit-risky bonds; reflects changes in the market's assessment and/or pricing of credit migration (or downgrade) risk and market liquidity risk.

Spurious correlation Refers to: 1) correlation between two variables that reflects chance relationships in a particular dataset; 2) correlation induced by a calculation that mixes each of two variables with a third variable; and 3) correlation between two variables arising not from a direct relation between them but from their relation to a third variable.

Stablecoin A cryptocurrency that aims to maintain a stable value relative to a specified asset or to a pool or basket of assets.

Stackelberg model A prominent model of strategic decision making in which firms are assumed to make their decisions sequentially.

Staggered board A structure of board elections in which only part of the board is elected simultaneously—for example, only one-third of the board may be up for election each year, so the board can be replaced over three years, not in one year if all seats were elected annually. This structure fosters greater continuity of board members but is an obstacle for shareholders seeking to effect change.

Stakeholder theory of corporate governance An expansion of the shareholder theory of corporate governance under which the objective of a business is to maximize value for, and balance the interests of, a broad group of stakeholders, including shareholders, employees, society, and the non-human environment.

Stakeholders Any party with an interest, financial or non-financial, in an entity or its actions.

Standard deviation The positive square root of the variance; a measure of dispersion in the same units as the original data.

Standard error of the estimate A measure of the distance between the observed values of the dependent variable and those predicted from the estimated regression. The smaller this value, the better the fit of the model. Also known as the standard error of the regression and the root mean square error.

Standard error of the forecast Used to provide an interval estimate around the estimated regression line. It is necessary because the regression line does not describe the relationship between the dependent and independent variables perfectly.

Standard error of the slope coefficient Calculated for simple linear regression by dividing the standard error of the estimate by the square root of the variation of the independent variable.

Standardization The process of creating protocols for the production, sale, transport, or use of a product or service. Standardization occurs when relevant parties agree to follow these protocols together. It helps support expanded economic and financial activities, such as trade and capital flows that support higher economic growth and standards of living, across borders.

Standards of conduct Behaviors required by a group; established benchmarks that clarify or enhance a group's code of ethics.

Standing limit orders A limit order at a price below market and which therefore is waiting to trade.

State actors Typically national governments, political organizations, or country leaders that exert authority over a country's national security and resources. The South African President, Sultan of Brunei, Malaysia's Parliament, and the British Prime Minister are all examples of state actors.

Statement of cash flows A financial statement that details the movement of cash over a period. The statement is classified into operating, investing, and financing activities.

Static trade-off theory of capital structure A theory pertaining to a company's optimal capital structure; the optimal level of debt is found at the point where additional debt would cause the costs of financial distress to increase by a greater amount than the benefit of the additional tax shield.

Statistically significant A result indicating that the null hypothesis can be rejected; with reference to an estimated regression coefficient, frequently understood to mean a result indicating that the corresponding population regression coefficient is different from zero.

Status quo bias An emotional bias in which people do nothing (i.e., maintain the status quo) instead of making a change.

Statutory voting A common method of voting where each share represents one vote.

Step-up bonds Bonds for which the coupon, be it fixed or floating, increases by specified margins at specified dates.

Stock dividend A type of dividend in which a company distributes additional shares of its common stock to shareholders instead of cash.

Stock exchange An exchange in which equity securities are traded. See *exchanges*.

Stock split An increase in the number of shares outstanding with a consequent decrease in share price, but no change to the company's underlying fundamentals.

Stockholder overhang The downward pressure on the share price of stock as large blocks of shares are being sold on the open market.

Stop order An order in which a trader has specified a stop price condition. Also called *stop-loss order*.

Stop-loss order See *stop order*.

Stranded assets A resource that is no longer economically valuable owing to changes in demand, regulations, or availability of substitutes—for example, a newly discovered oil well that will not be brought into production.

Strategic asset allocation A long-term strategy that establishes target allocations for various asset classes and aims to optimize the balance between risk and reward by diversifying investments.

Stratified random sampling A procedure that first divides a population into subpopulations (strata) based on classification criteria and then randomly draws samples from each stratum in sizes proportional to that of each stratum in the population.

Street convention For yield measures on fixed-income instruments that assume payments are made on scheduled dates and ignore weekends and holidays.

Stress testing A specific type of scenario analysis that estimates losses in rare and extremely unfavorable combinations of events or scenarios.

Strong-form efficient market A market in which security prices reflect all public and private information.

Structural budget deficit Also known as the cyclically adjusted budget deficit. The deficit that would exist if the economy was at full employment (or full potential output).

Structural subordination Refers to the positioning of debt, which is issued by a legal entity, typically a holding company, which is separate and therefore one step removed from an operating company, which holds assets pledged under a security agreement to senior secured debtholders.

Structured notes A broad category of securities that incorporate the features of debt instruments and one or more embedded derivatives designed to achieve a particular issuer or investor objective.

Subordinated debt A class of unsecured debt that ranks below a firm's senior unsecured obligations.

Subordination A form of internal credit enhancement that relies on creating more than one bond tranche and ordering the claim priorities for ownership or interest in an asset between the tranches. The ordering of the claim priorities is called a senior/subordinated structure, where the tranches of highest seniority are called senior, followed by subordinated or junior tranches. Also called **credit tranching**.

Subprime loans Lending to borrowers with lower credit quality, high DTI, and/or are loans with higher LTV, and include loans that are secured by second liens otherwise subordinated to other loans.

Sum of squares error (SSE) A measure of the total deviation between observed and estimated values of the dependent variable. It is calculated by subtracting each estimated value $\hat{Y}_i$ from its corresponding observed value Y_i, squaring each of these differences, and then summing all of these squared differences.

Sum of squares regression (SSR) A measure of the explained variation in the dependent variable, calculated as the sum of the squared differences between the predicted value of the dependent variable, Y ˆ_i, based on the estimated regression line, and the mean of the dependent variable, $\bar{Y}$.

Sum of squares total (SST) A measure of the total variation in the dependent variable in a simple linear regression. It is calculated by subtracting the mean of the observed values $\bar{Y}$ from each of the observed values Y_i, squaring each of these differences, and then summing all of these squared differences.

Sunk costs A cost that has already been incurred.

Supervised learning A type of machine learning in which the system attempts to learn to model relationships based on labeled training data.

Supervisory board In some jurisdictions, a corporation's board of directors is formally composed of a supervisory board and a management board. The supervisory board appoints and oversees the management board and often includes representatives of employees and other non-shareholder stakeholders.

Supply chain The sequence of processes involved in the creation and delivery of a physical product to the end customer, both within and external to a firm, regardless of whether those steps are performed by a single firm.

Supply shock A typically unexpected disturbance to supply.

Survivorship bias Relates to the inclusion of only current investment funds in a database. As such, the returns of funds that are no longer available in the marketplace (have been liquidated) are excluded from the database. Also see *backfill bias*.

Swap A firm commitment involving a periodic exchange of cash flows.

Swap contract An agreement between two parties to exchange a series of future cash flows.

Swap execution facility (SEF) A swap trading platform accessed by multiple **dealers**.

Swap rate The fixed rate to be paid by the fixed-rate payer specified in a swap contract.

Syndicate A group of lenders, typically made up of banks.

Synthetic protective put The combination of a synthetic long underlying position (i.e., a long forward and risk-free borrowing) and a purchased put on the underlying.

Systematic risk Risk that affects the entire market or economy; it cannot be avoided and is inherent in the overall market. Systematic risk is also known as *non-diversifiable* or *market risk*.

Systematic sampling A procedure of selecting every *k*th member until reaching a sample of the desired size. The sample that results from this procedure should be approximately random.

Systemic risk Refers to risks supervisory authorities believe are likely to have broad impact across the financial market infrastructure and affect a wide swath of market participants.

Tactical asset allocation A proactive strategy that adjusts asset class allocations within a portfolio based on short-term market trends, economic conditions, or valuation changes to capitalize on temporary market inefficiencies or opportunities to improve returns or manage risk more effectively.

Target capital structure Management's desired proportions of debt and equity financing, usually stated on a book value basis or indirectly using a financial leverage metric, such as net or gross debt to EBITDA or credit rating.

Target independent A bank's ability to determine the definition of inflation that they target, the rate of inflation that they target, and the horizon over which the target is to be achieved.

Target semideviation A measure of downside risk, calculated as the square root of the average of the squared deviations of observations below the target (also called *target downside deviation*).

Tariffs Taxes that a government levies on imported goods.

Tax base The amount at which an asset or liability is valued for tax purposes.

Tax expense An aggregate of an entity's income tax payable (or recoverable in the case of a tax benefit) and any changes in deferred tax assets and liabilities. It is essentially the income tax payable or recoverable if these had been determined based on accounting profit rather than taxable income.

Taxable income The portion of an entity's income that is subject to income taxes under the tax laws of its jurisdiction.

Taxable temporary differences Temporary differences that result in a taxable amount in a future period when determining the taxable profit as the balance sheet item is recovered or settled.

Technical analysis A form of security analysis that uses price and volume data, often displayed graphically, in decision making.

Tender offer A solicitation by a current or prospective shareholder to other shareholders to acquire a substantial percentage, including 100%, of shares at a specified price. This action is usually undertaken by a potential acquirer whose bid was rejected by the issuer's board of directors, prompting the potential acquirer to appeal directly to shareholders.

Tenor Remaining time-to-maturity for a fixed-income instrument.

Term repos Repos with a maturity longer than one day.

Term structure of interest rates Also known as the maturity structure of interest rates, refers to the difference in interest rates or benchmark yields by time-to-maturity.

Terminal stock value The expected value of a share at the end of the investment horizon—in effect, the expected selling price. Also called *terminal value*.

Terminal value The expected value of a share at the end of the investment horizon—in effect, the expected selling price.

Test of the mean of the differences A statistical test for differences based on paired observations drawn from samples that are dependent on each other.

Text analytics Involves the use of computer programs to analyze and derive meaning typically from large, unstructured text- or voice-based datasets, such as company filings, written reports, quarterly earnings calls, social media, email, internet postings, and surveys.

Thematic risks Known risks that evolve and expand over a period of time. Climate change, pattern migration, the rise of populist forces, and the ongoing threat of terrorism fall into this category.

Thin-tailed Describes a distribution that has relatively less weight in the tails than the normal distribution (also called platykurtic).

Tiered pricing A pricing approach that charges different prices to different buyers, commonly based on volume purchased.

Timberland investment management organizations Entities that support institutional investors by managing their investments in timberland by analyzing and acquiring suitable timberland holdings.

Time tranching Structure of a securitization that allows for the redistribution of "prepayment risk" among bond classes by creating bond classes of different expected maturities.

Time value The difference between an option's premium and its intrinsic value.

Time value decay The process by which the time value of an option declines toward zero as the option's expiration date is approached.

Time-weighted rate of return The compound rate of growth of one unit of currency invested in a portfolio during a stated measurement period; a measure of investment performance that is not sensitive to the timing and amount of withdrawals or additions to the portfolio.

Tokenization The process of representing ownership rights to physical assets on a blockchain or distributed ledger.

Top-down analysis An investment selection approach that begins with consideration of macroeconomic conditions and then evaluates markets and industries based upon such conditions.

Total probability rule for expected value A rule explaining the expected value of a random variable in terms of expected values of the random variable conditional on mutually exclusive and exhaustive scenarios.

Total return Measures the price appreciation, or percentage change in price of the securities in an index or portfolio, plus any income received over the period.

Total return index An index that reflects the price appreciation or percentage change in price of the constituent securities plus any income received since inception.

Total working capital The difference between current assets and current liabilities.

Tracking error The standard deviation of the differences between a portfolio's returns and its benchmark's returns; a synonym of active risk.

Tracking risk The standard deviation of the differences between a portfolio's returns and its benchmarks returns. Also called *tracking error.*

Trade creation When regional integration results in the replacement of higher cost domestic production by lower cost imports from other members.

Trade diversion When regional integration results in lower-cost imports from non-member countries being replaced with higher-cost imports from members.

Trade sale A portion or division of a private company sold via either direct sale or auction to a strategic buyer interested in increasing the scale and scope of an existing business.

Trade settlement date The date when the buyer and seller transfer consideration and securities.

Traditional investment markets Markets for traditional investments, which include all publicly traded debts and equities and shares in pooled investment vehicles that hold publicly traded debts and/or equities.

Tranches A grouping of securities within an issue with characteristics that vary from other tranches, such as different credit quality and seniority.

Transfer payments Welfare payments made through the social security system that exist to provide a basic minimum level of income for low-income households.

Transition risks Economic and financial losses from the transition to a lower-carbon economy in response to climate change—for example, the abandonment of an oil well that is no longer economical.

Treasury Inflation-Protected Securities (TIPS) US Treasury bonds with a principal that is adjusted for changes in the Consumer Price Index. TIPS are issued in 5-, 10-, and 30-year maturities.

Treynor ratio A measure of risk-adjusted performance that relates a portfolio's returns in excess of the risk-free rate to a portfolio's beta.

Trimmed mean A mean computed after excluding a stated small percentage of the lowest and highest observations.

Triparty repo A repurchase agreement in which the transacting parties agree to use a third-party agent that provides access to a larger collateral pool and multiple counterparties, as well as valuation and safekeeping of assets.

True yield Measures on fixed-income instruments use actual payment dates, accounting for weekends and holidays. The true yield on an instrument is always lower than the street convention yield.

Turn-of-the-year effect Calendar anomaly that stock market returns in January are significantly higher compared to the rest of the months of the year, with most of the abnormal returns reported during the first five trading days in January.

Two-fund separation theorem The theory that all investors regardless of taste, risk preferences, and initial wealth will hold a combination of two portfolios or funds: a risk-free asset and an optimal portfolio of risky assets.

Two-way table A table of the frequency distribution of observations classified on the basis of two discrete variables. Also known as *Contingency table.*

Two-week repo rate The interest rate on a two-week repurchase agreement; may be used as a policy rate by a central bank.

Type I error The error of rejecting a true null hypothesis; a false positive.

Type II error The error of not rejecting a false null hypothesis; false negative.

Uncommitted lines of credit Sources of bank credit that a bank can refuse to honor. Uncommitted credit lines are made up to a certain principal amount for a pre-determined maximum maturity, charging a market reference rate plus an issuer-specific spread on only the principal outstanding for the period of use.

Underfitted When a machine learning model treats true parameters as if they are noise and is unable to recognize relationships in the training data, making the model more likely to fail to fully discover patterns that underlie the data.

Underlying The asset referred to in a **derivative contract**.

Underwritten offering A type of securities issue mechanism in which the investment bank guarantees the sale of the securities at an offering price that is negotiated with the issuer. Also known as *firm commitment offering.*

Unearned revenue A liability account for money that has been collected for goods or services that have not yet been delivered; payment received in advance of providing a good or service. Also called *deferred revenue* or *deferred income.*

Unimodal A distribution with a single value that is most frequently occurring.

Unit economics The expression of revenues and costs on a per-unit basis.

Unitranche debt A hybrid or blended loan structure combining different tranches of secured and unsecured debt into a single loan with a single, blended interest rate.

Unsecured Without collateral; unsecured debt is backed only by cash flows of the issuer.

Unsponsored A type of depository receipt in which the foreign company whose shares are held by the depository has no involvement in the issuance of the receipts.

Unsupervised learning A type of machine learning in which the system tries to learn the structure of unlabeled data.

Utility tokens Tokens that provide services within a network, such as paying for services and network fees.

Validity instructions Instructions which indicate when the order may be filled.

Value added resellers Businesses that distribute a product and also handle more complex aspects of product installation, customization, service, or support.

Value at risk A money measure of the minimum value of losses expected during a specified time period at a given level of probability.

Value chain The systems and processes in a firm that create value for its customers.

Value proposition The product or service attributes valued by a firm's target customer that lead those customers to prefer that firm's offering.

Value-add real estate strategies Strategies that involve larger-scale redevelopment and repositioning of existing assets and that may allow the investor to earn a higher return compared with core-plus real estate strategies.

Value-based pricing Pricing set primarily by reference to the value of the product or service to customers.

VaR See *value at risk*.

Variance The expected value (the probability-weighted average) of squared deviations from a random variable's expected value.

Variance of a random variable The expected value (the probability-weighted average) of squared deviations from a random variable's expected value.

Variation margin The difference between current margin required and the current collateral price in a repurchase agreement.

Vega A measure of the sensitivity of an option's price to changes in the underlying's volatility.

Velocity The pace at which geopolitical risk impacts an investor portfolio.

Venture capital Private equity investment in a startup or early-stage company involving high risk and a high rate of failure.

Venture capital fund A hedge fund that seeks to buy, optimize, and ultimately sell portfolio companies to generate profits. See *private equity fund*.

Venture debt Private debt funding that provides venture capital backing to start-up or early-stage companies that may be generating little or negative cash flow.

Vest To become unconditionally entitled to.

Vesting date The day that an employee becomes unconditionally entitled to compensation.

Vintage year The year in which a private capital fund makes its first investment.

Volatility The standard deviation of the continuously compounded returns on the underlying asset.

Vote by proxy A mechanism that allows a designated party—such as another shareholder, a shareholder representative, or management—to vote on the shareholder's behalf.

Voting rights The power of shareholders to cast votes in corporate elections for directors and other matters submitted to a shareholder vote.

Warrant Debt feature or security granting the right to purchase additional common equity shares issued by the company at a predetermined price for a given period.

Waterfall structures These represent the distribution order for cash flows and risk to different tranches in a financing structure.

Weak-form efficient market hypothesis The belief that security prices fully reflect all past market data, which refers to all historical price and volume trading information.

Weighted average coupon rate (WAC) Rate calculated for a mortgage pass-through security by weighting the mortgage rate of each mortgage in the pool by the percentage of the outstanding mortgage balance relative to the outstanding amount of all the mortgages in the pool.

Weighted average maturity (WAM) Calculated for a mortgage pass-through security by weighting the remaining number of months to maturity of each mortgage in the pool by the outstanding mortgage balance relative to the outstanding amount of all the mortgages in the pool.

Weighted-average cost of capital (WACC) A weighted average of the after-tax required rates of return on a company's equity, debt, preferred stock, and other long-term financing sources, where the weights are the fraction of each source of financing in the company's current market value or management's target capital structure.

Winsorized mean A mean computed after assigning a stated percentage of the lowest values equal to one specified low value and a stated percentage of the highest values equal to one specified high value.

Write-off/liquidation Refers to a transaction that has not gone well, and the investment is likely to lose value. The private equity firm revises the value of its investment downward or liquidates the portfolio company.

Yield curve A graphical depiction of yields-to-maturity of bonds from the same issuer across maturities.

Yield spread The difference in yield-to-maturity between a bond and that of a another bond.

Yield-to-call An internal rate of return on a fixed-income instrument's cash flows assuming cash flows are received on scheduled dates and the bond is called at a certain call price and date.

Yield-to-maturity Internal rate of return on a fixed-income instrument's cash flows assuming all cash flows are received on their scheduled dates.

Yield-to-worst The lowest among a fixed-income instrument's yields-to-call and yield-to-maturity. A commonly cited yield measure for fixed-rate callable bonds.

Z-spread or zero-volatility spread is a constant yield spread for a bond over a government or swap curve.

Zero-coupon bonds Bonds that do not pay interest during their life. They are issued at a discount to par value and redeemed at par. Also called pure discount bond.